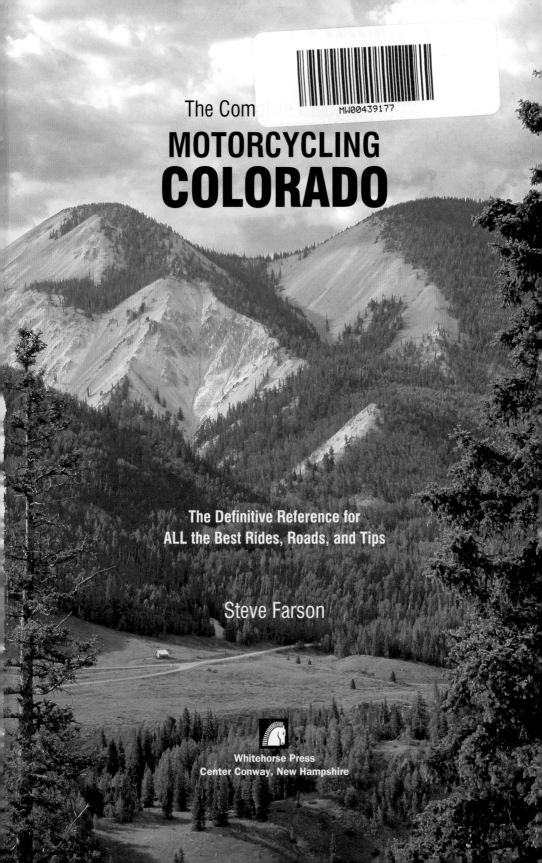

The Complete

MOTORCYCLING
COLORADO

**The Definitive Reference for
ALL the Best Rides, Roads, and Tips**

Steve Farson

Whitehorse Press
Center Conway, New Hampshire

Whitehorse Press books are also available at discounts in bulk quantity for sales and promotional use. For details about special sales or for a catalog of motorcycling books, videos, and gear write to the publisher:

Whitehorse Press
107 East Conway Road
Center Conway, New Hampshire 03813
603-356-6556 or 800-531-1133
CustomerService@WhitehorsePress.com
www.WhitehorsePress.com

ISBN 978-1-884313-92-9

5 4

Printed in China

This book is dedicated to Him above who makes all things possible, including the great sport of motorcycling, and to my wonderful wife and children . . . Bev, Brad, Ben, Matt, and Sarah.

Acknowledgments

With the deepest of gratitude I want to thank the Denver Public Library's Western History Collection for permission to use historical images from their archives for this book.

And I want to express a gratefulness for the many of you with whom I share the road. The cast of characters and bikes on the stage of Colorado's great byways makes this one of the best shows around.

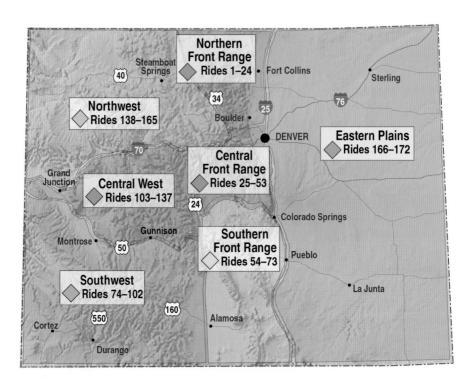

Key to Symbols

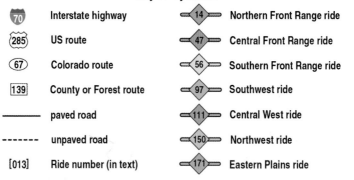			

Interstate highway	Northern Front Range ride
US route	Central Front Range ride
Colorado route	Southern Front Range ride
County or Forest route	Southwest ride
paved road	Central West ride
unpaved road	Northwest ride
[013] Ride number (in text)	Eastern Plains ride

CONTENTS

INTRODUCTION

Most of you don't really reach for your bike's keys merely so you can visit the bakery in Buena Vista, the ice cream shop in Idaho Springs, or the saloon in Salida. Sure, any of these may suffice as a destination, but your real reason for leaving the car at home will be the ride—just you, the bike, and the road. In fact, there may be times when you have dispensed with all such pretense, to point your front wheel in a general direction and soar like a bird surfing the thermals, going where the winds lead, content to avoid the efficiencies of travelling by the shortest or fastest routes. This book is written for the motorcyclist who considers the ride itself to be the destination.

With 172 rides, this book contains a greater depth of choices than other motorcycle guidebooks, with an unprecedented coverage of dual-sport riding opportunities. The rides are described in detail, as experienced from the saddle of a motorcycle—how to ride, what to look for, what to watch out for, and how to get the best out of each road.

A word or two about the images: occasionally, as I was capturing content for the book, the weather was uncooperative enough to spawn brief fantasies of my working from the luxury of a warm, dry car—nobody would know—but be assured, the feelings soon passed as I recognized the sleety gloom for what it was, a thing to be taken in stride, much as we do when we ride. After all, sometimes the less pleasant realities make for the most memorable occasions . . . and I deliberately chose not to return for a "prettier" picture.

During my research, I gained access to many historic photos, and where thick trees and buildings didn't get in the way, I often tried to recreate them from a spot as close as I could get to the original photographer's location. I find that archival images offer perspective and serve as a catalyst for reflecting on those who have passed before on horses of a different era; a pause that causes you to look back can help you better face the road ahead.

So how did I select the best of Colorado? Despite my being on the more anal margins of the spectrum, it didn't involve loading every road into a spreadsheet for mathematical quantification and comparison. My subjective "scoring" of a road gave more weight to those aspects most meaningful to motorcyclists, such as its:

- Fun Factor—Is it undulating? Entertaining?
- Lack of traffic
- Duration (the longer, the better!)
- Scenery
- Distinctiveness
- Destinations in addition to the ride itself
- Continuity and ease of connecting to other great rides

After adding it all up, confirming the alignment of the planets, checking to see if the whales were migrating on time, and stirring in the recognition that motorcyclists are a diverse group with different preferences and skill levels, I believe the 172 rides in this book represent the very best motorcycle rides in Colorado!

So what about dual-sport adventures? That was a dilemma. Forty rides are dedicated to off-pavement routes, mentioning more than 75 dirt roads, but I had to draw the line somewhere or this book could have been thousands of pages longer than it is. The journeys that made the cut can be traversed safely with a heavier dual-sport bike piloted by a rider of average skills, or by a game rider on a versatile street bike.

This book is divided into seven geographical sections, each beginning with an overview map that lets you see how all the different rides might be combined into loops and longer rides both within that section and with adjacent sections. The individual rides each have their own more detailed maps, along with route descriptions, photos, local points of interest, and historical background information.

Tips for Riding in Colorado

When riding in Colorado, it pays to be prepared! In a single day you can go from the rarified air at timberline to the sun-baked depths of a rocky desert canyon, or join a roiling river in a fertile glacial valley, or sweep into the open plains that fill the horizon. The temperature can change rapidly in only a few miles, so you need to dress in layers with heavily vented apparel.

In any month, anything known to fall from the clouds can grace your ride. Late summer monsoon-like showers can put a damper on things if you don't have something to ward off the moisture. Riding warm and dry in the rain can be sublime and serene, but cold and wet can be miserable and . . . well, miserable.

To illustrate the sort of extremes I'm talking about, let me tell you about a memorable ride I experienced one January day on the Southern Front Range. As I rode south from Fairplay on Colorado 9, the temperature had plunged from 35 degrees to 10 degrees by the time I reached the abandoned townsite of Garo! My heated gear was cranked up and the road was dry, but frost started coating my faceshield. Ten miles south of Hartsel, just as Colorado 9 becomes one of the finest riding roads around, the temps rebounded to 30 degrees and I felt like I was on a beach in Cancún. When I arrived in Guffey, at 49 degrees, it felt like I was cruising in Death Valley. I couldn't believe it—a change of almost 40 degrees in only 25 miles!

Also, note that better riding skills always increase one's fun level, to say nothing of improving safety. The roads in Colorado can be challenging, but that is also what makes them so engaging. If you haven't ever taken a motorcycle training course, or if it has been a while since you did, sign up for a Motorcycle Safety Foundation Beginner or Experienced Rider Course, or even a track-day

Motorcycling Colorado

school. Resources in your area can be found easily on the Internet.

Starting your ride early in the morning, say 8 a.m. or earlier, typically has the advantages of its being cool, sunny, and dry, and you can avoid the traffic that may be building by mid-morning (especially on weekends), as well as the afternoon thunder boomers. You can ride farther, stay longer, and experience more, in better conditions. Plus, the lower sun will light up the surroundings in a more magical manner. When you have traveled far to ride a certain road, you will want to optimize the chances for the perfect journey by getting an early start.

What if you have ridden for hours to arrive at a sweet stretch of tantalizing tarmac, only to spot a rolling roadblock just ahead, a ponderous or laboring vehicle poised to restrict your view and ruin your otherwise sublime experience? I say pull over, take a break, and then proceed only after a lengthy gap in the traffic. It isn't going to take you materially longer to get where you are going. It also will take the heat off the driver ahead and keep you from being tempted to make a crazy pass. It'll be safer and a lot more fun with an open road before you.

And lastly—believe it or not—some of the best motorcycle riding in Colorado can occur during the winter. You can wear protection without melting, there are no bugs and nasty thunderstorms to dodge, and there's something crisply beautiful and distinctly colorful about the season. Yeah, the roads may be a little grittier, but it's manageable, and heated gear will take the edges off the temperature. And, you can score a few points against Ole Man Winter.

Northern Front Range

REGIONAL OVERVIEW

To best enjoy this epic feast, bring your heartiest appetite to the Northern Front Range, a region from Boulder in the south, to the Wyoming border on the north, spanning the width between the Continental Divide and Interstate 25. With delights both savory and sweet, the menu includes glorious canyons, wandering backroads, dual-sport adventures, and tasty touring, spiced with gold-rush history and steeped in the world-class scenery of Rocky Mountain National Park—a varied selection of gourmet and down-home riding destined to please even the most discriminating of two-wheeled palates.

When it comes to corner-carving canyons, the regional choices are numerous and noteworthy. If you want 12 twisting miles of motorcycling bliss, sample St. Vrain Canyon. I can't praise it enough. And then there is Cache La Poudre Canyon, a long, deep cut in

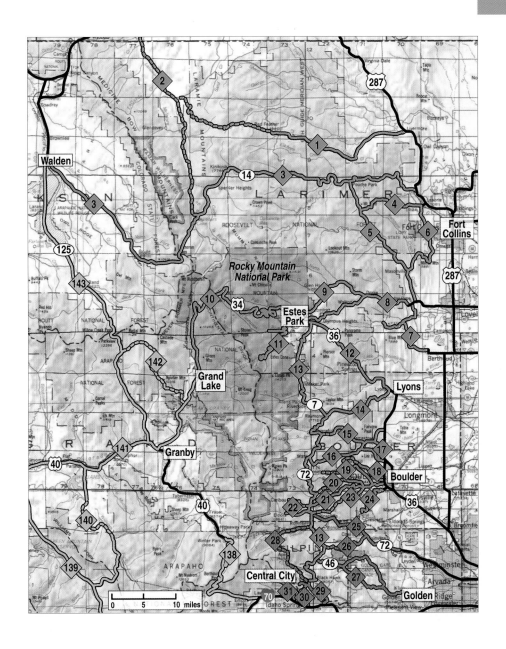

the mountains caused by the crashing water of the Cache La Poudre River. For years I would enter the canyon at the T-intersection of Stove Prairie Road and turn west for Cameron Pass and Walden, missing the eastern 16 miles of the canyon. One year, late in the spring, I finally placed two wheels on this overlooked stretch of two-lane magic, and discovered not only why the road is an official scenic byway, but also why the river has earned Colorado's only federal designation as a Wild and Scenic waterway. Riding the

bending asphalt ribbon beside that intense, roaring firehose of snow-melt is amazing and intimidating.

Most of the "ghost towns" along these routes might be more accurately described as semi-ghost towns, and they tend to be tucked away in the foothills above Boulder. Finding and riding to these nestled communities are a thrill, as there are no ho-hum journeys to any of these once-bustling places. The roads twist and turn, climb and descend, until you come upon the faded

tributes and testimonies to a vibrant mining past: Gold Hill, Wall Street, Sunset, Magnolia, Eldora, Caribou—all destinations worthy of the ride itself.

Were that not enough, the Peak to Peak Scenic Byway joins the western ends of all of these canyon roads, making it possible to return to Boulder via a route that is both different from and equal to the superlative one you chose for your outbound trek.

And towering over the Northern Front Range region are the majestic presence and peaks of Rocky Mountain National Park, with roads luring you into, through, and around its rugged beauty, to form impressions that will become magnified in the open air astride a motorcycle, and leave you convinced that this is one of America's greatest natural wonderlands.

Ride 1 **Red Feather Lakes**

Red Feather Lakes Road, Deadman Road, County 74E, 80C, Forest Road 162

A paved, sweeping ride of 23 miles to a lake resort area, followed by 25 miles of forested, dual-sport riding on a smooth dirt surface to a special river valley

Loggers and ranchers founded the Red Feather Lakes area around 1900, and not long after, enterprising sorts thought the scenic area had resort potential and thus proceeded to build dams and ditches. Today, dozens of scenic, azure blue lakes dot the landscape, making a ride to this region unique. The community was originally called Westlake, but was later renamed after "Princess" Tsianina Red Feather. She was an operatic singer, part Cherokee and part Creek Indian, who lived a storied life that included singing for U.S. troops in Europe during WWI. She was liked so much on the resort stage at Westlake that the residents decided to rename the town after her!

The launch for this ride is 20 miles northwest of Fort Collins, at the small roadside community of Livermore on US 287. Red Feather Lakes Road/County 74E presents a rolling introduction, up and down and left and right, but as the 23 miles are clicked off, there is a slight gain in intensity as pockmarked slopes of trees and rocky outcroppings cause the road to bob and weave more. Lakes along the roadside deliver not-so-subtle clues that you have arrived at the community of Red Feather Lakes.

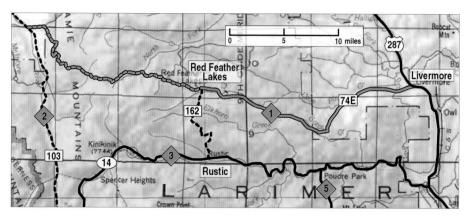

Turn your handlebars to the right/north at County 67J for a one-mile ride to the small town center with a general store, gas pumps, and other services. There are rental cabins and small resort properties all around, along with snack bars and delis. If you make a wandering tour of all the lakes, be on the lookout for the moose that call this area home. They wander over from the not-too-distant North Park release area, and find having lots of water with their salad irresistible.

At this point you will need to make a decision. To stay on a paved road, you can pull a 180 and head back east toward US 287. The dual-sport rider might be interested in the immense network of dual-sport roads north of Red Feather that can allow you to explore your way west, north, or east back to US 287. Be sure to top the tank off before embarking. Just a half mile farther west on Red Feather Lakes Road is the well-maintained, dirt County 162/Manhattan Road pointing south. In ten winding and zigzagging miles you will coast into the small community of Rustic on Colorado 14 in Cache La Poudre Canyon [003]. Check the current conditions, but this is an okay off-road journey for a capable street bike. A dual-sport bike would thrive on it. To be sure, ten miles off-road takes longer than anticipated for most, so be prepared, but you would land right at the great Cache La Poudre Canyon, setting you up for a looping, easterly ride back to Fort Collins on Colorado 14.

Your fourth choice would be to continue west on Red Feather Lakes Road, which leads to Deadman Road. In about a mile the pavement becomes gravel and you become a lonely adventurer on a secluded and remote road. I wonder if "Deadman" has anything to do with potential outcomes for the misfortunate? While a lightweight street bike could probably make the 25-mile traverse through woods and meadows to the Laramie River Valley, a dual-sport would be most at home. The Deadman option snuck into this chapter because it provides direct and scenic access to the outstanding Laramie River ride [002]. After miles of forested progress, it is quite something to break out into the open and see faraway vistas. The ride now becomes a 2,000-foot descent to the valley floor. Take note of the enormous bison ranch at Deadman's conclusion, where it intersects with County 103. It is the largest bison ranch I have ever seen, by far. Before venturing out this way, however, note that the Red Feather Lakes area will be your last chance for securing food and fuel.

Ride 2 **Laramie River**

Laramie River Road, County 103

A smooth 22-mile off-pavement ride through a secluded valley alongside a wild and scenic river

Laramie River Road takes you in solitude past impressive ranches, a sparkling river, and deep blue lakes with snowcapped mountains to the west. It heads north from Colorado Route 14 seven miles east of the Cameron Pass summit. This section of Colorado 14 is part of the outstanding Cache La Poudre Canyon ride [003]. The turnoff is well signed. Even if you have marginal interest in placing your bike on this smooth dirt surface, give it at least a two-mile trial run and take your bike to the header-pipe-blue waters of Chambers Lake. This 250-acre alpine lake is postcard pretty in its thin air setting. After a photo or a pause you can always return back to Colorado 14 and continue along on its stirring way. If you're up

for a deeper backcountry venture, then continue north into this wild river valley.

This descending ride gently loses 700 feet over the next 21 miles. The headwaters of the 216-mile-long Laramie River will be your constant riding companion this entire route. The river was named after 1820s French Canadian fur trader Jacques La Ramee, whose arrow-riddled body was found by others of his trade alongside the river now bearing his name. Sometimes I consider how wild this area must have been back then but, you know, while some things have changed in this valley, a lot probably hasn't. On your west side you have the 50,000-acre Rawah Wilderness, one of Colorado's five original wilderness areas established by the federal Wilderness Act of 1964. Towering above it are the 12,000- and 13,000-foot-high sentinels of the Medicine Bow Range. And in every direction, the Roosevelt National Forest extends beyond what you can see.

The winding, maintained, dirt-road base is tailored to, if not perfect for this kind of journey. And it isn't a dull traverse through a bunch of dense trees. There are wetlands (look for the moose), unpopulated meadows, and cattle-populated meadows. Secluded campgrounds and picnic areas invite a sidestand stop. Then there are the dude and guest ranches at the north end. Their picturesque settings will appeal to the photographer in you. At 22 miles there is a massive bison ranch and an intersection with

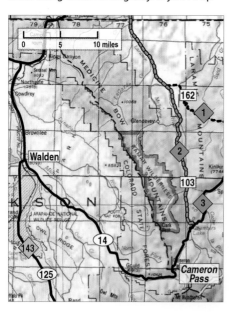

County 80C aiming east, which connects with the Red Feather Lakes–Deadman Road ride [001]. Continuing north is an option as well, with the Wyoming border 10 miles farther and a connection to paved Wyoming 230 another 10 miles distant, putting you at the scenic doorstep of the Snowy Range.

The unpaved Deadman Road access is probably best taken with a dual-sport bike. With the remoteness of this pristine place, know your tank range and plan accordingly. Walden is 37 miles west of this ride's junction with Colorado 14, but there's fuel at Red Feather Lakes. Archer's Poudre River Resort at Rustic, 20 miles east in Cache La Poudre Canyon, is also an option if they are open. A picnic along the Laramie River could be a meal choice. For a more formal affair, the Moose Creek Cafe in Walden or one of the seasonal resorts in Cache La Poudre Canyon could fit the bill and fill the belly.

Beside an out-and-back trip from Colorado Route 14, Laramie River Road could be combined with other roads for a couple of circling expeditions. From the Fort Collins area, connect the Laramie River Road ride with Red Feather Lakes–Deadman Road [001] and the Cache La Poudre ride [003]. A second option uses Walden as a base, taking Colorado 14 over Cameron Pass to the southeast, riding the Laramie River to Wyoming and Highway 230, and returning southwest to Walden. If on a dedicated dual-sport, consider connecting the ride of this chapter with adventures on the south side of Cache La Poudre Canyon in the Pingree Park area, and on the north side with the Cherokee Park area above Red Feather Lakes.

Ride 3 **Cache La Poudre**

Colorado 14

A 92-mile Colorado Scenic Byway following the Cache La Poudre River for more than 50 miles, that takes in a broad mountain pass, moose country, and sweeping high park views

When one enters Colorado 14 on the east and joins the Cache La Poudre–North Park Scenic Byway, a sign notes the small North Park town of Walden 92 miles away. That's 92 miles of canyon riding, mountain pass traversing, and high-alpine meadow cruising . . . all without a single stoplight. Even if you don't plan to let your bike take you all the way, for there are numerous sweet motorcycle turnoffs toward which you can point your front wheels, the anticipation of what lies ahead will make you very grateful you are in the saddle at that moment. This scenic byway delivers an exceptional motorcycle ride, however you choose to measure it.

The canyon takes its name from the river, which was given its name by French trappers in the 1820s when a snowstorm caused them to bury their gunpowder on the banks of the rushing water. Thus, the river was re-

ferred to as "The Hiding Place of the Powder" or Cache La Poudre. Entering the canyon from the east you can easily see why this is a scenic byway. The blend of roaring whitewater, precipitous canyon walls, inviting roadside parks, and mountain vistas will have you nodding in appreciation. Add an undulating and winding road and you will have more than enough reasons to call this the "perfect" ride.

At 16 miles into the journey, a great riding road, Stove Prairie [005] cuts off to the south. Turning the handlebars onto Stove Prairie, then returning to the Fort Collins area via Rist Canyon [004], or continuing on Stove Prairie to Masonville and then Horsetooth Reservoir [006], would be a tremendous two- to three-hour circuit.

Continuing west on Colorado 14 past Stove Prairie, you enter "The Narrows" of the canyon, with formations and debris left be-

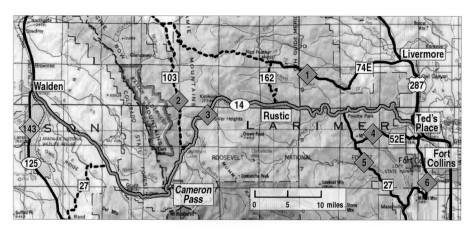

hind from receding glaciers. At 26 miles dual-sporters can cross the river and head south on Pingree Park Road to explore the Comanche Peak Wilderness, returning to Stove Prairie via links with Old Flowers Road or Buckhorn Road through Box Prairie. At 30 miles, you will reach the small community of Rustic. Back in the late 1800s this was a bustling summertime resort for travelers on horses of the four-footed kind. We on the two-wheeled kind can continue west toward Cameron Pass.

In Rustic, County 69 to the north (smooth dirt) connects to County 68, and Manhattan Road/County 162, which goes to the paved Red Feather Lakes Road [001] nine miles away. This would be a half-day loop back to Fort Collins. Before departing Rustic you can give your steed a pat on the tank for ascending 2,000 feet over the past 30 miles. Now you'll face 3,000 more sublime feet of climbing over the next 28 miles until you reach Cameron Pass on the Continental Divide. But before I get ahead of myself, at 51 miles—seven miles shy of the summit—the dirt-surfaced Laramie River Road/County 103 [002] wanders off to the north, passing the azure-blue waters of Chambers Lake, and continues north alongside the tumbling Laramie River toward Wyoming. I really like this riding road, and most any street bike can handle its smooth dirt surface.

The broad alpine summit of Cameron Pass at 10,276 feet is ultra scenic. The snowy surrounding peaks announce you are in the presence of a Colorado Classic. There is a parking area at the pass summit with restroom facilities, a picnic area, and short hiking trails. The west descent is a sweeping broad decline down toward the high-alpine meadows and valley of North Park. A Moose Visitor Center is eight miles west of the summit, and whether you place your sidestand down here or not, do keep an eye out for these impressive beasts. The North Park area is home to the state's largest moose population.

A warm Walden welcome, circa 1911

If you plan to head south on Colorado 125 over Willow Creek Pass [143] toward Granby, there is a dirt road cutoff (County 27) one mile north of Gould that will allow you to avoid going all the way up to Walden then back down south on 125. It is a 13-mile ride over high bluffs giving you massive views of North Park and the surrounding mountain ranges.

Continuing to the Jackson County seat of Walden, the only incorporated town in this remote mountain county, you experience a sweeping ride with the Medicine Bow Mountains dominating the landscape to the west. Walden is a good place to refuel and perhaps find some chow. The Moose Creek Cafe on Main Street is popular with motorcyclists. Between here and the eastern end of this scenic byway, 92 miles distant, you take your chances finding food and fuel, but the last time I checked, Archer's Poudre River Resort near Rustic was open year-round, and they sell gas and grub. Sometimes while making a transit of Cache La Poudre Canyon and Cameron Pass, I see other seasonal services in operation, but the next time I cruise through, the lights are off and the parking area is devoid of any vehicles. You might find what you're looking for on this scenic byway, but to be safe, your best bets are at Ted's Place or Fort Collins on the east, and at Walden on the west.

Ride 4 **Rist Canyon**

Rist Canyon Road, County 52E

A 12-mile ride up through a twisting canyon to lofty picture postcard pastures with a high ridge ascent and descent

Rist Canyon is one of those motorcycle roads perfectly placed near a metro area. For escaping the Fort Collins grid of city streets filled with buzzing traffic, Rist Canyon serves up a quiet and rural curving ride. In minutes your riding environment changes like a new act on a theater stage. The bends on the ribbon of road aren't just the sideways kind, for you ascend almost 3,000 feet

in the first ten miles. Temperatures will be cooler, the landscape puts on new clothes, and mountain vistas are seemingly only an arm's length away.

This road and ride is launched out of the small and charming community of Bellvue on the northwest side of Fort Collins. Bellvue, with its lush grass and trees, has attracted those on two and four feet for a long

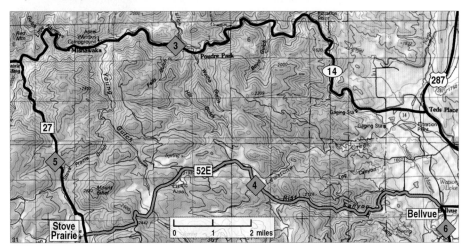

time. Teepee rings of the Arapaho Indians have been found in the vicinity. A large bison kill site was uncovered near the Cache La Poudre River two miles to the north.

Beginning in the 1860s, pale-skin settlers, drawn by the presence of fertile fields, dug irrigation ditches to siphon off some of the Cache La Poudre River's abundant water. The Union Pacific developed stone quarries nearby so they could have bridge building materials, and a worker town of Stout (now flooded by the Horsetooth Reservoir) flared to life for a decade or two. The inhabitants needed services, and thus were the humble beginnings of Bellvue. Several 1880s structures still remain and are visible from the saddle, including the 1884 sandstone building that hosted, over the decades, a general store, post office, barber shop, and saloon.

You can get your bike to Bellvue via Colorado 14 north out of Fort Collins. Turn left/west onto County 52E about a mile past the suburb town of LaPorte. However, if you are coming from the south you have the option of scooting over to Horsetooth Reservoir [006] and riding north on the fun County 23 road hugging the eastern hills and shoreline of Horsetooth Reservoir. This will deposit you right at Bellvue where you can turn your handlebars left onto County 52E and Rist Canyon Road. You will have a mile or two of pastures before you get swallowed by the narrow walls of the canyon.

After four miles of delicious back-and-forth, pendulum-like riding, you emerge onto picturesque mountain ranchlands. This diversity of landscape textures packed into a mere 12 miles is what distinguishes Rist Canyon Road. Nearing the ridgeline summit at 8,000 feet, the curves shorten their radii and it isn't uncommon to see the road surface coated with patches of sand and grit. So be forewarned! Continuing west, the tarmac unkinks itself and makes a rapid, 500-foot, descending encore through more idyllic fields, arriving at its Stove Prairie Road [005] conclusion two miles later.

Rist Canyon is ideal as a short, out-and-back ride any time of day. At low sun, some of those postcard fields and ranches will make you glad you brought your camera (or make you wish you had). The ride is also a link to others for some sweet longer journeys. I like to ride Rist over to Stove Prairie Road where a left turn puts the biggest chunk of this great road before your front wheel. A right turn will bring you to the inimitable Cache La Poudre Canyon [003] five miles farther. What great choices! Be sure to check your tank and hunger levels before venturing out, as options for satisfying both are slim to none along Rist Canyon and Stove Prairie.

Ride 5 **Stove Prairie**

Stove Prairie Road, Buckhorn Road, County 27

A rural 25-mile road with entertaining delights its entire length

This Stove Prairie adventure begins where County 27/Buckhorn Road takes off from US 34 a few miles west of Loveland. The first 5.2 miles through rolling countryside to Masonville is a fine warm-up to the meat of this ride. Looked at in this way, this is actually a lunchmeat sandwich ride. There's two meadowy slices of bread about five miles in length on the north and south, and between there's a 15-mile slice of the most savory riding you've ever consumed. Okay, the northernmost two miles are a little crusty as you approach Cache La Poudre Canyon, but you definitely don't want to leave this crust on the plate.

At Masonville coming up from the south, Buckhorn Road/County 27 comes to a T-intersection. There's a general store here that is sometimes open, sometimes closed. Regardless of its operating status, the small

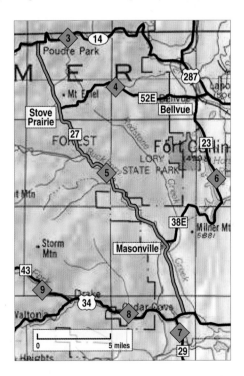

parking lot is where motorcyclists will often pause before continuing in one of two directions. A turn toward the east leads to Horsetooth Reservoir [006] five sweeping miles away. You are going to turn toward the west, however, and ride the heart of Stove Prairie Road. With the crooked Buckhorn Creek leading the way for the next 15 miles, you will have an amusement park of a ride— except better, and free.

At a little over ten miles from Masonville, Buckhorn Creek and this riding road part ways. County 44H or Buckhorn Road cuts off to the west and makes a dual-sport off-road ascent toward the Comanche Peak Wilderness. With the creek no longer taking the drunken staggering lead, there's a slight easing of the bends while the tarmac makes a 1,000-foot, curving climb through picturesque fields to the small, mostly spread out crossroads residential community of Stove Prairie. You will want to throttle down and approach sedately. The historic 1890s schoolhouse is here, as are the few additions made since. To the west, the dual-sport Old Flowers Road climbing to the Pingree Park

area gets its start. To the east is Rist Canyon Road [004] making an ascent over a shoulder of Buckhorn Mountain before engaging in a fun downhill bend-fest toward the north side of Horsetooth Reservoir and the small town of Bellvue, only a couple of miles from the northern reaches of Fort Collins.

From here to Cache La Poudre Canyon you have a 1,000-foot descent over five miles, passing through fertile grassy fields before a twisty forest finale. Speaking of forest, the shaggy tree-covered hills on this side of the Stove Prairie transit have experienced a lot of regrowth since the lumber years of the late 1800s. Much of the harvested wood was hacked into railroad ties and shipped north for the construction of the Transcontinental Railroad.

When you arrive at the world-class Cache La Poudre Canyon run on Colorado 14 [003], you can turn left/west toward Cameron Pass, or right for Ted's Place and a short scoot to US 287 and Fort Collins. Be sure to be fuel- and food-ready if venturing this far west of the Front Range. Service options are nil out here.

Ride 6 **Horsetooth Reservoir**

Centennial Drive, County 38E, 23

A 15-mile park-like ride along a reservoir with entertaining bends, grades, and views to the east

Horsetooth Reservoir was constructed in the late 1940s and is part of the Colorado-Big Thompson Project operated by the Bureau of Reclamation and the Northern Colorado Water Conservancy District. The same is true for Carter Lake [007] just south of Horsetooth, built a few years later in the early 1950s. The purpose of these water projects was to divert water from the west slope to a thirsty and thronged east slope for drinking, irrigation, and hydropower generation. Every time I ride along the bending shoreline of one of Colorado's reservoirs, I'm taken aback by the visual and reflective delights of these huge bodies. There's something about the lighting of Horsetooth Reservoir, the colors, and how the weather transforms this long and narrow lake into a different painting of nature every time I visit. My bike and I always looks forward to the times I let it run on the fun roads hugging the sides of Horsetooth Reservoir.

On the southern end of this ride is the crossroads community of Masonville, which is also the connection point to the Stove Prairie ride [005] and the journeys awaiting your bike in the Big Thompson Canyon area [008]. The northern terminus is Bellvue, which is also the launch point for the Rist Canyon ride [004]. To be sure there are other roads leading to Horsetooth, primarily from the Fort Collins area, as noted below, but the whole enchilada of this ride is the 15 miles from Masonville to Bellvue.

From Masonville on the south, County 38E

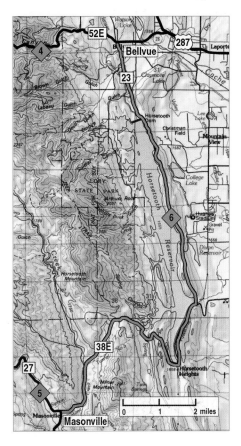

carves to the east and this sweeping ribbon of road will have you at the reservoir in five miles. After leaning your bike into the circling southern end of Horsetooth, 38E turns to the east and becomes one of the main access points (West Harmony Road) from the southern suburbs of Fort Collins. To continue the ride you can turn left/north where County 23/Centennial Drive becomes the giddy road following the hilly eastern contours of Horsetooth. A mile north of the 38E–23 intersection, there is the connection with Dixon Canyon Road. This is the other main road accessing Horsetooth from Fort Collins and it shoots right by Colorado State University's Hughes Stadium.

As your wheels spin north/south on County 23, you will see the ascents and descents before you, and the accompanying turns to negotiate. However, the distractions of leafy Fort Collins down below you to the east, and the beguiling water on the west will be begging for your attention! Fortunately there are plenty of pullouts and parking areas where you can pause if the contest for your attention becomes too burdensome. County 23 charts its course north all the way to Bellvue, following a 250-foot

descent from the elevations of Horsetooth, and is a charming place to rumble through as well. When your rpms settle down at the intersection with County 52E in Bellvue, you can turn the handlebars to the left for Rist Canyon, as mentioned earlier, or east toward north Fort Collins.

The Horsetooth Reservoir ride is a destination by itself, and a link to other rides in the area. If you are in the vicinity and are looking for an hour-long tour, taking your motorcycle to Horsetooth is a Grade A choice. Depending on the time of day, throw some food in your saddle or tankbag and ride to one of several picnic spots dotting the shorelines.

For a longer ride from Masonville, take Stove Prairie north to Rist Canyon, then return to this Horsetooth journey or go back to north Fort Collins—perhaps a leisurely 90 minutes. For a longer course, don't make the turn at Rist Canyon but continue north on Stove Prairie to the Cache La Poudre ride [003], turning east for the return, a two-hour-plus option. But all of them—Horsetooth, Stove Prairie, Rist Canyon, and Cache La Poudre—are outstanding two-wheeled ventures.

Ride 7 **Carter Lake**

County 8E, 31, 18E, Pole Hill Road

A refreshing 17-mile ride of fun hills and curving ascents to two lakeshores with views of the Northern Front Range

The Carter Lake–Pole Hill ride adds zip and pizzazz to a ride heading north or south in the Loveland or Berthoud area. It offers up-and-down grades, refreshing and scenic lakeside rides, and alluring curves in an area with mostly straight and flat roads. If you're in a hurry to get to your destination, then perhaps this excursion isn't your best choice, but if the ride *is* your destination, then these serpentine lakeside scoots are worth considering and exploring.

The 1,100-acre Carter Lake and nearby 327-acre Pinewood Reservoir are part of the Colorado-Big Thompson water reclamation project—a system of storage, tunnels, and creeks to divert west slope water to the populated east for drinking, irrigation, and electrical power generation. Both were completed in 1952. Both offer camping and picnicking, but there is a $7 fee to have

guilt-free use of the facilities. There is no fee to enjoy the lakeside breezes, views, and curving shore-side roads, however.

From the south side of Carter Lake, take

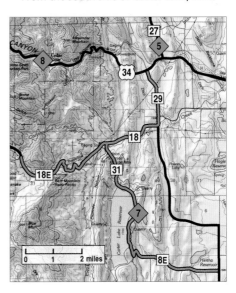

County 8E, which leads to the west off of County 23 and provides access to County 31 hugging the east side of the lake. The turn to Carter Lake is well marked. It doesn't take long for the flats and straights to shrink in your mirrors while curves and hills begin to swell before you. At the base of the lake area there is a sharp turn to the right for County 31. If access to the south side of Carter Lake is your aim, keep your front wheel pointed straight, but for the lakeside fling, you will want to hang a right onto County 31. From this semi-airy place you can look in practically every direction for competing views—from the sky blue waters of the lake on the west, to the greens of suburbia stretching to the eastern horizon. Now, of course, minimize the distractions, for the modest bends of the road up ahead will require some attention. The north side of Carter Lake has a marina with a restaurant. Other food service options are available upon leaving the lake area. Continuing north you have a 400-foot decline over 1.6 miles to County 31's conclusion at Pole Hill Road/County 18E.

By turning left on Pole Hill Road you will be treating yourself to five miles of twisting, fun-filled curves all the way to the paved road's conclusion at the Pinewood Reservoir.

I regularly ride Pole Hill to its scenic terminus when I'm in the area. The pretty azure blue lake may be a destination, but the pretzeled road itself is the bigger one for me.

Riding east on Pole Hill Road/County 18E brings you through nice ranches and farms before terminating at County 29 where you can head north to US 34, or south to make this a Carter Lake circle ride. If going north, Big Thompson Canyon [008] is west on US 34, and one mile to the east on 34 is the launch for the Stove Prairie ride [005]. Most of all, consider this Carter Lake–Pole Hill tour as perhaps a lunchtime thing or an evening cruise. And if your journey is longer, it provides a nice respite from the droning north-south alternatives farther east.

The eastern entrance of Big Thompson Canyon is known as "The Narrows."

Ride 8 **Big Thompson Canyon**

US 34

An 18-mile ride through one of Colorado's most renowned and scenic canyons, with easy access to other nearby rides and the Rocky Mountain National Park area

The tumbling Big Thompson River, and the canyon containing it, were named after Englishman David Thompson, a 19th-century engineer, astronomer, and trapper who explored many Rocky Mountain streams in search of prime trapping camps. Interestingly, in contrast to many other Colorado canyons, Big Thompson has never seen a train huffing black cinders as it labored up the 2,000-foot climb to Estes Park.

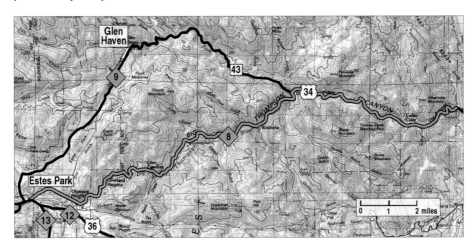

For more than 100 years, folks have been taking rides through Big Thompson Canyon.

Merchants in Loveland provided the impetus to build a road through the narrow canyon. The closeness of the canyon walls meant that the original wagon road was extremely tight in places. The Loveland–Estes Park stagecoach would have the right-of-way regardless of direction, and when meeting a freighter wagon coming the other way, the freighter would have to unhitch the horses, drive the team around the stagecoach, unload the wagon, remove the wheels, tip it over to squeeze it past, and then put it all back together again. Maybe the next time I come up behind a rolling roadblock RV I'll reflect with some gratitude that the road is no longer only one lane wide!

Take US 34 west from Loveland to get to Big Thompson Canyon. On the Estes Park side, US 34 is known as Big Thompson Canyon Road and extends from the main downtown area east to the canyon. When you approach from the Front Range, the ride begins with "The Narrows." This short section of the canyon is motorcycle enchantment with its tight and nicely cambered curves, punctuated by the river squeezing through a narrow chasm of vertical granite walls. The riding magic endures all the way to Estes Park as you are entertained with just about everything a canyon could present.

On July 31, 1976, a late afternoon thunderstorm parked itself above Estes Park and poured 12 inches of rain in a period of only four hours. Around 9 p.m. that evening, a raging wall of water 20 feet high raced down Big Thompson Canyon toward unsuspecting travelers, campers, and residences in an area where much less rain had fallen. Tragically, more than 140 lives were lost that summer evening. The final toll to property was equally staggering, with 418 homes, 400 cars, and 52 businesses destroyed. There are several roadside markers and memorials in the canyon and it is worth pulling over for some reflection.

The Big Thompson Canyon ride is surely a destination all by itself. That there are other great bike rides in every direction from its winding course is icing on the icing. At the eastern entrance, the Carter Lake [007] and Stove Prairie [005] rides extend a very appealing invitation. Seven miles west into the canyon at Drake, the sweet County 43 carves a path to Glen Haven and on to Estes Park [009]. Estes Park, at the western reaches of this journey, is ground zero for numerous other rides, such as the Little Thompson River [012], Peak-to-Peak Scenic Byway [013], Bear Lake Road [011], and Trail Ridge Road [010].

As for services of the food and fuel kind, there is little on US 34 between Loveland

Photographer Louis Charles McClure captured the ethereal beauty of the canyon in 1909.

and Estes Park. The historic Colorado Cherry Company near the east entrance is an interesting place to stop for a light snack or meal. The River Forks Inn at Drake, seven miles west into the canyon, is a full-service food place for the palate and more. Your best bet for fuel is either at the Loveland end or the Estes Park end of the ride.

Ride 9 **Glen Haven**

County 43, Devils Gulch Road, MacGregor Avenue

A 15-mile backroad alternative to US 34 that runs along a quiet twisting river to, and through, a quaint destination town

On the east side, the turnoff from US 34 to County 43 and the small town of Glen Haven is seven miles into Big Thompson Canyon at the canyon community of Drake. On the west, or Estes Park side, MacGregor Avenue at the first stoplight east of the

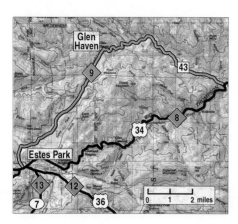

downtown area goes to the north off of the main East Elkhorn Avenue. In about a mile you'll find the eastward County 43/Devils Gulch Road. Regardless of direction, this is a fantastic road for motorcycles, and those in the know who consider the ride as the destination often choose this traverse over the trafficked US 34 main route.

From the canyon, turn onto County 43 going west, where a confirming sign lets you know that yes, indeed, you will arrive in Estes Park 15 engaging miles later. The riding introduction is sweet and polite, with the North Fork of the Big Thompson River showing some nice form. At three miles, and for the next five, things get intimate and you'll be leaning your bike into fun sets of tight, closely spaced curves as you ascend the narrowing canyon.

The rain is causing this biker to either grimace or grin. I'm gonna go with the latter!

The small roadside community of Glen Haven is a great place to stop and put the sidestand down. The Glen Haven General Store bakes killer cinnamon rolls and makes fresh deli sandwiches to your order. There are a couple of benches and tables outside where you can sit and watch life pass—or ride—by.

The slow down at Glen Haven is followed by a speed up toward an 800-foot climb, largely accomplished with two sets of tightly folded hairpin curves. Your reward at the top is a major photo op of the Continental Divide peaks of Rocky Mountain National Park. Their skyscraping lineup stands at attention for your eye or camera lens. A gentle descent through grassy meadows, which keeps the vistas before you, is the finale to Estes Park. Of course, if you're going in the other direction, the best sights would be in your mirrors, and I'd heartily advise your pulling over before you cruise down to Glen Haven!

On the east side of MacGregor Avenue, as you conclude or launch this journey, the famous and historic 138-room Stanley Hotel awaits your perusal. The Georgian-style hotel has hosted a Who's Who of guests over its 100 years, but to many, it is known as the place that inspired Stephen King to write his thriller, *The Shining.*

At the eastern entrance to Big Thompson Canyon, you can connect to the Carter Lake–Pole Hill ride [007] and the Stove Prairie scoot [005]. Estes Park is a base camp for all kinds of rides, such as the Little Thompson River [012], Peak to Peak Scenic Byway [013], Bear Lake Road [011], and Trail Ridge Road [010].

Ride 10 **Trail Ridge**

US 34

A 40-mile alpine ride on North America's highest continuous paved road through the world-class scenery of Rocky Mountain National Park

Even though Rocky Mountain National Park is well known and documented, I have to say that from the moment you enter the gates you will be struck by the grandeur of the vistas, and will understand why this was designated a national park. As you round every curve and ride over every rise of Trail Ridge Road/US 34, you'll realize that this is one extraordinary road, especially as experienced on two wheels.

The name Trail Ridge comes from its near-

ness to the foot trails established by Native Americans to cross these sky-reaching peaks. It was constructed from 1926 to 1932 after it was recognized that Fall River Road, built in 1920, was going to fall short as a touring road through the park. Careful thought went into the engineering and design of Trail Ridge Road, and its placement enhances the visual aspects of the park. Kindly curves and hills accommodate those transfixed by pleasant distractions, and the road has plenty of

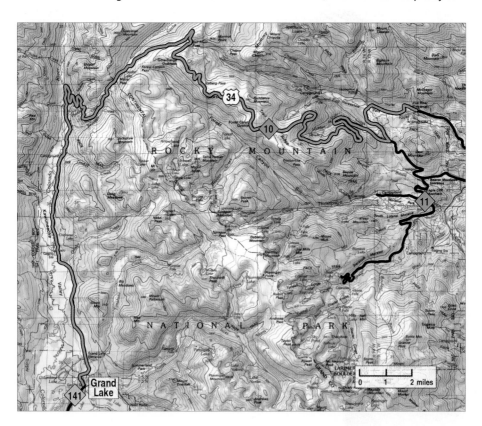

exposure to the sun's warming rays, which enable it to stay open more days during the winter, when fierce weather visits these awesome heights.

Trail Ridge runs a 40-mile route from Rocky Mountain National Park's eastern Fall River Entrance to the park's southwest portal just north of Grand Lake. Abundant signs in Estes Park will point the way. There is also the US 36 approach, leading south out of downtown Estes Park, which connects with Trail Ridge Road/US 34 six miles later. This southerly passage provides direct access to the Moraine Park–Bear Lake Road ride [011]. There is a $10 entrance fee if you are alone on a bike, but a passenger will increase the fee to the max of $20. This is good news for those of you who want to bring the entire family on your motorcycle!

The ascent up to Trail Ridge's highest point, at 12,183 feet, is dramatic at just about every moment. Be on the lookout for grazing deer and elk, and on the west side, their big moose cousins. Linger at the scenic pullouts and soak in the park experience. More than eight miles of the winding road on which you will be riding are above 11,000 feet. On the west side of the "I'm Above Timberline" segment, the Alpine Visitor Center can be a welcome and timely sight, depending on your needs and the weather. From here, the descent gains momentum as you cruise toward Milner Pass and then navigate a sharp series of tightly wound curves down to the headwaters of the Colorado River. The riding then levels out and sweeps toward the Grand Lake entrance, the Never Summer Range on the west guarding the way.

The Estes Park area at the east end of Rocky Mountain National Park is ground zero for numerous exceptional motorcycle rides— Big Thompson Canyon [008], Glen Haven [009], Little Thompson River [012], and the Peak to Peak Scenic Byway [013]. On the southwest end of the park, great riding connects to the Grand Lake entrance via the Colorado Headwaters [141]. If on a dedicated dual-sport, Stillwater Pass [139] climbs west from nearby Granby. Also, Fall River Road in the park, mentioned at the beginning, still exists and draws adventurous dual-sport riders every summer. Except for the comfort facilities at the Alpine Visitor Center, there are no services along Trail Ridge Road. You will need to prep for the ride at Estes Park or Grand Lake. Finally, you will enjoy Trail Ridge most by cruising, rather than rushing. Savoring it is the best way to experience it.

Ride 11 **Bear Lake**

US 36, Bear Lake Road

A ten-mile ride in Rocky Mountain National Park, through excellent elk-viewing habitat and an awe-inspiring meadow, to a high-alpine lake, with unsurpassed views all along the way

While you are in the Rocky Mountain National Park don't miss the ride up Bear Lake Road to magical Moraine Park, and then on to Bear Lake nestled at 9,500 feet along the Continental Divide. While Trail Ridge Road is the more famed journey in the park, the oft overlooked Bear Lake trip enchants one with

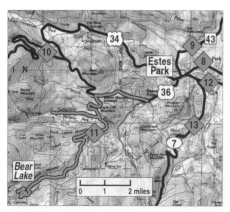

scenery that takes a back seat to no other ride in the state.

From downtown Estes Park, the way south to US 36 and Moraine Park Road is well marked. This is one of two main entrances on the east side of the park. The other is US 34 leading northwest out of Estes Park. Both roads meet later to join forces for the Trail Ridge Road ascent. For this ride, however, head south on Bear Lake Road, about one mile west of the US 34 park entrance.

Moraine Park appears a bit more than a mile after making the turn. If you just stay on Bear Lake Road, you get a tremendous view, but I heartily suggest you make a right/westward turn onto Moraine Park Campground Road 1.3 miles after joining the journey to Bear Lake. At 0.5 miles, turn left onto Fern Lake Road, and for two miles you can ride

the northern rim of Moraine Park, going deep toward its western edges at Forest Canyon. Moraine Park is embedded in a spectacular, jaw-dropping setting. Its namesake is a giant alpine meadow, teeming with herds of grazing elk, all guarded on the western ramparts by dramatic snowcapped peaks grazing the sky. All this is particularly memorable when experienced from an open-air motorcycle.

This cul-de-sac road will have you turning around at two miles. Upon returning to Bear Lake Road, turn right/south for the lake. A full view of Moraine Park, containing the headwaters of the Big Thompson River, makes an encore presentation before the road begins a twisting and scenic journey to its namesake lake seven miles farther. The fun road here is an attraction, but the main event is what you will behold over your handlebars, and it will serve to calm your throttle hand. Like other journeys in this book, this is most definitely a case where the destination road takes a back seat to its surroundings. Be in cruise mode, let the sights sink in, pull over for photos, and let the ride to Bear Lake linger. There are hiking trailheads and picnic grounds along the way. A parking area with a half-mile loop trail to Sprague Lake is a good place to park your bike. You may prefer this quieter lake to the one at the end of the road, but the view of Bear Lake is worth the anticipation.

Nearby Estes Park comes through with all kinds of services to refuel, refill, and relax. This Bear Lake ride can be linked with Trail Ridge Road [010], and the many rides in the area to which it connects.

Lyons celebrating Independence Day in 1901, and Lyons today

Ride 12 **Little Thompson River**

US 36, Colorado 66

A 20-mile link between the Front Range and the Estes Park–Rocky Mountain National Park area, with side journeys to hiking, picnic areas, and scenic attractions

US 36 between Lyons and Estes Park provides easy and alternative access between the Rocky Mountain National Park area and the Front Range. For many south of the Fort Collins and Loveland area, this route is probably the quickest, and fortunately it isn't a featureless, ho-hum scoot. You'll ride through small canyons, tight and sweeping curves, ups and downs, gulches and hilltops, and meadows and forests, with the added bonus of towering views of Estes Park and Rocky Mountain National Park.

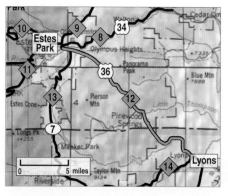

Lyons was named after Edward Lyon (an "s" was appended later), who came to the area to quarry the large red sandstone outcroppings and mountains in the surrounding country. The sandstone here is considered the hardest in the world, and railroad tracks laid to the town delivered a business boost to the quarries in the late 1880s. However, the invention of cement in 1910 delivered a business blow to the quarries, but not before their handsome stones were used in the construction of more than 15 sandstone structures in town, many of them listed on the National Register of Historic Places. The red stone was also hauled down to Boulder for construction at the new University of Colorado. So as you ride through Lyons to embark for Estes Park, count how many sandstone structures you can see, and if you spot the town library, note that you're looking at what used to be the train depot.

Lyons, sometimes known as the "Double Gateway to the Rockies," delivers a one-two riding punch to higher elevations. Spectacular Colorado 7 in St. Vrain Canyon [014] heads south out of town, and this journey counters with its own two-wheeled features as soon as you follow US 36 signs northwest to Estes Park. First up is a short and appetizing canyon run before a steady climb of 800 feet. Take a breather through Muggins Gulch with its nearby residential area, then ask for seconds. The Little Thompson River will be brought to the table, and up you'll go again for several hundred more feet.

Scenic grassy meadow riding is next on the stage with the dramatic peaks of Rocky Mountain National Park the backdrop setting. The dessert is a winding descent to Estes Park at the doorstep of the national park. US 36 takes on the name of North St. Vrain Avenue as it passes the south shoreline of Lake Estes. When you arrive at the first stoplight, think of it this way: you have just come to a hub of some of the best riding in the state. You came in on just one of the spokes. To the left/south is Colorado 7 and the introduction of the Peak to Peak Scenic Byway [013]. Rocky Mountain National Park is waiting with two rides—Bear Lake [011] and Trail Ridge Road [010]. Big Thompson

Canyon can't be missed either [008]. All this is just a sampling of what can be experienced in the area by motorcycle.

Four miles into this US 36 ride from Lyons, the dirt Longmont Dam Road leads south to Button Rock Reservoir, another four winding miles distant. This is not a recreation area, but there are trails and you can find a scenic spot for a picnic. At 9.6 miles, paved County 47/Big Elk Road follows the slightly crooked West Fork of the Little Thompson River south five miles to an area of several small lakes, where hiking and picnic opportunities also tempt one to deploy the sidestand.

With only 20 miles between Lyons and Estes Park, fuel and food options center around those two communities. There's a camp store or two toward Estes Park, but count on the refuel and refill at either end of this ride. Estes Park as a large community has just about everything under the sun—no matter what your taste buds might be clamoring for. The downtown area presents a menu of dining choices, as does US 34 heading toward Big Thompson Canyon. The Stone Cup in Lyons, just a block north of downtown's east-west Main Street is a popular coffee stop and deli for motorcyclists.

Ride 13 **Peak to Peak**

Colorado 119, 72, 7

A 60-mile ride alongside the Continental Divide providing stunning scenic views, historical mining towns and homesteads, and connections to a multitude of other special motorcycle runs

The Peak to Peak Scenic Byway runs from the Victorian mining towns of Central City and Black Hawk all the way to Estes Park at the eastern entrance of Rocky Mountain National Park. You can either ride the whole 60-mile serpentine byway as part of a daylong journey, or you can enjoy it as a link to other roads leading to or from the Front Range. This chapter highlights what to expect, what to look for, and what to take advantage of while traversing the entire length of this magnificent route.

This Colorado Scenic Byway makes its southern launch via Colorado 119, from the mining-turned-casino towns of Central City and Black Hawk. For a riding tour of the nearby semi-ghost towns, check out the Oh My God–Nevadaville–Russell Gulch ride [030]. Just north of town, 1.7 miles on the Peak to Peak, is the dual-sport Apex Valley Road to the ghost town of Apex and the scenic sights of Mammoth Gulch [028]. Three and a half miles farther, and 1,000 feet higher, is the western terminus of Golden Gate Canyon [027]. If you're headed north, pull over at the Golden Gate entrance and look back to the southwest for a glimpse of the Continental Divide. The tall, shapely mounts on the horizon are Grays and Torreys Peaks. At 14,270 feet, Grays Peak is the tallest point on the Continental Divide in the Lower 48.

Eight and a half miles from Black Hawk, Gap Road [026] cuts off toward Golden Gate Canyon State Park and the Twin Spruce descent to Coal Creek Canyon [025], which can also be reached via Colorado 72 at mile 15.4. One mile later is Magnolia Road [023]. In this area, expansive views of the Indian Peaks and the southern flanks of Rocky Mountain National Park will begin to fill the horizon above your handlebars, but a sweet series of lazy hairpin curves will keep you from lingering and looking for too long.

At 18 miles from the southern launch of this ride, the old mining community of Nederland extends a greeting. Historically, it was the site of a mill processing the silver from mines surrounding Caribou, which was five miles away and 1,600 feet higher (see the Eldora–Caribou ride [022]). A Dutch company owned several mines in the area, and gave this "lowland" area below Caribou the name "Nederland," which is Dutch for Netherlands. When you pass by the Bucyrus Steam Shovel on the west side of the roundabout, you're looking at an earthmover that helped excavate a big ditch called the Panama Canal. Several notable restaurants popular with motorcyclists—The Katmandu, Whistler's Cafe, First Street Pub & Grill, and Wild Mountain Smokehouse—are clustered around First Street and Jefferson Avenue. Nederland is also the connection point for the Boulder Canyon ride [021].

The remaining 42 miles to Estes Park are my favorite part of the Peak to Peak: the traffic thins, the panoramas thicken, and you'll be riding a bending, undulating ribbon of road surely meant for a bike. The parade of linking motorcycle roads will continue— Sugarloaf Mountain [020] at 21.7 miles; Lefthand Canyon [016] at the interesting

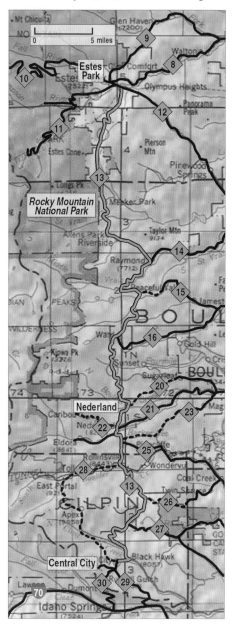

community of Ward at 30 miles; the Overland Road to James Canyon [015] at 34.4 miles; and the great St. Vrain Canyon [014] at 40 miles. Other rides nearby include dedicated dual-sport journeys on the Switzerland Trail and to Rollins Pass, as well as ventures launched out of Estes Park. On the north side of Ward, you will see a sign for Brainard Lake. You will have to pay a fee at the station but it is worth it for the five-mile-long, high-alpine, paved road, with gorgeous "Oh, my!" views. Claim a picnic table, unpack the food from your saddlebags, and as you munch away, appreciate this high country setting and the two wheels that inimitably delivered you here.

The drum beats of riding delights and scenic vistas increase in intensity as the southern ramparts of Rocky Mountain National Park grow ever closer. There's a pullout at Allenspark where you can pause before Mt. Meeker, rising to 13,911 feet. See if you can discern how neighboring Chiefs Head Peak to the west got its name! At 13 miles south of Estes Park, your bike will pass over North St. Vrain Creek. There's no indication you should throttle down here, but steal a glance to the west at Rocky Mountain National Park's stunning Wild Basin, and Mt. Copeland at 13,176 feet. Two winding miles closer to Estes Park you'll spot the stone chapel at St. Malo, with Mt. Meeker towering behind it. The famous 14,259-foot Longs Peak, with its diamond face, is just to the north.

There are numerous locations for getting food and fuel along the 60-mile Peak to Peak Scenic Byway. One of my favorite options is the B&F grocery store in Nederland, where they have a great deli serving warm and fresh food. I'll tuck some in my tankbag and have a picnic in downtown Nederland watching motorcycle traffic go by, or find a spot on the Peak to Peak for a scenery-filled, outdoor lunch.

Ride 14 **St. Vrain Canyon**

Colorado 7

A 14-mile ride up a lightly traveled canyon road laced with beautifully engineered curves

The St. Vrain Canyon is a ride destination if there ever was one. Plain and simple. The curves are gorgeously and intrinsically engineered, with cambers surely designed as a gift to motorcyclists. The smooth, yet grippy road surface tends to be grit-free. At 14 miles, the twistiness of St. Vrain Canyon lasts much longer than most, continuing to serve up curvy hors d'oeuvres after other canyons have closed their kitchens. And finally, with few residences in this cliffy and steep-walled place, even at its quieter western reaches, it is one of the more "unattended" Front Range canyons.

Colorado 7 south out of Lyons follows the corner-carving desires of the fast flowing South St. Vrain Creek. This is the case for

nine miles west into the narrow chasm. Above the confluence of the Middle St. Vrain and St. Vrain Creeks, the Middle St. Vrain shows the way. The ride up the canyon is a 2,600-foot ascent to the junction with Colorado 72 and the Peak to Peak Scenic Byway.

It is easy to find the well-marked Colorado 7

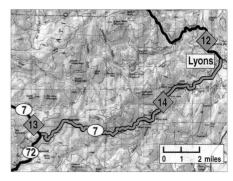

in the small downtown area of Lyons. The first few miles out of town will ease you into what's ahead. The landscape is pastoral (literally), the curves sweeping, and the views distant. Looking ahead you will see the hillsides becoming narrower and steeper, a hint of what Colorado 7 is about to serve. For the next 10 miles, a steady diet of sinuous, back-and-forth roadway is brought to the table. There's a nice variety here and it is all tasty. At 7.5 miles, the South St. Vrain picnic area will be on the south side of the road, but admittedly, one is often reluctant to interrupt the flow of this meal and put the fork . . . er, sidestand down.

At 11.6 miles from Lyons, County 103 branches off to the left/south to the cozy community of Raymond. Signs note the turnoff. This paved, four-mile, tree-lined, creekside road leads you through a quiet cluster of homes and an old resort-like community center with a general store, and provides a welcome a change of scen-

ery and pace. The county road concludes on the southwest end at the Peak to Peak.

At 14 miles when you arrive at Colorado 72, you'll join the Peak to Peak Scenic Byway [013], where you will have a dazzling array of choices. If you continue north on Colorado 7, ultra-scenic Estes Park awaits your two-wheeled arrival, from which you can tour Rocky Mountain National Park or return to the Front Range via US 36 alongside the Little Thompson River [012] or through Big Thompson Canyon [008]. Venturing south on Colorado 72 presents a stacked lineup of returning canyons, beginning with James Canyon [015] and Lefthand Canyon [016]. The town of Lyons at the base of this ride provides food and fuel services. The Stone Cup is a popular place for those on two wheels to grab a bakery sandwich, a coffee-bean brew, and a place outside to sit and contemplate momentous things . . . like where to ride to next.

Ride 15 **James Canyon**

Lefthand Canyon Drive, James Canyon Drive, Overland Road, County 94

A quiet, twisting 15-mile canyon ride through a historical community and varied terrain, connecting to the Peak to Peak Scenic Byway

James Canyon, north of Boulder, has a combination of features delivering serious ride benefits, which include an excellent road surface, a diversity of curves, a historical community to pass through, and a sweet ascent—and all this in a relatively quiet and secluded scenic canyon.

The canyon takes its name from the historic townsite of Jamestown eight miles into this ride. The area was first settled by George Zweck, who built a cabin in 1860 and brought cattle to the narrow, high-walled valley. Gold strikes nearby, like the one below Gold Hill, helped usher in the 1859 Gold Rush. By 1864, fortune-seeking miners were scampering all over the hills above Jamestown, but back then the miners called the place Buckhorn. It was subsequently re-

named to Camp Jimtown, and finally, to the more formal-sounding Jamestown.

The eastern door to James Canyon is off US 36, five miles north of Boulder where you turn west onto Lefthand Canyon Drive. At 5.2 miles, Lefthand Canyon Drive [016] makes a left-hand turn while you remain on this sweetly and tightly bound road, now called James Canyon Drive. There is some artistry to these bends, and your bike will be enjoying the leaned-over lines it will be drawing on this twisting canvas. *Pay attention* to the signs noting speeds for the upcoming curves. One can be lulled into a "motion of constant speed" until *bam!*—along comes the exception. There will be two right-hand curves looking innocently like many of the others, with the exception of a 15-mph

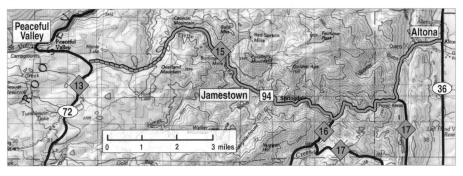

Jamestown in the late 1800s

Jamestown more than a century later

warning sign. You'll be in for a nasty surprise if you miss the sign and go in thinking it is another 30 mph bend.

Jamestown today is part ghost town and part tourist town. The main street, with its border of trees, is reached at almost eight miles and ushers you into a slow cruising ride through the community. Dual-sport riders can look for County 102J/Gold Lake Road, which follows Jim Creek to the west. It will deliver an adventure toward the Peak to Peak Scenic Byway [013], as will this smile-inducing James Canyon ride.

The western seven miles of James Canyon is distinct from the eastern eight. The light traffic becomes lighter. The eastern half is deep in the canyon, while the western portion rises above it. Views of narrow, rocky slopes expand to vistas of distant peaks. The four miles of road that climb west out of Jamestown are paved, but when you top out at 8,400 feet—three miles shy of the Peak to Peak Highway—the road base changes to smooth, maintained dirt, and the name changes to Overland Road. Any street bike should be able to handle this if the conditions are dry. I would give it a go, if just to make it to the stunning panorama of the Indian Peaks and the Continental Divide. This route ends with a finale at the Peak to Peak, just east of jaw-dropping Peaceful Valley, with views of photogenic Sawtooth Mountain at 12,304 feet.

There are no fill-the-tank options between Boulder and Lyons on the east side, and Nederland, 16 miles south of Overland Road's connection with the Peak to Peak, on the west. For food, there is a cafe in Jamestown, and the Millsite Inn in nearby Ward on the Peak to Peak is popular with motorcyclists.

Ride 16 **Lefthand Canyon**

Lefthand Canyon Drive, County 106

A quiet and forested 14-mile creekside canyon ascent to an eclectic community and the Peak to Peak Scenic Byway

Lefthand Canyon Drive is a ride on a path many have trod before. Climbing 3,200 feet over 14 gradual miles, Lefthand Canyon Drive has seen more than its share of fun- and fortune-seeking individuals. The gold strike that helped launch the 1859 Gold Rush came from Lefthand's southern valley walls, in a gulch just below Gold Hill. Discovery didn't come from an exploratory mine—a visible golden vein was spotted on the surface. But other golden harvests did come from mines bored into the sides of the hills above Lefthand Creek, with mills like the

Gale Mill and the Captain Jack Mill handling the extracts. Even though there is an old cabin or two, a decaying small building, and an "interesting" community at the top, you'll see little evidence of the past on this serpentine canyon road. For the most part, deep and dense conifers cover and cloak where enterprising souls toiled in years past.

Essentially, Lefthand is one of dozens and dozens of Front Range canyons carved by rushing streams draining snowmelt and water from higher elevations. Because you're on the east side of the Continental Divide,

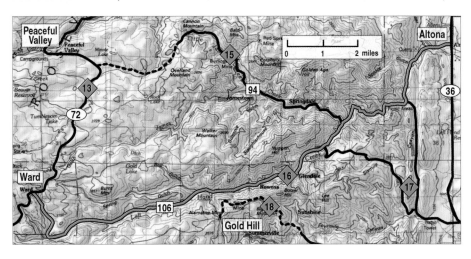

Back in 1900, maintaining your vehicle and its suspension were key to enjoying a ride through Lefthand Canyon.

the water here is just beginning its flowing march toward the Gulf of Mexico. As with the streams in neighboring canyons, Lefthand Creek charts a crooked course on its descent from high up, and this translates into another sublime riding road. You'll find Lefthand Canyon Drive pointing to the west off of US 36, five miles north of Boulder's northern extremities.

Lefthand Canyon brings two kinds of salad to the table. The first several miles is a Cobb salad, with a variety of greens in a bowl, multi-textured tasty curves, and a smooth creamy roadway dressing. When you ask for seconds at mile 5.2, where you make a "lefthand" turn to stay with this canyon, a different salad is served. The canyon is a darker spinach-y green, with a narrow-walled, shadowy tint, and a deep pine sameness. The curves are looser—not as tight and crunchy as the iceberg lettuce below. Dessert is brought when you idle down for the town of Ward at the top of the canyon.

Ward was, at one time, one of the richest towns in Colorado. The nearby mines were prodigious with their silver production. Named for Calvin Ward, who prospected an 1860 claim known as Miser's Dream, the town boomed for many decades while others flared then faded. Two separate, sweeping fires reduced much of Ward to charred wood and ash, but profitable mines nearby

rebuilt the town almost overnight. Over time, the silver became scarcer, as did the population. By 1920, Ward was mostly deserted. When the nearby Peak to Peak Scenic Byway was constructed in the 1930s, the population rebounded a bit but faded again in the 40s and 50s to only a dozen individuals. In the 60s it became a place of interest for "hippies" and has had a population of more than 100 ever since. Ward is now a zoning- and covenant-free community with plenty of character, and is an interesting place to ride through.

Lefthand Canyon is a fun, relatively quiet, 14-mile shot to the Peak to Peak Scenic Byway [013]. Once on the Peak to Peak, you can return to the Front Range via a variety of canyon descents. To be sure, Lefthand Canyon is always a top-grade descent choice. It's also a sweet connector to several other rides: 2.5 miles from US 36 to the south is Olde Stage Road [017]; bearing to the right at 5.2 miles you enter James Canyon [015]; and 6.2 miles south gets you to Lee Hill Drive [017]. At 10.1 miles, you can access dual-sport country to the south via steep Lick Skillet Road, one of the most vertical county roads around!

In Ward, you can pause for a sandwich or snack, and up on the Peak to Peak the nearby Millsite Inn is where many have put a sidestand down.

Ride 17 **Lee Hill–Olde Stage**

Lee Hill Drive, Olde Stage Road, County 75, 106

Two appealing alternative routes to access Lefthand and James Canyons, on 12 miles of winding, hilly backroads

If you are in the Boulder area or intend to ride Lefthand or James Canyons, these are two roads you might want to know about. They aren't amazing destination rides, but they are attractive and fun alternatives for traveling to and from the canyons northwest of Boulder. Plus, when you have only a limited amount of time, it's nice to have an inventory of short nearby rides from which to draw your diversion du jour.

Over the 1990 Thanksgiving holiday, on a day of 80-mph winds, mentally unstable Arnold Stein threw a burning mattress out the front door of his home along Olde Stage Road, starting a wildfire that burned ten homes, five outbuildings, and 3,000 acres. It was one of Boulder County's largest and

worst wildfires. While cruising along Olde Stage, your attention can be easily fixed on the remnants of this destruction, but you'd

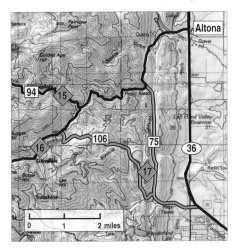

do well, instead, to keep your eye out for bears running across the road. I uncovered two recent accidents, in 2006 and 2008, where bicyclists collided with the bruins, the former during the cycling segment of a triathalon. The bear, estimated at 550 pounds, was reported to have just shrugged off the hit and continued on his way.

These two winding and hilly circuits offer a more involved route from Boulder to Lefthand and James Canyons. Instead of riding US 36 five miles north of Boulder's northern reaches, turn your handlebars west onto Lee Hill Drive off of Broadway, a half mile south of where Broadway merges with US 36 for its jaunt north to Lyons. One mile after joining Lee Hill Drive, Old Stage cuts off to the right for a rolling, 3.1-mile ride to Lefthand; staying with Lee Hill, you'll have a more crooked and undulating 4.4-mile traverse to the canyon.

Each alternative has its advantages. Olde Stage isn't as long or as engaging as Lee Hill, but it does deliver you and your bike to right where the fun stuff of Lefthand Canyon [016] begins, almost three miles before the access to James Canyon [015]. Lee Hill Drive is a more motivating ribbon of road, but you connect with Lefthand almost four miles deeper into the canyon, missing some of its more divine details. Really, however, the choice is simple—you ride both!

From Boulder, here's a nice looping ride if you're pressed for time: Olde Stage to Lefthand, north to Lee Hill, and back. If longer saddle time in on your agenda, then perhaps go out one way and come back another. Just go with what suits your fancy. 'Tis nice to have choices! And to be sure, the five cruising miles up US 36 can be great too, depending on your mood and motivation.

Ride 18 **Sunshine–Gold Hill**

Sunshine Canyon Drive, County 52

A twisting, hilly ten-mile ride (last four unpaved) to one of Colorado's oldest mining communities, where connections with other dual-sport rides await

Sunshine Canyon Drive is one of those fun and folded roads among the many in the Boulder area. The road goes every direction, horizontally and vertically. Your view from the saddle ranges from forests and meadows, to ranches and old homesteads. At the end of this ten-mile ride, after gaining 3,000 feet in elevation, you'll find historic Gold Hill, the site of Colorado's first permanent mining camp. In January of 1859, a lode discovered at nearby Gold Run helped launch the Gold Rush to Colorado. In the 150 years since, Gold Hill has seen population ups and downs, often coinciding with the boom and bust of ores mined in its vicinity. It has survived two major fires, but numerous old structures remain and stand in recognition of those who have passed by before.

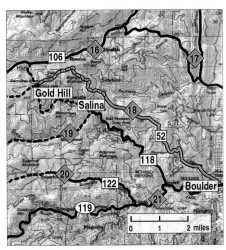

To access Sunshine Canyon Drive, ride west on the east-west Mapleton Avenue, which is three blocks north of downtown Boulder's well-known Pearl Street. On

Sunshine Canyon Road, in the aftermath of the Fourmile Canyon fire of September 2010.

Mapleton, you will pass rows of charming older homes, and at Fourth Street this engaging and scenic ride begins. There's a nice back-and-forth, curving rhythm to the climb. As for its name, the southern exposure makes "sunshine" an apt description, but the canyon portion of it doesn't last long. After a mile of so, you will climb out of the cut in the hills and begin a weaving ascent formed by hillside contours. There will be some nice respites along the way as you crest into several gentle and scenic meadows. At five miles, there is a small parking area on the south side (with a portable restroom) for the Bald Mountain Scenic Area. A one-mile hike brings you to 360-degree, bird-in-flight views.

As you approach the upper reaches of this ride and continue on toward Gold Hill, you will enter the burn zone of Colorado's most expensive wildfire ever, the Fourmile Canyon Fire of September 2010. You will note a mosaic of damage—places where the inferno charred everything in its path, and patches where the winds and whims of the fire skipped over swaths of forests and tucked-away homes.

At six miles, the paved surface becomes smooth and maintained dirt. You can turn around here or continue the fun for four more miles to Gold Hill. In dry conditions, there would be no issues handling it on a street bike. Just be smooth and enjoy the views. And vistas there are! At this altitude, many of the forested slopes that surround Boulder will be below you, and the shimmering Indian Peaks on the western horizon above you.

After joining the off-road portion of this journey, there is a series of elevation-gaining

switchbacks, then a 1,000-foot, gorge-like valley on the north before you emerge to a sweet, flat, meadow-covered hilltop. A short, 200-foot descent brings you to rustic Gold Hill. A slow westerly cruise of the main street is a trip through time. The restored inn is on the National Register of Historic Places. The Gold Hill two-room schoolhouse, in use since 1873, is the oldest continuously operating school in Colorado. The General Store is worth a stop. Lunch and bakery items are available and one can sit at a table near the old woodstove or do some munchin' outside with the time warp all around.

In addition to turning around and retracing the route up, you will have three dirt-road options. If you are astride a dedicated dual-sport bike, the Lick Skillet Road/County 90 drops northward to Lefthand Canyon [016] only one mile away. It is one of the steepest county roads in the country! Gold Hill Road/County 52 goes north and is a maintained dirt road, which gently meanders to the Peak to Peak Scenic Byway [013] seven miles distant. Finally, on the east end of town, Boulder Street winds south, dropping 1,700 feet over four smooth miles to the old mining community of Salina, where you can pick up the Fourmile Canyon ride [019].

There aren't any fuel options in the area, but with Boulder so close, it shouldn't be an issue. For a meal, the Gold Hill General Store is the only game in town. I had a decent barbecue sandwich there the last time I passed through. The Sunshine Canyon ride is a great, one- or two-hour ride out of the Boulder area, and can easily become a longer venture when linked with one of the dirt-road options out of Gold Hill.

Looking west down Gold Hill's main street

Ride 19 **Fourmile Canyon**

Fourmile Canyon Drive, County 118

A divine ten-mile creekside canyon ride to historical sites, with links to dual-sport options and connections to other Boulder area rides

To find this route, take Colorado 119 west out of Boulder. Two miles after you enter Boulder Canyon, turn right at the sign for Fourmile Canyon. The tight, tree-lined, bend-fest of a road serves up a steady stream of curves following the steady streams of Fourmile Creek. At 3.7 miles you will pass the few remaining homes of the 1875 mining camp of Crisman. At five miles, a downshift for the fork in the road will mark your arrival at Salina, founded in 1874 by a surveying party from Salina, Kansas. Many of the old structures remain, including the 1885 schoolhouse and 1902 church. There is a nicely detailed street sign here, pointing the way north to Gold Hill, and west to Wall Street and Sunset—which is where you're headed. Before you continue on, look north up Gold Run Road. You will see the steeple of a historical church, and

the route to the very historic Gold Hill [018] only four miles away, but almost 2,000 feet higher!

Here at the halfway point of this two-wheeled journey, the road shifts from a tightly snaking, paved road, to a smooth, straight, dirt surface. Any street bike would be fine on this maintained surface. Follow the sign's arrows to the west and enjoy a slow cruising ride up the narrow valley to Wall Street and Sunset. In only a couple of miles, the historic Wall Street Assay Office (now a museum) appears on the north side of the road. This was a place where the fortunes of many prospectors would turn. The assayer would examine ore samples and determine the mineral content. Dreams were both confirmed and dashed inside the doors of this office.

In September, 2010, just east of the his-

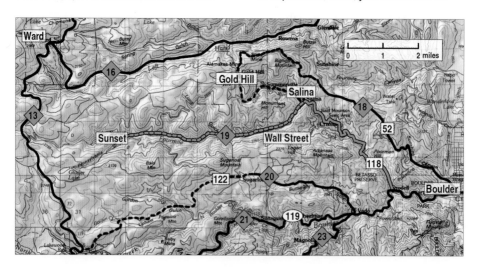

Wall Street Mill at the turn of the 20th century

Sunset in 1884

Wall Street Mill today

Sunset today

toric Assay Office, a controlled slash-pile burn became an uncontrolled one, and the Fourmile Canyon Fire was launched. Over the span of two weeks, the flames consumed enough property to become Colorado's most expensive wildfire ever.

A hundred yards to the west are the remains of the once immense Wall Street Mill. Its name didn't come from the Wall Street kind of money it generated, but rather from the money generated by Wall Street to fund its construction! It never met investor expectations and operations were disappointingly concluded. But the ride doesn't end here, for you have three easy dirt miles to the once-bustling place of Sunset. It is easy to imagine what it must have been like to roll in on a set of rails instead of a set of motorcycle tires. This portion of the Fourmile Canyon ride is on the old narrow-gauge train bed. In Sun-

set, the rails that used to be here would link with tracks coming over the Switzerland Trail (so named to encourage tourism). Today, Sunset is a quiet cluster of new, and not-so-new homes. Back then, it hosted a busy depot for trains carrying supplies and passengers.

From here, the option for most is to turn around and ride the five easy and pleasing miles back to Salina, where you can continue this tour of Boulder County mining history with a turn north, up the dirt Gold Run Road. A turn south, down Fourmile Canyon, delivers five snaking (s)miles leading back to Boulder Canyon. If you are astride a dedicated dual-sport, you don't have to make the turnaround at Sunset. The dirt-and-rock Switzerland Trail/County 93J runs north-south through town. A northern venture ascends Gold Hill Road, and the route south winds to Sugarloaf Mountain and Road. Both deliver tremendous Indian Peaks views on the Continental Divide.

Ride 20 **Sugarloaf Mountain**

Sugarloaf Road, County 122

A ten-mile alternative route between Boulder and the Peak to Peak Scenic Byway, consisting of a mix of pavement and smooth dirt, through hilly forests with a gently winding ascent offering views of the high plains

Sugarloaf Road is another great motorcycle destination road connecting with Boulder Canyon. What's nice about these sweet options is how they differ from one another. Sugarloaf has an airy and open feeling to it. The curves aren't as dense, and the hillsides are less steep and don't shutter you in. There is meadow riding with far-horizon vistas, and big sky—if not sunshine—seems to abound.

The turn to Sugarloaf Road is west of

Boulder on Colorado 119, four miles into Boulder Canyon—an intense introduction to this mellow ride. When you turn right/north into its embrace, you're given a tight, hearty hug that lifts you off your feet. One twisting mile and 500 feet higher, things calm down and you'll enter a different, but sublime riding zone. It doesn't take long for your bike to break out into the open, and as you climb higher, views of Boulder begin to fill your mirrors. Sugarloaf Mountain, up ahead on

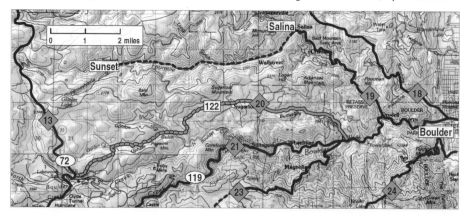

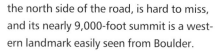

The eastern end of Sugarloaf Road twists its way out of Boulder Canyon.

The western end consists of smooth dirt.

the north side of the road, is hard to miss, and its nearly 9,000-foot summit is a western landmark easily seen from Boulder.

At the crest of this ride, with Sugarloaf Mountain slightly to your northwest, pause for a moment and look around at the 360-degree views. You will be at the historic townsite of Sugarloaf, but there isn't much remaining to see, for you are also at ground zero for one of Colorado's most devastating wildfires, in terms of property loss. On July 9, 1989, a discarded cigarette started a fire that charred 44 homes and structures in just the first six hours of that Sunday afternoon. The fire was extinguished four days and 2,100 acres later.

Fortunately, there was no loss of life, but the old Sugarloaf town structures literally went up in smoke. The flames engulfed both sides of the road here, and if you look toward Sugarloaf Mountain, you can see scattered, charred trees still standing. Just ahead of you will be dirt County 93J and the dual-sport road north to the historic Switzerland Trail. The narrow-gauge train bed it once contained is described in the Fourmile Canyon ride [019].

A turnaround here, back toward Boulder Canyon, is a fine option, as is continuing west toward the Peak to Peak Highway. Your wheels will be on asphalt for another 1.5 miles before a smooth and compacted, dirt-road base takes over escort duties for the remaining 3.5 miles.

This western side of Sugarloaf Road changes the TV channel of the ride. The program consists of a curving journey through hills and pine-covered slopes, and the seclusion of this area means you and your bike will have a starring role. There might be a supporting actor or two, but for the most part you will have the scenes to yourself before the credits start rolling upon your arrival at the Peak to Peak.

Sugarloaf Mountain is one of many out-and-back options from the Boulder area. Every one of these short rides has its own flavor. If you aren't hesitant about putting your bike on smooth dirt, this ride doesn't have to be an out-and-back. This Sugarloaf alternative gets you around all but four miles of busier Boulder Canyon, and places you and your bike on the great Peak to Peak Scenic Byway [013] three miles north of Nederland.

Back in 1880, well-attired, hat-wearing visitors pose before Boulder Falls.

Ride 21 **Boulder Canyon**

Colorado 119

A curving, scenic 16-mile ascent through a historical canyon, connecting to numerous sweet motorcycle destinations

Colorado 119 aims west out of downtown Boulder and enters Boulder Canyon less than a mile from the city. It invites you to come along on a 2,700-foot climb to Nederland 16 miles away, following the crooked and tumbling designs of Boulder Creek as it drains the moisture from up high. The first motorized access to the canyon was the Colorado and Northwestern narrow gauge, which provided rail access to the fortune-seeking communities, supporting the gold and silver mines up near Eldora and Caribou.

It was a challenge keeping the tracks in shape and the train operational. Floods dev-astated the canyon often until the construction of the Barker Dam and Reservoir in 1909. Today you'll ride the old train bed on a layer of Colorado 119 asphalt. The winding canyon is one to be experienced in cruise mode, as it is a canyon with traffic, given its proximity to Boulder and the access it provides to numerous communities up in the foothills. Nevertheless, it is a scenic and satisfying road, worthy of placing your bike upon.

The canyon action begins right away once you leave Boulder heading west. There is no lull or gradual introduction. Watch for bicyclists laboring up and coasting down, and

Boulder Canyon near Lover's Leap, circa 1900

vehicles pulling over at small parking areas. In a way, you'll feel as though you're on a stage in a theater, part of a grand production, for much always seems to be happening in Boulder Canyon. At two miles in, take note of the Fourmile Canyon [019] turnoff to the north. At four, the wickedly curving Magnolia Road [023] takes a turn to the south. Only a few hundred yards away on the north side, serpentine Sugarloaf Road [020] awaits.

One grand stop worthy of a sidestand deploy is Boulder Falls, eleven miles into the canyon. During spring snowmelt, a firehose-like fountain shoots out of a north-side rift in the rocks. For years this waterfall and the nearby rocks were known as the "Yosemite of Boulder Canyon."

At the top of the canyon, you'll ride through an uphill right-hand sweeper, and Barker Reservoir will come into view to your left. The town of Nederland and the Continental Divide are scenic anchors to the west. The Peak to Peak Scenic Byway [013] can be joined here—turn either south or north for great canyon rides back to the Front Range. If you've a yen for exploration, the semi-ghost town of Eldora [022] is accessible via a paved road on the south side of Nederland. If a dual-sport is between your knees, the ghost town of Caribou [022] is close by—launch from the west side of town. For a meal, check out these popular motorcycle-rider spots on First Street and nearby Jefferson in Nederland: The Katmandu, Whistler's Cafe, First Street Pub & Grill, and Wild Mountain Smokehouse.

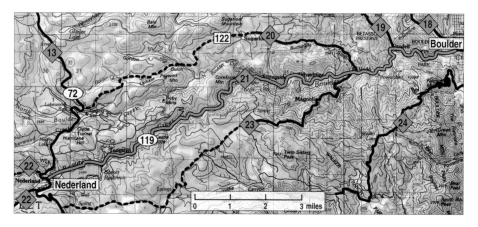

The road to Caribou

Ride 22 **Eldora–Caribou**

Eldora Road, Caribou Road, County 130, 128

Two short excursions from Nederland—a three-mile paved road to the semi-ghost town of Eldora that becomes a dirt road to historical sites beyond, and a six-mile unpaved road to the ghost town of Caribou

Though these are two distinct rides, because of their short duration and close proximity, I have linked them together for a brief two-wheeled tour. The Eldora leg is paved but the Caribou leg is not, and is probably best ridden on a dual-sport or a capable, lightweight, street bike. Both ventures deliver a fine ride, but admittedly, their inclusion in this book is largely based on the value of the historical and scenic experiences they deliver. Only a few minutes away from the Peak to Peak Scenic Byway, they are interesting side trips worthy of inclusion.

Eldora can trace its existence to productive nearby mines, including the 1890s Happy Valley placer mine, and prior to that, the hugely profitable Fourth of July silver mine,

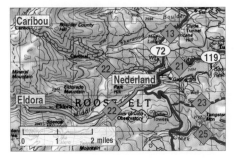

four miles west of town. The Hessie mining camp, two miles to the west, contributed to the founding of this "consolidating" community. Initially, the town was named Eldorado—that is, until the postmaster told the residents the name was already taken in Colorado. Their solution was to simply lop off the last two letters!

The well-marked Eldora Road is found on the southwest side of colorful Nederland off the Peak to Peak Scenic Byway. The three-mile ride to the townsite is flanked by trails through the Caribou Flats meadows on the right, the steep Shelf Road to the Eldora Ski Area on the left, and scattered residences on both sides. The old Main Street appears soon after passing over the precisely named South Fork Middle Boulder Creek. The paved surface holds out for a half mile past Eldora, then transitions to an easy dirt-and-rock road base for another mile and a half to the historic townsite of Hessie. A dedicated dual-sport can take you two miles farther up a deeply scenic alpine road to the distinguished Fourth of July Mine.

Caribou is one of Colorado's more famed,

and faded, mining communities. Boasting a population estimated at 3,000 in 1875, it dwindled to fewer than 50 by 1920, and dropped to zero in 1944 when the last resident passed away. It was known as "The Place Where Winds Were Born," but the word itself comes from the Micmac Indian language and means "snow shoveller." Well, with its 9,800-foot elevation, I can see some relevance, but the name of the district was actually derived from the prodigious Caribou silver mine, bored in the 1860s. Access to the mostly smooth, dirt-and-rock Caribou Road is on the northwest side of Nederland, less than half a mile west of the roundabout on the Peak to Peak Highway.

Eldora, in its heyday, celebrating Labor Day in 1901

This excellent, six-mile, off-road ride manages most of its 1,400-foot ascent during the last four miles. At mile three, take note of a clearing with a large pleasing field on the south side of the road, and a smaller, aspen-filled meadow to the north. This is the location of the old-and-gone town of Cardinal. The Caribou city leaders didn't want any "shady" ladies or other riffraff plying their crafts in the community, so those who were evicted built their own cabin community down the road and decided the first word of "cardinal sin" would be an appropriate, tongue-in-cheek name. When the high and mostly vacant site of Caribou comes into view, note the parking area on the west side of the road as a convenient place for a sidestand deploy and pause for reflection. If you are on a dedicated dual-sport, there are rocky trails here heading north to the Rainbow Lakes and south to Eldora. The Peak to Peak Scenic Byway ride [013] goes into detail on the numerous ride options in the area, and where one can stop for a meal in Nederland.

Eldora in 2009

Caribou in 1920

The remains of Caribou today

Ride 23 **Magnolia**

Magnolia Road, County 132

A destination route from Boulder to the Peak to Peak Scenic Byway, involving five miles of tightly paved twists and turns up a canyon, followed by seven miles of easy-going, high meadow riding on well-maintained dirt

The Magnolia Road is another one of the enticing roads leading off from Boulder Canyon. Each one has its own personality, but this one is particularly lively. Sugarloaf and Magnolia Roads both leave Colorado 119 at four miles west into Boulder Canyon. Think of them as twins, but not identical—not even very fraternal. Sugarloaf Road [020] going north, is bathed in warm southern exposure sunshine, and is very accommodating and easy to live with. Magnolia, on the other hand, goes to the south, toward dark, moody, forested slopes, throwing hairpins and curves at you and climbing 1,000 feet in

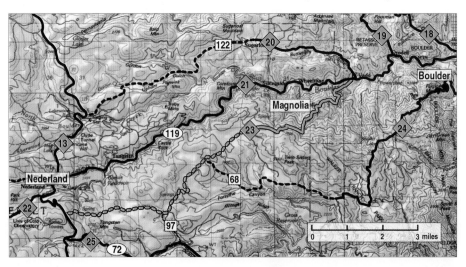

the first two miles. But this kind of spunky personality is often welcomed by motorcyclists who enjoy a little challenge. The road gets its name from the somewhat discrete Magnolia mining camp nearby.

At 2.1 miles into this ride from its Boulder Canyon kick off, just after one of the few lazy left-handers, you will see Old Whiskey Road off to the left/south. A quick detour down this road will reveal some of its scattered remains. After making the turn, you will skirt the contours of a forested valley that once contained a grocery store, a drug store, a dry goods store, an assay office, a few ore mills, three hotels, and a post office.

At five miles, your bike will have hustled you another 1,000 feet higher to an elevation of 8,200 feet. There are a couple of wide shoulders to the side where you can pause for a breather and test your ability to spot landmarks to the north, both near and far. The first five miles are motorcycle exhilaration, but so are the next seven, though in a different kind of way, as the surface changes over to a smooth, county maintained, dirt surface. The tight bends cease and the grades lose steepness. Meadows and farms will be your spectators, with a few hardy homesteads still standing strong and able to watch as well. Along the way, you will be treated to distant, lonely panoramas of the foothills to the east.

At 6.6 miles, County 68 to the southeast can take you to Gross Reservoir and on to Flagstaff Road [024] for a return to Boulder. The quality of this dirt surface is closer to the dual-sport end of the spectrum. At nine miles, smooth dirt County 97 carves off to the left/south for a mile to its intersection with Colorado 72 [025], requiring you to decide in which tantalizing direction to tip the handlebars. Finally, three miles later, the superb and diverse Magnolia Road journey concludes at the Peak to Peak Highway [013] just to the south of Nederland.

The Magnolia Road, like Sugarloaf Road, provides alternative access to the Peak to Peak Highway from the Boulder area, and vice versa. And it does so in a special and joyful manner. As I've noted elsewhere, 'tis nice to have choices. Magnolia can also guide you back to the Front Range via Gross Reservoir or Coal Creek Canyon/Colorado 72, as mentioned above. An enjoyable one- to three-hour adventure from the Boulder area would be to scoot up Boulder Canyon [021] for four miles, and turn left onto Magnolia Road. Enjoy the quiet ride to the Peak to Peak, have a snack in Nederland, and return via Boulder Canyon or Sugarloaf Road.

These enthusiastic cruising riders told me they hit the Magnolia Road every autumn.

Ride 24 **Flagstaff Mountain**

Flagstaff Road, County 77

An amusement park ride up Flagstaff Mountain on a steep, tightly twisting road with a roller-coaster conclusion in nine miles at Gross Reservoir, where there is access to several dual-sport roads

Flagstaff Road was originally constructed as a cliffy, dirt-road trail winding up Flagstaff Mountain, which peers down on Boulder

from the southwest. The summit has long been a destination for thrill seekers and sightseers, along with the Chautauqua Park located adjacent to the beginning of this ride. Both places have been attracting visitors since long before there were motorized means to get to these mountain parks.

To get to Flagstaff Road, follow Baseline Road west out of South Boulder. For a short spell, Flagstaff Road enters Gregory Canyon and then it makes a sharp right. From here, the views, curves, and climb begin. Like a tightly coiled cobra rising out of a basket, the Flagstaff ascent offers the tightest of hairpins and 15 percent gradients as 1,200 feet of elevation is quickly gained. You will pass Panorama Point, the Halfway House

Restaurant, and Crown Rock in the first three miles. At 3.5 miles there is the junction with Summit Road to the right at a place known as Realization Point. The half-mile summit road escorts you to the top of the mountain, where you will find the Flagstaff Nature Center, with exhibits and a knowledgeable volunteer staff.

At four miles, the Lost Gulch Overlook, with parking, lures you to take a peek, as views of the Continental Divide to the west will have been tantalizing you through the dense trees. As Flagstaff Road leaves the Boulder Mountain Park boundary at five miles, you'll pass through another turnstile in this amusement park ride and should buckle in for the roller-coaster portion of the transit.

The Walker Ranch Open Space Park can be seen to the left as the ride approaches Gross Reservoir. This park area was the site of the Eldorado Wildfire, of unknown origin, which consumed 1,100 acres over three days in Sep-tember 2000. Just past the burn area, you come to the dirt-road turnoff to the Gross Reservoir. Make this left-hand turn onto Gross Dam Road and to the parking lot on the right, only 50 yards after making the turn.

This parking area is a good place to take a break, enjoy a picnic, or embark upon a hike—possibly down to the water's edge. From here, you can continue on the unpaved Gross Dam Road along the eastern side of the water, and turn the wheels for 6.7 winding miles to Coal Creek Canyon [025]. Another prime choice would be to continue north on Flagstaff Road past the parking area mentioned above, where the pavement turns to dirt (and County 68), and delivers a 5.4-mile venture to Magnolia Road [023]. Both selections are dual-sport friendly, but if you're on a lightweight street bike, let a glance at the current conditions determine your willingness. There is always the option of returning the way you came.

Northern Front Range

RECOMMENDATIONS

Short Canyon Loops

1. Ascend via Boulder Canyon [021] five miles to Magnolia Road [023] on the left/ south. Ride it to the termination at the Peak to Peak Scenic Byway [013]. Turn right/north, pass through Nederland, and continue north for 3.5 miles to Sugarloaf Road [020]. Point the bike east on Sugarloaf for a descent to Boulder Canyon.

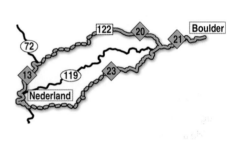

2. Two miles up Boulder Canyon [021] take the north-side turnoff for Fourmile Canyon [019]. Five miles into the canyon at Salina, turn left for a quick, two-mile detour to the old Wall Street Mill. The abandoned train-depot community of Sunset is another few miles west. Return to Salina, and if you're up for a dirt-road climb to the historic community of Gold Hill, point the handlebars north through Salina for the four-mile, switchback ascent. At Gold Hill's east end, Sunshine Canyon Drive [018] heads up and to the northeast, before dropping southeast to Boulder's western side.

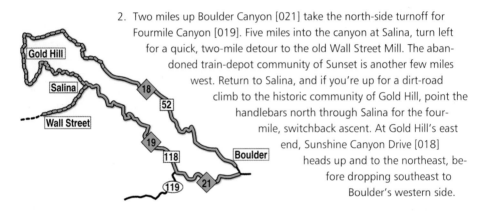

3. Follow US 36 north out of Boulder five miles to the entrance of Lefthand Canyon [016] on the west. Alternately, take Lee Hill Drive or Olde Stage Road [017] on Boulder's north side. Sixteen miles up, you'll find the community of Ward on the Peak to Peak Highway [013]. Ride north 4.7 miles to catch Overland Road to James Canyon and Jamestown [015], which returns you to lower Lefthand Canyon.

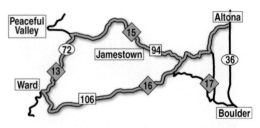

Circling Foothills Journeys—Three Figure 8's

1. From Lyons, ascend via St. Vrain Canyon [014], staying with Colorado 7 as it passes through Allenspark, skirts the southern slopes of Mt. Meeker and Longs Peak, and enters Estes Park from the south. Return to Lyons via US 36 and the Little Thompson River ride [012], or head toward downtown Estes Park. Just east of the town center, MacGregor Avenue/Business US 34 departs to the north. MacGregor Avenue becomes Devils Gulch/County 43 which leads to Glen Haven [009], and then the descent via Big Thompson Canyon [008]. Consider the Carter Lake ride [007], with the side attraction of Pole Hill Road, as a motorcycle-friendly route between Colorado 66 and Lyons, and US 34 to the north.

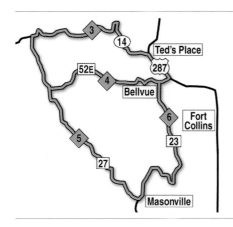

2. From Fort Collins (noting the accompanying map), circle Horsetooth Reservoir [006] with Rist Canyon [004] on the north, or make a larger circle with the Poudre Canyon [003] farther north. The Stove Prairie Road [005] is the western backbone. And if you're really up for it, ride the entire Figure 8!

3. For a longer Figure 8—with dual-sport sections—from Livermore north of Fort Collins, ride Red Feather Lakes Road [001] to the community of Red Feather Lakes. Ten miles south on the dirt Manhattan Road/County 182 is the small community of Rustic in Cache La Poudre Canyon [003]. For a longer dirt-road adventure, continue past the community of Red Feather Lakes onto Deadman Road/County 162 [001]. This is a largely forested ride to Laramie River Road [002], which you can enjoy southbound all the way to Colorado 14 just east of Cameron Pass. A turn east here will get you back to Fort Collins via the Cache La Poudre Canyon.

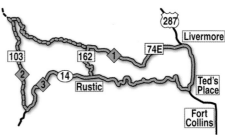

Favorite Rides

The Twistiest Circuits

[009] Glen Haven Road
[014] St. Vrain
[016] Lefthand to James Canyon
[018] Sunshine Canyon
[019] Fourmile Canyon
[023] The Magnolia Road
[024] Flagstaff Road

Best Cruising Journeys

[001] Red Feather Lakes Road
[003] Cache la Poudre Canyon
[006] Centennial Drive along
       Horsetooth Reservoir
[007] The ride along Carter Lake
[008] Big Thompson Canyon
[010] Trail Ridge Road,
       Rocky Mountain National Park
[011] Bear Lake Road,
       Rocky Mountain National Park
[012] US 36 from Lyons to Estes Park
[013] The Peak to Peak Scenic Byway
[016] Lefthand Canyon
[021] Boulder Canyon

Best Longer Journeys

[005] Buckhorn Road and Stove Prairie Road
[010] Trail Ridge Road
[013] The Peak to Peak Scenic Byway
[031] Cache la Poudre Canyon

Best Backroads

[001] Red Feather Lakes Road
[004] Above Rist Canyon
[005] Stove Prairie Road
[009] County 43 to Glen Haven
[020] Sugarloaf Mountain

Worthy Destinations

[001] The Red Feather Lakes area
[002] Chambers Lake on Laramie River Road
[003] Moose Visitor Center at
       the western base of Cameron Pass
[008] Memorials of the Great Flash Flood
       in Big Thompson Canyon
[009] Glen Haven General Store
[011] Moraine Park,
       Rocky Mountain National Park
[013] Brainard Lake off the Peak to Peak
[018] Semi-ghost town of Gold Hill
[019] Wall Street Mill and Assay Office
       in Fourmile Canyon
[021] Boulder Falls
[022] Semi-ghost town of Eldora
[024] Flagstaff Nature Center via Flagstaff Road
[024] Gross Reservoir via Flagstaff Road

Little-Known Gems

[001] Red Feather Lakes Road
[002] Laramie River Road
[007] Pole Hill Road
[011] Bear Lake Road
[015] James Canyon all the way
       to the Peak to Peak
[016] The road to Brainard Lake
       off the Peak to Peak
[018] Sunshine Canyon
[019] Fourmile Canyon
[020] Sugarloaf Road
[023] Magnolia Road
[024] Flagstaff Road

Central Front Range

REGIONAL OVERVIEW

The Central Front Range region essentially encompasses the maze and mosaic of terrain contained by the foothills west of the Denver metro area, stretching between Monument and Woodland Park on the south, Coal Creek Canyon on the north, and as far west as Guanella Pass. This riding area may be the smallest in geographic size of the seven regions covered in the book, but the choices run deep.

The proximity of populous Denver means there is an abundance of roads crawling all over the hills and mountains at the fringes of her western skirt. Some who work in the Mile High City choose to make a longer commute so they can reside 1,000 to 5,000 feet higher, in ever more oxygen-challenged air. Residents want access, however, and county road and bridge departments have come through with an abundance of improvements in the form of potato-peel-like roads curling through and around the forested spuds of hills.

You can spend days exploring the Central Front Range, and more than a few of the circuits will strike a chord, the harmonies of which you will want to play again and again. Enjoy!

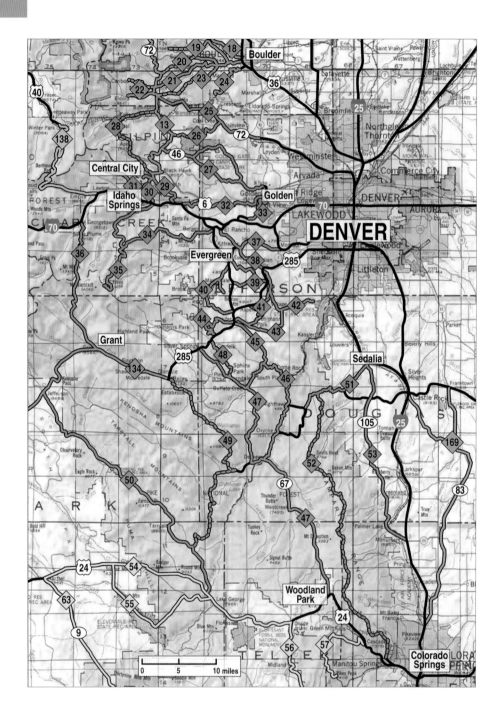

Rides in This Section

Ride 25 **Coal Creek Canyon**

Colorado 72

An entertaining 19-mile road delivering sharp ascents and descents with sweet curves in between, all wrapped up with a diversity of classic Colorado scenery

Colorado 72 cuts into Coal Creek Canyon about 20 miles northwest of Denver. There is scant historical information on the area, but one can trace the prominence of trains in the canyon's development. The name Coal Creek Canyon may be connected to the coal trains that have been making their way through and around the mountains surrounding this scenic, creek-carved canyon

for years. The famed Union Pacific Moffat Line operates its big diesels here, and over a 24-hour period it isn't uncommon for 18 to 24 trains to laboriously ascend the grades of these rocky foothills.

Route 72 leaves the northwest corner of Denver heading for Coal Creek Canyon. After you engage the canyon on your bike, the train tracks bid you adieu as they bend more

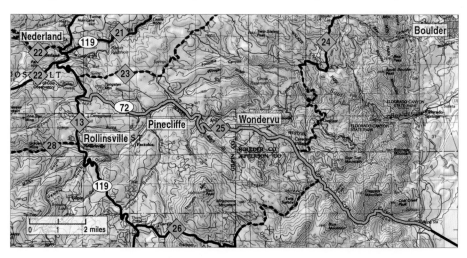

Motorcycling Colorado

to the north. Get ready to gain some elevation. Some of the curves are sneakily tight, so watch the signs carefully. As the climb continues, so does the snaking act of the road, and it is a fine, entertaining show. Nine miles into this curve-fest, you crest at the small community of Wondervu. Look to the west and you won't wonder long where the name comes from—and the scenery gets even better as you ride the sunset side and start the descent to Pinecliffe. But before you continue, and if it is timely to do so, you might want to stop and have a meal at the motorcycle destination Wondervu Cafe.

As you continue to motor west, the visual delights of the Continental Divide on the horizon start competing for your attention. But don't get distracted for too long—there are curves here you don't want to mess up on. To add to the challenge, the road delightfully and rapidly descends 600 steep feet to the Upper South Boulder Creek at Pinecliffe. Heading west, it is downhill tight, but if you reversed the direction of this narrative, it would be uphill tight. You may have a preference for how you want to tackle this.

It seems that every time I ride this road I gasp at the slide show of scenic views, thinking . . . that would be a good photo stop, that would be a good photo stop, and then I keep passing them by because I can't seem to break up the dance with this road!

For many along the Front Range, it would take 30 to 60 minutes to arrive at the eastern entrance of Coal Creek Canyon. If you stop at the cafe in Wondervu and continue on to the Peak to Peak Scenic Byway [013], this becomes an ideal entrée as part of a half- or full-day riding meal depending on where you let the Peak to Peak escort you. See the Peak to Peak ride [013] for circuit options. Consider nearby Golden Gate Canyon [027] or Gap Road to Twin Spruce Road [026] as shorter return alternatives.

If a graveled surface causes no major angst, three miles east of Wondervu there is a turnoff north to Gross Reservoir. This 6.7-mile, dirt-and-gravel road delivers sweet views of the reservoir while it takes you to Flagstaff Road [024] and its gnarled descent to Boulder.

Finally, if you're just interested in an hour-long exercise of your bike—with all kinds of lefts and rights and ups and downs—then head west on Colorado 72, through Coal Creek Canyon, all the way to the Peak to Peak, and then turn around and ride it again. This is one of those roads that acquires a very different taste simply by changing the direction in which it is consumed!

Ride 26 **Twin Spruce–Gap**

Gap Road, Twin Spruce Road, County 2

A high and diverse ten-mile ride—half on the paved Twin Spruce Road, and half on the easy-dirt Gap Road—passing through Golden Gate Canyon State Park, and packed with a variety of classic Rocky Mountain scenery

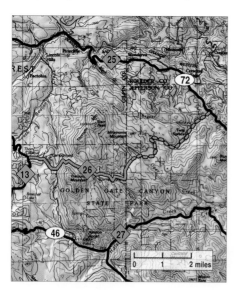

This is a delightful and scenic ten-mile ride, with the Gap and Twin Spruce Roads linking seamlessly up high about halfway. The easy-dirt Gap Road sidepasses through Golden Gate Canyon State Park, and sweetly paved Twin Spruce makes a 1,000-foot change of elevation on a road only a pretzel maker (or a motorcyclist) would like.

Heading east on Gap Road from the Peak to Peak Scenic Byway [013], you will pass through a cluster of homes nestled in the high pines surrounding Golden Gate Canyon State Park. You will enter the park shortly after and begin an ascent to Panorama Point at 1.6 miles. There is a scenic pullout here, and the views to the west of the Continental Divide are worth a sidestand pause.

Gap Road then passes through a series of high rock outcroppings as it winds around and through the hills of Golden Gate. It is a fun, dirt-road scoot and any bike should be able to handle it. The road changes name to Twin Spruce at just under five miles, by a beautiful high meadow with far views to the east, and shorter views of old homesteads. The views here would be hard to surpass.

From here, Twin Spruce escorts you and your bike on a wonderful descent to Coal Creek Canyon [025]. The twisty road up high morphs into a gentler creekside ride down low. In five miles, after cruising through meandering S-curves below steep hillside slopes thickly covered with trees, you will come to a stop sign in Coal Creek Canyon. It is completely understandable and excusable if you find yourself having the urge to turn around immediately and re-ride this road in the other direction!

If you aren't eager for the dirt Gap Road section, you can always just ride up Twin Spruce to the top and turn around at the Golden Gate Canyon park entrance. There is a pullout there, and this high meadow place is a fine one for a pause. Conversely, you might just want to ride the western Gap Road side in the park, with its craggy high rocks and tremendous views to the west. To be sure, all ten miles are excellent and I think they are waiting for you!

At the western entrance to Golden Gate State Park off Gap Road, there is a three-mile-long, ultra-scenic and ultra-twisting paved park road heading south. This Mountain Base Road connects to neighboring Golden Gate Canyon [027] and requires a $6 park fee payable at the park visitor center.

There are no food or fuel services along this ride, but they are readily available at both ends. There is a gas and food stop nearby in Coal Creek Canyon, and in Nederland, ten miles away from where Gap Road concludes at the Peak to Peak Scenic Byway.

Ride 27 **Golden Gate–Crawford Gulch**

Golden Gate Canyon Road, Drew Hill Road, Ralston Creek Road, County 70, 46, 57

A diverse 18-mile canyon ride with entertaining hilly ascents and descents, passing by parks and a variety of terrain, directly connecting Golden with the Peak to Peak Scenic Byway

I think canyons are great. There's nothing like experiencing canyon curves on a bike, or looking up at steep canyon walls guiding your journey. It isn't the same when you're in a four-wheeled thing with a roof overhead and doors enclosing you. Some canyons go about their duty, following the course of a rushing stream for a few miles before they conclude. Not Golden Gate. You get miles of canyon riding before ascending a hilltop, and then plunging down for more deep valley curves. You'll go up again, then down again. It repeats, delightfully so, for 18 miles—and that doesn't even include the adjacent and juicy Crawford Gulch Road.

This ride begins a little more than a mile north of Clear Creek Canyon's [032] intersection with Colorado 93. There are signs on Colorado 93 pointing out the entrance to Golden Gate Canyon. You will be introduced

to the canyon's seductive and bending pavement almost immediately. Several of the curves can be unexpectedly tight, so have your riding wits dialed in.

At four miles into the canyon, Crawford Gulch Road leads off to the right/north. It rivals Golden Gate as a crooked and devilish road, not knowing whether to go up or down, or this way or that.

If you select the Crawford Gulch Road option, you will pass the entrance to White Ranch Open Space Park at four miles. The paved surface continues for another mile before turning into dirt Drew Hill Road, but it is a very finely maintained road base, easy for any bike.

Pavement will return after a mile or so and then you're seamlessly on Ralston Creek Road, and you'll follow its namesake as you ride through and along the southern edge of

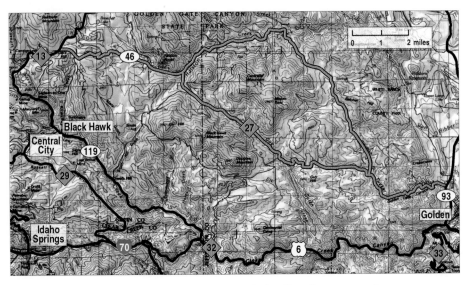

Golden Gate Canyon State Park. Ralston Creek Road concludes at the Golden Gate Canyon Road five miles after entering the park boundary.

Of course, choices are nice, and I understand how you could have foregone the dessert of Crawford Gulch—the main course is enough to fill you up big time. You will pass old cabins and new, homesteads and ranches, fields and trees, with views near and far, especially as you crest hilltops. This glorious journey concludes 3,400 feet higher at the Peak to Peak Scenic Byway [013],

which offers direct connections to numerous other destination rides.

The Golden Gate Canyon road and ride is a versatile one. You can make it a quick 60 to 90 minute journey going out and back, perhaps by looping through Crawford Gulch, or you can link it to longer rides via the Peak to Peak. There are no food or fuel options, but this doesn't mean you can't pack some grub to enjoy roadside in one of the parks along the way. Turning left or right at the Peak to Peak will bring you to services within ten miles.

Ride 28 **Apex–Mammoth Gulch**

Apex Valley Road, Elk Park Road, Mammoth Gulch Road, Rollins Pass Road, County 4N

An 18-mile dual-sport ride through a mining ghost town to an ultra-scenic place

Apex Valley Road branches off the Peak to Peak Scenic Byway [013] just two miles north of Black Hawk. However, if you take County 3 out of Central City, a mile or two past the Teller House you will come to three cemeteries. According to local residents, all three are haunted. For sure, they do look spirit-filled. Continue on, and the easy-dirt county road will connect with Apex Valley Road, which is unsurfaced, but can be ridden by most street bikes in dry conditions. There will be a gentle ascent for about five miles and then you will arrive at the old townsite of Apex.

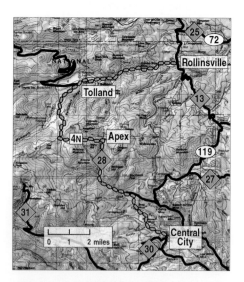

In 1900, Apex had two hotels, a miners' hall, a dance hall, and much more, including a population of 1,000. The town was founded when (according to legend) a miner named Dick Mackey was left with only $400 after his partner vanished with $30,000 in gold ore. Down to his last few dollars, he placed his remaining dynamite at the end of a tunnel he

Gathering for the July 4th parade in 1900

Main Street in Apex today

had dug, lit the fuse, and went home. Well glory be! The next morning he checked out the results of his exploding firecrackers and a serious gold strike was revealed!

From here, the road becomes rougher, and I recommend it only if you are riding a dual-sport bike. County 4N/Elk Park Road climbs and wanders to the west from here, passing another ghost town (on private property) called American City. You might catch a glimpse of a cabin or two through the trees on the right/north. Continue on, down through a drainage, then up toward a hilltop.

The road is a little rocky here, but this is the roughest part of the ride. You will ascend toward the west with anticipation because you will have sneaked peeks of enough grand scenery ahead to know there is something special at the top . . . and indeed there is. At an intersection with the forest and county road at the top, you will want to take the one leading to the north, which continues as County 4N/Mammoth Gulch Road. It will escort you to Rollins Pass Road and Tolland.

Here is where you will want to pause and

soak it all in—classic Colorado scenery, with a postcard-perfect valley down below you, rising up to the heights of James Peak at 13,294 feet above you. Maybe it is named Mammoth Gulch for the mammoth scenery. You might hear cows bellowing, and if you ride this during a peak time for wildflowers, there will be carpets of color all around you.

The road continues to be easily "dual-sportable" as you descend toward the junction with Rollins Pass Road. You can venture west on this famous road to where—at this time—it concludes at the closed pass, or you can ride to the road's east-end conclusion at Rollinsville on the Peak to Peak Highway [013]. Along the way, you will scoot past the semi-ghost town of Tolland, a key train stop at one time.

I get a kick out of roads and rides like this, with history presented right before you, and scenery happening all around, almost as if you are on the stage at a theater-in-the-round. The journey described here is almost 18 miles in length, but it will take nearly two hours to complete if you pause along the way. And don't get caught at the Central City cemeteries after sunset!

Ride 29 **Central City Parkway**

Central City Parkway

A quiet eight-mile, four-lane parkway ride with perfectly engineered sweeping curves and grades

Back in 1990, Colorado voters gave the nod to limited-stakes gambling in three historic mining towns—Black Hawk, Central City, and Cripple Creek. Prior to the 2004 construction of this Parkway, access to Black Hawk and Central City for Front Range residents was primarily via US 6 through Clear Creek Canyon and Colorado 119. It is a great ride [032], but for the town officials of Central City, great riding or not, there was a problem. Motorists coming up the canyon from Golden would find Black Hawk too enticing to pass by on the way to Central City. Thus Black Hawk became the big gambling kahuna beating out its neighbor one mile up the hill. "Well, what are we going to do about this?" was a question asked more than once by Central City planners. "How can we get drivers to come directly to Central City, bypassing Black Hawk?" After back-and-forth lawsuits between the two

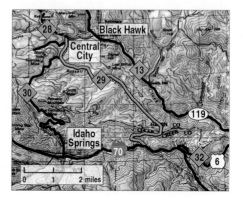

towns, counter claims, and property ownership issues, the legal wrangling resulted in an eight-mile parkway designed and constructed to escort people directly from Interstate 70 to Central City. The ribbon cutting ceremony took place in November of 2004, when 1996 Indy 500 champ Buddy Lanier christened the new tarmac in a 1996 Dodge Viper Indy Pace Car with a run of just over three minutes. Reportedly, he averaged 155

mph over the 8.4-mile race course . . . er, parkway! Let me tell you, on certain kinds of high-octane bikes, it is tempting to do something similar. Alas, however, it is something not to be risked with the artificially slow parkway speed limit of 40 mph.

From I-70 take Exit 243 to enter the parkway. This is just a few miles east of the Idaho Springs exit. The sweepers are outstanding, the cambers are perfect, and the radii consistent. It is "Exhibit A" of modern highway construction, and it delivers the goods for motorcyclists. As four-laners go, this is a sweet one. One can just savor the ride and smell the wildflowers along the way, or let the willing and eager bike lean over a bit more through the divine curves.

The rich history of this area can't be overstated. Mining brought many from the east to the Colorado territory, and the Central City and Black Hawk area was a big magnet for early fortune seekers. You certainly can make this area a destination for your bike. The meals at the casinos are inexpensive. You're likely to see a few bikes outside the Red Dolly Casino, between Central City and Black Hawk, their owners inside enjoying an inexpensive prime rib meal—$5.99 the last time I checked! The Dostal Alley in Central City will also surprise you with their calzones.

If you are ready for more riding and are astride a dual-sport, check out nearby ghost-town ventures to Apex [028], or Russell Gulch and Nevadaville included as part of the Oh My God route [030]. Paved journeys are ready to be served by joining the Peak to Peak Scenic Byway at Black Hawk [013], as well as US 6 south to Clear Creek Canyon [032] for a return to the Denver area.

Central City in 1898

Reminders of times gone by

Ride 30 **Oh My God**

Oh My God Road, Virginia Canyon Road, Nevadaville Road

A nine-mile ride through history, past countless mines and a couple of semi-ghost towns, with a road surface mix of pavement and easy dirt

This tour launches from Idaho Springs, a place laden with history, and concludes nine miles away at Nevadaville, a community that was once one of the most populous towns in Colorado, boasting more than 4,000 residents in the 1860s. Today it is mostly an empty place, with mines, mills, and hollow buildings standing in silent testimony to those who toiled and lived in the area 150 years ago.

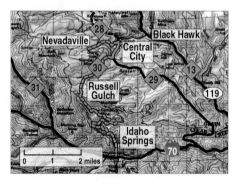

The route to Oh My God Road and Virginia Canyon Road is well marked by signs on the north side of downtown Idaho Springs. Say goodbye to pavement at around 0.2 miles. The hard-packed dirt is maintained well and should be okay for most street bikes. I know of Gold Wings that have navigated this without any issues. Keep following the signs for Oh My God and Virginia Canyon. Put on your figurative seatbelts, for you will climb 2,500 feet in only five miles!

At the top of the ascent, and after winding through a forest for a mile, you will come to the semi-ghost town of Russell Gulch, named after William Greeneberry Russell, who discovered gold deposits in this valley in 1859. Take time to wander some of the mostly deserted streets, abandoned homes, and decaying structures.

The ride continues above Russell Gulch toward the northeast. There are mines all along the way and even an old mill you will pass under. Central City appears in two miles and you will soon make a descent right to the downtown area. Hang a left going south onto the Central City Parkway [029]. Instead of riding

A backward glance will put Oh My God Road in perspective.

Ore teams make ready to depart for the nearby mines on a typical morning in 1898. Idaho Springs is still a bustling place.

this gem, however, just 0.2 miles from the entrance you will see a sign pointing the way to Nevadaville, which is only one mile up an easy, packed-dirt road.

Even if the roads here didn't put the past on display, they would still be a kick to ride! I would set aside an hour or two for exploring. Idaho Springs offers places to fuel the stomach and gas tank. Popular spots downtown on Miner Street include Two Brothers Deli, Tommyknockers, Buffalo Restaurant

and Bar, and Beau Jo's Pizza. The Central City and nearby Black Hawk casinos have many restaurants. On the Central City side of Black Hawk, you'll likely find motorcycles parked outside the Red Dolly Casino, which offers inexpensive prime rib dinners.

From Idaho Springs you can connect with the Colorado 103 ride to Echo Lake [034] or the Fall River ride [031]. Apex Valley is nearby [028], as is the Peak to Peak Scenic Byway [013] and Clear Creek Canyon [032].

Nevadaville City Hall in1933

Nevadaville City Hall in 2009

Ride 31 **Fall River**

Fall River Road, County 275

A 20-mile out-and-back ride along a river, through a legacy of mining, up to a high lake and glacier with supreme scenery all around

The Fall River Valley, with its proximity to the mining boomtowns of Idaho Springs, Central City, and Black Hawk, has had its share of mining, with its requisite hopes and

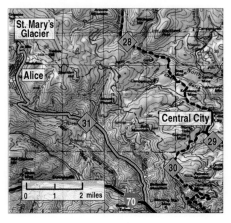

dreams, despair and departure. One of the larger gold deposits was found up high, just below St. Mary's Glacier in the 1880s. The town of Alice was built to accommodate the industry, but the gold ran out quickly, as it did in many of the camps in this valley, and in less than 20 years the town closed its doors. The beauty of this high-alpine place—with visitors traveling to see St. Mary's Glacier and Lake—drew enough lingering admirers that a community was built above Alice in the 1950s. One can see it is still a challenge to make a go of it here—resorts, buildings, and cabins, all boarded up. Nevertheless, there are vacation homes and year-round dwellings thriving in the area,

Motorcycling Colorado

and it is definitely a scenic ride for you and your bike.

From Interstate 70, take Exit 238 just west of Idaho Springs to Fall River Road leading to St. Mary's Glacier. Immediately after you turn, twisting the throttle up Fall River Road, you can see serious mining activity from 100 years ago. Look up at the hillsides as you ride along the river and you will see more evidence of hardy souls in a time long past, looking for that golden and rich vein. Typically, rides along a quickly descending stream are quite curvy, but not this one. The bends are gentle, as are the first several miles of the ascent.

But altitude must be gained before reaching Alice and the lakes, so watch for a series of hairpin curves as the river is left behind and the road points your front wheel ever more skyward. The scenery becomes more dramatic as snowcapped mountain peaks begin blocking your view to the west. At about nine miles, there will be a faint sign to the left for the townsite of Alice. Though it is a dirt road, go ahead and check it out, as the dirt is easy enough for any street bike. Structures withstanding time and elements stand as silent witnesses to a long ago era.

About a half-mile farther up Fall River Road, the pavement will end at Silver Lake and you will be treated to a classic alpine view. You will also be "treated" to the presence of several decaying commercial buildings telling tales of hope and struggle. Personally, I find their presence adds to the personality of this place and ride.

There are no food or fuel services along the way, but Idaho Springs is only a mile from the Fall River Road turnoff. If you have a serious dual-sport bike, you can point it northeast and ride over the nearby ridgelines to Apex Valley and the Mammoth Gulch area [028]. If you want to go on a great hike, there is a trail just before Silver Lake that will lead you to St. Mary's Glacier and Lake three-quarters of a mile away. The snowfield is permanent and offers a slope where you could carve a few ski or snowboard turns in the middle of summer. The only hitch would be how to carry your gear on the bike!

Ride 32 **Clear Creek Canyon**

US 6

A 14-mile ride through one of Colorado's most beautiful canyons, with five tunnels and a crashing river to provide visual and audio entertainment

Clear Creek drains the high peaks near Loveland Pass and the Continental Divide. Along the way, many small tributaries join the whitewater-fest and the party culminates in the deep gorge just west of Golden. This was the location of the Colorado Gold Rush of 1859, with numerous communities—like Black Hawk, Central City, Idaho Springs, Georgetown, and Silver Plume—

springing to life to serve those toiling in the nearby hills. To help bring the ores to market, the Colorado Central Railroad constructed tracks in the 1860s alongside Clear Creek.

Today, the pavement of US 6 and Interstate 70 overlays on the old train beds, and delivers two-wheeled riders up and down the Clear Creek Canyons, just like two rails

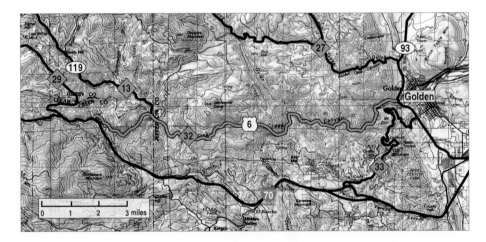

did more than 100 years ago. While technically the canyon extends all the way to Georgetown, before Interstate 70 makes its sharp ascent up toward Loveland Pass, the description here is of the 14 great miles from Golden to where US 6 joins the interstate. As you head west up the canyon from Golden, you are greeted almost immediately with the first of five tunnels (six if you count the one on I-70 just east of Idaho Springs). You might find yourself grinning as the tunnel walls amplify the roar of the internal combustion between your knees.

With trucks hauling gravel from the pit at the interstate and casino buses going to and from Black Hawk and Central City, this is not a ride on which you'd want to overtwist the throttle. It is a busy canyon, and passing opportunities are limited. So just go with the flow. Take in one of the most scenic canyons in the state. Observe the rock climbers up high, and the plunging whitewater down low. Lean the bike long into the many extended curves. Pull over at the turnouts and read the interpretive signs, or just sit along-side the river and consider the passages this canyon has seen over many years—yours among them.

US 6 though Clear Creek Canyon has proximity to Denver and offers quick access to great long rides, including the Peak to Peak Scenic Byway [013], the ghost towns of Russell Gulch and Nevadaville [030] above Central City, and the climb to Echo Lake [034]. If you're just looking for a scenic hour-long scoot, continue up US 6 to Black Hawk. Stay right at the light for 12 canyon miles to Highway 119, and return the same way, or via nearby Golden Gate Canyon [027].

Fuel and food options are plentiful in Golden and in Idaho Springs. The downtown main street areas of both are popular with motorcyclists and present a variety of restaurants capable of pleasing your taste buds. The casino towns have food options as well, and are typically inexpensive at that. The Red Dolly Casino on the Central City side of Black Hawk often has a few bikes in the parking lot with riders taking advantage of inexpensively priced prime rib dinners.

From Lookout Mountain Road, Clear Creek Canyon rolls into the distance.

This road was almost identical 100 years ago; its designers were thinking like motorcyclists.

Ride 33 **Lookout Mountain**

Lookout Mountain Road, County 68

An eight-mile, tightly twisted hoot of road up to a historical site with great views to Golden and Denver below

Just to the west of Golden is an eight-mile-long, twist-fest of a road. It rapidly ascends Lookout Mountain in a demented kind of way, providing you with multiple views and

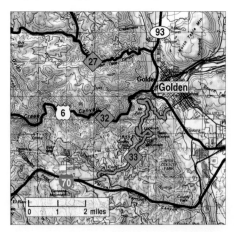

attractions along its length. Even back in 1918, enthusiasts in devices with wheels and an internal combustion engine would delight in the tantalizing Lookout Mountain ride. Some things never change.

From Golden, at the traffic light intersection of US 6/40 and Nineteenth Street, take Nineteenth Street to the west where it becomes Lookout Mountain Road. The climb and curves begin immediately and you may want to pause at one of several wide spots along the way to check your progress.

At four miles, there will be a pullout where you can gaze west toward the jagged ridgeline of the Continental Divide, then focus lower and deeper at the serpentine US 6 deep in Clear Creek Canyon [032]. At five miles, there is the turnoff for the William F.

Pausing at the same wide spot along the road, 75 years after the original photo was taken

Cody (Buffalo Bill) gravesite. While there is controversy as to why he was interred here— rather than in Cody, Wyoming, say—the widely published reason is that he simply wanted to be buried in a lofty place overlooking the high plains he loved so much. He lived a full life, from Pony Express rider to gold miner, buffalo hunter, and U.S. Army scout. Adjacent to the gravesite is a small museum and snack bar, with ample parking and views to the east and north.

Only a stone's throw up the road, there will be a turnoff to the north (Colorow Road) leading to the Lookout Mountain Nature Center, which shares a parking area with the historic Boettcher Mansion. Both places can

be toured for free, and the short journey to them has its fine riding moments. Two miles later, the Lookout Mountain Road concludes at US 40 where you can turn left for a return to the Denver area, or head right for other mountain journeys—and without any regrets, you could certainly turn around and go back the way you came! Colorado mountain roads often deliver a different experience simply by changing the direction in which they are ridden!

For a longer journey, you can link this ride to others, such as Clear Creek Canyon [032], but be sure to put Lookout Mountain Road on your dance card whenever you feel like doing The Twist.

Looking back on the road from the parking lot of the Buffalo Bill Museum and gravesite

Ride 34 **Echo Lake**

Colorado 103

A 32-mile scenic high-altitude traverse that will overdose you with a rich diet of divine riding curves, while providing access to Echo Lake, the Lodge, and Mt. Evans

Colorado 103 runs from the Evergreen Parkway at Bergen Park west of Denver, to Interstate 70 at Idaho Springs. This ride is part of the Mt. Evans Scenic Byway and it gives you stunning views the entire length. In addition, the ride offers a tasty buffet of curves, sweepers, and delicious straights. No need to choose among them as the road serves them all up in sweet order.

From its eastern end at Bergen Park, Colorado 103 begins with a cruise along the edge of the Elk Meadow Open Space Park. After several miles, the pastoral curves become a devilish brew of tight, mostly right-hand curves as the road rapidly gains altitude. Be careful as you approach, and read the signs carefully, for some of the curves are hairpin tight and can surprise you.

At around eight miles in from the east, the road begins to stretch its legs and you will find yourself on a more open and sweeping ride all the way to the top at Echo Lake. You will scoot over two passes—Squaw, in the middle of a corridor of trees and marked faintly with a painted line across the road, and Juniper at a wide spot with a scenic view to the north. From here you can sweep your eyes over the Continental Divide to the northwest, and Rocky Mountain National Park more than 70 miles to the north-north-east. Down below, the mines near Idaho Springs, Central City, and Black Hawk dot the hills, looking like tiny prairie dog colonies. If you look down the road where you're headed, you'll see the sister peaks of Mt. Evans extending a greeting.

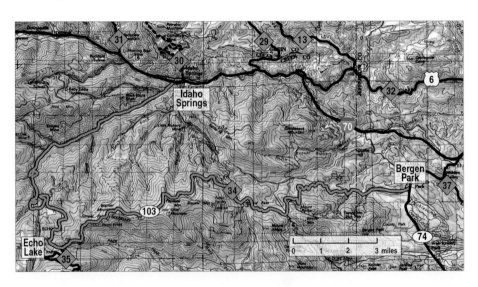

Echo Lake, as seen from the Mt. Evans Scenic Byway

At mile 18, relax the throttle for Echo Lake and the Echo Lake Lodge. During the summer months you can visit the lodge for a meal, a souvenir, or a place to warm up! You can also buy some food for an outing at the nearby lake or at one of the picnic grounds you've passed, or are going to pass. I have often parked the bike and enjoyed an open-air repast at the Ponder Point picnic area about three miles west of the Echo Lake area.

The section of 103 from Echo Lake to Idaho Springs is about 13 miles long and is similar to the eastern approach in that it begins with a gentle climb before transforming itself into a gorgeous serpentine creature. The curves on this west side are beautifully and sublimely cambered.

Set aside two hours to ride this gem of a road. If you have the time, turn it into a half-day journey with lunch at the Echo Lake Lodge, a picnic along the way, or a meal in Idaho Springs or Evergreen. If you're up for a longer day, and the weather looks accommodating, ride the Mt. Evans Scenic Byway [035] from its Echo Lake access entrance.

The weather at Echo Lake (elevation: 10,600 feet) can be much different, not to mention much cooler, than at the lower elevation starting points for this ride. There is no place for fuel along the 32-mile road, so you will need to fill your tank before you take off, especially if you are planning to ride to the top of Mt. Evans.

When riding Highway 103 from end to end, I prefer to start in Bergen Park and conclude at Idaho Springs, mainly because I favor ascending tight curves to descending them, and the Bergen Park side is more tightly kinked.

Ride 35 **Mt. Evans**

Colorado 5

A rarified, unmatched journey along the highest paved road in North America, running 14 miles from Echo Lake to the summit of Mt. Evans at an elevation of 14,264 feet

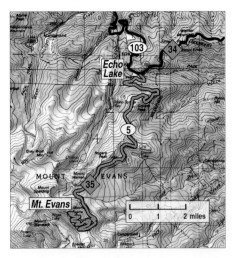

Mt. Evans is the 14,264-foot sentinel to the west of Denver. It scrapes the sky on the western horizon and can be seen from far out onto the eastern plains. In the early 1900s, after a toll road was built to the top of Pikes Peak 80 miles to the south [057], Denver's jealous mayor, Robert Speer, found funds to do the same with Mt. Evans. It was a ten-year project, but on October 4, 1927, it was completed, and today you can enjoy the fruits of this labor.

The Mt. Evans Highway begins at Echo Lake on Colorado 103, which runs from Idaho Springs at I-70 on the north, to Bergen Park (Squaw Pass Road) on the south [034].

The highway climbs steadily to its lofty terminus. Several miles into the ascent you will come to the Mt. Goliath Scenic Area and will ride through a patch of gnarled, wind-carved, bristlecone pine, the oldest living or-

The Crest House at the summit parking lot as it appeared in 1941

More often than not, a welcome party of mountain goats will hail your arrival to the summit of Mt. Evans.

ganisms on Earth. One of the trees in this area is more than 1,500 years old. There is an interpretive center here, and a rest stop.

Few motorcycle journeys anywhere compare to what you will experience on one of the highest paved roads in the world. The airiness, the curvature of the earth—not to mention the curvature of the road—makes this a special traverse. And all of this seems magnified by the tiny machine transporting you. At the summit there is a large parking area with nearby restrooms and viewing platforms. The stone foundation of the Crest House, once containing a restaurant and gift shop, is all that remains after a 1979 fire consumed the structure. A University of Denver Observatory is also at the summit which, at 14,148 feet, contains the second-highest optical telescope in the world. If you have legs and lungs at this altitude, there is a path climbing 120 feet to the very top of Mt. Evans.

This is a unique and must-do ride, whether you live nearby, or are visiting from afar. The Pikes Peak Highway [057] above Colorado Springs is a similar alternative. The Evans ride offers a paved ascent all the way. The Pikes Peak journey does have unpaved sections (for now), but also has that warm

and cozy restaurant and gift shop at the summit. On more than a few days at these altitudes, that can be classified as a bonus.

The Mt. Evans trip is a great half-day ride out of Denver, or if you are within an hour of the Highway 103 access points. There are no fuel options once you start accelerating toward Echo Lake on 103. During the summer months, the Echo Lake Lodge near the Mt. Evans Highway entrance is open, and this historic structure contains a restaurant and gift shop. It is worth a stop to check it out. Be prepared for significantly different weather as you go above timberline and approach the summit on that ultimate convertible of yours.

One other tip: if you explain to the ranger at the entrance station that you're only planning to ride to the top and back down, you will not have to pay the entrance fee, which is intended for travelers who will be spending time above timberline, using the facilities, visiting the interpretive places, and hiking to the summit from the parking areas.

Ride 36 **Guanella Pass**

County 62, Forest Road 118

A 23-mile high-altitude, ultra-scenic ride close to the Front Range on a mix of paved and well-maintained dirt surfaces

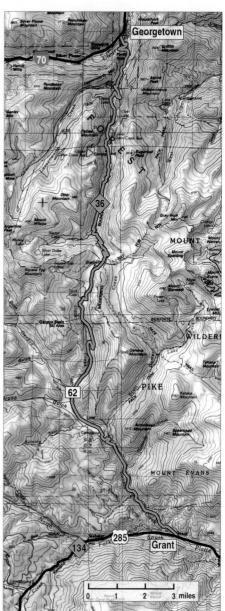

Guanella Pass Road was built over an old burro trail and named for the Department of Transportation engineer who designed and led the construction back in the 1950s. It scales heights from Grant on US 285 in the south, to Georgetown on Interstate 70 at the northern end. The highest point on the road is well above timberline at 11,66 feet. The ride to this place, whether from the north or south, is filled with diverse terrain and sights, including possible encounters with bighorn sheep and mountain goats. Keep your eyes peeled for golden eagles as well.

This is a ride with a fine combination of paved and dirt surfaces. There is nothing tricky about the dirt, for it is well maintained in the summer months and you should have no problem navigating the entire 23-mile journey. For this narrative, you begin from the south, or Grant side, on Highway 285. There are no services in Grant, so Bailey, about ten miles to the east, is where you should gas up and perhaps throw some grub into your saddle or tankbag.

The road turns to dirt about a mile from Grant and finds a path through a deep and steep forest, following the tumbling of Geneva Creek. Pavement will return after a few miles, and you'll gain elevation through a series of switchbacks up to the incredibly beautiful Geneva Park. The forests around the Geneva Park area are teeming with big game, and hunting success is quite routine in the vicinity. One of my wildlife memories

is of scratching on a lonely forest road to the west of this park, where I watched a beaver diligently work on his homestead as the sun was setting.

In a few miles, if you look west, you will see the remains of the Geneva Basin Ski Area, open off and on from 1965 to 1984. The dramatic pass summit is attained soon after, and to the east you will see 14,060-foot Mt. Bierstadt, named after famed western painter Albert Bierstadt. Albert tried to get neighboring 14,264-foot Mt. Evans named after his wife—and he was successful for a while—until the Colorado legislature said, "Hey, wait a minute," and moved her gentle name to a lower mountain nearby. Behind, and to the south of his namesake, is hers—Rosalie Peak at 13,575 feet. Just to the north of Mt. Bierstadt are the jagged and intimidating crags of the Sawtooth ridge. To

the north, you get a preview of the descent toward Georgetown, with the Continental Divide scraping the sky in the distance.

The north, or Georgetown side of the pass has gentle switchbacks near the top that will help you change elevation rather quickly. You will also pass rapidly moving whitewater, harnessed by the Cabin Creek Hydroelectric Plant. Soon, you will be riding a shelf road above Georgetown, a National Historic Landmark District. If you don't like my picnic idea (I can handle it), you will find numerous great dining places in the downtown area, as well as also near the entrance to Interstate 70.

Give yourself 60 to 90 minutes to make the transit. Be prepared for the weather to be significantly different up high. The Georgetown (north) side can be cooler and the road conditions more unsettled than on the sun-warmed, south side.

Before there was Evergreen Lake, there was the Dedisse Ranch.

Ride 37 **Bear Creek–Kerr Gulch**

Colorado 74, County 23

A 12-mile ride through a twisty rock-walled canyon close to Denver, leading to historical communities and featuring an optional ride on a narrow shelf road to a secluded backroad

The small community of Morrison at the western edge of Denver is the location of the famed Red Rocks Park. Morrison provides entrance into the mountains via a sweet ride running through Bear Creek Canyon alongside Bear Creek, which carries the runoff from Mt. Evans and her sister peaks. Before the Evergreen Dam was built at the top of the can-

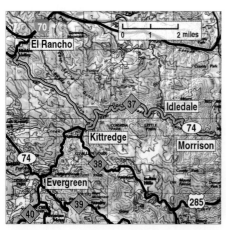

yon, flooding the Dedisse Ranch and creating Evergreen Lake, Bear Creek was an unpredictable, and frequently rampaging stream that wreaked havoc on the lower communities of Kittredge, Idledale, and even Morrison. Today the tamed creek provides accompaniment to a very scenic and twisting ride into the mountains that ascend 1,400 feet from Morrison to Evergreen.

The road through the canyon tends to be in good shape year round because much of it has good exposure to the sun. The entrance to the canyon, however, has steep walls, so it can be shady in places, but the road is sand-free for the most part. The first section of the ride near Morrison has the most twists. Be careful if ascending the canyon, for there are two right-handers about two miles in that have decreasing radii, and they have caught more than a few motorcyclists unaware.

At almost four miles, the will road pass through the small town of Idledale. From here the canyon opens up somewhat, and a mile later there will be a passing opportunity if you need one. Right about here, the Lair of the Bear Open Space Park offers hiking and picnics along Bear Creek. The road enters the forest at six miles, and at seven miles Kittredge appears over the handlebars.

At Kittredge there are two fine roads to consider. Just as you throttle down for the community, there is a road on the right to Kerr Gulch, just past a maintenance depot. It ascends quickly on a narrow chip-and-seal shelf road. For one mile it can be a hair-raising experience, but then the surface improves to a glassy-smooth, asphalt texture providing a secluded and scenic ride that climbs four more miles all the way to the El

Rancho area and I-70. If you ride this on a summer evening, the chances are excellent you will see elk grazing in the fields.

The other Kittredge alternative, if you are not heading all the way to Evergreen, is to turn left onto Myers Gulch Road, the first main road. See the Parmalee Gulch chapter [038] for details. From Evergreen you can connect with the Stanley Park ride [039], or go a short distance down County 73 to the Brook Forest ride [040].

Food and fuel options are plentiful along the way here. It all depends on what you're in the mood for. For breakfast or lunch, check out the Country Road Cafe in Kittredge. A ride up to Kittredge or Evergreen on a summer's evening can be quite special as the sun resists slipping behind the mountains until late into the evening.

The entrance to Bear Creek Canyon in 1896, and today

Ride 38 **Indian Hills**

Parmalee Gulch Road, Myers Gulch Road, County 120

A backroad, six-mile, 700-foot ascent and descent that connects two sweet canyons

The Parmalee and Myers Gulch Roads connect the Turkey Creek and Bear Creek drainages. In doing so they pass mountain parks, climb up to Indian Hills, exchange road names, and wander briefly through meadows and a foothill community, before adhering to the maxim, "What goes up must come down."

The Parmalee Gulch side of this ride begins as a well-marked turnoff to the north as US 285 emerges from the high canyon walls of Turkey Creek. Mixing in a series of tight curves with several straight sections, the road passes through one of the oldest foothill communities west of Denver, with aged cabins, homes, and structures on either side of the ascent.

At just under three miles, there is a turn you can make if you want to check out Mt. Falcon Open Space Park. The 2.7-mile road has recently been chip sealed and is easy for

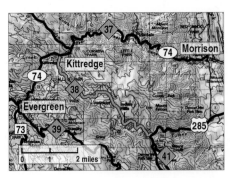

any street bike. If you go, make the easy hike to the remains of John Brisben Walker's castle-like home that went up in flames in 1918. He owned 4,000 acres at the top of Mt. Falcon and had visions of building a western or summertime White House on a nearby ridge, at which U.S. presidents could reside and work. The project never went beyond the laying of a foundation and cornerstone, despite a well-publicized effort to raise funds, which included a campaign that solicited ten-cent donations from thousands of Colorado school children. Alas, while several of his investments returned rich rewards, others did not—including his purchase of the Stanley Steamer Company—and he passed away in 1931 with little to his name.

The downhill side of this ride (uphill if coming up Myers Gulch from Kittredge in Bear Creek Canyon) is one of forested accompaniment, with Pence Park on one side and O'Fallon Park on the other. You will pass a few homes as you approach Kittredge and the canyon.

In Kittredge you can connect with the Bear Creek Canyon ride [037] for a loop back to Denver, or link to the nearby Kerr Gulch Road. From Evergreen, you can make a turn toward the Stanley Park [039] or Brook Forest [040] journeys.

Ride 39 **Stanley Park–North Turkey**

Little Cub Creek Road, Stanley Park Road, High Drive, North Turkey Creek Road

A quiet, backroad, 15-mile roller-coaster ride near the Front Range, offering a collection of perfectly appointed bends

The roads of this ride are among the curviest you will come across in the Front Range. They take you alongside winding creeks and also up, over, and through tightly bunched hills and valleys. From the western hills leading to Stanley Park there are great views of Mt. Evans and her sister peaks.

This ride begins in Evergreen, just 100 yards to the south of the Evergreen Lake Dam, where you will see Little Cub Creek Road leading to the south toward Stanley Park. This portion of the 12-mile curve-fest is actually three roads seamlessly connected to each other. Little Cub Creek becomes Stanley Park Road, which then becomes High Drive. Reverse the order, and you find an alternative route to Evergreen from North Turkey Creek where High Drive has its entrance or conclusion, depending on the way you are going.

Little Cub Creek Road follows its namesake for several miles before beginning a sharp ascent up to Stanley Park. Try not to gaze at the snowcaps on the near western horizon, for you and your bike will be facing a series of tight, back-and-forth curves.

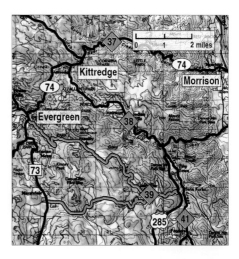

After topping out at Stanley Park, enjoy the winding tarmac as it weaves its way through quiet homes and quiet fields. Around dusk on a summer evening, the area is an active place for grazing elk and deer. On the descent, as the road becomes High Drive, be wary of several tight, almost Z-like curves. High Drive ends at North Turkey Creek Road, which by itself offers a diet of pretzeled pavement as well. You can also reach North Turkey Creek Road directly from US 285, just two miles past Turkey Creek Canyon to the west.

North Turkey Creek Road follows the creek bearing its name for two miles before leaving it for an ascent to a fertile meadow where the elk treat the area like a big salad bowl—especially at dinner time! Just before North Turkey Creek ends at County 73, you will pass Evergreen Memorial Park on the south side of the road. This is an area with bison in large fields, and with deer, elk, and other large herbivores in big enclosures. The bison herd includes two or three white (well, sandy colored if you ask me) shaggy beasts. See if you can spot them.

By riding North Turkey Creek Road from US 285 directly to County 73, you can connect with the Conifer rides by turning left, and with a right turn toward Evergreen, you can connect with the Brook Forest backroad journey [040], and Bear Creek Canyon [037].

For those in the Front Range, these roads are close by and can take you on a fun quarter-day ride, perhaps during a summer evening with a meal stop in Conifer or Evergreen. You will be challenged by the curves, but my guess is more than a few of you would be up for this! Note, however, the many quiet residences along the way, and ride accordingly.

Ride 40 **Brook Forest**

Brook Forest Road, Shadow Mountain Road, Blue Creek Road

A 12-mile winding backroad that ascends and descends 1,200 feet and serves as an alternative route between Evergreen and Conifer

There are roads you enjoy, and there are roads you endure. Often, Colorado 73 between Evergreen and Conifer is the latter for me. It is fairly straight and typically heavy with traffic. I find myself creeping along and constantly changing gears. This ride offers alternative routes between these two towns. Granted, they are longer and you will probably lose a few minutes of time, but after sampling their curving and unimpeded liberties, you won't find it hard to justify the choice.

From downtown Evergreen at the main intersection, ride Colorado 73 one mile toward Conifer, then turn right/south onto Brook Forest Road. From the Conifer side, head toward Evergreen on Colorado 73 for a little over a mile, turning left/south onto Shadow Mountain Road. This is one of those roads that changes names along the way. Just keep your front wheel on the main road and you won't have any problems.

From Evergreen, the road twists and turns as it climbs steadily up the south slopes of Black Mountain. It is a fun road without any lights or stop signs, but you will be passing by homes with driveways to the left and right. Many of these on the Evergreen side

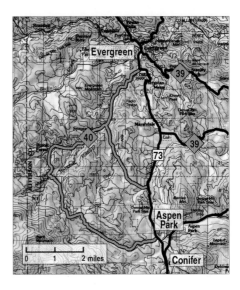

are of an older vintage. At around five miles, relax the throttle for the historic Brook Forest Inn. Opened in 1919 by a couple from the Alps, it offered the latest in luxury for the times, including running water, electricity, baths, and lodging for up to 130 visitors. The inn was expanded over the years and became quite the destination for many. It has changed ownership and business focus over time, but most recently it has returned to its roots as a place for rest and refreshment.

Continuing on, the road gains altitude as it cuts through a swath of piney woods in the Arapaho National Forest. The curves can sneak up on you here, as can sand on the road, so take it easy. After a series of S-curves you will drop down into a bowl where vehicles may be parked along the side the road near the trailhead for the very fine Maxwell Falls hiking trail.

Homes will begin to appear among the trees again as the road leads you on toward

Conifer, then there will be another gap before the forest, like a regrouped army, charges forth and reclaims the open space. This is a sweet section of curves and sweepers as you descend to Colorado 73 four miles away. Be sure to acknowledge the historical homesteading cabins flying past on the way toward your destination. Oh, wait a minute—the ride *is* the destination.

A little less than three miles after turning onto Brook Forest from Evergreen, Blue Creek Road, as an alternative, departs to the left. It is a three-mile detour back to Colorado 73, and while it's shorter than the Brook Forest and Shadow Mountain route, it makes up for its brevity in scenic backroad beauty.

Plenty of services are available in the towns at either end of this ride. Also, you can always pack some food and stop at one of the quiet picnic places along the stream, or bring it with you on your two-mile hike to check out Maxwell Falls!

Ride 41 **South Turkey–Hilldale**

South Turkey Creek Road, City View Drive, Crystal Way, Oehlmann Park Road

A quiet, curving 13-mile creekside ride on a historical road that bypasses a busy highway, with an option to ascend a tightly twisting road delivering far views and access to the Conifer area

When riding southwest out of Denver on US 285, consider taking South Turkey Creek Road, which roughly parallels US 285 for eight miles. Though a few minutes longer, it is a more peaceful, curvy, and scenic ride than nearby US 285.

As the steep walls of Turkey Creek Canyon give way to more open hillsides, you will pass under the entrance ramp from Indian Hills [038] to US 285. Drift over to the left lane, nudging the handlebars toward South Turkey Creek Road a few hundred yards away. In about a mile you will see Tiny Town on your right. This popular summertime attraction was built on the site of a Denver–Leadville stagecoach stop, beginning as a place where a father built miniature replicas of buildings to delight his daughter. In 1939 a Tiny Town Railroad began operation. Since then the place has survived floods, fires, and economic winds, but sometimes just barely. Today it thrives, as the small train circles the grounds, you might recognize a building or two.

As the road follows the meandering and flowing path of its namesake, take note of the eclectic collection of homes you ride by, for you are on one of the oldest mountain roads around. This was the original US 285, and before that it was a dirt road for stage-coaches journeying southwest out of Den-

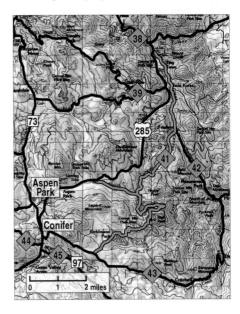

Three steeds resting after a successful conquest of Hilldale Pines

ver—and before that it was a Ute and Arapaho path between the plains of Denver and the high mountain meadows of the Conifer area and beyond.

At three miles you'll pass the turnoff to Deer Creek Canyon [042] and at eight miles you will re-link with US 285 just east of Aspen Park. If you're "up" for more, and I mean this literally, at six miles into this ride—two miles before South Turkey Creek's conclusion—there is City View Drive off to the south/left. You will be challenged if you make this turn. The curves and turns are demonic but, you know, the bikes are always willing! Also, there is an enticing array of roads leading off City View that will take you to a cul-de-sac or through a subdivision maze. But there's really only two key turns not to miss: at 1.2 miles, stay on City View by making a 90-degree turn to the left, and at 3.0 miles turn left onto Crystal. That's it. It will take you to Oehlmann Park Road and all the way to Pleasant Park [043] at six miles.

There's a good reason the road climbing up through the homes of Hilldale Pines is named City View. At around two miles you will have panoramas of Denver and the plains that will have you thinking you can see all the way to Kansas. You do climb 800 feet in only a few minutes on this hillside scoot. Be careful, for some of the curves are of the hairpin variety. There is a roller-coaster feel to the road before you get to a meadow and the ride joins Crystal and then Oehlmann Park. The journey concludes at Pleasant Park [043], where you can turn left for Denver or right to Conifer only two miles away.

The convenience store at Tiny Town is occasionally opened for food and fuel, but no other options exist until you reach the Aspen Park and Conifer area.

Ride 42 **Deer Creek Canyon**

Deer Creek Canyon Road

A short but incredibly sweet eight-mile canyon scoot southwest of Denver on smooth, sand-free pavement providing access to open-space parks and other rides in the foothills

Although Deer Creek Canyon Road is only eight miles in length, its texture, cambers, and design make it worth putting on your agenda. It follows the tight and snaking course of Deer Creek as it drains the foothills southwest of Denver, emptying into nearby Chatfield Reservoir. The road climbs out of the canyon, up over Firehouse Hill, and ends at South Turkey Creek Road.

You can find the entrance to the canyon via Wadsworth or Kipling Boulevard. Access can also be made by Valley Road south out of Ken Caryl. The delights begin right away when your wheels touch this finely surfaced ribbon of road, recently widened to accommodate bicyclists. This extra lane width has minimized the awful practice of vehicles cutting corners through dirty shoulders, flinging gravel or sand onto the roadway.

In Deer Creek Canyon the surface tends to be very clean with nicely cambered curves. that go back and forth as you gain altitude up into the foothills. The first road to the left, at four miles, leads to another great ride, High Grade Road–Pleasant Park [043].

After passing the South Deer Creek turnoff, the canyon road enters into a mile-long series of very tight and decreasing-radius curves. The road also narrows somewhat and can be grittier. Be on your guard here! Three miles later, after ascending, then descending Firehouse Hill, the road ends at South Turkey Creek Road [041].

You can extend your visit to this canyon area by visiting one of three open space parks nestled alongside this scenic road. Hildebrand Ranch Park is just before the mouth of the canyon between Kipling and Wadsworth Avenues. Just a mile into the canyon is the South Valley Park and another mile farther is Deer Creek Canyon Park with signs indicating a turnoff to the south.

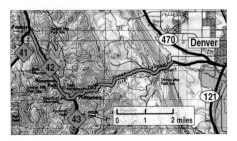

After heavy, wet snow collapsed two other buildings several years ago, only one structure remains standing in Phillipsburg.

Ride 43 **High Grade–Pleasant Park**

South Deer Creek Road, High Grade Road, Pleasant Park Road

A quiet and diverse ten-mile backcountry route between Conifer and southwest Denver, with a mountain-hugging ascent to lovely meadows and pastures

Sometimes you want to ride something new. Sometimes you want to ride a wickedly bent road. Sometimes a backroad cruise is high on your list. Maybe you just want to get to the Conifer area and perhaps beyond, and US 285 is a "Been There Done That." Well, this chapter is for you.

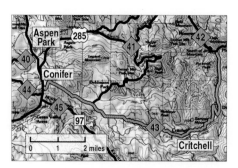

This ride consists of three relatively unknown roads, seamlessly connected, that bring you through a 2,000-foot elevation change in ten miles. The journey essentially follows a twisted old wagon trail to the US 285 corridor. High Grade Road in the middle presents you with a demented hunk of hillside sandwiched between two slices of superb rural riding.

This run starts from a turnoff about three miles into Deer Creek Canyon [042]. You will see South Deer Creek Road leading off to the south at a small clearing called Phillipsburg. The road gently passes a small number of residences as it swings alongside a branch of Deer Creek. At around three miles the road joins High Grade Road and dramatically ascends about 700 feet in only three miles. This is one coiled, wretched, mountain-hugging road.

Keep your riding wits about you as your bike cuts between steep slopes on one side and a deep creek gorge on the other. The tight and blind curves can be sandy from cars cutting the corners, so have this in the back of your riding mind. At another small clearing called Critchell, about three miles after starting the High Grade climb, the road changes names again and you will have your two wheels on Pleasant Park Road.

A little bit of historical trivia: the infamous cannibal Alferd Packer (Silver Thread Scenic Byway [079]), lived out his paroled and elderly years at this small Critchell crossroads location.

As your ascent continues on Pleasant Park Road, you will see that it lives up to its name. You will pass fields, ranches, and old cabins on this pastoral county road, with enough tight bends to keep you in grin mode. When you arrive at Conifer you will have choices: you can head north on US 285 for a return to Denver, or you can head south 200 yards and turn right onto Kennedy Gulch Road, just past the shopping center; this is the launch for the Conifer Mountain ride [044]. At the bottom of the exit, a left turn will take you onto Foxton Road [045], which is a sweet and swerving descent all the way to the South Platte River [046].

Here's a little detour you might want to take: when you pass through that smidge of a community called Critchell, you will see Kuehster Road leading off to the south. It is a dead-end, semi-chip-and-seal road climbing toward a ridgeline. No problem on a street bike. Ride to the top then descend a bit, down and to the left. Look to the south and if the skies and lighting are cooperating . . . well, I hope you brought a camera. That's all I'm gonna say!

Ride 44 **Conifer Mountain**

Kennedy Gulch Road, Conifer Mountain Road, Marks Drive, Pike View Drive, Kings Valley Drive

A ten-mile hoot of a ride with serious twists and turns up, over, and down Conifer Mountain

Put your seat belts (figuratively) on for this one! The straights are few and the curves are many. If you like the taste of tight twisty tarmac, then make plans to take your bike to Conifer Mountain.

Just past Conifer on US 285, right after the shopping center on the right/west side of the highway, there is the exit for Foxton Road [045] and Kennedy Gulch Road. At the bottom of the exit, turn right on Kennedy Gulch to begin the ascent of Conifer Mountain. This road lures you in with a nice weaving

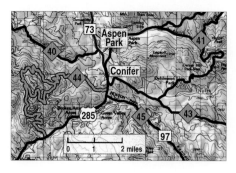

ride through the forest before snaring you with a series of wickedly tight curves.

If you escape and make it five miles farther and 1,000 feet higher you will come to a Y in the road. You can go either way. Conifer Mountain Drive will take you to the right and it winds away for several miles before coming to Marks Drive—which is also where Conifer Mountain Road takes you if you bear to the left. Both routes pass by quiet homes tucked into the trees as you continue to gain elevation. The key differences between the two routes is that if you go right you have a longer ride to Marks Drive, and if you turn to the left you will be presented with bigger views to the south and southeast.

Note that you have to find Marks Drive to make it down the south side of Conifer Mountain. On some maps and signs it is noted as South Marks Drive. From the start of this ride, if you turn left on Conifer Moun-

Looking down on the start of Marks Drive

tain Road (versus to the right and Conifer Mountain Drive), it is 5.4 miles to Marks Drive. To be sure, if you don't find it, you can always have a fun scoot back down the east side via your approach . . . and this isn't a bad option!

The descent to the south and east is somewhat like the beginning, with a winding road drawing you through a corridor of trees before the kinks in the road become serious. Because you are going downhill, you will find it easier to notice the views before you, and if you manage to sneak glances at the rock formations through the pines to your right, you will see one of Colorado's newest state parks, Staunton State Park, due to open in 2012.

Finding the route on this descent is not easy. While it will seem like you haven't made a turn off the road, it will change names several times! Along the way it becomes Pike View Drive, and when you get to Kings Valley Drive, turning left, you soon will be arriving at US 285. The best advice I can give you is, when you have a choice, keep heading downhill. Eventually you will be deposited three miles farther southwest on US 285.

Stay alert as you will be passing by driveways and homes, and some of the curves can catch you if you are distracted. That said, I've paused numerous times with riding friends at a wide spot on Marks Drive, and the grins and whoops coming from under the helmets is perhaps the best testimony for this road and ride.

Back in 1904, the ranch surrounding the Foxton Barn was a center for community social gatherings. Today it stands silently by, as drivers rush past on their way to other destinations.

Ride 45 **Foxton**

Foxton Road, County 97

An eight-mile winding ride down a quiet and scenic road providing alternative access to journeys in the South Platte River area

Just south of Conifer on US 285 is the exit for Kennedy Gulch Road and Foxton Road. To the west is the excellent twisting journey over Conifer Mountain [044] and to the southeast is Foxton Road. Pointing the handlebars toward Foxton provides you with a lonely and sweet escort down to South Platte River Road [046]. It isn't as tightly sinuous as its Conifer Mountain cousin on the other side of US 285, but if you're in the right mood, it is perfect.

Two Denver mountain parks make their appearance in the first two miles, in an area of pleasing meadowlands between forested slopes of emerald pine. Foxton Road continues its meandering and descending ways for an additional five miles when the boundaries of Reynolds Ranch Open Space Park begin appearing on both sides of the road. The park is named after John Reynolds, who donated much of the property to Jefferson County.

This area is where some of Colorado's earliest foothills pioneers settled. The ranch house on the east side of the road across from the park was a stop for pack trains making their way to Leadville from Denver, in the days before the Denver, South Park &

Pacific narrow-gauge train would blow its whistle in the nearby Platte River Canyons.

After passing through the Open Space Park, this journey changes clothes and soon you'll be riding a seriously wrinkled garment of tarmac as you approach the river. This is one of those times when a motorcyclist says that wrinkled is good!

Take it easy in these tight, sometimes sandy curves. The dramatic river scenery, with its craggy spires and rocky outcroppings will be vying for your atten-

tion. When you reach Foxton Road's conclusion at the river, you can turn right for an easy, five-mile easy chip-and-seal ride to Buffalo Creek and Deckers Road, or turn left for Nighthawk at ten miles and the ascent to Sprucewood and Jarre Canyon [051]. At 14.5 miles, if you turn left you will reach Deckers [047]. It should be noted there is a four-mile section north of Nighthawk that is dirt, and not sealed. It is no problem on a street bike, but it can be dusty.

Though no longer in use, the Foxton post office building still stands.

The South Platte Hotel, shown here in 1899, still marks the confluence of the Middle and North Forks of the South Platte River.

Ride 46 **South Platte River**

Platte River Road, County 97

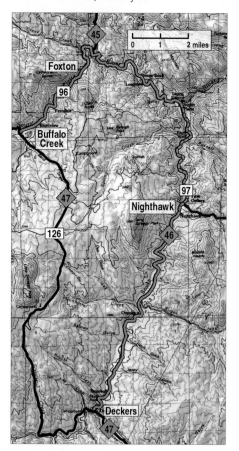

A delightfully curving 25-mile ride alongside the South Platte River that passes through historic old communities and underneath intimidating rock formations on a mix of paved, chipped, and easy-dirt surfaces

This ride follows two forks of the South Platte River. Narrow-gauge trains started making their way up the South Platte River canyons 130 years ago, opening up transportation access to the booming central district mining camps. For decades it was a prosperous time, with the railroads carrying not only ores, but also tourists who now had easy access to the mountains. Indeed, resorts were built all along the rail line to attract and serve vacationing visitors who rarely, if ever, had made it far into the mountains. Some of these towns still remain, and others have long since faded.

From Deckers [047] heading north on Platte River Road (Highway 67 for five miles before it departs the river), you will find

Just before reaching Nighthawk, a photographer in 1900 stood at this bend in the river to take a photo of 8,812-foot Long Scraggy Peak. That is one scraggy peak, eh! My riding friend placed his bike in the foreground as we sought to replicate the scene.

yourself on a paved, twisting ribbon of road, dancing with the river as it bends left and right, left and right. Only a mile from Deckers is the old townsite of Trumbull.

The river road remains paved for another five miles to another small community—Nighthawk. After Nighthawk, the road becomes dirt, and it remains this way to the old townsite of South Platte and the South Platte Hotel. Despite the lack of asphalt, it is an easy ride for a heavy street bike if you don't mind the potential for dust. You will find the river and surrounding country a rockier place, with huge, train-car-sized boulders scattered around like a giant game of marbles.

At the South Platte, the road becomes a primitive chip-and-seal atop the old train bed. A popular stop for day picnics 100 years ago was Dome Rock just past the South Platte townsite. Pause, turn off your engine, and see if you can spot it on the other side of the river. If you listen carefully, you may be able to discern the faint sounds of a train whistle, with joyous hints of laughter from those visiting a century ago.

Continuing on, you'll wind past the semi-ghost town of Foxton. The old cabin post office remains right next to the road. The first resident of Foxton back in the late 1800s was a dentist who decided to quietly retire here along the river. The tranquility didn't last long when the Denver, South Platte & Pacific placed narrow-gauge tracks in front of his place in the 1870s. Determined to not let this stand, the dentist tried to take advan-

Trumbull in 1899

Trumbull today

The Cathedral Spires then and now

tage of the slight incline here and would soap the rails in an attempt to make the train wheels spin and slip when passing! I guess he found his efforts ineffective and the disruption unbearable, so he packed up and moved to Oregon.

The road base in the Foxton area of the ride decays into a crumbling chip-and-seal. It is still an easy street bike ride, but keep the wheels pointed true and on your side of the narrow road as you go around the curves. You will see occasional homes and cabins on the other side of the river, some with footbridges, and others without any visible access. This is mostly due to a flash flood in July of 1996, caused when heavy rains fell on the baked soil of the nearby area burned by

Buffalo Creek Wildfire in May of that year. Without soft soil to absorb the rain, it roared down the river 20 feet higher in places than it is now, blasting out most footbridges, leaving cars and debris wedged high up in the rocks.

Not only is this a destination ride, but the motorcycle roads it connects with are blissful, including the Jarre Canyon ride [051] and the Deckers ride [047]. Additionally, there is the Foxton road access [045] just a mile north of Foxton. Deckers is a popular place with bikers and you will find food services here. However, there is no fuel, and the nearest places to gas up are 14 miles away in Buffalo Creek where there is a pump, or 25 miles away in Woodland Park on US 24.

Peter Head in 1900

Peter Head today

Ride 47 **Deckers**

Pine Valley Road, County 126, Colorado 67

A special 48-mile mountain road ride renowned for its diverse riding attractions, with a motorcycle gathering place midway

The Deckers ride offers much to the two-wheeled enthusiast. For almost 50 miles it weaves through the Pike National Forest and small communities, going this way and that way, up and down. The ride can be engaged at Woodland Park (US 24) at the south end, or at Pine Junction (US 285) on the north. It also can be joined midway at the small roadside community of Deckers via the Platte River ride [046]. On any day of the week during the season, and especially on weekends, Deckers is a place where many on two wheels gather for a snack, a little tire kickin', and watching an assortment of bikes pass by.

The lowest elevation of this ride is at Deckers, with Horse Creek joining the Middle Fork of the South Platte at the bridge. Temperatures are often ten degrees warmer here year round than at the higher altitude bookends of Pine Junction and Woodland Park. South of Deckers, Colorado 67 provides the riding delights. North of Deckers, Jefferson County 126, then Pine Valley Road handle the honors.

When heading north from Woodland Park you are first greeted with a leisurely scoot through trees and fields for about ten miles. As you descend to Deckers, the curves tighten. Here, evidence of Colorado's largest wildfire ever—the monstrous Hayman Fire of June 2002—extends in every direction. The heat was so great where the road starts its descent that even the pavement caught on fire.

In a short distance you will pass the small community of Westcreek on the left. It isn't easy to see, for it is down the hill and behind trees on the south, but CDOT tends to actively dump sand here during off-season months for the residents, so scan the road for any grit. The downhill ride continues toward Deckers and the delights of this winding road become visibly apparent as you weave your bike through a maze of rocks and trees.

On the north side of Deckers you can spur your bike toward the first of two ascents. The warm-up is tightly twisting for several

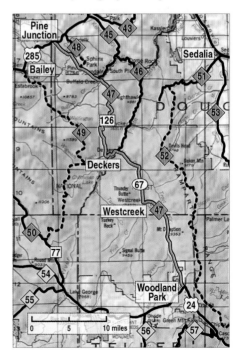

miles, followed by the climb up "Horse-power Hill." More than a few bikers claim this is one of best riding stretches around. At the top, you will be introduced to a series of marvelous sweepers. A scenic pullout mid-way through this riding wonderland is some-what inconveniently placed, giving you a tough choice: continue the dance, or pause the song and take a break.

A descent to Buffalo Creek and the North Fork of the South Platte follows. You will pass through another wildfire area—The Buffalo Creek Fire of May 1996, started by a campfire not being completely extinguished. Here, the North Fork of the South Platte joins the ride and shows you the way to Pine Grove before you make the final ascent up to Pine Junction and US 285.

This is a versatile ride. One you can enjoy whether you have only a few hours, or if you have all day, for it takes you by other nearby rides like Sphinx Park [048], the South Platte River [046], and Jarre Canyon [051] out of Sprucewood. If you have a dual-sport bike, you can gain access to the Matukat [049] ride just west of Deckers, and there's also the Rampart Range ride [052] and all kinds of forest roads leading to the south out of Westcreek and just north of Deckers.

Except for a single gas pump at Buffalo Creek (when the general store is open), there are no places to refuel for the 50 miles be-tween Woodland Park and Pine Junction, but snack food and light meals are available at Deckers. Also, Zoka's Restaurant and Bar in Pine Grove is popular with motorcyclists, as well as the historic Bucksnort Saloon in Sphinx Park, a couple of chip-and-sealed miles north up scenic Elk Creek Canyon out of Pine Grove.

Ride 48 **Sphinx Park**

Elk Creek Road, County 83

A short side trip off Pine Valley Road on a street-bike friendly chip-and-seal surface, through a spectacular canyon to a historic community that is the epitome of the Old West

One hundred years ago the Denver, South Park & Pacific narrow-gauge train belched cinder-laden smoke as it labored up the South Platte River canyons southwest of Denver, aiming for the high meadows of South Park. It stopped along the way in Pine (also known as Pine Grove) on the North Fork of the South Platte River. To the north of town, up a narrow, boulder-filled, slab-rock canyon, a dirt road was hacked through ledges to the small community of Sphinx Park. Stagecoaches would run back and forth in this impressive gorge, carrying passengers from the trains seeking a weekend respite in the mountains.

There are two entrances into the canyon harboring the cabin community of Sphinx Park. The more dramatic (and shorter) approach, mentioned in the preceding paragraph, is from Pine Grove. A ride on Deckers–Pine Valley Road [047] will bring you and your bike right to this small and historical train-stop community. The journey up Elk Creek Canyon to Sphinx is only a few

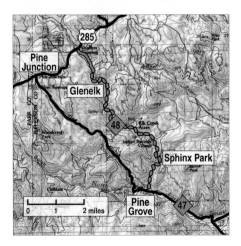

miles long, but it is one for the memory book. Look for South Elk Creek Road leading to the north from the center of Pine Grove. While it is a chip-and-seal route to Sphinx Park, heavy street bikes can make it without a problem.

Along the way, take in the massive outcroppings and magnificent formations. This is a rock climber's paradise. You're going to feel pretty insignificant as you pass through the towering cliffs on your suddenly puny motorcycle. You will note, if not hear, the cascading Elk Creek falling through and over rocks as it does its share of draining the high peaks of the Mt. Evans area to the west. After gazing down at the bold stream, look up for the equally bold cabins perched high on apartment-sized rocks, and remnants of cabins that used to be perched high on apartment-sized rocks. Some of these have one very big step out the front door!

Arrival at Sphinx Park is special. It feels almost like a movie set for an old western town, but it's the real thing and authenticity hangs thickly in the air. Old cabins abound, and are clustered in every direction. The setting and atmosphere is hard to beat. The highlight of the place is the Bucksnort Saloon. Many tales can be told about this tavern. A local once rode his mule into the bar. He was kicked out, but the mule was permitted to stay.

If you find yourself enjoying a ride on the great Deckers Road [047], you will enjoy a ride and a stop here as well. On a summer evening, few places typify quintessential Colorado like Sphinx Park. If US 285 is your destination following the Sphinx Park visit, consider scooting up Elk Creek Road all the way, as opposed to returning to Pine Grove. The easy dirt-surface road is hardened with pavement a few miles from US 285. Be sure to ride slowly through the rustic and charming community of Glenelk, not far from 285. The cabins are close to the road and the soft lights inside on a summer's night doubly warm the soul.

Ride 49 **Matukat**

Wellington Lake Road, Stoney Pass Road, Goose Creek Road, Matukat Road, County 68, Forest Road 560, 211

A 40-mile backcountry dual-sport ride through the Pike National Forest, past a lake and over a pass, with scenic vistas, serious rock formations, rustic homesteads, and a recovering fire-burned forest

This is an impressive ride through the heart of the Pike National Forest. For 40 miles, high scores are given for how this series of connected roads inspires dual-sport riders. From the roads you ride to the sights you see, this route delivers big time. The deeper you ride into this journey, the deeper the experience becomes.

On the northwest side, the ride begins at the bottom of Crow Hill in Bailey. On the other end, it is kicked off at a T-intersection with the superb Tarryall Road [050], seven miles north of Lake George. Saddle up and start off on County 68 or the Wellington Lake Road as it departs to the southeast on the east side of Bailey. Only the first mile is paved; the rest is a graded dirt surface. If you are interested in train history, at 2.1 miles lean the bike to the left and make a turn to the north onto Insmont Drive. In a few hundred yards, the 120-year-old train-stop resort town of Insmont comes into view with many historical structures still standing.

Continuing on Wellington Lake Road, at 3.5 miles the small, inviting valley of Estabrook appears over the handlebars with its old homesteads and resort cabins on the south side. The North Fork of the South Platte cuts through a visible canyon on the north side, where plans were made to dam the river and flood Bailey, creating an Estabrook Reservoir. It didn't happen, but I guess the plans are

filed away somewhere for that possibility someday.

Forest riding is next on the stage. At 10.5 miles, the impressive spires of The Castle tower above, making you feel like a lowly peasant passing by. The private Wellington Lake with its campgrounds and camp store

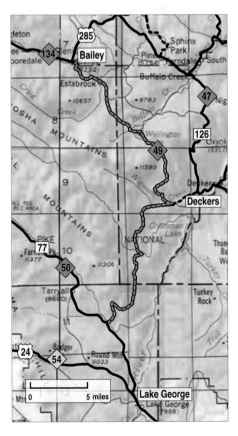

is just ahead. For what it is worth, this is black bear central, and they love coming down from Buffalo Peak on the south side of the lake, messing with the campers, then taking a few slurps of refreshing Wellington aqua.

Up to this point the road conditions are dirt-road decent. Ride around the north side of scenic Wellington and conditions decay a bit. There is a fun creek crossing, and then there is a somewhat stony surface for about a mile as you ascend 400 feet to aptly named Stoney Pass! It is sections like this where I hesitate to endorse a lightweight street bike. However, with some good suspension, worthy tires, and a spirit of laughter and adventure, let your fun, non-dual-sport loose on these enticing 40 miles. Except for this mildly rocky section, the surface is quite placid.

The sweetness of the ride continues on the south side of Stoney Pass. Old rustic homesteads, cabins pre-dating the National Forest designation, and tucked-away meadows complete the landscape as the easy dirt road winds through it all as if you're on some kind of paid scenic tour.

It is unavoidable. You cannot miss the desolation and destruction of the 130,000-acre Hayman Fire of June 2002. It will be all around you as the ride ventures deeper into what was once a vibrant forest. On the Sunday after its Saturday afternoon ignition, the inferno consumed 60,000 acres—becoming, in just a single day, Colorado's largest fire. But that pre-2002 forest is slowly making its comeback, as countless bouquets of wildflowers cover the hills as if a nursery is nurturing the area in preparation for high school prom season. Aspen stands in sheltered gullies and gulches are thriving like weeds fed Miracle-Gro. Someday, the fiery color will return here, but it will be from aspen gold.

At 22 miles, you will come to a well-signed intersection. To continue this journey on the remaining 18 miles to Tarryall Road, make a sharp right and continue on Goose Creek Road/Forest Road 211. A turn to the left will bring you to paved Jefferson County

126 just a few miles east of Deckers [047]. If you were acquainted with this area before the flames came through, you will notice a major change in the uncovering of amazing rock formations and outcroppings. Not that they weren't visible before, but they have become much more apparent in the currently denuded forest.

At 31 miles, if there is a hiker in you, a turnoff to the Goose Creek Trailhead is on the west side of the road. It is one of best hikes in the state, with Yosemite-like splendor surrounding you along the way. At about two hours into this magical hike you will come to a playground of apartment-sized rocks jumbled and tumbled together, forming a network of cave-like tunnels. There's also a little history just past the rocks, but I'll leave that for those making the two-footed trek!

Several winding and ascending miles later,

a panorama will unfold to the north and west. Put the sidestand down here and take it all in. You're at an inspiring vista many do not see. The reward is yours for making the trek, but the greater return will be experiencing all of this without doors or a roof. Amen!

The conclusion of the ride will be seven or so miles farther at Tarryall Road [050]. The community of Lake George on US 24 [054] seven miles to the south is where you can top off the tank or take care of the appetite. Florissant, three miles farther east, presents more choices. Numerous rides pour out of US 24, like bats from a cave at dusk. On the north end, Bailey is the place to prepare thyself or refill thyself. The Cutthroat Cafe in Bailey is a popular place for motorcyclists to chow down. Dual-sport enthusiasts will also note that Pike National Forest area has many other great dual-sport rides for secluded exploration. Go for it!

Ride 50 **Tarryall**

Tarryall Road, County 77

A 42-mile ride of lonely and scenic beauty passing through places time has hardly touched

Tarryall Road/Park County 77 delivers a journey through a countryside that has hardly changed since early settlers settled and hardy miners mined. Pioneering homesteads and cabins are present the entire route. Some are rather drafty and some are lived in. One ghost town and one semi-ghost town tell a tale in silence. However,

recently placed interpretive signs help you hear and understand some of the whispers from the past.

Tarryall Road is a link between US 285 and Jefferson on the north, and US 24 at Lake George on the south. The monstrous Hayman Fire (Colorado's largest wildfire ever) was ignited from a campground along this road in June of 2002, just a few miles north of Lake George. As funds become available, the road is being resurfaced to improve the route for any future fire or emergency needs. At this time, the first seven miles heading south out of Jefferson are newly paved—and it is a world-class job. You will be riding in the zone as you pass through old ranches, sweeping back and forth on a pristine road base following the wandering course of the Tarryall River.

Coming from the north, at seven miles near the Stagestop Saloon, the road surface changes to a texture of broken chip-and-seal. The road continues like this, along with short scattered dirt sections, for the next 28 miles. You should have no problems riding this on any street bike, but watch where you point your front wheel. At the southern terminus of this road near Lake George, the road is also smoothly paved. It's that 28 miles of old road base in the middle that is, in a way, consistent with the character of this ride!

At eleven miles from Jefferson heading south, you will pass by vacant structures close to the east side of the road edge. These are the standing remains of Bordenville, founded by Timothy Borden of Iowa who was one of the first white settlers in the area. As the road curves, look east up the forlorn and windswept hillside to see the pioneer cemetery of Bordenville, which stands in testimony to those enduring spirits who tried to make a go of this long-winter, short-summer place.

At risk of being morbid, one past pioneer resident is not buried here. Benjamin Ratcliff, furious at gossip directed toward his children by the head of the school board, showed up at a meeting and emptied his gun at the board members, killing all three. He was tried and subsequently hung at Cañon City, but was buried in an unmarked grave somewhere outside of the Bordenville cemetery fence.

You will cruise the northern shoreline of Tarryall Reservoir until about mile 18, and then enter an area of wild and pristine beauty. The tour here is outstanding, with a winding road that entertains and roadside scenery that enchants. I can't think of many, if any, places in Colorado that look quite like the rock-formation-filled paintings here. This is a sweet and special ride. A few minutes farther, the semi-ghost town of Tarryall appears over the handlebars. The population of this community 120 years ago was near 800, largely supported by the flare of nearby mining activity. At that time, it also went by the unflattering name of "Grab All." Guess it wasn't known for fair and equitable business practices. Indeed, the name of the nearby county seat of Fairplay came from its mining-days motto "We Play Fair."

Be fuel-ready for these 42 miles as there are no gas pumps along the way. Jefferson and Lake George on each end are your nearest choices. The Stagestop Saloon at seven miles from Jefferson serves a killer steak sandwich and real onion rings if it is open. The Twin Eagles Campground, a few miles northeast of the Tarryall townsite, is a favorite picnic stop of mine. I stuff the bags in Lake George or Jefferson and have the place to myself most of the time. There's a picnic table on the other side of Tarryall Creek that has seen my rear on numerous occasions. The Jefferson Market on the north side has an excellent grill open Thursday through Monday. As for nearby rides, excellent US 285 [134] and US 24 [054] will get you and your bike to Tarryall's riding delights. Dual-sporters have a network of South Park adventures branching out from here. County 23 embarking south at the Tarryall Reservoir Dam will deliver breathtaking views of South Park's grandeur and bring you over to US 24 at the western base of Wilkerson Pass.

Ride 51 **Jarre Canyon**

Colorado 67

A 13-mile journey into the foothills delivering a variety of ride attractions, from canyons and meadows, over hills and through valleys, past ranches and homesteads, to national forest facilities and dual-sport connectors

From Sedalia, Jarre Canyon Road/Colorado 67 begins its ascent into the foothills by passing gently through grassy fields, horse farms, and small ranches. Near the mouth of the canyon, and a few miles above, you'll ride by the old Jarre Creek and Woodbine Ranches.

The Jarre Creek Ranch was noted in 1882 as a good place for growing small grains, corn, and potatoes—but not so good for hay production. It lies at the base of Wildcat Mountain, a landmark for both Indians and settlers named for the large mountain lions that roam the area. The history of the Woodbine Ranch is more checkered. In the 1920s during Prohibition, it was the location of a

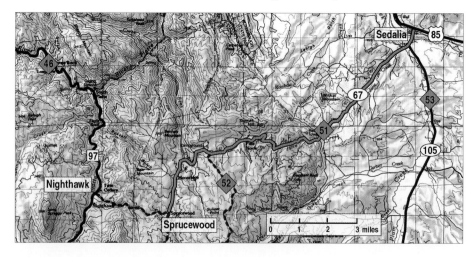

speakeasy and brothel, with an illegal casino operating on the grounds. The Rocky Mountain News in 1936 called Woodbine the hottest gambling spot between Kansas City and Reno.

In a poker game, a gangster once won half-interest in the nearby Roundup Ranch, three miles west of Woodbine, where he decided to host rodeos and deer hunting parties where the sporting gun of choice was a Thompson sub-machine gun! Woodbine has burned down several times over the years, and in the 1950s it was sold to a Baptist Youth Camp Association.

You will whisk through small communities, such as Pine Nook and Moonridge as you ascend and make your way west from Sedalia. You will pass old cabins and homesteads as well as Pike National Forest trailheads, restroom facilities, and nearby picnic grounds.

At 13 miles, you'll come to a fork in the road anchored by the Sprucewood Inn. The pavement ends here. This area is ground zero from which dirt bikers can ride the great single-track trails in the Pike National Forest and nearby Rampart Range area [052]. If you continue on County 67 to the left, you will have an almost nine-mile, dirt-road ride to South Platte River Road [046]. It is well maintained and scenic, but it can be dusty.

If you continue down and to the right you will be on County 40/Pine Creek Road. Locals call it "Nighthawk Hill," and it's a hill all right—a steep one at that! The county spreads a chloride solution on the dirt and the surface texture often resembles that of a roughly paved road. It drops you to the river in only 3.3 miles. Of course, after a burger at the Sprucewood Inn, you can always turn around and ride the sweet 13 miles back to Sedalia or Colorado 105 [053].

Jarre Canyon is a great destination for two wheels, offering a fun and historical ride of potentially varying length, depending on your interest and time. From Sedalia you can ride to the Sprucewood area and back in under an hour, or you can have a meal and easily return in less than two hours. You can turn it into a half day or longer by riding Rampart Range Road (dual-sport recommended) that Jarre Canyon passes by at around mile ten, or continue on to a great South Platte River ride a few miles past Sprucewood. There is no fuel after Sedalia, nor is there fuel in Deckers [047] if you continue that far. Food can be found at the Pine Nook Mountain Market, the Sprucewood Inn (if it is open), and in Deckers.

Ride 52 **Rampart Range**

Rampart Range Road, Forest Road 300

A 60-mile dirt-road ride high on the ridgelines of scenic foothills with numerous side forest roads, trails, and single tracks, accompanied by many camping and picnic sites along the way

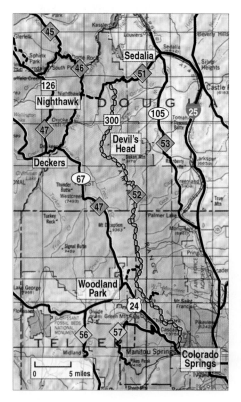

This is a well-known road, and not just in motorcycle circles. Many drive it in their cars for its easy and scenic access to lakes, rock formations, hikes, picnics, and even a fire lookout. You can do the same on your bike—and more—to explore the options available on and off this great road.

From Jarre Canyon [051] near Sedalia on the north, to Garden of the Gods in Colorado Springs on the south, you have a 60-mile-long menu of just about everything a dirt road can offer. If you don't have much time, just have an appetizer and return the way you came or take a forest road back. Want to ride the whole enchilada? Go for it! Heading south from its northern terminus, Rampart Range delivers a gentler amplitude of curves and hills than its southern conclusion. This area of the road and ride is stocked with parallel-running single tracks, campsite pullouts, and viewpoints—primarily to the rolling plains of the east.

A great spot to give your iron horse a breather

As you approach rocky Devil's Head at around nine miles, the road becomes more demented with twists and elevation changes. There is a turnoff to the east that will take you to a well-marked hiking trail where you can visit one of Colorado's last fire lookouts. Continuing south, there is a return to a more serene journey, but this is where the views start to challenge your brain for attention. I have, on occasion, almost overcooked a couple of loose curves as I craned my neck at those darn vistas! Kinks in the road will give you opportunities to look back at Devil's Head's rocky ramparts. Of course, coming up from the south, the rocky fortress will often be in front of your visor. Views to the west will start to open up as you make progress south, with the Tarryall Mountains trying to seduce you. There will be some flat rocky outcroppings and ledges where you can park your steed and pause for a view or a picnic.

As you approach Woodland Park, there are some fun sections where you can open the throttle and have quite a breezy ride through the forest! It is here, also, where Rampart Range presents the most mesmerizing sights and views. If there is an advantage to going from north to south, it is in seeing a looming Pikes Peak growing around each and every turn. Also, if you elect to head toward Colorado Springs, emptying out at the Garden of the Gods Road, instead of bailing out at Woodland Park (County 22), you will have bird-in-flight views of Queens Canyon and the Garden of the Gods, and the views of Pikes Peak from here are flat-out unrivaled. You can also take a short side ride down Forest Road 306 and check out the Rampart Reservoir Recreation Area.

This is a long 60-mile ride, with most of it on dirt except for a few miles near Woodland Park. I lean toward this being primarily a dual-sport ride, but a hearty street bike, ridden in calm fashion, should be okay. It's up to you if you want to make it a 30-minute exploration, a three-hour adventure, or an all day or overnight thing with the network of side forest roads, but these tend to serve up less certain surfaces and are more suitable for a dual-sport bike.

There are no food or fuel services along this road, but Woodland Park is a short two-mile exit before rejoining the fun. As noted at the beginning, this road is known and used by many, but despite its recognition, every time I ride it I find myself mostly alone. Those 60 miles sure do spread things out!

Ride 53 **Perry Park**

Colorado 105

A sweeping 27-mile alternative to Interstate 25, with grand views of ranches and Front Range foothills

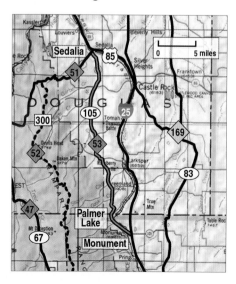

If I need to get from Colorado Springs to Denver or vice versa, and I have extra time, I'll take one of two roads roughly parallel to Interstate 25. One is Colorado 83 on the east side of I-25 [169], and the other is Colorado 105, winding along small creek beds and weaving through pastoral ranches. Actually, I'll ride down from the mountains just to experience 105 and then return.

To ride north from Monument on 105, take Exit 161 on I-25. From the west side of the interstate, your first mile will be through the Monument interstate commerce area before passing through a three-mile straight-line break to the small

On Colorado 105, the views are as open and expansive as the fields and pastures.

community of Palmer Lake, where the ride really begins as you point your front wheel north on 105.

The visual delights will begin right away as you look left and right (especially left), to see idyllic farms and ranches nestled below the first lumpy hills and ridgelines of the Rocky Mountains. Don't let your eyes wander too much, for there are several sharper curves stirred into the mix of mostly gentle bends. You will also find elevation change as the road, like a rumpled carpet, passes through several creek drainages. It may not be noticeable, but there is a 1000-foot descent (from 6,900 feet to 5,900 feet) over the 27 miles from Monument to Sedalia.

As this ride unfolds to the north, the vistas roll farther and the road stretches out more. The ranches and farms seem to grow in size, as well. Colorado 105 concludes on the north side at Highway 67 as it meanders toward Jarre Canyon [051]. Just to the east is Sedalia, where there are services, in-

cluding several motorcycle-friendly establishments.

This is a worthy north-south alternative to running the gauntlet of Interstate 25 between Denver and Colorado Springs. There are services at both ends, including two restaurants especially popular with motorcyclists. At Palmer Lake, check out O'Malley's Steak Pub on Colorado 105, and in Sedalia there is the Sedalia Grill at the corner of Colorado 67 and 85, just a half-mile to the east where Colorado 105 connects with Colorado 67.

For a diversion while riding Colorado 105, you can scoot over to the small town of Larkspur on the east by way of Perry Park Avenue or Spruce Mountain Road. On weekends during the summer, the Colorado Renaissance Festival takes over the Larkspur area with its medieval attractions. If you're on a more dirt-worthy bike, Dakan and Jackson Creek Roads adventurously leading to the west off of 105 will take you to the Rampart Range area [052].

Central Front Range

RECOMMENDATIONS

Especially Twisty Rides

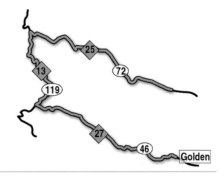

1. Ascend Coal Creek Canyon [025] to the Peak to Peak Scenic Byway [013]. Ride south ten miles on the Peak to Peak–Golden Gate Canyon [027], turn left and descend to Golden.

2. Ride Bear Creek Canyon [037] to Evergreen, turning left at the light; ride 0.3 mile to the Little Cub Creek–Stanley Park [039] circuit on the left. Descend to North Turkey Road, turning left for US 285 to Denver.

3. Climb Bear Creek Canyon [037] to Kittredge, turning right onto Kerr Gulch, and ascend to the Evergreen Parkway. Alternatively, ride Lookout Mountain Road [033] to Interstate 70W. Exit at El Rancho, joining the Evergreen Parkway. Pass Bergen Park and turn right onto Squaw Pass Road [034] to Echo Lake. Descend Colorado 103 to Idaho Springs and return via I-70 or Clear Creek Canyon [032].

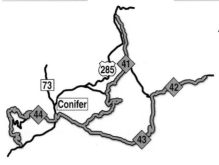

4. Ride Deer Creek Canyon [042] to High Grade Road–Pleasant Park [043], or ride South Turkey Creek Road to Hilldale Pines and Crystal Way to Pleasant Park [041]. Take Pleasant Park west to Conifer. Head south a half-mile on US 285, exiting at Kennedy Gulch Road. Ride Conifer Mountain [044] to Kings Valley on US 285. Return to Denver.

Backroad Tours

1. Take US 285 through Turkey Creek Canyon, turning right onto Parmalee Gulch [038] to Indian Hills. Descend to Kittredge, turning left onto Bear Creek Road for Evergreen. At the light, turn left onto Colorado 73 for Conifer, but in one mile turn right on Brook Forest Road [040] for a 12-mile journey winding back to Colorado 73 just north of Conifer. Turn right for US 285 and a return to Denver.

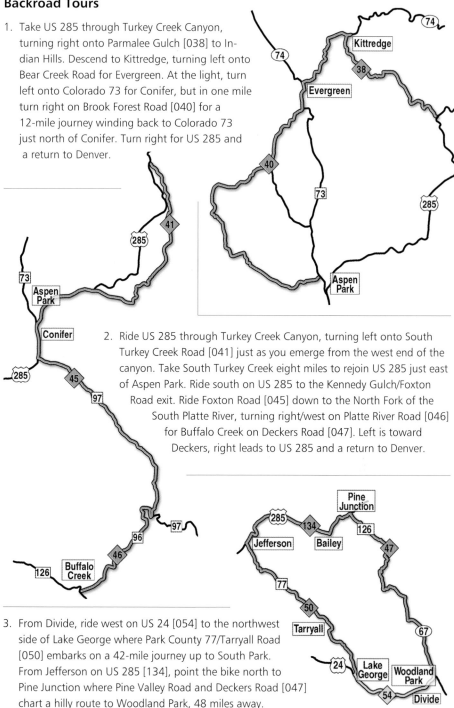

2. Ride US 285 through Turkey Creek Canyon, turning left onto South Turkey Creek Road [041] just as you emerge from the west end of the canyon. Take South Turkey Creek eight miles to rejoin US 285 just east of Aspen Park. Ride south on US 285 to the Kennedy Gulch/Foxton Road exit. Ride Foxton Road [045] down to the North Fork of the South Platte River, turning right/west on Platte River Road [046] for Buffalo Creek on Deckers Road [047]. Left is toward Deckers, right leads to US 285 and a return to Denver.

3. From Divide, ride west on US 24 [054] to the northwest side of Lake George where Park County 77/Tarryall Road [050] embarks on a 42-mile journey up to South Park. From Jefferson on US 285 [134], point the bike north to Pine Junction where Pine Valley Road and Deckers Road [047] chart a hilly route to Woodland Park, 48 miles away.

Dirt Roads to Old Places

1. Ride Jarre Canyon [051] to
   Sprucewood. Descend steep
   West Pine Creek Road 3.5 miles
   for South Platte River Road [046].
   Turn right/north on River Road for
   the historic South Platte Hotel, Dome
   Rock, Foxton, Ferndale, and Buffalo Creek. From here,
   a left delivers Deckers [047], a right leads to US 285.

2. Ride to Idaho Springs, taking Oh My God Road
   [030] up Virginia Canyon to the semi-ghost town of
   Russell Gulch. Continue to Central City, turning left
   onto the Central City Parkway [029]. Before the
   Parkway leaves the Central City limits, turn right for
   the ghost town of Nevadaville one mile up the
   hill. Return to Central City, taking Eureka
   Street northwest past the historic Central
   City cemeteries for Upper Apex Road.
   Follow it to Apex Valley Road[028] for
   the ghost town of Apex. Optionally,
   continue for Mammoth Gulch or return
   back to Central City.

3. Take Deckers Road [047] to Pine
   Grove, turning north for Elk Creek
   Canyon, Sphinx Park, and the Bucksnort
   Saloon [048]. Continue on South Elk Creek
   Road for US 285 and Shaffers Crossing.

Favorite Rides

Most Scenic Rides

[034] Squaw Pass Road
       to Echo Lake to Idaho Springs
[035] Mt. Evans Scenic Byway
[036] Guanella Pass
[046] South Platte River Road
[048] Elk Creek Canyon to Sphinx Park
[049] South of Stoney Pass
[050] Tarryall Road

Best Longer Journeys

[025] Coal Creek Canyon
[027] Golden Gate Canyon
[034] Squaw Pass Road to Echo Lake–
       to Idaho Springs
[036] Guanella Pass
[047] Deckers Road

Sweet Riding Sections

[025] The west side of Coal Creek Canyon
[027] Golden Gate Canyon
[033] The tight twists of
       Lookout Mountain Road
[034] The ten miles on each side of Echo Lake
[042] The middle three miles
       of Deer Creek Canyon
[043] High Grade Road
[044] The ascent of Conifer Mountain
[046] The cruise along the Platte River
       from Deckers to Nighthawk
[047] The sweepers of Jefferson County 126
       and the Deckers Road

Worthy Destinations

[025] Wondervu Cafe, Coal Creek Canyon
[028] Ghost town of Apex via Apex Valley Road
[030] The ghost towns of Russell Gulch
       and Nevadaville
[033] Buffalo Bill's Grave,
       the lookouts of Lookout Mountain
[034] Echo Lake Lodge
[035] Summit of Mt. Evans
[036] Summit of Guanella Pass
[037] Breakfast at the Country Road Cafe
       in Kittredge
[047] Deckers
[047] Joanie's Deli, Woodland Park
[048] The Bucksnort Saloon in Sphinx Park
[050] Twin Eagles Picnic Area
[050] Tarryall Reservoir
[051] Pine Nook Mountain Market
       and Sprucewood Inn, Jarre Canyon
[053] O'Malley's Pub on CO 105, Palmer Lake

Little-Known Gems

[026] Twin Spruce and Gap Roads
[027] Crawford Gulch and Ralston Creek Roads
[031] Fall River Road from Alice
[033] Lookout Mountain Road
[037] Kerr Gulch
[039] Little Cub Creek Road through
       Stanley Park to High Drive
[040] Brook Forest Road to
       Shadow Mountain Road
[041] City View Drive to Crystal Way
[044] Kennedy Gulch Road to Conifer Mountain
[045] Foxton Road
[049] Matukat

Southern Front Range

REGIONAL OVERVIEW

As you move south of Colorado Springs, into the Southern Front Range Region, you will notice that population centers are smaller and more scattered, the land more open and sweeping. Mountain ranges declare buffer zones around their rocky fortresses, with sizeable park-like gaps between the Sangre de Cristos, the Wet Mountains, and the Culebra Range, and solitary giants like Pikes Peak defy other sentinels to come any closer. As elsewhere in the state, rivers chart wild courses, but like their towering guardians, are more spread out, resulting in fewer canyons and valleys for the two-wheeled pilot.

What is there to attract enthusiasts to this rectangular area between Interstate 25, US 24, US 285, and the New Mexico border? Alpine entrées like Pikes Peak, and Cuchara and Cordova Passes are served up on silver

Rides in This Section

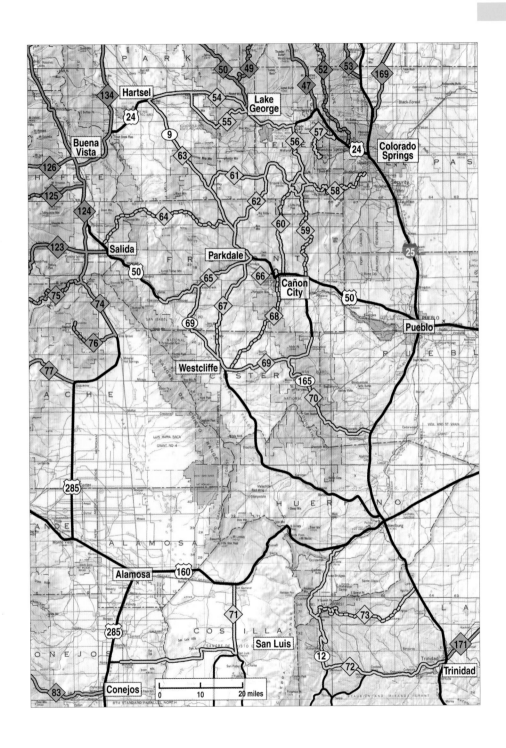

Southern Front Range   135

platters, complemented by the cuisine of Arkansas, Phantom, and Hardscrabble Canyons. Numerous old mining camps and historical places serve up endearing appetizers—but it's best to save room for a dessert of the finest collection of backroad journeys in the state: the roller coaster of High Park Road, sweeping Colorado 9, time-forgotten Park County 102, and the rollicking Greenhorn Highway to Bishop's Castle—all enchanting and entertaining. And let's not forget the delicious scenery of the local dual-sport roads, seasoned thoughout by a robust mining history.

With so many plates on such a small table, there is much to sample from the saddle in a single day. Have your bike gulping the thin air of Pikes Peak in the morning. For lunch, you could nibble on three tasty miles of tarmac on Colorado 67 between Victor and Cripple Creek, in anticipation of an afternoon snack of backcountry sweepers on Park County 102 on your way to Guffey, with more of the same on Colorado 9, before turning north to dine on historic Phantom Canyon Road, built on the old Florence & Cripple Creek Railroad train bed.

Your route isn't far from the ancestral trail used by the Utes for a ceremonial passage in 1912.

Ride 54 **Wilkerson Pass**

US 24

A historic 38-mile trail through old towns and a rocky canyon, and over a mountain pass with sweeping views

This stretch of US 24 is filled with just about everything a motorcyclist could possibly seek from a ride. From towns to a trail, parks to a pass, and a canyon to a course through high-altitude meadows, this ride presents it all in fine fashion to those passing through on two wheels. There is no real defining aspect to these 38 miles. The west side near Hartsel is starkly different from Divide on the east, and in between is riding entertainment, from the sweeping road beneath you to the scenery sweeping past you.

US 24 follows the Ute Pass Trail. From the shadows of Pikes Peak to the vast meadows and hunting grounds of South Park, with camps along the way, this was, in a sense, the Ute's US 24 back then. The community of Divide will be the starting point for this ride. Ute Pass, at 9,165 feet, is only a tomahawk throw west of the US 24 and Colorado 67 intersection in Divide, but the town name derives from the way water supposedly runs off in every direction from the crown of the pass sum-

mit. A little imagination is needed to believe that, but take a look the next time you cruise by!

At 1.6 miles west of Divide, Lower Twin Rocks Road dives off to the southwest at a sneaky junction and delivers a delightfully twisting ride over 4.8 miles to a T-intersection with Teller County 1. A turn left/south onto County 1 serves up a backdoor entrance to, or exit from, Cripple Creek, and delivers two other roads tailored to motorcycles—High Park Road [062] and Park County 102–Guffey [061].

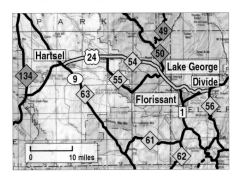

The rock outcroppings of Florissant Canyon will be the next riding feature to appear, as your bike sways gently in sync with the road. It isn't the most dramatic canyon, but the highway's meandering two-step through its piled, stacked, and balanced rocks is one of the gems of this journey. Eight miles from Divide, just before you arrive at Florissant, pull over at the interpretive sign on the north side of the road. It will tell you a lot more about the Ute presence and history in the area than I have room for here. Plus, it will point out visible features in the surrounding terrain.

Teller County 1 leads to the south from Florissant to the Florissant Fossil Beds National Monument only a few miles away. It is something to see the petrified giant redwood tree stumps from the time when the area had a much warmer and moister climate!

Lake George is four miles farther along US 24. From this small community next to a small lake of the same name, you can connect with County 90 to scenic Elevenmile Reservoir and State Park [055] and the Tarryall Road trip through time [050]. Continuing from Lake George to the west, there is a thinning of traffic, a thinning of roadside development, and a thinning of the air as you climb 1,500 sweeping feet over ten

miles to gentle Wilkerson Pass. The Forest Service operates a visitor center here with facilities, a small bookshop, viewing areas, and on occasion, a timely warm cup of coffee. The expanse of South Park unfolds below to one of Colorado's more distinctive pass panoramas, proof that despite the modest heights here, pass elegance is not necessarily driven by sheer elevation.

A descent down the west side of Wilkerson will have you letting off the throttle in Hartsel, 15 Ute-arrow-straight miles later. A turn left/south onto Colorado 9 [063] will put you on one of the best motorcycle roads around. If there is a growl in your digestive tract, the Hob Cafe and Saloon in Hartsel serves worthy burgers. So does the Thunderbird Inn in Florissant. The Costello Street Coffee House, also in Florissant, serves up more than just warm brews of coffee beans—deli sandwiches and bakery goodies are only a few dollars away. As for topping off the tank, fuel is readily available in every town along this ride.

Though this scenic and history-laden stretch of US 24 serves as a connector to many fine rides in the area, its own show is exemplary as well. I am reminded of watching a warm-up band at a concert that easily could have been the main act!

I turned the bike around moments after taking this photo. As foretold by those dark and lovely clouds, a tornado touched down a few minutes later!

Ride 55 **Elevenmile**

County 90, 92, 59, 23

A 20-mile paved backcountry and reservoir ride, winding through ranches and past old homesteads to a scenic state park and lake resort community

The Elevenmile Canyon Reservoir was one of Denver's early water storage projects. Completed in 1932, it was the largest body of water in the state at that time. Built to slake the city's growing thirst, three small towns—Idlewild, Freshwater, and Howbert—were sacrificed and flooded by the dammed waters of the South Platte River. Actually, there was some substance to

Howbert, with a grocery store, drug store, butcher shop, hotel, schoolhouse, sawmill, two saloons, and 25 homes among the structures meeting a watery end. Another effect, more beneficial to us who ride the area, was the relocation of the road, which previously ran next to the South Platte, to its present-day US 24-course over Wilkerson Pass.

County 90 toward Elevenmile is about a

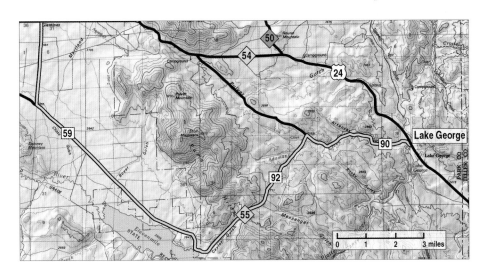

half-mile northwest of Lake George. The chip-and-seal surface, which extends the entire 20 miles, isn't bad, and fits with the character of the ride. You will pass a scattered mix of old and newer homesteads. A few aged structures have valiantly withstood the trials of a high-altitude sun and high-country winters. At four miles, in the middle of fine pastoral fields, County 90 jaunts off to the northwest as you lean the bike left and the sealed road becomes County 92.

In the six miles to the big lake you will pass through a big meadow, then a big forest, and then descend to the ambitious 1932 City of Denver endeavor. There is a general store just before County 92 turns closer to the deep blue lake and the state park area. I sometimes grab some chow at the store and sit at the bench or picnic table. The sparkling blue waters can reflect the southern sun like a mirror shattered into a million pieces, and in the background, South Park is held in by the Mosquito Range to the west. Anglers who have hooked a big one can get their fish officially measured by the Division of Wildlife at the store. I once interrupted a lunchmeat

munch to see a giant rainbow trout up close. I think it could have fed a family of four for months.

County 92 winds through the state park area—where you can pay a small fee to take advantage of the facilities and services—then you'll makes a beeline toward the northwest for seven more miles, the county designation changing to Road 59 along the way. Just follow the chip-and-sealed surface and you'll be fine. It makes a turn north at the seven-mile mark, reconnecting in three miles with US 24 on the west side of Wilkerson Pass.

As your bike idles at US 24, to the left will be Hartsel and the great Colorado 9 [063] south toward Guffey, then on to the Royal Gorge area. If you are coming from the Colorado Springs or Cañon City area, I would recommend connecting US 24 and Elevenmile with the superb riding roads of Colorado 9 [063], Park County 102 [061], and High Park Road [062] for a fantastic day of riding. If a dual-sport is underneath you, the Elevenmile Canyon area is a center for dirt-road exploration, including what is across from you and your idling bike at US 24. Head north on San Juan Street (a road in a grid of roads for a development that never happened), then follow its turn west where it becomes Turner Gulch Road/County 23. It will present a dazzling tour above South Park amid lumpy hills, bringing you all the way to the Tarryall Reservoir and the superb County 77 ride [050].

Your nearest food and fuel options, beyond the general store at the reservoir, will be in Hartsel and Lake George. Both communities have a fine grill and diner. If you've got a great burger on your brain, the Hob Cafe and Saloon in Hartsel is worthy of tying up your iron horse at the post out front.

Ride 56 **Cripple Creek**

Colorado 67, County 81

A 30-mile curving and ascending ride to two historic mining towns connected by four miles of a twist-fest of motorcycling fun

Few towns in Colorado, if not the country, can match the mining history of Victor and Cripple Creek. Not only are tales of their past rich with ores, but tours of their present are rich with lore. You'll know when you are entering the vicinity of these two Victorian towns, not by roadway signs, but by the visible proliferation of old mills and mines dotting the landscape like giant prairie dog mounds.

It was a nearby gold strike in 1890 that transformed the nature of these high hills from cattle bellowing above to miners boring below. In three years the population of the area zoomed from 300 to 10,000. The last gold rush of Colorado was on, and the lodes harvested from some of these mines were among the richest anywhere. But the local history also includes devastating fires and labor strife. As you ride the roads of these great gold camps, it won't be difficult to reflect on the stories of this place, for storytellers will be all around.

Join this ride by turning southeast at the only stoplight in Divide on Colorado 67, where it diverges from US 24 and heads for the Cripple Creek area. The first five miles won't be the most inspiring, as you cruise a long straight, but views of Pikes Peak and her attendant sub-peaks do energize, as do the buffet of curves delivering a 1,000-foot ascent in the following nine miles. When the climb levels out at the high park where County 81 departs southeast for the back

way to Victor, look around and behold where the town of Gillett used to be. Little remains of this ghost town, which once

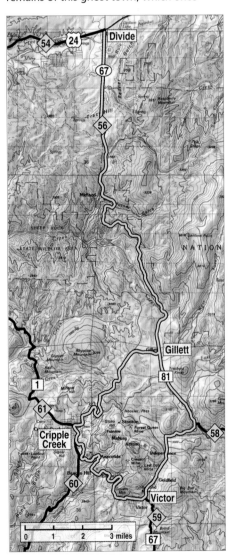

boasted a population of 700. Gillett can also boast of having hosted the only sanctioned Mexican bullfight to ever take place in the country, back in 1895.

In Gillett, turn onto County 81, a blissful motorcycling road that leads to Victor in seven miles through a veritable "minefield " of the past. Both the road and that sights are outstanding.

Victor's Main Street downtown, running east and west, is Colorado 67, and it goes directly to Cripple Creek by way of a tangled, four-mile, twist-fest of a road. In my opinion it signs, seals, and delivers one of the most sporting, fun stretches in the state. What it lacks in quantity it makes up for in quality. I know riders who turn 100-plus miles on their odometer just to lean into these series of sublime S-curves.

With Colorado voters approving legalized gambling in 1991, the casinos have brought a fading Cripple Creek back to life. One can find excellent mealtime bargains in one of the many casinos.

Check out the Cripple Creek & Victor Narrow Gauge Railroad for a riding tour of a different kind. The Molly Kathleen Mine, on Colorado 67 north out of Cripple Creek, delivers a real gold mine tour deep below the surface. Even a ride on the double-decker skinny elevator is a hoot. Across the highway is the fairly new Pikes Peak Heritage Center. The exhibits are impressive and free.

For fuel, about a mile west out of Cripple Creek on Teller County 1 there is a grocery store and gas pump combo. The ride delivered by County 1 as it connects to Park County 102 is described in Ride 61. The other end of this journey is US 24 from Divide, over Wilkerson Pass to Hartsel [054]. For the dual-sport set, three nearby rides await your worthy bike—Gold Camp Road [058], Phantom Canyon [059], and Shelf Road [060].

Victor at the turn of the last century, and at the turn of this century

Ride 57 **Pikes Peak**

Pikes Peak Highway

A famed 19-mile, mostly paved, tightly twisting ride that climbs 6,700 memorable feet to the top of "America's Mountain"

Pikes Peak is said to be the second most visited mountain in the world after Mt. Fuji in Japan. It is named after Zebulon Pike, who led a Lewis-and-Clark-like expedition to map the southern area of the Louisiana Purchase in 1806. He tried to climb the mountain in November of that year, but gave up after two days in waist-deep snow. He allegedly proclaimed to others that no one would ever reach the top.

A carriage road was built to the top in 1890, and significantly improved in 1915 as the Pikes Peak Highway. In 1893 Katherine Lee Bates, while spending the summer teaching at Colorado College, was inspired by the train ride west and by the vistas at the summit to write a poem first titled *Pikes Peak*. Later it was matched to music and published in 1910 as *America the Beautiful*.

Since 1916, on the last Saturday in June, the Pikes Peak International Hill Climb takes over the mountain and thrills fans with cars and motorcycles racing to the top.

The well-marked entrance to the Pikes Peak Highway is off US 24, a little over nine miles west of Interstate 25. The entrance gate is about half a mile after making the turn. From May through November, the "in season" fee is $12 (off-season $10). The highway at higher elevations and the summit used to be closed during the winter but now stays open, weather permitting. My son climbed Pikes Peak one day in January, and found five cars at the top and the Summit House open for business! On a dry balmy winter's day, take a ride to the top of Pikes

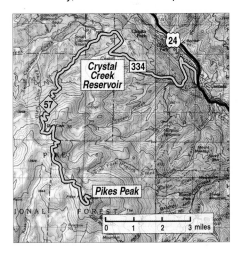

Peak. Only a few hardy souls will be on the mountain, and a grill inside the Summit House will have a sizzling burger ready for you! Besides, you'll save two bucks.

The Pikes Peak Highway is one tightly bending road to ride. All those curves that might be tedious in a car can be exciting on a two-wheeled steed. Of course, the tables will be turned if you're caught by a nasty weather system up high. I've looked at Pikes Peak from a distance with a menacing dark thundercloud swallowing the summit, and had a flash of gratitude I wasn't up there in the middle of that mayhem . . . on a bike no less! Plus, a rain-drenched dirt road—even if it is graded smooth—isn't on my short list of favorite road conditions. So, best plan to make the assault in the morning, before the afternoon thunder boomers develop (the gate opens at 9 a.m.), or make it a mission

on a day with low humidity and abundant deep blue skies.

Most of the highway is paved, and with each passing year more of the dirt surface receives the asphalt treatment, but there are still stretches two to three miles in length that are smooth-graded dirt. I've come across reports noting it will be fully paved by 2012. Six miles into the journey there is a gift shop and interpretive center at the Crystal Creek Reservoir. At 13 miles, the Glen Cove Inn invites a sidestand deploy for a snack and a scenic pause. The place at the top is called The Summit and in addition to a grill menu, they are known for their fresh-baked donuts. Plan to spend some time at the top, for not only the warming Summit House, but also the world-class views in every direction from this famous 14,110-foot giant. And bring that camera!

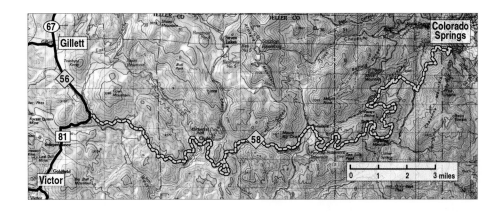

Ride 58 **Gold Camp**

Gold Camp Road, Old Stage Road, Forest Road 368, 370, County 8

A scenic 25-mile dirt-road ride on a historical train bed with a winding ascent past rock formations, reservoirs, and old homesteads

Gold Camp Road follows, in part, the tightly curving course of the former Colorado Springs & Cripple Creek Railway, which was one of the railways servicing the gold camps around Victor and Cripple Creek. As the glory days of trains came to an end, the railway was sold under foreclosure. The tracks were pulled up, a road base was put down, and bridges carrying trains were replaced by piles of rock and dirt filled in to support cars. For ten years, until around 1939, this was a private toll road known as the Corley Mountain Highway. When the toll road became a free road, the name was aptly switched to Gold Camp Road.

President Theodore Roosevelt once rode this route, and he described its beauty as "bankrupting the English language." So who am I to try to describe the visual bombardment one experiences on this 25-mile journey? What's special about this route is the textbook tour of Front Range foothills topography that it delivers.

The ride starts in Colorado Springs at the intersection of West Cheyenne Mountain Boulevard and Penrose Avenue, just a few hundred yards north of the entrance to the Cheyenne Mountain Zoo. Take Old Stage Road or Forest Road 368, which climbs to the west.

Old Stage Road joins Gold Camp Road in 3.5 wickedly winding miles. When you can spare a moment for diversion, glance through the trees to the north at the massive rock formations anchoring the eastern slopes of Pikes Peak. The initial ascent out of the Springs is the steepest part of this 25-mile, 3,500-foot climb.

As elevation is gained, the space between geographic features increases. There is a broadening of the terrain, both vertically and horizontally. Water storage projects for Colorado Springs appear, and if you are on a dedicated dual-sport bike, you can access other mountain lakes by the numerous forest roads branching off this Gold Camp vine.

a pause for reflection. The molten rock spires on the north side look like giant waxed candles subjected to a long flame. The grandeur of the Bison Creek Valley to the northwest provides a spectacular setting, one fit for a place of worship.

This ride ends at a T-intersection with Lazy S Ranch Road (also known as County 81). A turn to the left brings you to the great mining districts of Victor and Cripple Creek [056] only a few paved miles away. A push of the handlebars to the right/north, will deliver Colorado 67, where you can connect to the town of Divide and US 24. If you are in need of fuel, gas pumps can be found at Cripple Creek or in Divide. Victor has a fun bar and grill downtown, and the casinos at Cripple Creek deliver robust meals at a less than robust price. If you are in the picnic frame of mind, throw some food in the bags and find a big rock at one of many idyllic places along Gold Camp Road.

You will ride through an old curving train tunnel, one of the original nine that hasn't collapsed. Proponents of the paranormal believe these 110-year-old tunnels harbor haunting spirits, and attribute various vaporous sightings to the wandering souls of the men who worked this line—just some warm and fuzzy thoughts for you as you enter the dark and unlit tunnel on your open and unprotected bike.

At about 18 miles, you will enter the church-like setting of Cathedral Valley. This quiet and seemingly spiritual place is worth

From Colorado Springs, a great half-day trip would be an exploratory ride up Gold Camp to the mining districts, returning via US 24. If you are up for longer off-road adventures, consider Phantom Canyon [059] out of Victor, or Shelf Road [060] departing south out of Cripple Creek. And if you are wondering about Gold Camp's dirt surface, this is primarily a dual-sport journey, but an easy-to-ride street bike should be fine in dry conditions.

Gold Camp Road starts its journey east, as seen from Lazy S Ranch Road.

Ride 59 **Phantom Canyon**

Phantom Canyon Road, Colorado 67

A 30-mile graded dirt-road ride on an old train bed in a special canyon with rock-wall and hidden-meadow scenery

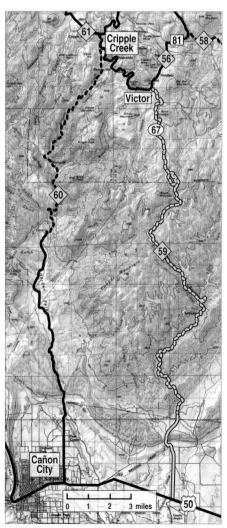

Phantom Canyon Road is a leg of the Gold Belt Tour Scenic Byway, and as canyons go, few rival its scenic package of pinnacles perched atop craggy rock faces, with quiet streams feeding lush gardens tucked away below. From the saddle of the bike, this isn't a canyon you carve up, but rather one you soak up.

Phantom Canyon Road lies on the train bed of the narrow-gauge Florence & Cripple Creek Railroad, which was the first railroad to service the Cripple Creek–Victor mining region in the 1890s. If you, on your skinny little bike, think this course is narrow, consider how they squeezed train cars on rails up through this rocky gorge—trains hauled by coal-fired locomotives belching thick black smoke as they labored up to the mines. Twelve stations were built along the way to service the trains heading up to Victor and Cripple Creek with their loads of coal and supplies, returning on the descent with golden ore for the smelters in Florence. Amazingly, the gold mines of Cripple Creek and Victor produced more gold than the combined production of the California and Alaska Gold Rushes.

To ride Phantom Canyon Road from the north, follow the Gold Belt Tour Scenic Byway signs to the east of Victor, which plainly

show the way. From the south, Phantom Canyon Road heads north from the intersection of Colorado 67 and US 50, about four miles east of Cañon City. From here, the first five miles are paved, then the road surface switches to a graded, texturized mix of small gravel and dirt. Since this is a scenic byway, it does get some maintenance attention. Near this five-mile-into-the-journey mark you will be welcomed into the domain of the deep canyon.

Over 30 miles there is an ascent of 4,500 feet, with Eightmile Creek as your swerving guide for almost 20 miles. The appearance of numerous, small, garden-like meadows about the size of volleyball courts, will surprise you as you round a tight corner. The contrast of the meadows to the surrounding rocky terrain can be striking. These streamside fields would also make comfortable campsites. While the ascent is gradual in the first half of this ride, it becomes more pronounced during the second half as you climb above the creek bed, and instead of looking up cliffy canyon walls you'll begin to peer down them. The tight switchback curves will distract you with views of where you were only minutes before. Once you reach the top of the canyon, you'll have a few miles of aspen-ringed, lush, grassy meadows, which would delight any animal of the grazing persuasion.

The many scenic byway signs along the way can fill you in on much of the history of the area. I've seen all kinds of bikes on Phantom Canyon Road. If you are comfortable on dirt with small chip rock mixed in, the graded surface is decent for any kind of bike. But understandably, a soaking rain can make the grip less certain. Remember, a stray thundercloud can wander by on any day during the summer—though, it seems like every time I turn two wheels into this canyon, the dust is evidence that it has been awhile since significant rain has graced the area. It isn't a busy canyon, but you can minimize your contact with airborne grit from other vehicles by making the transit earlier in the morning or later in the day.

The 30-mile length shouldn't cause any fuel-range apprehension, but you can top off the tank in Cripple Creek or in Florence. Both areas are generous with restaurant options. Inexpensive meals can be found at the Cripple Creek casinos, as the operators hope the the low food prices will lure you in to gamble. And there is always the option of stuffing some food and drink in the bags and putting your sidestand down at one of the many quiet park-like places near the tumbling creek.

Dual-sport riders can make a loop by combining this ride with the Shelf Road ride [060], or head to Colorado Springs on the Gold Camp ride [058].

Ride 60 **Shelf–Red Canyon**

Shelf Road, Red Canyon Road

A 25-mile dirt-and-rock ride (lower 12 miles are paved) on a shelf-like, historical wagon road over and through a secluded canyon

Riding above and through lonely canyon valleys dwarfed by intimidating cliffs and rock outcroppings, Shelf Road easily sets itself apart from others. Even its nearby neighbor, the Phantom Canyon [059], is cut from a different bolt of cloth.

Shelf Road, constructed in 1892, was the first hacked and blasted-out path between the Arkansas River Valley and the Cripple Creek mining district. As a wagon road, it enabled access for eager entrepreneurs in the valley to tap into the booming trade of the exploding gold camps just north in the hills above. Its status as the only route was short-lived, however. A few years later, the Florence & Cripple Creek Railroad completed a narrow-gauge rail line up the Phantom Canyon [059]. To be sure, Shelf Road astounds as well, with its narrow ledgy perch

tucked between cliffs looming above and steep slopes falling away below, but in be-

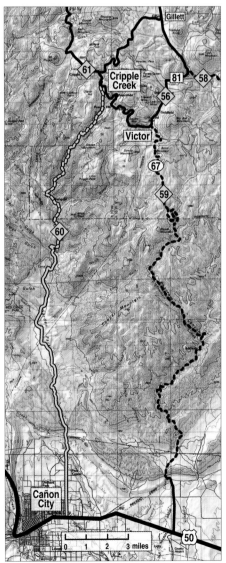

tween the rock shows are sweet intermissions of secluded, vividly green meadows. The winding course through all of this makes for a special motorcycle ride.

The easiest way to join Shelf Road from the south side is by following Field Avenue north out of the downtown area of Cañon City. It connects with Red Canyon Road about 2.2 miles north of downtown, which performs a seamless meld with Shelf Road about ten miles later. From the north end, take Colorado 67 toward Victor from Cripple Creek. At the southern end of Cripple Creek's town edge, about 0.3 mile from the Main Street, the signed Shelf Road makes a gentle dirt-road departure to the south. This is a leg of the Gold Belt Tour Scenic and Historic Byway, so it is well marked, but the rustic and somewhat primitive nature of this narrow old stagecoach route has been preserved. You can also connect with Shelf Road closer to Victor via a second marked Shelf Road off

of Colorado 67 [056], right in the middle of that divine set of riding curves.

The descent south out of Cripple Creek begins to entertain right away as the road drops deeper into a jumbled and tumbled rock world, while canyon walls narrow the sky above. Window Rock at the top of a granite spire is easily recognizable, as modest Cripple Creek tumbles down through the nearby boulders. This will be mighty fine riding, as the descent produces things to gawk at in every direction from your ultimate convertible. This is a rock climber's paradise, and the narrow, one-lane road serpentines through it all, providing a little extra pizzazz when one must squeeze over to the edge to accomodate the rare vehicle coming from the other direction.

You'll pass the ghost town camp of Marigold, but little remains after its nearby mines had little more to give. Farther south, as you ride above the scenic floor of the canyon,

however, is the old tollkeeper's cabin. The tollkeeper would watch for the freighters or stagecoaches and hike up to the road to collect the toll each time anyone deigned to pass. Ain't no toll for us on horses of a different era, but as you ride Shelf Road, you're basically in the middle of a landscape that has not changed during the past century, and you're making the journey much as they did with their horses and wagons. Well, maybe our suspension is a little better. I hate to think of driving a team of horses and a wagon, meeting another of the same coming the other direction on this one-wagon-wide trail!

As progress is made south, there is a widening of the panorama as the Arkansas River Valley unfolds. The road widens as well, and is paved for the remaining twelve miles to Cañon City. Cripple Creek will have joined Fourmile Creek, which leads the road here as it wanders toward the Arkansas River. As mentioned previously, the southern ten miles of this ride are on Red Canyon Road.

Just turn your head to the west and you will understand how the road came to be named. By the way, this is a park area and your can point your dual-sport bike west onto County F24, under a faded Red Canyon sign, and take a tightly twisting tour of this red rock country.

Shelf Road is best done on a dual-sport bike. A lightweight street bike would probably be okay, but the rocky texture of the surface would be tedious. An easier alternative would be Phantom Canyon Road to the east—speaking of which, linking the two of these together for an out-and-back ride would be a fine loop. The Cripple Creek area is ground zero for great rides, including Colorado 67 mentioned above, Gold Camp Road [058], Teller County 1–High Park Road [062], and County 102–Guffey [061]. On the south end, the Arkansas River Canyon [065] is in the vicinity, as is Colorado 9 [063], Copper Gulch [067], and the Oak Creek Grade [068]. There aren't any 7-Elevens on Shelf Road, so load up in Cripple Creek or Cañon City!

Ride 61 **Guffey**

County 1, 11, 112, 102

A twisting, sweeping 30-mile backcountry ride amidst historical homesteads, between two different towns, and past rock formations to scenic vistas

Guffey, at the western side of this ride, is on County 102, about a mile east from Colorado 9 (see Ride 63). The town, founded late in the 19th century, was supported by a combination of mining, lumbering, and ranching. The mines didn't last long; the lumber business faded not long after, but ranching has had the legs to sustain the community, though not without some speculation as to whether Guffey would become a ghost town. Today, the community has

preserved an eclectic, 100-year-old feel to the place. While some new structures are present, the majority are original and historic.

County 102 continues east through Guffey, ascends a 500-foot grassy hill two miles later, and then delivers a simply beautiful pastoral (literally and figuratively) journey for fifteen miles to where it links up with High Park Road at a three-way yielding intersection. I never, ever, tire of this 15-mile

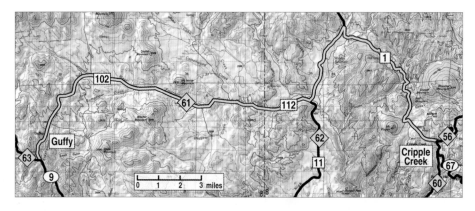

stretch. A cast of cattle, chewing lazily in front of old homesteads (I don't think there is a modern ranch building anywhere along County 102), will lift their grazing heads to ponder the strange thing flying by. If you lift your riding head to the horizon over your handlebars, you can try to figure out all those distinct ramparts leading to the summit of the seriously scenic Pikes Peak.

At the three-way intersection, continuing straight serves up the high riding drama of High Park Road [062]. Leaning left or riding toward the north onto County 11 takes you to Cripple Creek. Seven fun riding miles after making the turn, you will arrive at a T-intersection. Turning left to the north onto County 1 takes you on an enjoyable scoot past the biggest llama ranch I've ever seen, as well as other mixed-use sites on the way to Florissant and US 24 [054]. However, this ride takes you right/south on County 1 toward Cripple Creek. There is an Evergreen Station at this T-intersection with gas pumps

and convenience store food. Pull over for a pause here, and you will likely see numerous bikes passing by with pilots aboard "in the know" about the riding allure of this area.

Arrival at Cripple Creek is a twist- and hill-fest seven miles later. It is an excellent dessert or appetizer to this ride—depending on your direction. I have no preference which way to make this traverse between Cripple Creek and Guffey. It over-delivers regardless of direction. Cripple Creek is covered in detail in Ride 56 devoted to Colorado 67, Victor, and Cripple Creek. Numerous other rides can be joined from this area, like the smooth dirt road of Gold Camp [058] and Phantom Canyon [059], as well as the dual-sport Shelf Road [060].

For a Cripple Creek area meal, the casinos offer decent fare at an inexpensive fare. They sure hope you will stop by the slot machines! In Guffey, I'm not the only two-wheeled enthusiast who enjoys stopping for a meal at Rita's Place. It is highly recommended.

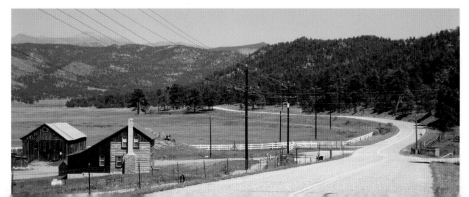

Ride 62 **High Park**

High Park Road, County 11

A grand, paved, 18-mile, sweeping, high country, roller-coaster ride of amusement, delivering all the attractions sought by those on two wheels

High Park Road gets high marks for the exhilarating ride it delivers. The best analogy I can come up with is how this traverse is like an exhiliarating 18-mile roller-coaster ride. It dips and whoops, sweeps and curves, has blind rises and distant views. It tickles the innards with its array of riding delights, and like an amusement park ride, there is a tinge of regret when you coast to the conclusion, but what makes this different is how at each High Park end, another ride awaits without your having to wait in line.

At the south end, High Park Road/Teller County 11 gets its traction off of divine Colo-

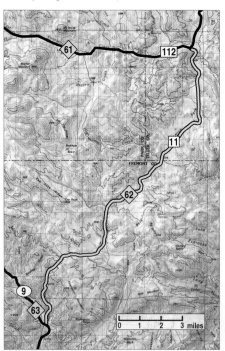

rado 9 [063], eight miles north of where Highway 9 connects to US 50. On the north end it meets Teller County 112 at a sort of three-way intersection. When hitching a ride with the launch to the north from Colorado 9, you'll begin a 500-foot weaving climb up Miner Gulch. At four miles, you will top out at 8,000 feet and get your first hint regarding the source of this road's name.

The high parks or meadows are not of the flat or unvarying kind, but rather resemble a throw rug that has been bunched up. Somehow, the road finds a path through the ripples by going around or over them. Sometimes this means a glorious sweeping curve and sometimes a tightly folded one. There are gentle rises, but also series of sharp hills with hidden bottoms that swallow anyone riding ahead of you. It's like riding several giant letter M's in row . . . like MMMM, but at font size 2,000,000. Two cautions are worth noting here. At just over ten miles north of the start, if you are coming up from the south, there is a tight curve posted at 15 mph. It can catch the unaware or distracted. Judging from the black rubber laid down here, it has caught more that a few. The other thing is to remember is that this is open range country. A cow could be standing next to the road, on the road, right around that blind curve, or at the bottom of that steep roller-coaster hill. Tragically, a small group of cows did catch a sportbike rider several years ago as they stood like

states at the bottom of a blind and sharp descent. Of the two- to three-dozen times I've ridden High Park Road, though, there was only one instance I can think of when I saw open range cattle within the vicinity of the road. Nevertheless, let the occasional cattle guard you cross over remind you of the situation. And in any case, having your alert antenna fully deployed on any ride is good counsel.

While the serpentine course is the main star here, stupendous views of Pikes Peak's shy southern slopes will compete for your attention, as will the supporting cast of rustic ranches and old homesteads. This is a quiet and out-of-the-way place, in many ways unchanged over long years. And the empty ribbon of road before your handlebars is perhaps one of the greatest features of High Park Road.

At the northern end, 18 miles from the south terminus, High Park Road has a 90-degree turn at Teller County 112. If you continue straight, you'll be on County 112 or the road leading to Guffey (it becomes Park County 102 at the county border), 15 miles away. This side of a possible riding triangle is described as part of the ride from Guffey to Cripple Creek [061].

If you point the front wheel toward Guffey, be sure to stop at Rita's Place for a great meal. It is not uncommon to be sharing parking space with other bikes. If you make the 90-degree turn north, High Park Road and County 11 continue for four more winding miles to County 1. There is an Evergreen Station here with gas pumps, as well convenience store snacks. There isn't any fuel out here except at this station, so plan well! If you continue past the Evergreen Station on County 1 (described in the Guffey ride), Cripple Creek is a fun, eight miles later, where other great rides await. When journeying to the High Park area, plan on at least a half day, if not a full day, of riding enjoyment as you explore the area's roads.

Ride 63 **Currant Creek Pass**

Colorado 9

A 46-mile ride serving delicious sweepers and curves through a lonely scenic patchwork of forests and meadows, ranches and old homesteads, with postcard views to the north

I am going to say right up front that Colorado Highway 9 between US 50 and US 24 is one of my favorite stretches of roadway in the state to ride.

This road scores high in the following measures: emptiness, duration, closeness, exquisiteness, and coolness. It's a road you will share with few other vehicles (emptiness) and it lasts for 48 miles (duration). Colorado 9 goes directly by (closeness) the great High Park Road—another favorite of the-road-is-the-destination set with which Colorado 9 can be linked to form a longer circuit. There is a classy layout to the road (exquisiteness), with how it delivers serpentine curves over the rolling and undulating ter-

rain. Finally, there is the rusting and rustic cabin community of Guffey (coolness) just two miles off of Colorado 9, very much worthy of a short visit or a mealtime pause.

The famous tourist destination of the Royal Gorge is off US 50 ten miles west of Cañon City. If you have some bills in the wallet you can ride your bike across the also famous bridge suspended 1,530 feet above the Arkansas River. Just 1.3 miles west of the Royal Gorge entrance, near Parkdale, is the southern terminus of this ride, where Colorado 9 has its quiet send-off to the north. The north end of this ride is at the small South Park roadside town of Hartsel on US 24.

When you head north from the Royal Gorge area, the first eight miles ease you into what is ahead with a descent through Cottonwood Gulch, before ascending 1,200 feet through a cut between Cottonwood Ridge and Eightmile Mountain. You'll lean your bike into a left-hander on the other side and be introduced to Currant Creek, your brilliant guide for the next 26 miles. At this eight-mile mark is heavenly High Park Road/ County 11 [062], which unfairly tempts you with a turn toward the north.

Continuing northwest, Colorado 9 knows how to put on a good show, with a line up of stars and supporting actors and actresses. Look for beaver dams on the southwest side of the road, old homesteads telling old stories, and the lovely Thirtynine Mile Mountain

to the northeast putting on an encore of nature. At 11,561 feet, this isn't the highest peak around, but as the ribbon of road curves around her grassy slopes rising up to a burr haircut of pine with earrings of aspen stands, I've always thought it was one of the prettier mountains in the state.

Currant Creek Pass, at 9,300 feet, is a few miles farther northwest, then there will be a descent to Buffalo Gulch, where you might actually see some of the hairy beasts grazing on the nearby ranchlands. This is also where you'll see mountain panoramas filling the space above your handlebars. The grand meadows of South Park begin to extend before you with the high-rise peaks of the Mosquito Range absorbing the sky above.

When you arrive at US 24 and Hartsel, a right turn takes you to Wilkerson Pass [054] toward Woodland Park, and a left turn delivers a US 24 route toward Buena Vista or a Colorado 9 ride to Fairplay. Both of these communities connect to other rides. Linking

to the fantastic High Park Road mentioned above with Park County 102 on the north side, and a return to Guffey, is a magical riding triangle. Or, don't make the County 102 turn, but continue north on County 11 to County 1 for a rousing scoot to Cripple Creek. This is all part of the Park County 102 ride [061]. For dual-sport riders, fine forest roads sprout in every direction like a well-fertilized garden. On the Tallahassee Road/ County 175 [064] west toward Salida, you will be overcome by the scenic experience.

On the south end of this journey, you can get food and fuel at Cañon City or in the Royal Gorge area—but Cañon City has more choices. Hartsel has a fine grill (Hob Cafe and Saloon) and a convenience store with gas pumps. When I travel in this area I try to time this ride so that the two-mile exit to Guffey is midway in the journey. At Rita's Place in Guffey, you can grab a great meal. It isn't unusual to find other motorcycles parked at this rider-friendly diner.

Ride 64 **The Ute Trail**

Tallahassee Road, County 175, 2

A 43-mile ultra-scenic dual-sport ride through lonely meadows, hills, and valleys, past ranches and homesteads, with an alpine setting at the western end

This dual-sport ride rewards you with special sights of a magical landscape not often seen in Colorado. The rumpled carpet of high-alpine meadows swallows you up as if you are a Lilliputian wandering through Gulliver's mountain abode. Lonely 11,000-foot-high mountains ring the giant playground we pass through on our tiny toys. The ride climaxes on the west end with the descent to Salida and the Arkansas Valley. You'll be

grateful for the for the dual-sport bike in your garage.

This Ute Trail ride, in my humble opinion, offers one of the finest off-road ventures around. Numerous dirt roads branch off this sweet vine of a journey, and are worthy of exploration.

The west end of this ride, County 175, leaves Colorado 291 northwest of Salida, just a few hundred yards past the downtown

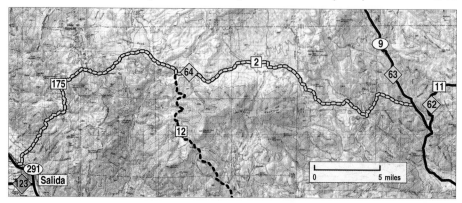

area with a sign pointing the way northeast, or to the right. On the east end, look for Tallahassee Road, or County 2, departing west from Colorado 9 [063], 11 miles north of the US 50 junction. In a way, the Ute Trail and Tallahassee Road contain scenes from three movies. From the east, the first third is John Wayne's forest-ringed meadow action in 1969's *True Grit*. The middle third is Julie Andrews singing, "The hills are alive with the sound of music," and the western third is straight from *The Lord of the Rings.*

From the east, a descent is made into Smith Gulch, and a winding tour of forests and fields with small ranches is up first. Cottonwood Ridge is the wall heavy with trees to the south. After a five-mile skirt around the ridge and out of the gulch, the panoramas teasingly begin to open up. There are several dirt-road intersections along the way, but it is easy to stay with Tallahassee Road/County 2. There is a low mountain pass, or

divide, between Waugh Mountain and Wall Mountain at 11 miles, and once on the western side you will unconsciously let off the throttle as you drink in all that is around. You will now be at 9,000 feet in elevation, a good gap higher than the 7,500-foot launch at Colorado 9. Black Mountain, straight ahead at 11,654 feet, and Waugh Mountain (11,718 feet) on the left/south side will compete for your attention. They are prime examples of picturesque beauty that is not dependent on high altitude. The aspen on Waugh Mountain's northwestern side would be a golden spectacle come autumn.

At 23 miles, County 12 cuts off to the south. This is an excellent 24-mile descent to the town of Cotopaxi in the Arkansas River Canyon [065]. At 30 miles you will cross from Fremont County to Chaffee County, and the road changes number from 2 to 175, but the Ute Trail moniker remains. Spur your bike for four more miles, then pause for

an epic vista. The serrated 14,000-foot monarchs of the southern Sawatch Range to the west will stand almost 5,000 feet above you, while the Arkansas River winds through its valley 2,000 feet below you to the southwest. The contrast between the two is striking. In between is a fairytale land of lumpy hills showing the way down to Salida. Last time I rode the Ute Trail, as I was stopped here, a local resident in a beater truck came up from the valley and paused beside me. Rolling down his window he said with a grin, "Quite a special place, isn't it?" From here it will be a snaking ten-mile downhill to Salida, with a series of gulches branching off to the side. The final descent is accompanied by Ute Creek (appropriately so) before it empties into the Arkansas.

Reflecting on the Ute Trail, it is easy to comprehend why the Utes would resist those seeking to claim this land, whether they were other Indian tribes or European settlers. With the exception of scattered dirt roads and ranches, not a whole lot has changed along these 43 miles.

While this is dual-sport motorcycle country, if the conditions are dry and you are aboard a light and easy-to-ride street bike, it should be okay. Be food- and fuel-prepared. Salida on the west end presents the most choices. On the east end, gas can be found at the Royal Gorge area, 11 miles south of the Tallahassee entrance. For a great food stop, pay a visit to motorcycle-friendly Rita's Place in Guffey, off Colorado 9, ten miles north from Tallahassee Road.

The grand entrance to the Arkansas River Canyon, heading west from Parkdale

Ride 65 **Arkansas Canyon**

US 50

A 30-mile canyon-river ride with both sweeping and tighter curves amidst serious rock formations, delivering access to recreation sites, picnic areas, scenic pullouts, and other nearby rides

When you ride US 50 through the Arkansas River Canyon (also known as Bighorn Sheep Canyon), you will be on a stretch of a highway that runs 3,011 miles from Ocean City, Maryland, to Sacramento, California—almost coast to coast. Though you will only be riding one percent of this distance, it is a memorable fraction as it runs through the canyon carved by the mighty Arkansas River.

This is a beautiful ride. The tortured rocks all around tell a tale of serious geologic forces, which are even more evident in the famous Royal Gorge farther downstream to the east. It's my opinion that though the stretch of US 50 we can ride through is a broader and longer canyon, it isn't any less regal than its more renowned extension a few miles away.

This ride enters the long and snaking canyon at Parkdale just two miles west of the main Royal Gorge entrance on US 50. It is hard to fathom that the wide rushing river is

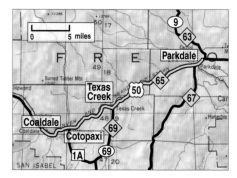

The Denver & Rio Grande Western train ran through the canyon near Cotopaxi in 1920, and Texas Creek in 1940.

just a skinny little watery thing you can jump over at Fremont Pass 80 miles away [132]. The road begins its tantalizing mixture of curves and sweepers immediately from Parkdale. This is a precisely engineered roadway, with a fine surface on which to turn two wheels. I could go back and forth in this canyon all day long, just goin' with the flow.

Let this ride be one you savor and let soak in. While there are times and places where the canyon is utterly lonely, there can be moments when traffic will have its way. Just be in a riding zone and, as I said, go with the flow.

Speaking of flows, a westward transit will have you ascending 500 hardly perceptible feet over the 30-mile ride. On this side of the Continental Divide, the Arkansas will be making its way east, and has 1,400 miles to go until it empties into the Mississippi River. On a summer's day, you will likely encounter whitewater rafters on this preeminent river,

following the same canyon-carving course as we motorcyclists.

There are numerous scenic pullouts along the way for breaks, picnics, and photos. There are reasons this is also known as Bighorn Sheep Canyon. There are also small fuel and food stores dotting the canyon, as well as casual restaurants.

At Parkdale, on the east end of the canyon, the superb Colorado 9 [063] starts its journey north. The Copper Gulch ride [067] aims south for Westcliffe; at Texas Creek, Colorado 69 [069] also departs for Westcliffe. If coming from the west, check out the County 1A shortcut to Colorado 69, as it runs south from Cotopaxi. Farther west on US 50 there is the full-service and fully sweet town of Salida, with numerous notable rides branching out in different directions. The same goes for Cañon City on the east side of the Royal Gorge, which is another launch pad for several rides.

Ride 66 **Skyline**

Skyline Drive

A riotous 3.3-mile ride on a one-lane, one-way, hoot-filled road just west of Cañon City

Skyline Drive was constructed in the early 1900s as a tourist road, using labor supplied by inmates from the nearby state prison. Back then, lengthy sentences for crimes often included the words "hard labor." Well, the toils of the inmates' picks and shovels have resulted in a trail of grins and shivers for motorcyclists. Only a car-width wide, it can only be driven (or ridden) in one direction. The blind rises will test your faith and confidence that there is a surface for your tires on the other side. If ever there was a road like a roller-coaster ride, this is it, and it will give you the same sort of thrills.

Find Skyline Drive on the east side of US 50, three miles west of Cañon City. Signs point the way. You basically ride an 800-

Enjoying a ride on Skyline Drive 1905

The same rise a century later

foot-high crest of the Dakota Hogback. Long before we were riding motorcycles, this hogback, along with others up and down the Front Range, was more horizontal and at the bottom of a shallow inland sea. As the Rocky Mountains sprouted to the west, it caused these sandstone layers to jut upward.

Fossil records are found throughout these ancient seabeds. In December 1999, while on a Sunday morning drive of Skyline, a University of Colorado paleontology student was astonished to see what he thought were dinosaur tracks embedded in the Dakota sandstone. Turns out he was right! Be sure to pause at the interpretive signs for views of these prints.

I think I know why it wasn't a motorcyclist who discovered the tracks of a Cretaceous period reptile. It's because he'd have been riveted on the bunched-up narrow ribbon of road in front of him! Have fun on this thing.

Though it is only three miles in length, this is a memorable road. Toward the end, before Skyline makes a dive down to the left toward Cañon City, there is a wide spot where you can put the sidestand down and gaze at the city to the east and Fremont Peak to the west. You might also look back at what you've just ridden. As with anything on a bike, the experience is amplified in every measure.

Unless you are from the Cañon City area, chances are a venture onto Skyline Drive will be a part of a longer ride planned for the day. Rides taking off from the Cañon City area toward the Cripple Creek area include Phantom Canyon [059] and Shelf Road–Red Canyon [060]. To the south are Copper Gulch [067] and Oak Creek Grade [068]. West of here a few miles off of US 50 is the famous Royal Gorge, and the entrance to the grand riding canyon of the Arkansas [065].

Ride 67 **Copper Gulch**

Copper Gulch Road, County 3, 28, 27A, 30, 215

A 27-mile backcountry ride (the middle eight miles are smooth dirt) winding through secluded gulches and over high plateaus, with the Sangre de Cristo Range filling your view to the south

The Copper Gulch Road and ride is a quiet journey through ranchlands, gulches, plateaus, and small developments. Like nearby Oak Creek Grade [068], it is a fine alternative route between the Cañon City area and Westcliffe, and even if either community isn't on your "get to" list, Copper Gulch is still a worthy destination for your two-wheeled steed.

On the north end, Copper Gulch Road branches off US 50 at Parkdale, three miles west of the main road to the Royal Gorge. At 2.5 miles south into the journey, County 3 jaunts to the east on a curving four-mile traverse to the backside of the Royal Gorge Park. This more secluded approach to the famous gorge is a worthy alternative to the more tourist-busy northern entrance. Actually, County 3 divides one mile after the turnoff from Copper Gulch. It becomes County 3A heading for the Royal Gorge, while County 3 changes into dirt-road clothes and becomes Temple Canyon Road back to

Cañon City—highly recommended with the right bike.

Continuing south on Copper Gulch Road, now becoming County 28, you'll scoot through a couple of ranchland miles before entering the namesake of this journey—a

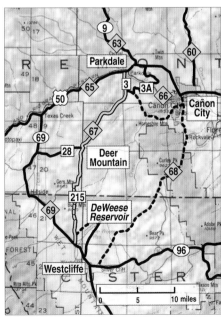

seven-mile-long ribbon of tarmac wrapping around a series of shrubby hills. It is almost canyon-like in nature, though I suppose the hillsides aren't steep enough for us to use that particular descriptor. Still, it isn't wholly expected, and it is a fun, twisting intervention between the big green fields of the ranches bordering the gulch.

On the south side of the gulch, the road meanders through and over 8,000-foot-high knobs. The small community of Deer Mountain is named after one of them. On the east side is Iron Mountain. A 2002 wildfire named after this promontory claimed 4,400 acres and dozens of homes. An overturned barbeque grill is said to have been the source. Charred trees stand in contrast to shaggy green grasses on the hillsides. County 28, also known as Gulch Road, departs west out of Deer Mountain for Colorado 69 only 6.5 miles away, but it isn't paved all the way.

Pavement also ceases south of Deer Mountain, but it makes a return several miles before the conclusion at Colorado 69, three miles northwest of Westcliffe—but to be sure, this is a treated and smoothly fast section of dirt for about eight miles. In dry conditions, most any motorcycle would be mighty fine. This part of the ride delivers mesmerizing, if distracting views of the Sangre de Cristo mountain range with its serrated summits and ridgelines cutting the sky to the nearby west.

Two miles north of throttling down for the tour's conclusion at Colorado 69, consider making a lean and turn east for DeWeese Reservoir and its State Wildlife Area. It is only three miles away on County 220, but if you don't like the road surface, paved County 241 north out of Westcliffe can escort you there. This lake is an old one, as water storage projects go in Colorado. It was built by Dall DeWeese and C.R.C. Dye as part of a vision to manage water from Grape Creek, so the Lincoln Park area of Cañon City could thrive as a fruit producing area. In the 1930s the dam's height was increased by 12 feet with labor from the Cañon City State Penitentiary. It is gorgeous on this high plateau, with shimmering Pikes Peak the lone sentinel to the north, and the peaks of the Sangre de Cristo Range guarding the western horizon. Whether you make the turn to DeWeese or not, sweeping alpine panoramas will be all around you as you cruise south to the intersection with Colorado 69.

Options for food and gas exist in the Cañon City area or in Westcliffe. From the Cañon City area, you could ride Copper Gulch one direction and return via the Oak Creek Grade [068]. You also have Colorado 96 and the Frontier Pathways Scenic Byway [069] east out of Westcliffe.

Ride 68 **Oak Creek Grade**

County 255, 277, 143

A wonderful, 30-mile, smooth dirt ride through quiet rural communities and rustic ranches, with national forest access, canyon country, and scenic vistas throughout

This journey charts a course between the Westcliffe area and Cañon City. Along the way it weaves a secluded path through fields and forests, hidden valleys, and not-so-hidden mountains, all bookended by the Sangre de Cristos thousands of feet higher, and Cañon City thousands of feet lower. This ride passes by rural homes, through small community clusters, and around century-old ranches, which always adds a little pizzazz to the ride.

The northeast end of this 30-mile traverse is at the southwest corner of Cañon City, just west of the intersection of Elm Avenue and South Ninth Street. From the Westcliffe side, ride to the eastern side of Silver Cliff, looking for paved County 255/Oak Creek Grade departing toward the northeast. The first three miles are paved before a graded, smooth-dirt surface takes over. For a fine historical introduction of the area, pull over at an interpretive sign area not far into the dirt road changeover. You'll be at the south end of the high DeWeese Plateau here, and this

pause-for-the-sign place is also a fine pause-for-the-view of the Sangre de Cristo Range, cutting the high western sky with their knife-edge ridgelines.

About halfway, the Oak Creek General Store comes into view. This is one of those

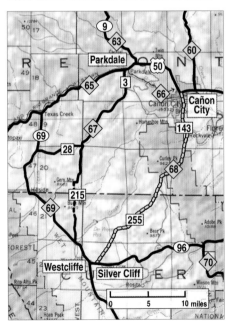

destinations within "the ride is the destination." Time your journey to breeze by here at lunchtime for their roast beef sandwiches, or if you really want to delight those you ride with, as well as the morning taste buds, get your saddled rear here before 10 a.m. for a breakfast like your ma or grandma would make. We're talking biscuits 'n gravy, pancakes, waffles, etc.

The scattered rural dwellings and rustic ranches will gradually phase out as you enter the San Isabel National Forest. The road connects with its namesake, Oak Creek, and lets the stream figure out how to get through the maze of rock outcroppings populating the ridgelines and slopes of the Wet Mountains. This is mighty fine riding.

The encore of riding this direction is the presentation of Cañon City and the Arkansas River Valley on the stage two thousand feet below. This would also be a great opening act if you were coming from the Cañon City area instead.

Despite the dirt-road nature of this ride I think an easy-going street bike would be fine in dry conditions. Be fuel-ready for the 30

miles. Cañon City and Westcliffe have plentiful food choices if you are skipping the Oak Creek Grade General Store option. You can also toss some vittles in the saddlebags and have a picnic at the Oak Creek Campground in the national forest.

This journey parallels the Copper Gulch ride [067], with which it could be combined for a sweet loop. Right where the Oak Creek Grade connects with the southwest side of Cañon City, take McDaniel Boulevard a half-mile west to Valley Road on the right. In a few hundred feet this will connect with Mariposa Road. Turn right to join County 3/ Temple Canyon Road to the west. I highly recommend this mostly dirt-road journey. Those motoring on dual-sports will find exploration options all along the Oak Creek Grade, as well as on the other side of Cañon City, such as the historic routes to the gold camps of Cripple Creek and Victor via Shelf Road [060] and Phantom Canyon [059]. On the west side, Westcliffe, where Colorado 96 connects with Colorado 69 [069], stands ready to serve up more great riding.

Approaching Westcliffe and the Sangre de Cristos from the east

Ride 69 **Westcliffe**

Colorado 96, 69

A glorious, paved, 50-mile mountain ride along a scenic byway delivering every kind of feature sought by motorcyclists

With the abundance of two-wheeled journeys in this area, Routes 96 and 69 often become part of another ride. But what should be appreciated is that by themselves, these superb highways—which are part of the Frontier Pathways Scenic Byway—offer a lengthy half circle of great riding, with the Arkansas River Canyon [065] closing the loop.

The ten miles from Wetmore to McKenzie Junction on Colorado 96 are an example of how special and diverse a motorcycling road can be. The first five miles or so consist of a serene valley, while the second five toward Hardscrabble Canyon and the junction with Colorado 165 conduct a hair-raising mountain ascent of 1,500 feet. It should be noted that there is a very tight, right-hand turn in this series of climbing curves, so be on the lookout for a sign warning of this wicked bend. At McKenzie Junction, a left turn on the renowned Greenhorn Highway 165 will serve up an inimitable ride to Bishop's Castle

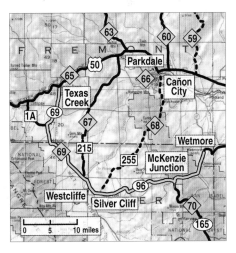

and beyond [070]. An option I would recommend is riding to Bishop's Castle, then returning to this junction and continuing on west toward Westcliffe.

This intersection with Colorado 165 in McKenzie Junction is where the historic Hardscrabble Ranch was located. As you motor west, other old homesteads and ranches tell tales of the past as they breeze and whisper by. Several small valley descents function as a warm-up for the big introduction to the Wet Mountain Valley. Through the trees, you will be teased with glimpses of a skyscraping mountain range on the horizon. Then the taunting ceases and the glimpses become gawks as the Sangre de Cristo Range, with its jagged 13,000- and 14,000-foot sentinels, comes into full view. Regardless of season or time of day, the panoramas as you arrive from the east are heart-stopping. Thankfully, the road is fairly straight on the descent to Westcliffe—can't have pesky little views getting in the way of keeping the rubber on the road!

Westcliffe and her sister community of Silver Cliff, a few steps to the east, can be a great place to refill food and fuel. There are a variety of cafes and diners here and all are good.

Westcliffe was founded as a railroad town when the Denver and Rio Grande Railroad

bought cheap land a few miles "West of Cliff" around 1880, and thus drew commerce and services with all that freight activity near the depot. Soon, Westcliffe had surpassed Silver Cliff as the bigger town. The tracks were pulled up decades later but the people didn't pull out. To the northeast of Westcliffe are great dual-sport rides toward and through the Wet Mountains via Copper Gulch [067] and Oak Creek [068].

The 24-mile ride to the small roadside community of Texas Creek in the Arkansas River Canyon starts on Colorado 69 north out of Westcliffe. This leg starts with an airy openness and slightly bending roadway as the Sangre de Cristo Mountains shadow your progress. As the miles click off, the openness becomes more confined, as do the curves. The road then follows Texas Creek as it carves a sweet winding course for the final seven miles. In some riding circles, this lonely section of tarmac is known as the Texas Creek International Speedway, but you didn't hear that from me.

At Texas Creek you can link up with the Arkansas River Canyon ride described in Ride 65. On Colorado 69, seven miles before its conclusion at the canyon, County 1A drifts off to the west, directly to Cotopaxi. This chip-and-seal road will save you time if your ultimate direction is west on US 50.

Westcliffe 100 years ago, and today, after someone clearly came by with a sack of seeds

Ride 70 **Bishop's Castle**

Greenhorn Highway, Colorado 165

A 36-mile premier motorcycle ride along a section of the Frontier Pathways Scenic Byway, which tracks an undulating course through valleys and mountainous terrain, passing a destination castle and lakeside resort along the way

Colorado 165, also known as the Greenhorn Highway, runs from Route 96 at McKenzie Junction southeast to Colorado City.

This highway gets its non-numerical name from the great Comanche Chief Cuerno Verde (Green Horn) who was known for wearing a headdress with a green horn emerging over his forehead. He was also known for resisting colonial Spain's encroachment into the southwest, constantly raiding small settlements in the New Mexico territory. Spanish governor Juan Bautista de Anza of New Mexico, fed up with the constant sieges, gathered a 600-man army along with several hundred unfriendly Comanches, and marched north in 1779 on a quest to find Green Horn and his warriors.

And find they did, at the base of today's 12,347-foot Greenhorn Mountain overlooking the town of Rye at the southern end of

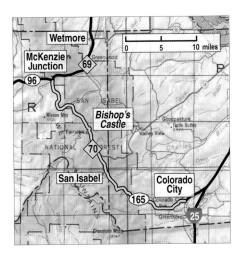

and it is a mesmerizing 12.6 miles with curves and swoops.

Bishop's Castle will amaze you when you see it towering over the tops of the pine and aspen. There are wide areas on the roadside for parking, and you will probably see other motorcycles with their sidestands down. Take a walking tour of the place. It is open and you can wander inside. Watch your step, for it wasn't necessarily built to code, and this was a cause for some of the historical tension between Jim Bishop, the builder, and the local government. Nevertheless, officials now seem to "accept" what he has accomplished and now even publicize its interesting, if not impressive, presence.

Six more crooked riding miles usher Lake San Isabel into view with the small community of San Isabel hugging the northwest shoreline. The Lodge, a family-owned restaurant and gift shop with cabins for rent in San Isabel, is excellent for a meal any time of day. For a photo op, ride across the dam and snap an image of the lake with the quaint San Isabel village on the other side. There is a forest service parking area here with restroom facilities.

Ten wonderful miles south, and the small town of Rye will appear over the handlebars. The full-service town of Colorado City near Interstate 25 is six miles farther. If you do not want to go all the way to Colorado City, you can always turn around at the castle or at San Isabel and head back toward McKenzie Junction, then point the front wheel west on great Colorado 96 for Westcliffe and the ultra-scenic Wet Valley. Westcliffe is a good place for food and fuel; choices are limited elsewhere along Colorado 96.

this ride. The long battle was one of the largest in the early west, with Green Horn and several key sub-chiefs killed in the conflict. The outcome solidified Spain's—and subsequently, Mexico's—hold on territory south of the Arkansas River for the next 70 years. So as you ride the Greenhorn Highway through the fields near Rye, turn toward the southwest and consider what happened here more than 230 years ago!

You connect with the Greenhorn Highway, or Colorado 165, at empty McKenzie Junction, where Colorado 96 [069] passes through on its way from Wetmore to Westcliffe. It is 12.6 miles to Bishop's Castle,

Ride 71 **Los Caminos Antiguos Scenic Byway**

Colorado 159, 142

A 50-mile ride through some of Colorado's oldest communities on a high desert road with a historic river crossing

On this ride you will travel on two legs of the Los Caminos Antiguos (Spanish for "Ancient Roads") Scenic and Historic Byway, deep in the southeast corner of the San Luis Valley, the world's largest alpine valley at three million acres. This broad ancient seabed was a lure for Spanish explorers, settlers, and missionaries from the south, before underground ores up north drew fortune seekers from the east. Colorado's oldest church, in nearby Conejos, was established three years before the big 1859 gold strikes west of Denver. This area is steeped in Colorado history and a journey here is a nice change of pace from a typical Centennial State ride.

As you approach the small town of Fort Garland where this ride begins, you will be dwarfed by the Blanca Massif soaring high to the north. Back when measurements weren't as precise as today, it was thought that Blanca Peak, at 14,345 feet, was only a dozen feet or so from being Colorado's highest mountain. An enterprising person in Alamosa thought it would be good for business if the community could boast of having the tallest peak nearby. Thus began the project of piling rocks with a pole at the top to see if could be made into the state's highest pinnacle. Well, I've been at the summit and

there just ain't that much room on that narrow precipice! Anyway, it is now known that while Blanca is the fourth highest in the state, it still falls almost 100 feet short of Mt. Elbert's 14,433 sky-reaching feet.

Turn south on Colorado 159 at Fort Garland, named after the nearby and historic garrison. This fort is one of Colorado's oldest (as is just about everything else on this ride), and in 1858 it was charged with protecting San Luis Valley settlers. Frontiersmen like Kit Carson were on assignment here, but after a 25-year run it was decommissioned in 1883, following the relocation of the Utes to reservations.

The Colorado 159 ride to San Luis is a 15-mile, cue-stick-straight road south out of

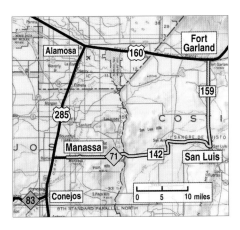

Fort Garland. The serrated peaks of the high Culebra Range will draw your attention to the east, as will carpets of fertile irrigated fields. This is an excellent cruising ride. Just take it all in. And take in Colorado's oldest surviving settlement by riding through the small and quaint Spanish-heritage town of San Luis. Established in 1851, it isn't the oldest town in Colorado, but no town has been continually settled for as long. You'll have a riding option from San Luis in addition to continuing this Los Caminos Antiguos tour. If you head south on Colorado 159, in 18 miles you will cross into New Mexico. The highway is renumbered to New Mexico 522 and in 41 lonely, fantastic miles you will be in the Taos area, ground zero for superb day rides in every direction.

Sticking with the Scenic and Historic Byway, from San Luis point the bike west on Colorado 142 toward Manassa. This is also divine cruising country. Turn the engine and the wheels at the right revolutions and you'll wish it would go on and on. The greenery of San Luis in your mirrors is in contrast to the brownery of the high and dry San Luis Hills before you. At their base, 19 miles west of San Luis, the mighty south-flowing Rio Grande River quenches the thirst of an arid land. The river doesn't look so mighty now, but it was hundreds of years ago. An interpretive sign at the river crossing describes how Spanish explorer Don Diego de Vargas crossed the "big river" at this location, fearing angry Pueblo Indians were in hot in pursuit after he'd raided their settlement in Taos. Back then, the unmanaged Rio Grande was 250 feet across and ten feet deep!

The birthplace of Jack Dempsey, the "Manassa Mauler," is 11 miles farther. He was the World Heavyweight Boxing Champ from 1919 to 1926, and he was known for being a ferocious fighter always on the offensive.

Manassa is a small San Luis Valley town, yet the largest in Conejos County. The town fathers purchased the land here with the assurance that the Denver and Rio Grande Railroad would pass through, but the tracks ended up three miles farther west at Romeo! Nevertheless, the town prospered, and you can too, whether staying here for a spell or riding on to Romeo as the trains did 100 years ago.

At Antonito, seven miles south of Romeo, you can connect with the La Manga and Cumbres Passes ride at Antonito on Colorado 17 [083]. As for food and fuel, while the choices are limited, nice diners and cafes await in Fort Garland, San Luis, or Manassa, as well as stations to fill your fuel tank.

Ride 72 **Cuchara**

Colorado 12

A 70-mile scenic byway presenting first-class ride amenities, from low valley and high mountain traverses to charming towns and lakeside attractions

Colorado 12, in the minds of some, is Colorado's most beautiful ride with its valleys, rivers, lakes, hills, mountains, towns, and historic places. For the motorcycle connoisseur, it has curves, sweepers, straights, ascents, and descents, with a sweetly paved surface along the way. Factor in the solitude and the 70 miles without stoplights, and you have a road worth bringing your bike to.

The area is soaked in history, with Native American cultures giving homage to the spiritual Spanish Peaks above, to Spanish explorers taking gold from below those very mountains. From mining to railroads and ranching to outfitters, from geologists studying unique formations and fortune seekers following legends of gold buried nearby—adding it all up, one can see how

the Highway of Legends became one of Colorado's first scenic byways.

From the north, Colorado 12 branches off US 160, ten miles west of Walsenburg. The

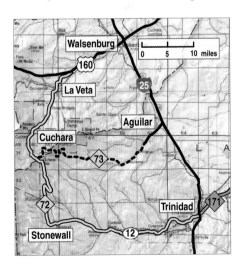

The stone wall just west of Stonewall in 1900 and 1933. And today. That dirt road is now paved. Alas, I turned in the wrong direction and didn't get a view identical to the older photos—but you get the idea.

welcoming town of La Veta is a short five miles away, and is not only a good place to top off the tank and partake of a meal, but invites a longer stay to explore its shops and old Spanish fort. The valley setting is idyllic and lends credence to the reported words of John Francisco, one of La Veta's earliest settlers, "This is paradise enough for me." By the way, La Veta is Spanish for "The Vein," but no one seems to know the source for this.

The best riding will be the next 34 miles. First, at eleven miles south of La Veta, you will pass through Cuchara—a rustic, western town still in the 19th century, with a saloon, general store, and hitching posts. This place entices you to do more than just slowly pass through, suggesting you let off that throttle completely and stop for a spell. From here, you'll bid farewell to the valley-carving Cucharas River and say hello to a dreamy, 1,300-foot climb up to the pass summit at 9,941 feet. Immense forests of aspen contain the twisting six-mile climb, and then before you know it, you will have attained the grassy summit. The dirt road to the east, climbing through the forest, is the Cordova Pass Road [073]. The serpentine stretch continuing and descending to the south is where you will be headed. North of the pass, the road is shaped like a cobra still coiled in the snake charmer's basket, but the south side is where the snake begins to rise and uncoil itself. You'll sweep up, down, and around, thanks to those pesky mountains slopes and lakes in your way.

As you slow down for the small town of Stonewall, you will recognize how this old tourist town came to be named. The many trees give the place a camp-like feel, popular with the RV crowd. The Middle Fork of the

Purgatoire River feeds the fields and delivers the route through the Stonewall Valley before it is joined by its North Fork and South Fork cousins. From Stonewall to the east, it will be a meandering 30 miles of Purgatoire River riding through old Spanish communities until its flow is intercepted by the dam at Trinidad Lake. The high peaks of the Culebra Range fill your mirrors as you ride toward the east, and are a tremendously scenic draw if you are riding in the opposite direction. As you scoot around the north side of Trinidad Lake State Park, you will pass through the old coal mining town of Cokedale. It can look a little gritty, but compared to the industrial scene here 100 years ago, someone clearly took a big vacuum cleaner to the place.

Trinidad on the southeast end is a nice place for the termination (or commencement) of this scenic byway journey. The downtown area has brick-lined streets, which are enjoyable to explore and ride around on, observing how well things have been taken care of. If you want to take care of your appetite, consider popular Tequila's Family Mexican Restaurant at Exit 11 on I-25 south of town.

The Comanche National Grasslands tour [171] is northeast out of Trinidad, and north at Exit 30 is access to Aguilar and the Cordova Pass ride [073]. I certainly recommend pulling over at Exit 27 for the Ludlow Massacre site only a mile west of the interstate. For those feeling adventurous, the dirt County 44 continues west through serious coal country, and one of the sites passed is the Hastings Mine where a catastrophic explosion killed more than 100 miners.

As for fuel, you have one option for the 70 miles between Trinidad and La Veta, and that would be the gas pumps at the general store in Stonewall. Other than the restaurant options in Trinidad and La Veta, you can grab a light lunch in Stonewall, and the old western town of Cuchara presents a few rustically themed options, as well.

Ride 73 **Aguilar–Cordova Pass**

County 43.7, 46

A 35-mile paved and unpaved ride through historic coal country, amidst enticing meadows and rock formations, and over a deeply scenic high mountain pass

Back in 2001, this ride over Cordova Pass in the shadows of the Spanish Peaks was incorporated into the Highway of Legends Scenic Byway [072]. Despite its unsurfaced texture, it is highly deserving of this special designation. The road was originally constructed in

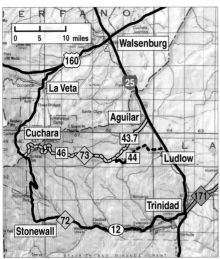

the 1930s by local county jurisdictions and the depression era Works Progress Administration and Civilian Conservation Corps (CCC). It was a rough, hacked-out thing back then, but over the years improvements have come, especially when it became a state designated byway. One of the earlier "moments of improvement" came in 1978 when the pass was renamed after long-time county commissioner José de Jesus Cordova, who put forth the vision for this special road. Prior to then, it was known as Apishapa Pass, from the Apache word meaning "stinking water."—don't worry, however, you can breathe easy as you ascend Cordova along the slender Apishapa River. The Apache, with noses pinched closed, observed that when the stream evaporated on the plains, it left behind stenchy pools of tepid water.

From the east, the ride over Cordova Pass

begins by following the Main Street west out of the small town of Aguilar, near Interstate 25. On the west end it is easily joined at the top of Cuchara Pass where well-signed County 46 takes off for its short, six-mile, 1,300-foot climb to Cordova's summit. So, which direction to ride? Well, if you're interested in touching the top of the pass summit quickly, make the climb from Cuchara Pass for the superb dose of scenery displayed up Cordova's western flanks. If a long savoring ride through historical places, with the Spanish Peaks looming larger after every turn pricks your heart, make your way to Aguilar and point the bike west.

The road west out of Aguilar on County 43.7 is paved for the first five miles. Graded gravel takes over at that point and so does a feeling that the area has seen more populous times. The area is rich with early 1900s coal mining history, and with the decline of productive mines came the decline of producing people. At 11 miles there will be a fork in the road. Take the right tine toward Cordova, and the wisdom of your choice will be confirmed when, just after a short rise,

the Spanish Peaks fill up the horizon. The Apishapa continues to guide for another five miles before giving way to the 3,200-foot climb for the remaining ten miles to the summit. Take notice of the vertical granite dikes scattered throughout the piney woods above and below you. These were formed long ago by splits in the earth's surface with molten lava filling in the cracks. Back in the 1930s, the CCC bored through one of the dikes, constructing an arch that you will pass under.

The pass summit contains one of the largest stands of bristlecone pine in the world. These are the world's longest living organisms, capable of reaching 5,000 years in age. It is interesting how they find it easiest to thrive at high and harsh environments, like the one hosting the bristlecone stand on the ascent of Mt. Evans. Maybe it has something to do with the clear and pristine environment. Or maybe they are just inspired by the vistas of nearby mountain giants like the Spanish Peaks. The western descent has steeper portions near the top before delivering a sweet tour alternating between mead-

ows and aspen stands, meadows and aspen stands . . . This is a mesmerizing place in autumn. At about a half-mile before arriving at Cuchara Pass, pause at the scenic Farley Wildflower Lookout. The granite gray of the volcanic dikes in the distance, with wildflower-carpeted fields in the foreground, all backed up by the towering peaks of the Culebra Range, is more than just a Kodak moment.

Be sure to gas up and be food-ready before venturing into the Cordova Pass area. Aguilar on the east end, and either La Veta or Stonewall on the west end, are your choices. A picnic along the way could be an ideal table setting. If you're up for exploring, grab a detailed local map around Aguilar and feast your eyes on the network of dual-sport explorations in the area. Most of these can be ridden with an easy-to-ride street bike, but I'm not advocating a street-bike assault on Cordova Pass. When this area was hot with coal mining, road building in the area was feverish as well. The bitumen visible on the surface is evidence of what is under the soil all around. Old miners' cabins and places where the inhabitants worked are scattered throughout the region. The fork in the road 11 miles out of Anguilar (mentioned above) is County 44, which winds back to the east, passing by locations that include the Hastings Mine Disaster of 1917, and the site where the Colorado National Guard engaged striking miners in 1914, resulting in what is called the Ludlow Massacre. This whole area is worth a motorcycle journey to get here, perhaps staying in Trinidad for the evening.

Southern Front Range

RECOMMENDATIONS

Backroad Journeys

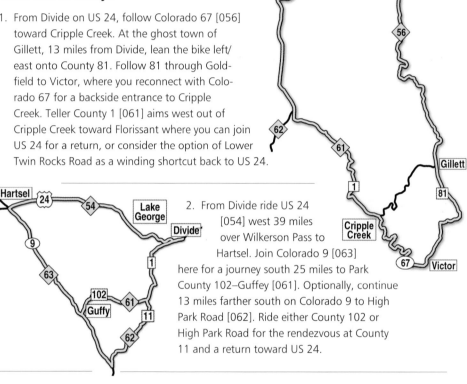

1. From Divide on US 24, follow Colorado 67 [056] toward Cripple Creek. At the ghost town of Gillett, 13 miles from Divide, lean the bike left/east onto County 81. Follow 81 through Goldfield to Victor, where you reconnect with Colorado 67 for a backside entrance to Cripple Creek. Teller County 1 [061] aims west out of Cripple Creek toward Florissant where you can join US 24 for a return, or consider the option of Lower Twin Rocks Road as a winding shortcut back to US 24.

2. From Divide ride US 24 [054] west 39 miles over Wilkerson Pass to Hartsel. Join Colorado 9 [063] here for a journey south 25 miles to Park County 102–Guffey [061]. Optionally, continue 13 miles farther south on Colorado 9 to High Park Road [062]. Ride either County 102 or High Park Road for the rendezvous at County 11 and a return toward US 24.

3. From Divide, ride west 1.6 miles on US 24 to catch Lower Twin Rocks Road sneaking off to the left/southwest. Follow its curving ways four miles to County 1. Turn left/south, cruising for six miles, where you make a right turn onto County 11. The Evergreen Station convenience store is at this junction. County 11 leads to one corner of a tremendous riding triangle. The direction doesn't matter as you enter the three-sided motorcycling zone of High Park Road [062], Colorado 9 [063], and Park County 102 [061]. Once back at the Evergreen Station, return toward Lower Twin Rocks, or if time permits, follow County 1 [061] to Cripple Creek and take Colorado 67 [056] back to Divide.

4. From Florence, ride Colorado 67 south where Colorado 96 takes over at Wetmore. Follow 96 [069] southwest up through Hardscrabble Canyon to the Greenhorn Highway/Colorado 165 at McKenzie Junction. Ride 165 for 13 miles to Bishop's Castle [070]. Return to McKenzie Junction and lean the bike left/west on 96 for Westcliffe. Colorado 69 will escort you from Westcliffe to Texas Creek in th Arkansas River Canyon [065] where an eastward cruise on US 50 completes the circle back to the Cañon City andFlorence area.

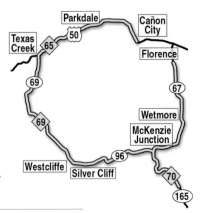

Dirt Road Explorations

1. From Colorado Springs, ascend Gold Camp Road [058] to County 81, where a turn south brings you to Victor and a connection with Colorado 67 toward Cripple Creek. The main entrance to Shelf Road [060] is on the east side of Cripple Creek, but there is a cutoff south to Shelf Road halfway into the short twisting traverse between Victor and Cripple Creek. Descend Shelf Road all the way to Cañon City, where you can ride US 50 east to the main Florence stoplight, with County 67 aiming north for Phantom Canyon [059], which you ascend to Victor.

2. Ride US 50 west out of Cañon City, past the Royal Gorge to the entrance of the Arkansas River Canyon at Parkdale. County 3 toward Copper Gulch [067] is located here. Follow it all the way to the north side of Westcliffe, joining Colorado 69 south to the intersection with Colorado 96 [069] in Westcliffe. A mile east on 96, just past Silver Cliff, will introduce Oak Creek Grade [068] toward the northeast for a journey back to Cañon City.

Favorite Rides

Best Cruising Roads

[056] Colorado 67 through Cripple Creek
[061] County 102 east out of Guffey
[065] US 50 in the Arkansas River Canyon
[069] Colorado 96 from Wetmore to Westcliffe
[071] Colorado 159 and 142,
        north and west of San Luis

Best Sporting Curves and Sweepers

[056] Colorado 67 between Victor
        and Cripple Creek
[062] High Park Road
[063] Colorado 9 from Parkdale to Hartsel
[070] Colorado 165/Greenhorn Highway
[072] Highway of Legends, Cuchara Pass

Most Scenic Spots

[054] Wilkerson Pass
[055] Eleven Mile Canyon Reservoir
[056] Cripple Creek from Colorado 67 overlook
[057] All along the Pikes Peak Highway
[058] Cathedral Valley on Gold Camp Road
[058] County 81 on the backside of Victor,
        looking north at Pikes Peak
[059] Deep in Phantom Canyon
[060] All along Shelf Road
[061] Homesteads on Cty 102 east of Guffey
[063] Thirtyninemile Mountain from Colorado 9
[064] County 175 and the Ute Trail above Salida
[065] The Arkansas River in its canyon
[066] Roller-coaster ride and views from Skyline
[068] Above Cañon City from Oak Creek Grade
[069] Colorado 96 approach to Westcliffe
        with the Sangre de Cristos
[071] The Rio Grande River from Colorado 142
[071] 14,000-plus peaks of Mt. Blanca
        and Culebra Peak from Colorado 159
[072] The Cuchara Valley
[073] Cordova Pass

Best Dirt-Road Adventures

[059] Phantom Canyon
[060] Shelf Road
[064] Ute Trail, County 175, Tallahassee Road
[068] Oak Creek Grade
[073] Cordova Pass

Worthy Destinations

[052] Pantry Restaurant in Green Mountain Falls
[054] Florissant Fossil Beds National Monument
[054] Colorado Wolf Center near Divide,
        off Lower Twin Rocks Road
[055] Elevenmile Canyon Reservoir
[056] Mines, mills, and town of Victor
[056] The inexpensive restaurants, rooms,
        and casinos of Cripple Creek
[057] Pikes Peak Summit House
[061] Rita's Place, Guffy
[067] Backside approach to the Royal Gorge
        via County 3 and Copper Gulch
[068] Oak Creek Grade General Store
[070] Bishop's Castle
[070] The Lodge family restaurant
        and cabins, Lake San Isabel
[071] San Luis, Colorado's oldest
        continuously inhabited town
[072] Town of Cuchara
[072] Brick streets of downtown Trinidad
[073] Hastings Mine site south of Aguilar
[073] Ludlow Massacre site south of Aguilar

Little-Known Gems

[055] County 90 to Elevenmile Canyon Reservoir
[056] County 81 and the back way to Victor
[061] County 102 east of Guffey
[067] Copper Gulch Road
[068] Oak Creek Grade
[071] Colorado 159 and 142,
        north and west of San Luis

Southwest

REGIONAL OVERVIEW

Southwestern Colorado has a tremendous variety of motorcycling roads tucked into a relatively small area between US 285, US 50, and the borders of New Mexico and Utah. In many other parts of the country you might have to travel days to find such diverse motorcycling. Here, in less than an hour, you can ride from the alien landscape of the Canyons of the Ancients near Cortez, at 5,000 feet in elevation, to the chilly alpine

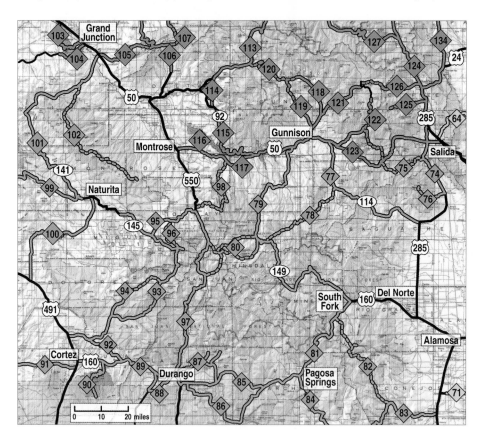

terrain of Lizard Head Pass, more than a mile higher. The Silver Thread Scenic Byway traverses two mountain passes, a gap, and two fertile river valleys, before winding through dry and hilly sage country to offer up an inviting break at a couple of old mining towns—all in only 117 stoplight-free miles! It's one of the best roads you will ever set your front tire upon.

Today, the roads on which we ride our modern iron horses often run along the same routes traveled in previous centuries by Ute Indians, fortune-seeking miners, stagecoach drivers, and wagon freighters, and the history they have lived will give your own journey an extra dimension. The landscape is replete with old mining claims, faded homesteads, and historical markers. Maybe I'm a bit nostalgic about such things, but reflecting on the adventurers of the past gives me a richer perspective on my own present-day adventures. Welcome to the riding wonderland of southwest Colorado.

Rides in This Section

Looking north toward the Arkansas River Valley and Poncha Springs, from the lower elevations of Poncha Pass

Ride 74 **Poncha Pass**

US 285

A sweeping 22-mile mountain pass ride traversing from one mountain valley to another, with visible history and grand scenic views

Linking the fertile Arkansas River Valley with the vast San Luis Valley, the Poncha Pass ride follows a route formerly used by Native Americans, Spanish explorers, mountain men, and early settlers. Famed road builder Otto Mears built his first toll road here in the 1870s, later selling it to the Denver and Rio Grande Railroad so its lines could be extended to the big valley. The San Luis Valley is the world's largest alpine valley with more than three million acres at 7,500 feet of elevation. It is bordered on the east by the shapely Sangre de Cristo Range, and on the distant west by the San Juan Mountains. In prehistoric times, an inland sea covered this land. Today, only shallow pools of water scattered throughout the flat valley floor remain, and they attract waterfowl, both permanent and migratory. National and state wildlife refuges protect the lakes and their inhabitants.

If there is a motorcycle riding crossroads in Colorado, the intersection of US 50 and US 285—hosted by the small commercial junction town of Poncha Springs—could be it. Great rides await in every direction, and they lead to other exemplary excursions for the enthusiast. For this ride, scoot south on US 285, over Poncha Pass to the San Luis Valley. It is a ride wearing two suits. The first half is loose fitting, a bit rumpled, with curves sweeping you to the top of the pass. The second half is flatly pressed, with straight, linear creases, giving you a gun-barrel escort to Villa Grove in the San Luis Valley.

As you ride south, ascending the northern slopes of Poncha Pass, the old train bed of the Denver and Rio Grande can be spotted along the way, mostly on the brushy hillsides to the west. At five miles, Forest Road 202 departs southwest for Marshall Pass [075]. A railtoad line was also extended to the heights of Marshall Pass, linking the

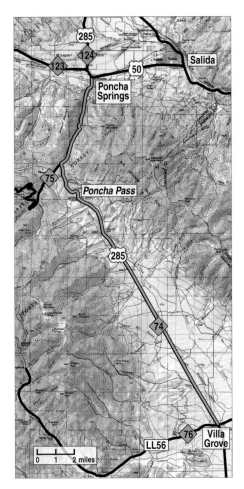

Heading out of Poncha Springs for a ride at the turn of the last century

Gunnison Valley to those of this ride. The spot where the rails divided was known as Mears Junction, named for Otto Mears.

Some quick scrutiny here as you lean into the corners will reveal evidence of the area's active railroading past. The remaining 600 feet of elevation gain to the pass summit are delivered gradually and lazily over the next two and a half miles, although several of the sweeping curves have been known to induce more than a few grins.

The 9,010-foot pass summit isn't the highest or most dramatic, but views abound and there always seems to be a feeling of

achievement about making it to the top. There's a wide parking area on the southwest side of the pass with interpretive signs, inviting a sidestand pause to view the Sawatch Range to the south and the 14,000-foot pinnacles of Mt. Shavano and Tabeguache Peak dominating the vistas back to the north. I've always enjoyed the panorama to the south with the jagged rooftop of the Sangre de Cristos scraping the sky off into the distance. When these summits are overloaded with stark white snow, lit up by

brilliant sunshine against a deep blue backdrop—we're talking major postcard setting.

Riding the 1,000-foot descent over ten miles to the San Luis community of Villa Grove is like coming through a funnel from the small end—things expand all around you. The Sangre de Cristo Mountains grow in stature and the valley widens. At Villa Grove one can refuel or refill. Put the sidestand down at the Villa Grove General Store, in operation since 1882. A smooth dirt road to the boom-and-bust, semi-ghost town of Bonanza [076] heads west out of town. Continue 19 more miles on US 285 as it bends toward the southwest, and you will be at the town of Saguache and the entrance to the superb Cochetopa ride [077]. From there, you could take Cochetopa's Colorado 114 up to US 50, push the handlebars east toward Monarch Pass, and be back where this Poncha Pass ride started. It would be a sweet half-day circuit.

From the beginning of this ride—that special motorcycle intersection of US 50 and US 285—you can ride to the west on US 50 toward Monarch Pass [123]. North on US 285 is the Top of the Rockies Scenic Byway [124], and an eastward turn onto US 50 takes you to the great town of Salida only a few miles away, and the riding canyon of the Arkansas River [065]. There's an overdose of fantastic riding in every direction.

Ride 75 **Marshall Pass**

Marshall Pass Road, County 243, XX32, Forest Road 200, 243

A 30-mile dual-sport ride over a high mountain pass on an old train bed, in a place with a storied past

The discovery of Marshall Pass can be traced to someone's travails with a toothache. Army Lt. William L. Marshall was charged by the Wheeler Survey of 1873 to complete a military survey of the San Juan Mountains in southwest Colorado. That autumn, the encampment was near present-day Silverton as winter began to strengthen its snowy, icy

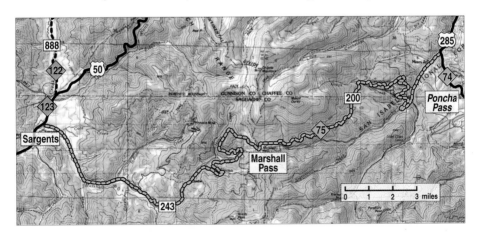

grip. The camp packed up and started for Denver via the traditional Cochetopa Pass route but a festering tooth in Lt. Marshall's mouth developed into a raging pain, enough so that he could only consume thin, soupy food through his tightly clenched jaws. A blacksmith with the party offered to pry open his mouth and pull out the offending molar, but the lieutenant declined the kind gesture, opting for the professional services of a dentist in still far away Denver. With pain mounting, Marshall and his packer Dave Mears took off to find a quicker route for Denver. They aimed toward a lower ridgeline in the distance and spent six days trudging through snow, around rocks, and over fallen timber to reach the top. This gap had promise. It pointed in the right direction and its approaches weren't steep. Despite the dental agony, Marshall and Mears stayed put for a day diagramming the area before continuing on toward Denver, arriving four days before their survey camp did.

Word circulated during the ensuing years about the discovery of this pass route from the Arkansas River Valley to the "Gunnison City" area. In 1877 Otto Mears was given a charter to build a wagon road over the pass named for its discoverer, and three years later it was open for business. Only a year later, the Denver and Rio Grande Railroad reached Salida, and offered to buy Mears's

toll road for $13,000. Six months after that, the first train rolled into Gunnison on August 6, 1881. This line survived the demise of the mining industry and carried passengers until 1940, then cattle and coal, before the railroad sought permission to vacate the line in 1953. The rails came up in 1955, and one year later, a county road for general traffic (and that means motorcycles!) was opened.

The eastern end of the Marshall Pass road is off US 285, five miles south of its intersection with US 50 in Poncha Springs. The turnoff to the southwest is well marked, and is just north of Poncha Pass [074]. The west end of the road departs from US 50 at the Sargents townsite, near the base of Monarch Pass [123]. Sargents was a gritty depot for the train traffic, except for a general store and cafe with gas pumps on US 50. Think of Marshall Pass as a secluded dirt-road alternative to the south, parallel to the paved Monarch Pass.

The ascent and descent of Marshall Pass is on shelf roads carved into forested hillsides, with tantalizing breakouts into the open, revealing deep valleys below and peaks scraping the sky above. The east side of Marshall is dominated by views of the solitary giant, Mt. Ouray. At 13,971 feet, Ouray is 29 feet shy of being a member of the "fourteener" club, and thus just missed being one of the state's "must climb" destinations.

There is a gentleness to the terrain as the

10,842-foot pass summit is approached, an indication your bike will soon be able to take a made-it-to-the-top rest. Grassy meadows appear, pine trees give each other more room, and a genial grade delivers the final traverse. I can understand if you gaze awhile at the far-reaching views to the western horizon. I certainly would! But shift your focus closer and notice the scattered debris of rotting wood along the road just northwest of the summit. This would be the remains of the sheltering wood tunnel, built for the trains at this high-alpine place.

I classify this as a dual-sport ride. There are some rocks, and some ruts, and some bumps, and so forth, but there are also miles of smooth dirt. I wouldn't be surprised to see a light and capable street bike make it to the top. The journey is 30 miles from end to end, with the west side approach slightly longer and more gradual at 16 miles. You will find an excellent cafe, along with fuel, at the Sargents General Store mentioned above. On the east side, Poncha Springs and Salida are just four and nine miles away, respectively.

You could really make this a part of a longer area ride. The dual-sport ride to the semi-ghost town of Bonanza [076] is not far south from the east entrance of Marshall Pass. You could always just make a big circle of Marshall and Monarch Passes. Only a mile northwest of Sargents is the door to the dual-sport pass rides of the Pitkin area [122].

More than 11 decades separate these views looking north from the Bonanza area.

Ride 76 **Bonanza**

County LL56

A 15-mile dual-sport ride to a historical semi-ghost town across open rangeland and up a scenic mountain valley

Bonanza is a Spanish word meaning "rich mineral deposit," as in when a prospector exclaims, "It's a bonanza, boys!" The mines in this area weren't the largest in Colorado put they sure did pump out the silver. Bonanza is a classic boom-and-bust town. Following the big strikes of 1880, the town flared to life. Hearing Bonanza could be the next Leadville, more than 40,000 people passed through or stayed in the first two years, including former president Ulysses S. Grant. As you ride through the area, try to imagine how this ghost town and the surrounding communities once supported saloons, dance halls, banks, hotels, doctors, attorneys, grocers, a furniture store, a candy shop, a bakery, a bowling alley, a newspaper, and even a baseball team. Perhaps they were called the Bonanza Riders!

By the 1930s, most of the mines had flickered out, and residents began to filter out. A 1937 blaze charred many of the tightly packed buildings, accelerating the decline. Today it is a place of few residents living in a pretty spot rich with history. Just as daily stagecoaches did over 100 years ago, we can ride a fine route to this special destination.

The road to Bonanza is on the north side of Villa Grove, a small town hugging the sides US Highway 285 in the northern San Luis Valley. County LL56 to Bonanza points to the west off US 285, between the northern edge of town and the old Villa Grove Cemetery. The introductory road surface is pavement for the first five miles or so, and it is possible that grumpy, open range cattle will be your welcoming committee. These five miles will be riding fine as the road shoots straight then quivers slightly to join the meandering Kerber Creek most of the rest of the way.

The dirt surface is all right for street bikes, if it isn't wet. Watch for ruts, but otherwise, enjoy the relatively smooth surface. Old homesteads, some livable and some rather drafty, dot the roadside here and there, as do a few resort ranches and bed and breakfasts. The lovely Antora Peak, at 13,266 feet, with a mosaic of aspen and pine on her lower slopes, graces the view over the handlebars as you ride northwest.

At 14 miles, the county road bears to the right and the remains of Kerber City, one of Bonanza's "suburbs" comes into view, primarily on the right/southeast side of the road. A bend to the left, past the historic Bonanza cemetery and you'll arrive at the town, where the road is lined with a scattered history book mix of decayed, refurbished, and modernized structures. The 2000 census tallied 14 residents, making this the smallest incorporated town in Colorado. There is a small intersection on the north side with interpretive signs describing the toils, trials, and triumphs of this once-booming mining camp and town. It is difficult to observe some of the historical slopeside min-

ing action, for aspen stands have claimed and cloaked much of the unused space. This would be a pretty autumn visit.

With a worthy dual-sport bike, you have several exploration options up high on crustier forest roads. The road leading north divides into two, with the rightward venture ascending past old mines and continuing on to a rendezvous with US 285 just south of Poncha Pass.

Back at Kerber City and farther south at the bend to the north, forest roads lead to the aptly named ghost town of "Spook City." Many will simply enjoy the short return to Villa Grove where a diner in the historical general store, a cafe, and fuel pumps can quench the need to refill.

To the west is Saguache with additional services described in the Cochetopa ride [077]. North of Villa Grove is Poncha Pass [074], and if you are in the mood for more dual-sport riding, there is the ascent of historic Marshall Pass [075]. Regardless of where you are riding from or to, this 15-mile Bonanza excursion on the north end of the San Luis Valley will not disappoint.

Ride 77

Cochetopa Canyon–North Cochetopa Pass

Colorado 114

A divine, secluded 60-mile paved ride over a mountain pass and through backcountry wilderness, with twisties and sweepers galore

This is a special ride for those who declare the ride to be the destination. For 60 mind-mending miles you fly, lean, and dance with this circuit. Then you climb a mountain pass. Then you repeat the tango. And you probably won't mind that it is a show with few spectators, for this is a lonely and secluded production. Colorado 114 cuts through the middle of some serious backcountry, with the La Garita Wilderness to the west, the Gunnison National Forest all around, and meadows containing streams along the road.

Cochetopa is the Ute Indian word for "pass of the buffalo." The pass and canyon of this ride are named after the surrounding Cochetopa Hills. In the mid-19th century, the area was explored as a potential location for the Transcontinental Railroad, but the rugged terrain encouraged placing the tracks farther north in Wyoming. The original pass summit is actually five miles south of this paved "North" Cochetopa Pass, and was a historical stagecoach route. Its dirt surface can easily be traversed today by a dual-sport or a decent street bike. A charter was issued in the late 1800s to build an improved wagon road over a more favorable, northerly route. In 1916 it became state highway, although it wasn't paved until 1962. In a way, we are the beneficiaries of the trailblazers and surveyors who explored these hills and mountains 160 years ago. Their efforts resulted in an exceptional road for us intrepid adventurers on motorcycles!

The northern terminus of Colorado 114 is six miles east of Gunnison off US 50, and it ends in the small town of Saguache. The first few miles riding south dangle the bait of a winding roadway through working ranches and small farms. The hook is then set and you are reeled in to a reddish, rocky canyon carved by Cochetopa Creek, which contains some of the best canyon riding in Colorado. For 14 miles, you will be entertained with series upon series of dense and beautiful curves. What might be a chore in a car is a blast to ride on a motorcycle. You'll emerge from the canyon into a terrain that is a little more sane. To the right/west, County NN14 aims for distant, forested hills. This is the off-road Los Piños Pass ride described in Ride 78.

Next on the agenda are sweepers climbing to the North Cochetopa Pass summit ten miles away and 1,100 thin-air feet higher. It is easy to be in a riding zone here is well, with the motion of the bike in sync with the road, as if one. The pass summit at 10,149 feet is not as dramatic as some others, but you are at the Continental Divide, and this adds a little pizzazz to the place. When you are ready for more sweepers, descend southeast toward Saguache. You'll ride through beautiful high parks, and if you glance toward the southwest, the wild 130,000-acre La Garita Wilderness, as designated by the United States Congress in 1964, absorbs the horizon. When you look in that direction—and really, any direction for most of this ride—little has changed since the Utes rode their ponies through this land.

You make somewhat of a commitment in placing your bike on Colorado 114, especially with the vast San Luis Valley at the eastern end. On the north side, however, US 50 is a gateway to numerous nearby rides, including Monarch Pass [123] and the dual-sport journeys of Marshall Pass [075] and the Pitkin area [122]. Gunnison, just to the west of 114's conclusion at US 50, is in the midst of motorcycle journeys in every direction.

Gunnison or Saguache are where you will want to top off the tank—of both the fuel and food kind. The Firebrand Deli at the corner of US 50 and Colorado 135 in downtown Gunnison is a draw for motorcyclists. The Dessert First Kitchen just north of Saguache, a few hundred feet away on County 47 at its intersection with Colorado 114, is also an excellent place for a meal.

Ride 78 **Los Piños Pass**

Los Piños–Cebolla Road, Forest Road 788, County 50, KK14, NN14

A 43-mile dual-sport ride over a forested pass, through a remote backcountry landscape of valleys, meadows, canyons, and open range

Los Piños is Spanish for "The Pines." There's plenty of 'em on this ride, but the scenic open meadows, separating secluded rocky canyons, joined with vast leafy aspen groves does have one questioning the singular selection. This route utilizes an old stagecoach toll road built in 1874 on a well-used Ute trail. At one time, bands of Utes from the San Luis Valley were relocated here under the supervision of the Los Piños Indian Agency. Today, the old agency, on the east side of this ride a few miles west of Colorado 114, is a forest service work center. It isn't difficult to pass through these 43 miles on your two-wheeled horse, reflecting on

how little has probably changed since four-hoofed horses made the same journey. This is an isolated ride, connecting quiet and lonely highways. Unless it is hunting season, expect to be able to count the number of passing vehicles on just your non-throttle hand.

On the west side, Los Piños Pass Road takes off from Colorado 149 nine miles east of Lake City, about a mile past the Windy Point Lookout at Slumgullion Pass. On the east end, the ride is joined at County NN14, off Colorado 114, 19 miles south of US 50. When you turn the handlebars east toward Los Piños from the lofty heights of Slumgullion Pass, you are extended a welcome by the first of numerous campgrounds located near the path of this old dirt road. While this is a dual-sport-declared journey, there isn't really anything hair-raising along the way. A few more embedded stones appear in the surface near the Los Piños Pass part of the ride, and in a few other spots, but for the most part this is a decent and not overly bumpy journey. A light and easily maneuverable street bike would probably be okay without causing any "What am I doing here?" moments.

Mill Creek is the first of several charming creeks showing the lonely and scenic way. It hands the reins to Cebolla Creek at four miles, and for the next eleven miles Cebolla charts a dirt-road dream of a ride. The tumbling and sparkling stream is often only a few feet away from the road as you squeeze through narrow rocky passages before emerging into bucolic water-fed ranchlands.

Campgrounds continue to make an appearance in nicely chosen locations. With all the forest road tracks extending off the entire route, a campground here not only could be a one-night stay, but also a base camp for days of dual-sport exploration. You'll probably have the campground all to yourself. Pack a hiker's fishing pole and invite some brookies from the nearby creeks to join you for dinner.

At fifteen miles, you'll find the ghost town site of Cathedral. This is where there is a fork in the journey. To the left/north is the dirt Cebolla Road heading toward Powderhorn and back to Colorado 149. Taking this turn is certainly a fine riding option. For Los Piños Pass, lean toward the right and prepare for the 1,400-foot climb to the summit, five

twisting miles away. The ascent up the western, aspen-filled slopes serve up penthouse views of where you have been (or where you are going). To the south, the vast La Garita Wilderness, with its above-timberline peaks, enhances the wild and remote feel of the place. The faint old wagon road will be the only visible intervention, and riders on idling bikes see the same scene as those riders in bucking stagecoaches. The eastern descent from the pass is a wandering tour of open range with cattle as curious spectators. There is some sweet high-speed riding on smooth dirt here, as you fly by ranches and the old Ute Agency facility. The east side is a fun encore.

Los Piños Pass could be considered as a "go between" with heavenly Colorado 114 [077] on one side, and the Silver Thread Scenic Byway of Colorado 149 [079] on the other. But with the remote experience of this special traverse, Los Piños Pass Road is more than just a link between two highways. The descriptions of the Colorado 114 and 149 rides note the food and fuel options at each end. There is some distance here (70-plus miles) between Lake City and your nearest choices in Gunnison or Saguache and, as always, it can take longer than expected when the surface isn't paved and there are pauses to soak in the panoramic surroundings.

Ride 79 **Silver Thread Scenic Byway**

Colorado 149

A 117-mile world-class ride along two rivers, over two mountain passes, and through two inviting towns, with deep and scenic wilderness all around

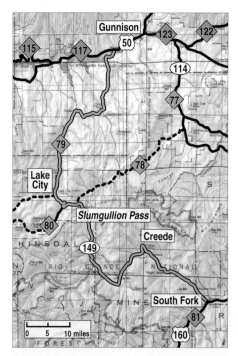

The Silver Thread Scenic Byway, named for the silver mining camps on and near its course, is one of the finest, most exquisite motorcycle roads in Colorado. It is 117 miles of undulating, twisting, enchanting travel with minimal traffic, no stoplights, and two historic towns.

The northern starting line is seven miles west of Gunnison off US 50, and the finish line is at South Fork on US 160. (Unless you swap direction, as you may with any road in this book). At a bridge over Blue Mesa Reservoir [117], signs point the way to Colorado 149 to the south. A shoreline cruise is the get-acquainted session; soon after comes the initiation. At around mile eight, you'll become a dues-paying member, with full rights and privileges. Exhilarating could be the word to use here. A riding friend once told me about leading some of his riding buddies from the east onto this coiled course, but he couldn't figure out why one was pulling over to the shoulder in the middle of the "flow." The rider disembarked, walked to the center of the road, got on his hands and knees, and bent down to kiss its asphalt surface.

The curving ride along the Lake Fork of the Gunnison River is a beautiful cruise, as the distance to the Hinsdale County seat is narrowed. When you arrive at the 1870s mining camp of Lake City, you're basically where almost all the population of Hinsdale County resides. With slightly more than 1,000 year-round residents, Hinsdale is one of the least populated counties in Colorado. This is understandable, considering the preponderance of wilderness areas in the county. Numerous fine and friendly establishments for a food break are waiting in Lake City. Take your pick. If the scent of barbecue stimulates at the moment, the Sportsmans Barbecue on Gunnison Avenue will not disappoint. The town's Main Street is one block west of Colorado 149's path through the community. Speaking of meals, famous cannibal Alferd Packer consumed his during the harsh winter of 1874, two miles west of town. You pass the "site of consumption" on the very steep ascent to Slumgullion Pass, only six miles away but 2,500 feet higher! The pass is named after a still-visible cataclysmic landslide 700 years ago. Its yellow-shaded dirt reminded early settlers of the color of slumgullion stew. Nearby Lake San Cristobal was formed when the huge slide blocked flows of the Gunnison River's Lake Fork. Be sure to check all this out by turning left/north to the Windy Point Scenic Lookout just shy of the pass summit. It is worthy of a sidestand deploy—few panoramic vistas in Colorado compare.

On the other side of the pass is a gradual and twisting eight-mile descent to Spring Creek Pass. Initially this is a curve-after-curve course through spectator trees before a magical route is plotted through a series of meadow-covered hills. Be on the lookout for moose here. They have been thriving since a 1990 introduction of 100 of the leggy beasts. Eight miles after the gentle pass crest, follow a sign pointing east for North Clear Creek Falls. The parking area is only a few hundred yards away, but what a sur-

prise! The next 16 miles are descend into sweeper heaven. Signs will announce that you are entering the Rio Grande Headwaters Area. Glance west at the humble stream and realize that this water is just starting out on a 1,800-mile voyage to the Gulf of Mexico.

Ease off on the throttle as the historic mining town of Creede comes into view. Make a turn into this small town and cruise its cozy streets. If there is a hunger twitch, there are numerous restaurants by which you could park your bike. The Creede Smoke-house Barbecue is popular with bikers and the restaurant in the old firehouse is worth checking out.

The remaining 21 miles from Creede to South Fork could merit its own ride descrip-

tion. The Rio Grande will have swelled, seemingly in only a few miles, and the winding course it has chosen, with Colorado 149 following, will have you in hearty agreement.

At Wagon Wheel Gap there is a resort with a restaurant, and a selection of food and fuel services await at South Fork, where a turn to the southwest would put you on the Wolf Creek Pass ride [081]. It wasn't mentioned above, but if your gas tank is thirsty, there are stations in Lake City and Creede.

Finally, there are two linking dual-sport rides in addition to the others noted. In Lake City, the renowned Alpine Loop [080] is launched to the west, and just east of Slumgullion Pass is the Los Piños Pass ride [078].

Creede in 1892 and Creede today

Ride 80 **Alpine Loop**

Cinnamon Pass Road, Engineer Pass Road, County 20, 30, 110

A renowned 60-mile alpine dual-sport adventure, delivering world-class scenery and riding, with ghost towns along the way and a destination town on each end

Due to some challenging sections, I hesitated for a brief moment about including the Alpine Loop in this collection, as my criteria for including a ride excluded those that required a small, off-road thumper to make the traverse safely. However, the Alpine Loop can be navigated, with some care and capability, on a large and comfy dual-sport bike. Many riders consider this off-road adventure to be the greatest and most famous in Colorado.

Though much could be written about the lives, fortunes, and tragedies of those who pioneered and settled these soaring timberline places, let me just mention that the rocky roads you ride here were hacked out by 19th-century miners hauling their min-

eral-based harvests downhill on mule-drawn wagons to places like Lake City, Ouray, and Silverton. Left in their wake are the rustic and rusting remains of mines, mills, cabins, and community centers. Tales of a time passed will be whispered as you slowly ride by. Stir this in with the grandeur of the al-

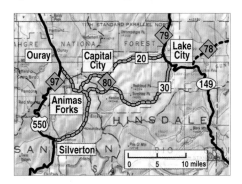

pine scenery, and you'll have a experience unlike any other, especially when the immersion comes from the saddle of a bike.

There are two main passes on the Alpine Loop—Engineer at 12,780 feet, and Cinnamon at 12,640 feet. I will cover both briefly, riding up and over their thin-air crests from Lake City, joining them together at the ghost town of Animas Forks for the descent to Silverton. For Engineer, head to the south side of town, turning west on First Street for two blocks where County 20 begins its ascent. For Cinnamon, ride south out of Lake City two miles on Colorado 149, turning the handlebars southwest onto paved County 30, which first starts out as a sweet and winding lakeside ride around the western shore of Lake San Cristobal. Think of it this way: the Alpine Loop is basically fish-shaped. The scaly thing is facing east with its head at Lake City. The backbone is the road to Engi-

neer. The distended stomach is the Cinnamon route. Both converge at the tail near the ghost town of Animas Forks, and there is a fishing line snagged on the bottom corner of the tail leading southwest to an angler named Silverton.

Both ascents to the west start out on the mild side of the spectrum. Rocks gain in diameter as elevation increases. The ruts, washouts, and granite ledges you'll throttle over appear more often as trees appear less often. On the Engineer side, check out the ghost town of Capitol City at 9.4 miles, where residents hoped the clever community name would give them an edge as the state's capitol! There is a fork in the road here, and you will want to point the bike to the left/southwest. At 22 miles on the Cinnamon Pass route there will be another fork, and you will want to bear right for the pass summit. However, a quick detour south at

The historic townsite of Animas Forks lies at the western base of the Engineer and Cinnamon Pass ascents.

this fork brings the amazing American Basin into view, with a trailhead to the summit of 14,048-foot Handies Peak at the end of the road. A few years ago on a climbing trip to the top of Handies, we beheld the most incredible wildflower scene ever at this basin. The verdant and dense flowers carpeted the earth like a scene from the *Wizard of Oz*. They were enormous, as if it had rained Miracle-Gro daily from the clouds.

Both pass summits are airy with rooftop views of the Rocky Mountains. Five nearby peaks over 14,000 feet scrape the blue above. The ride down from either pass, in either direction, can have its uncertain moments as loose scree can break traction. Keep things slow and in control, modulating with the rear brake and having a light touch on the front brake. The remains of Animas Forks appear over the handlebars several steep miles later. This mining camp once was a buzzing place in the late 1800s, more so in the summer, since many of the residents

would hustle down to "balmier" Silverton during the winter. Blizzards and avalanches made it a challenging place to work or visit for all but a few months each year. One blizzard in 1884 dumped 25 feet of snow over a three-week period. You can explore the ghost town's buildings, stabilized in 1997 and 1998. From here you have the option to ride north for a rocky journey to Ouray, or south to Silverton with a graded dirt road winding through one of the most mine-intensive areas in Colorado.

Silverton and Ouray sit on the famed San Juan Skyway [097], and Lake City is parked right on the Silver Thread Scenic Byway [079]. Both ends of this Alpine Loop have myriad places for food, fuel, and fun. One last observation—the road names of the Alpine Loop are inconsistently labeled on maps, both electronic and paper. Fortunately, because the Alpine Loop is an official Scenic Byway, the route itself is well-signed and marked.

Ride 81 **Wolf Creek Pass**

US 160

A classic 42-mile high-alpine pass journey, with river valley riding and sweeping, multi-lane ascents to the pass summit

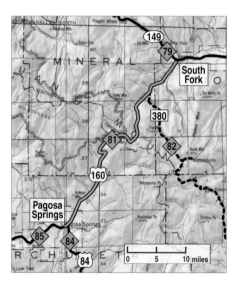

There's something about the name Wolf Creek Pass that makes it sound serious. At 10,863 feet, straddling the Continental Divide, it doesn't take a pillion seat to any other ridable pass. Whenever one approaches Wolf Creek, whether from the east or west, there is an anticipation, a quickening of the pulse rate. It's almost like finally getting on an amusement park ride after a long wait. In addition, this road has an attribute not found on most paved Colorado mountain passes—passing lanes much of the way up. This means the curves aren't as tight, but it makes the road a sweeper dreamland, with few to no impediments in front. Oh for sure, I get a sweet mule kick out of tightly pretzeled roads, but beautiful high-speed arcing curves pack an equally welcome wallop. So, welcome to Wolf Creek Pass and what it delivers to those who find the ride to be the main destination.

On the northeast end, US 160 passes through the roadside community of South Fork on its way to meeting the Wolf Creek challenge. It must be noted South Fork is also at the southern terminus of the magnificent Silver Thread Scenic Byway [079]. Linking these two top-tier rides together is a common and commendable idea.

A luscious tree-lined ride along the South Fork of the Rio Grande River will be the first attraction. At 7.4 miles from South Fork, note Forest Road 380 charting a path on the south side of US 160 for the ghost town of Summitville, and the heart-stopping beauty of the Stunner Pass area [082]. It is one of the great ones, but best for dual-sport bikes. As progress is made toward Wolf Creek Pass, the valley walls will narrow and steepen, becoming canyon walls. During spring snowmelt, the squeezed river roars through here in a show of white fury. Soon, the walls will widen, as does the road with the addition of a climbing lane. Have fun, but watch out here. There is a curving tunnel, or snow shed, below the pass summit. Inside, it hides a curve tighter than others that can catch an unprepared rider just cooking through. A few years ago I was descending on dry pavement. Upon entering the tunnel, I was greeted mid-curve with a river of snow melt crossing the lanes and a plodding, lumbering vehicle hidden by the tunnel walls. Not an experience I'd want to repeat!

The pass summit is broad, with parking on the south side for a pause to look at the view

The Rhoads family stopped atop Wolf Creek Pass in 1925, on their way to Mesa Verde. The view below, taken in 1930, is slightly more primitive in appearance.

and read the interpretive signs. Scenic wooded and meadowed views are presented east and west. The west side of Wolf Creek is a major riding blast. Back in 1975, country music artist C.W. McCall recorded "Wolf Creek Pass," a song about two truckers in an out-of-control Peterbilt on the pass descent he called "37 Miles O' Hell." The drama included these lyrics:

I looked at Earl and his eyes was wide

His lip was curled, and his leg was fried.
And his hand was froze to the wheel like a tongue
To a sled in the middle of a blizzard.
I says, "Earl, I'm not the type to complain
But the time has come for me to explain
That if you don't apply some brake real soon,
They're gonna have to pick us up with a stick and a spoon . . . "

At the bottom of the pass on the west side, turn the bike into a parking area for nearby Treasure Falls. It is worth interrupting the ride. The remaining 15 miles to Pagosa Springs are a nice wind down with the San Juan River showing the way. It is ultra-scenic here, especially with intimidating Wolf Creek Pass filling up the northern sky with her how-do-I-get-up-there rocky cliffs and outcroppings. Before making this transit, make sure you are prepared with food and fuel. There's no recourse between South Fork and Pagosa Springs. For a brief account of the interesting history of the mineral hot springs town of Pagosa Springs, see Ride 85.

Ride 82 **Stunner Pass**

Forest Road 250, 380, Park Creek Road

A magnificent 55-mile dual-sport ride along a river and past an old town, before scaling heights to a place of supreme beauty

Few dual-sport rides in Colorado impress me as much as this one. Perhaps I'm giving too much weight to how magical it is. The last time I made the traverse, somber rain clouds were parting and the sun's rays were shining spotlights on paradise-like meadows and rainbow-hued mountains—then again, I've also ridden it in a gray and steady rain. I would still take my bike on Forest Road 250 and 380 again and again. In my subjective view, this is a Top Ten off-road journey.

On the south end, Forest Road 250 leaves Colorado 17, right where the highway makes a big bend to the south toward La Manga and Cumbres Passes. The small townsite of Horca is at this bend, 22 miles west of Antonito. There are several launch locations on the north side, as noted below. From the south, the Conejos River will be

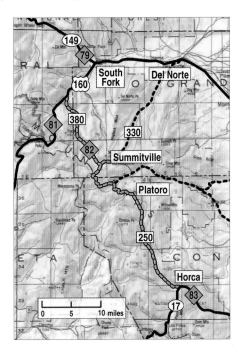

Platoro back in 1933, and today

your riding partner for the 22 miles to the old mining town of Platoro. This Gold Medal trout stream carves a winding path, broad enough for distant vistas, up through a valley laden with meadows, aspen, and steep rock faces.

For its entire length, the road surface for this tour is mostly a smooth and graded combination of dirt and gravel. A light and easy-to-ride street bike should be okay in dry conditions. When you arrive at Platoro, take a spin through the dirt streets of this old mining camp, or perhaps pay a shoreline visit to deep blue Platoro Reservoir 1.6 miles farther.

From Platoro, Stunner Pass at 10,541 feet is reached with a modest 800-foot riding ascent over four miles. There's a hardly noticeable ghost town here. The towns of Stunner and nearby Platoro never struck it big, and it didn't help when floodwaters of the Conejos wiped out this forest road. The government

opted not to make repairs following the closure of nearby forts at Pagosa Springs and Fort Garland. Plus, the narrow-gauge train out of Antonito laid tracks to the south over Cumbres Pass. For the hardy residents at these remote locations, it all added up to a major bummer, with cargo—such as mail—only deliverable by pack trains or riders. When winter paid a long visit, even those who were really hardy became fewer in number.

Two miles past the Stunner Pass summit, Forest Road 250 jogs to the east, also becoming the Alamosa River Road, and offers a return to the south side of the Alamosa area. The amazing mix of colorful, iron-laden peaks here, clothed in aspen above a park-like valley, is spectacular. But resist the turn toward Alamosa, and turn the handlebars left onto Forest Road 380 toward Summitville, for a wonderland of amazement awaits, in a setting straight out of a

Evidence of the 1915 mining operations near Summitville has since melted into the landscape.

fairy tale, or perhaps some kind of fantasyland movie. The road winds perfectly through this high-altitude landscape garden with stop-you-in-your-tracks sights on both sides and around every corner.

At eleven miles, Forest Road 380 departs northwest on a nice, 14-mile descent to US 160 near South Fork. Bearing to the right/ northeast onto Forest Road 330 will bring you to the very visible ghost town of Summitville. This mining camp was the largest and richest in the area. A gold strike in 1870 opened the door to a flood of miners and entrepreneurs, leading to a community boasting of 14 saloons, a newspaper, several hotels, and nine mills—all serving and employing the 600 residents. (That's one saloon for every 42 people!) If you continue past Summitville on Forest Road 330, it becomes Piños Creek Road and 28 miles of excellent dirt-road riding will have you and your idling bike at Del Norte on US 160.

Except for a small store and diner in Platoro, your food options will be at the lodge in Horca at the southern side of this ride, or someplace at the end of one of the three arteries extending out from the Stunner Pass area—Alamosa to the east, Del Norte to the northeast, or South Fork to the northwest. The South Fork option via Forest Road 380 and Park Creek Road is the shortest route to the Summitville area. Be sure you have the fuel for this 55-mile adventure, and even more in the tank if Del Norte is your start or end point. Camping and picnicking opportunities abound in the Rio Grande National Forest area. Recognize that a 50-mile off-road ride can take longer than you think, particularly if you're pausing at the town and nature sites along the way. With US 160 on the north side [081] and Colorado 17 on the south [083], the two-wheeled venture to and from this Platoro and Stunner ride can be a special addition.

Ride 83 **La Manga–Cumbres**

Colorado 17

A quiet and sweet 40-mile motorcycle journey along a beautiful river, over two mountain passes, and through high-alpine meadows, while delivering train history and a connection to an alternate route in New Mexico

Hey, I shortchanged this ride by calling it a 40-miler, because that is only the distance from Antonito to the New Mexico border. Most of you riding this made-for-motorcycles highway will cross the border and continue to Chama eight miles farther south, and the leg here will be part of a longer and more luxuriant trip. And if this isn't the case, just for the record, I could go blissfully back and forth on Colorado 17 all day

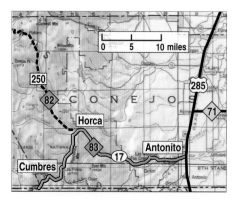

long, with the bike humming rpms below and me humming tunes above. This journey scores high in just about every ride-for-the-road measure, and it is worth the effort to cover the distance to get your bike there.

Cumbres Pass, at 10,022 feet, is modestly lower than its more northern sibling, La Manga Pass, at 10,230 feet, but Cumbres is the only reason for the existence of this lonely highway traversing two mountain passes between two rural towns. The pass was on the main line of the mighty Denver and Rio Grande narrow-gauge railroad between Alamosa and Durango. Much of what existed in the 1880s remains today, mainly because of the ongoing operations of the Cumbres and Toltec Scenic Railroad out of Antonito. Train enthusiasts consider the 64-mile trip through the Toltec Gorge to Cumbres Pass, then Chama and back, to be one of the most spectacular and magical

railed rides anywhere in the world. I'm not sure it's much different for those riding Colorado 17 on two wheels.

A few months ago I asked a fly-fishing guide operating out of Deckers, "If I could instantly teleport you to any fishing stream in Colorado, which one would it be?" He looked off into the distance for a second or two then responded, "The Conejos." As you ride Colorado 17 west out of Antonito along the crystal-clear waters of the Conejos, you will have a scenic and wild river as your entrancing companion. The first ten miles also contain a couple of faint communities and ranches of various acreages. Look to the north along the way and you will spot an elk

ranch. The Rio Grande National Forest imposes its forested will on the terrain at around 12 miles and the riding fun is kicked up a notch as the road sweeps horizontally and vertically alongside the Conejos.

At 22 miles riding west out of Antonito, you will come upon the small community of Horca, with the magnificent Forest Road 250 beginning its journey northwest toward Platoro and Stunner Pass [082]. The personality of this ride will change as you twist the throttle south on 17 toward the two passes. You'll gain 1,300 feet over the next six miles to the broad and grassy summit of La Manga Pass. The next twelve miles to the New Mexico border will be a high-altitude riding para-

The Cumbres curve in 1881, just below the pass summit

dise as you and your bike become as one, flying in tandem through a scenic, lonely, and undulating terrain you won't want to end. You will make a big circling lean around the historic Cumbres snow shed site. Soon after, you'll reach the top of Cumbres Pass before making a gradual, splendid descent to the border, and on to Chama, New Mexico, eight wonderful miles later. Yes, New Mexico has sweet riding as well!

There are minimal food and fuel service options between Antonito and Chama. The Conejos River Valley contains campgrounds and picnic areas, and a resort or two might have a general store open. At Horca, 22 miles into this journey, there is a lodge with the Chuck Wagon Cafe and Restaurant, but as with many remote and secluded places, there could be seasonal hours. Chama has an excellent High Country Saloon and Res-

taurant at the intersection of New Mexico 17 and US 84. Antonito's US 285 downtown contains several restaurants, but give them a look over. Your "confident" fuel choices are Antonito on the north and Chama on the south.

For sure, use New Mexico's Chama as a connector to continue this motorcycle venture. US 84 to the west [084] winds through scenic countryside all the way to Pagosa Springs on US 160. This has the potential of being an excellent circling ride, as does US 64 south then east of Chama back to US 285. If pointing your bike north on this ride toward Antonito, consider turning east at Manassa on Colorado 142 [071] for a pleasing ride to Colorado's oldest town. Oh, and one other thing! The huge and green aspen groves visible on this Colorado 17 ride would be huge and golden in the autumn.

Ride 84 **Chromo**

US 84

A winding road through the backcountry (28 miles in Colorado, 20 miles in New Mexico), crossing creeks and passing through hills, flats, mesas, meadows, and forests

To limit ourselves only to roads within Colorado is to shortchange this ride, as well as Colorado 17 to the east, drawing a figurative line at the New Mexico border. Southern Colorado possesses some of the best riding in North America, and things don't change just because of a man-made border. US 84 aiming southeast from US 160 in Pagosa Springs finds Chama, New Mexico, 48 miles away, or 20 miles "south of the border." While I don't think the New Mexico Board of Tourism was thinking of motorcyclists when they came up with the state motto "Land of Enchantment," northern New Mexico is an enchanting place to ride, and US 84 is a sweet route through Chromo, across the border to Chama and points beyond, including the Taos area.

You find well-marked US 84 on the far eastern edges of Pagosa Springs. After a mile or so of commercial presence, there is a thinning of suburban riding and a thickening of

the rural kind. Ranches, farms, and fertile meadows begin to appear, as does seemingly every kind of terrain lump and bump under the sun. In the first chunk of this ride, you'll fly through, over, or around Eightmile Mesa, Winter Hills, Kenney Flats, Klutter Mountain, and Mesa Cortado—I could keep listing other landscape features lined up all the way to New Mexico, but you get the idea!

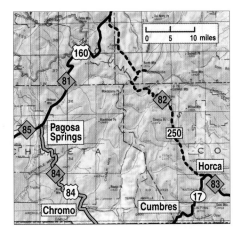

At 3.7 miles, Echo Canyon Reservoir stretches off to the right/west. It was built by the Colorado Division of Wildlife in 1968 as a fishing lake. An easy dirt road can take you to its shores for a picnic or for watching the action. And there is action at this stocked 73-acre lake. The state record largemouth bass at 11 pounds, 6 ounces, was hauled out of its 50-foot depths back in 1997. But feel free to continue spinning your two wheels on US 84, for its winding ways can seriously lure you.

The diverse landscape along US 84 contributes to its riding value. In addition to the terrain features and reservoir mentioned above, you'll come upon Halfway Canyon, and the Rio Blanco, along with numerous smaller streams. After your bike rounds a curve and you're facing east, before you will be an immense and impressive wilderness. The Stunner Pass ride [082] traverses this majesty of the South San Juan Wilderness. US 84 doesn't contain the alpine scenery observable from many other Colorado roads described on these pages, but it presents riding vistas that will serve as reminders of how you are venturing farther south in latitude.

Farther south, you will come to the small valley community of Chromo, a name derived from the Greek word for "color." The Navajo Peaks to the northeast are especially colorful when the rays of the setting sun light them up. This is horse ranch country nurtured by the Navajo River. A general store and gas station here can be a place where you pause and tie up your iron horse. Five miles later you'll come to the border with New Mexico, but fine riding continues 20 miles farther to Chama.

If you like a steady diet of sweepers interspersed with curves of a tighter nature, then welcome to a meal you can have every day and never grow weary of. If you prefer a quiet cafe versus a boisterous buffet, then welcome to a secluded and lonely journey with minimal traffic standing in line before you. You have a couple of connecting ride options from the Pagosa Springs area. To the west, US 160 to Bayfield is described in Ride 85. To the east is Wolf Creek Pass [081]. From Chama in New Mexico, turning the handlebars north on Highway 17 delivers the Cumbres and La Manga Pass ride [083], where you can make this a looping tour by connecting to US 160 on the north. The Pagosa Springs area is stocked with food and fuel options, so plan accordingly, with Chromo the only meager choice along the way to Chama. Where US 84 connects with New Mexico 17 in Chama, there is the well-regarded High Country Saloon and Restaurant.

Ride 85 **Pagosa–Bayfield**

US 160

A rolling 60-mile countryside ride through fields and forests interspersed with attractions, communities, and history

US 160 crossing Colorado's lower latitudes is one of the finer motorcycle passages across the state. Rather than discuss the whole of it in one piece, I have divided it into smaller portions, which is how many riders will consume the delectable motorcycling morsels found in this area. The stretch of US 160 described here runs from Pagosa Springs to Bayfield, then ten more miles to Durango.

The Pagosa Springs area is rich with history. For centuries, Native American cultures were drawn to nearby mineral hot springs. This is understandable, since hot water showers weren't found in many teepees. Tribes would fight to defend, if not seek ownership of, what the Utes called "pah gosah," meaning "healing waters." By the way, this translation is given by folks from the city of Pagosa Springs, but those less connected with the city's commerce say it more closely translates into "strong-smelling water." The Navajos and Utes frequently clashed over the sulphur-rich springs and decided in 1866 to settle the conflict with a one-on-one fight. Interestingly, the Utes

Albert Henry Pfeiffer

picked Albert Henry Pfeiffer, a U.S. agent in New Mexico who was well liked and respected by the Utes, but less so by the Navajos. Pfeiffer chose as his weapon a long 15-inch Bowie hunting knife. The Navajo fighter charged hard and fast to gain the upper hand, but Pfeiffer hurled his sharp instrument through the air, burying it in the Navajo's chest for a quick and decisive end. The Utes thus claimed the hot springs, and for 14 years it was so, until big daddy U.S. Govern-

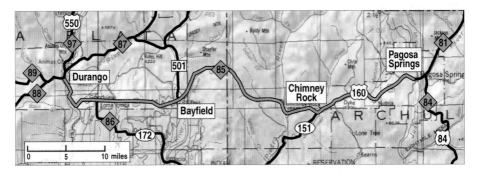

ment moved in declaring ownership in 1880. Bath houses and other structures appeared soon after, and thus Pagosa Springs got its heated start. Today it is a fun place to ride through, pause at, or stay a spell. Great motorcycle journeys branch off in every direction.

Pointing the front wheel west out of Pagosa Springs on US 160 will be rather uneventful for the first few miles as you pass through a sort of suburbia.

At 16 miles from Pagosa Spring's center, Colorado 151 [086] departs to the south, skirting around the Chimney Rock Archaeological and Historic Site, continuing to the massive Navajo Reservoir, and then on to a tour of the Southern Ute Indian Reservation before rejoining US 160 just east of Durango. Consider this as a longer, but equally enticing route to Durango.

US 160 presents some of its best riding on the segment between Colorado 151 and Bayfield. For 24 miles there is an enhancement of all that really matters when it is just you and the motorcycle out in the wind. After cresting the modest Yellowjacket Pass, at 7,770 feet, there is a meandering 800-foot descent which will deliver you to Bayfield ten miles farther. If you find yourself pondering your choices at the traffic light in Bayfield, and you're up for more, push the handlebars to the north onto County 501/Vallecito Road [087], which offers outstanding riding all the way to Durango. Things on US 160 from Bayfield to Durango, the next 12 miles, are less impressive as traffic increases along with the straightness of the road.

The two big towns at either end of this ride are your best bets for food and fuel fill-ups. There's little to nil between Pagosa Springs and Durango, though Bayfield has convenience stores with gas pumps. As for ride suggestions, there is the momentous Wolf Creek Pass [081] to South Fork via US 160 east out of Pagosa Springs. There are numerous dual-sport journeys north and south of US 160, but if going south takes you into the Southern Ute Indian Reservation, be sensitive to the fact that off-road riding may not be acceptable. To the north, the spectacular Weminuche Wilderness and other wild areas await, but many of the forest roads are out and back. Here are two circling or looping ideas for you out of Pagosa Springs: ride Colorado 84 [084] south to Chama, New Mexico. Take Highway 17 [083] back to Colorado, over Cumbres and La Manga Passes, and on to Antonito. Ride up US 285 to Alamosa, and then take US 160 over Wolf Creek Pass back the Pagosa Springs. Set aside an unrushed day for this spectacular tour. The other loop is toward Durango on US 160, returning to Pagosa Springs via Colorado 172 and 151. This would be a sweet half-day ride.

Ride 86 **Chimney Rock–Ignacio**

Colorado 151, 172

A 50-mile tour through the Ute Indian Reservation, passing by a massive recreation area, as well as the Chimney Rock National Archeological Area and Historic Site

This motorcycle excursion covers 50 miles, with most of its rolling course within the borders of the Southern Ute Indian Reservation. The Utes are the oldest continuous residents of Colorado. Today there are three main Ute Tribes. The largest in number are the Northern Utes, with headquarters at Fort Duchesne in Utah. The Ute Mountain Utes are located in Towaoc, Colorado, just southwest of Cortez, and the Southern Utes are headquartered in Ignacio, which you can pass through or pause at during this ride.

This journey through hilly ancient lands is kickstarted on the east side, where Colorado 151 connects with US 160 west of Pagosa Springs. At the west end seven miles east of Durango, Colorado 172 departs south for Ignacio, named for the long-lived Ute Chief. This route roughly parallels and is a longer alternative to the busier US 160 [085] to the north. Whenever I cruise US 160 between Pagosa Springs and Durango, I often push the handlebars south for this alternative route that probably takes twice as long . . . but you know, that's fine with me.

Heading south on Colorado 151 on the

east side of this traverse, you will be presented with a different view of the Chimney Rock Archaeological Area and Historic Site than you get from the US 160 side. Designated in 1970, the site contains more than 200 homes and ceremonial structures of Ancestral Puebloan Indians, with their lofty locations probably driven by a desire to be near the high and sacred rock pinnacles. A small visitor center three miles into this ride on the right is staffed in the summertime and worth a visit.

To be sure, the ride is also the destination here. Colorado 151 is a lonely and winding ride, through a brushy and hilly landscape filled with emerald pinyon pine, juniper, and

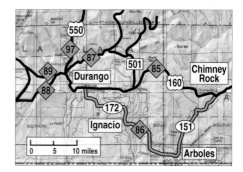

Chief Ignacio in 1880

Ute scouts crossing the nearby Los Piños River

A Ute Camp in 1880

cottonwood. The Piedra River draining the San Juan Mountains north of Pagosa Springs joins the show at eight miles and leads well for seven more before it empties its cold contents into the enormous Navajo Reservoir, which extends five miles south to the New Mexico border and then another 20 miles farther. It has been called Colorado's answer to Utah's massive Lake Powell. You don't get much of a sense of its size from Colorado 151, but there are state park facilities for camping, picnicking, fishing, boating, and the like. It is a full-service recreation area and the nearby community of Arboles does have a small store for supplies.

The composition of the ride changes after you make the turn west through Arboles. There is a widening and flattening. Views are farther, crops appear, and farms dot the fields for the next 16 gentle miles to the center of the Southern Ute Indian Reservation at Ignacio. The community here has a downtown area with food and fuel options, but so does the Sky Ute Lodge and Casino north of Ignacio on Colorado 172 with 146 rooms, eight luxury suites, five restaurants, and even a bowling alley. Ignacio Bike Week is the host of the Four Corners Motorcycle Rally, scheduled annually the week before Labor Day. There have been a few times in its 16-year run when it didn't happen, but it has returned the past several years and is a well-received and well-attended event.

The last one-third of this "ride through the reservation" is a 16-mile jaunt on Colorado 172 to its northern conclusion at US 160 east of Durango. The Los Piños River, also a watery contributor to the Navajo Reservoir, is the escort north out of Ignacio before it gives away to fertile green hay fields and unimpeded views of the towering San Juans to the north and the La Platas to the west on its way to US 160. Durango is a big town, ground zero for several motorcycle journeys. Don't be surprised to see riders and bikers everywhere!

Ride 87 **Vallecito**

Florida Road, Vallecito Road, County 240, 501

A winding, rural, 35-mile road to two reservoirs, past picturesque farms, ranches, and old homesteads

If I lived in the Durango–Bayfield area with a bike in the garage, I would ride this route all the time. If I had ridden to the area—perhaps to experience the great San Juan Skyway, or just passing through—I'd still probably make time for Florida Road. It is one of my favorite backroad rides. There's a manner, maybe even a politeness to how perfectly it curves around tidy country farms surrounded by thick fields of hay. One could ride alongside Florida River just for its artistic setting, but as with other river-led rides, the course chosen by this flowing stream adds to the motorcycling enjoyment. This road, tailored for motorcycles, is very much a destination, along with the sights and sites along the way.

On the west side, access to Florida Road begins on the north side of the downtown Durango area. Just before US 550 crosses over the Animas River, a sign points the way right to the Vallecito Reservoir. On the east end, turn the handlebars north onto

Vallecito Road at the main US 160 stoplight intersection in Bayfield. Florida Road has a humble beginning, passing through Durango suburbia for two to three miles. A few attractive residential areas dot the landscape, but the dots spread out and then are overtaken by forested countryside as you reach the Florida River.

Enjoy pastoral riding, literally and figuratively, for the next seven miles. Cattle will be dining in some of the narrow, river-fed pas-

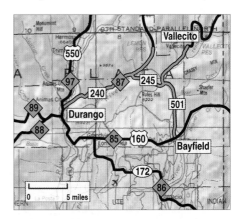

tures, and in other fields, shaggy growth is reserved for an autumn hay harvest. The river, transporting the snow melt of the southern San Juans to feed these fields, will also feed your bike that diet of bends and dips it thrives on.

A fork in the road will present two options. The left tine is a slightly bending road toward Lemon Reservoir less than two miles away, and the right tine is the direction to lean toward for Vallecito. Lemon Reservoir is a quieter lake, less developed, and in a more rustic setting. The shoreline is steep, but at the north end, the water of this stocked fishing lake is more accessible. Two campgrounds with picnic areas are available, and small camp stores on the south side might be open, but count on meeting your fuel and food needs at Durango, Bayfield, or even at Vallecito.

You will have three more enchanting miles from the Lemon Reservoir turnoff to the one you'll take for Vallecito. This time, ease off on the throttle at a T-intersection. A turn of

the bars to the right on Vallecito Road (County 501) brings 8.7 miles of gentle countryside riding to Bayfield on US 160. A push to the left places you at the razor blue lake in five sweet riding miles.

Vallecito is Spanish for "Little Valley," but there's nothing petite about this big sparkling body of water. There's also a fair amount of amenities for the motorcyclist—from restaurants, stores, and topping off the tank, to lodging, camping, and picnicking. Take a tour around the west side of the lake before making your return toward Bayfield or Durango.

In a way, this close-by ride on the northeast side of Durango is a cousin to the Wildcat Canyon ride on the southwest [088], in that both are shorter-duration journeys. If you have 60 to 90 minutes to relish some time with your bike, take a cruise on Florida Road to one of the two reservoirs, then on to Bayfield or back the way you came. US 160 at Bayfield is covered in Ride 85, and the San Juan Skyway at this ride's western end is detailed in Ride 97.

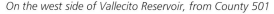

On the west side of Vallecito Reservoir, from County 501

Ride 88 **Wildcat Canyon**

Wildcat Canyon Road, County 141, Colorado 140

A rural 19-mile ride with curves and sweepers, through open fields, and past country homes, farms, ranches, and the site of a historic fort

This road and ride fit in the category of "If you're in the area, you should check out this nearby ride." Well, Durango is the area, and Wildcat Canyon to Colorado 140 is the ride. This little scoot adresses myriad concerns: you don't have much time, don't want to go far, want to explore, want to go a different way . . . you name it!

This backroad jaunt is found two miles west of the US 160 and US 550 intersection on the south side of Durango. Point the bike west on US 160 then make the turn south onto Wildcat Canyon Road. There's no warm-up here. You'll be fielding curveballs right away—you'll get three miles of them as you goose the bike up 500 feet to a high

rangeland area of farms and fields. The transition will be a nice one as you pass over a blind rise through a hillside cut.

Five miles of sweeping through high and hilly meadows will be up next. There is a green crew-cut of trees on the grassy knobs

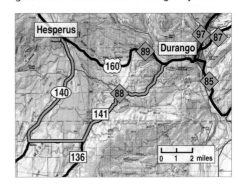

and ridgelines. Farms appear and fields expand, as do the views as another 300 feet is climbed. At this eight-mile mark, you'll make a bending turn to the west for a 3.3-mile-long fastball to a T-intersection at Colorado 140. Before leaning the bike into the bend, note that continuing straight on County 136 can provide a continued journey to the southwest.

There are all kinds of wandering county roads in this direction, all the way to the New Mexico border. County 136 is the most entertaining from a rider's perspective, permitting a 16-mile trek above Spring Gulch, concluding at Colorado 140 two miles north of the border. The Cinder Buttes to the south are the landmarks to look for.

From Colorado 141, a push of the bars north onto Colorado 140 will place you at Hesperus on US 160 in only eight miles. The La Plata Mountains loom large and larger as you approach US 160 on this excellent cruising road. Before making too much progress however, remember to make a few glances

to the left at around three miles after joining Colorado 140. This is the historic Fort Lewis area, named for a Colonel William Lewis, who died in a Kansas conflict with the Cheyenne in 1878. Initially, his name graced a military installation near Pagosa Springs, which was charged with maintaining civility in the area between the Southern Utes and settlers. Later the post became a fort, was moved to the area you are now riding past and then, with a diminishing need for frontier forts, it was transformed into Fort Lewis A&M College, the predecessor of today's Fort Lewis College in Durango.

So what to do with Wildcat Canyon? Well, first, it is a Durango area option when you're looking for a fine hour-long scoot away from congestion. Second, it can lead to exploring rides—some dual-sport—in the area west and southwest of Durango. And third, if a ride on US 160 between Mancos and Durango [089] is on the agenda, make the leg between Hesperus and Durango a Wildcat Canyon run.

Ride 89 **Durango–Mancos**

US 160

A 43-mile southern leg of the San Juan Skyway Scenic Byway that travels through farms and meadows, with sweeping ascents and descents

Many ride this stretch of US 160. Often it is a component of a longer journey and seen as a route to other motorcycle destinations, including the mighty San Juan Skyway Scenic Byway described in this and three other chapters. That said, this segment of the Skyway is worthy as a destination for your bike and can stand alone.

As you ride east or west on US 160, you will be following a well-worn path. With the rugged La Plata Mountains and her 13,000-foot peaks imposing a barrier to the north, and the dozens of north-south running canyons and mesas to the south, there was this narrow gap between the obstacles, chosen by many for east-west transit. For a sixty-year run, from 1892 to 1952, the Rio Grande Southern Railroad connected Durango to Mancos, then made a gradual turn north toward Rico and Telluride where it linked up with the Denver and Rio Grande Railroad. As you cruise along US 160, look for the old

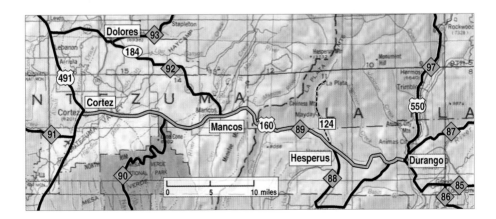

train bed on the side of the road. You can also reflect on earlier travelers—those journeying before motorized transportation—for this stretch of US 160 follows the path of the Navajo Trail and the Old Spanish Trail.

US 160 is the main east-west highway, cutting through Durango on the east and Cortez on the west. When riding west out of Durango, Wildcat Canyon [088] at 2.1 miles, is an alternative route to Hesperus ten miles to the west of Durango. After Hesperus there is a more rural and country feel to the scoot, as residences and other structures become fewer in number, and ranches and untamed acreage begin to dominate. The La Plata Mountains are an impressive towering sight as they stand watch on your north side. Take a look at the old Hesperus Ski Area on the south side of the road. When I passed through this area by car in 1978 with a friend, this was the first ski resort I had ever seen, with skiers carving down the slopes right next to the highway!

At 20 miles, a nice sweeping 300-foot ascent up the La Plata Divide and around Madden Peak will be before your handlebars, and it is tempting to twist the throttle a bit more on these high-speed curves. The sizeable town of Mancos is at the bottom of the other side. There you can push the bars right at the main stoplight onto Colorado 184 [092] and enjoy the reservoir-filled ride to Dolores. From there, connect with Colorado 145 for the world-class ride over Lizard Head Pass to Telluride and beyond [093]. Mancos calls itself "The Gateway to Mesa Verde" for good reason. Stay on 160 through Mancos seven more miles and your bike will be idling at the entrace of Mesa Verde National Park [090]. Cortez, eight miles farther, has full services, as well as ride connections to the Canyons of the Ancients National Monument [091] and the western leg of the San Juan Skyway via Colorado 145.

Connecting rides from the Durango area on the east side include the inimitable US 550 to Ouray [097], the Florida Road to Vallecito [087], US 160 to Pagosa Springs [085], and the Southern Ute Indian tour from Ignacio to Chimney Rock [086]. And this short list doesn't include the dual-sport routes suggested in other parts of the book. Speaking of dual-sport ventures along US 160, you should check out County 124 on the north side of Hesperus. It follows the La Plata River past the ghost town of Mayday and on up to the remains of old mines, such as Gold King and Cumberland.

Ride 90 **Mesa Verde**

Mesa Verde Park Road

A scenic, 60-mile, round-trip tour of a national park, serving up a series of fun riding bends and climbs, and culminating with a visit to significant archaeological sites

Riding through state and national parks can deliver truly special moments on the bike. Mesa Verde National Park is no exception, and as a riding road, it has few peers. For 30 miles, as the main park road climbs to the top of the mesa, it makes turns in the soil like a sidewinder does on sand. As the road twists back and forth, the distant views keep changing. The amazing archaeological sites at the end of the road form a grand finale, and the experience is repeated on the way out!

Mesa Verde National Park was established in 1906 by President Theodore Roosevelt to "preserve the works of man." It was the first national park to protect this kind of attraction—4,000 archaeological sites providing a glimpse into the lives of the Ancestral Puebloan people who made the area their home for more than 700 years, from AD 600 to AD 1300. The main attraction for many is the spectacular cliff dwellings tucked under massive rock overhangs and squeezed onto small ledges in cozy rock crevices. You undoubtedly will be trying to fathom how they made it to, or departed from, their adobe-walled structures without falling hundreds of feet! Mesa Verde means "green table" in Spanish, and it is descriptive of the park terrain with its summertime emerald green juniper and pinyon pine. There are more than a dozen table-topped mesas you ride by and

over, with numerous named ridgelines and canyons completing the landscape.

Access to the park is off US 160 eight miles east of Cortez, seven miles west of Mancos. The park entrance fee is $10 per vehicle, good for seven days, and well worth it. The riding

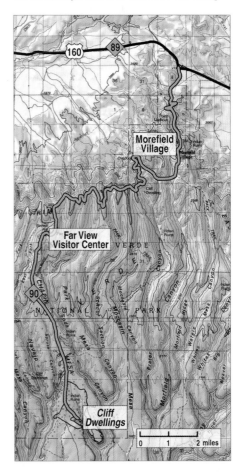

joys begin immediately as you wind up and around Point Lookout. After 3.5 miles, and 1,000 feet of elevation gain, there is a fine scenic lookout to the east with the Mancos Valley far below. US 160 [089] is seen sweeping through the checkerboard of farms in the valley. About a mile past the lookout, the park headquarters and Morefield Village Visitor Center will be on the right.

Ride through a tunnel and then you'll en-ter a seemingly endless series of S-curves of varying duration and radii. The Montezuma Lookout will compete for attention with Park Point Lookout, so keep your riding wits intact. At 15 miles, the Far View Visitor Center and Lodge will appear on the right. This is another place for a pause, or perhaps an overnight stay.

From here at the halfway point, the ride flavor and texture changes significantly. In-

stead of carving through green shrubby trees, around and over blocky mesas, the ride becomes a relatively flat cruise through the blackened trees on top of Chapin Mesa. Views south to the distant horizon are of New Mexico. You will be entering the main exhibit areas of the park. For the renowned Cliff House, Balcony House, and Sun Temple sites, follow the route directly south from the Far View Center—signs point the way. At five miles, you will approach a stop sign at a crossroads. A sign with arrows indicates the viewing sites ahead and to the left. Parking areas a short stroll from overlooks, and balconies are available for a sidestand deployment.

The trip down from the Far View Center is often through a gauntlet of charred trees, the aftermath of the 1996 Chapin Mesa Wildfire sparked by lightning, which consumed 4,781 acres. The 2000 Bircher Fire, elsewhere in the park, torched 19,709 acres.

Since 1934, 11 wildfires over 35 acres in size have rampaged through Mesa Verde, every one of them ignited by lightning. Occasionally, new archaeological sites are uncovered by the flames thinning the dense underbrush, but fortunately, damage to the exisitng ancient structures and sites has been light.

The nearby towns of Cortez and Mancos offer food and fuel options before entering the park. The Morefield Village Visitor Center on the right, 3.6 miles into the park, has gas pumps and a general store. Camping is available in the park at designated areas, and lodging exists at Far View, 15 miles into the journey.

If I were to offer one suggestion, it would be to visit and ride the park early in the morning, before the heat and before the traffic. There's something about having a place like this almost to yourself, with the road empty before and behind you.

Ride 91 **Canyons of the Ancients**

McElmo Creek Road

A paved 26-mile curving backroads journey through scenic farms and red-rock canyon country to the Canyons of the Ancients National Monument, Utah, and beyond

This motorcycle road in Colorado's southwest corner follows the weaving, rock-carving whims of McElmo Creek. The terrain here is consistent with other rides bordering Utah, and they all bring an enchanting difference to the typical Colorado Rocky Moun-

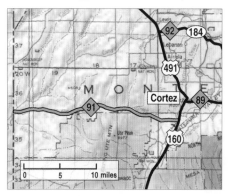

tain ride. The deep presence of an immense archaeological area increases the value of this ride.

Because of the remoteness and isolation of this region, few visitors (or riders) pass through the specially designated areas on this road. The McElmo Creek Natural Area, a 433-acre state preserve on the north side of the road, is recognized for the rare reptiles living among its unique rock formations. Later, the road cruises through the Canyons of the Ancients National Monument, home to more than 6,000 archaeological sites. In parts of the monument, the concentration of structures—dwellings, small villages, etc.— exceed 100 per square mile. These are ancient lands of numerous Native American cultures, which existed from hundreds of years ago to thousands of years ago.

Access to McElmo Creek Road is from US 160, about three miles south of Cortez. There is a stoplight here where you will point the front wheel toward the west. The first few miles will be rather ho-hum as you skirt the airport area and other commercial entities. A few bends and dips liven things up a bit as rural homes and farms establish a presence. Soon you'll start to sneak in views of McElmo Creek as it wends its watery course through the salmon-colored rocks of numerous canyons, with names like Trail Canyon, Goodman Canyon, Moccasin Canyon, and Yellowjacket Canyon. Formations like Cannon Ball Mesa, Battle Rock, and Big Point will loom above you.

In step with the improving visual delights is the quality of the riding, as the road wraps around rock outcroppings, descends into dry and sandy washes, then climbs again for a repeat. There is an unevenness to the road surface, as if the soils have shifted beneath

it, but this is minor. The sense that you are entering the monument area is confirmed when signs and pullouts make roadside appearances. You can hike this area for days and not see a living two-legged soul, but round a cliff or outcropping of apartment-sized rocks and you could stumble across the structural remains of dwellings used by those living here many moons ago.

The ride continues into Utah, where a network of primarily dual-sport roads can take you through a lunar landscape of history, mostly protected by the Hovenweep National Monument. On the right bike, you could continue this excursion and wander south to Utah 262, then turn east back to US 160, making this a circle ride. There are also dirt-road journeys to the north eventually connecting with US 491, for a more northerly loop. If motorcycle camping is your accomodation of choice, this would be my kind of "get lost" place. On the east end, Cortez is where you will want to make sure you are food- and fuel-ready.

Ride 92 **Mancos–Dolores**

Colorado 184

A sweeping 26-mile backroad ride through and over high plateaus, delivering far-ranging views and access to numerous nearby lakes and reservoirs

Colorado 184 delivers a rural, 26-mile ride around the northern reaches of Cortez, following a zigzagging course from 18 miles east of Cortez, to 11 miles northwest of town. The views of the 13,000-foot La Plata Mountains to the east are ever-present, while the table ridgelines of Mesa Verde National Park absorb the southern horizon. Farms, fields, and forests fill the foreground. When the bike crests low hills along the way, you can see the Canyons of the Ancients National Monument and Sleeping Ute Mountain Ute Indian Reservation as the distant landmarks to the west.

On the east end, Colorado 184 takes off to the north at US 160's main traffic light in Mancos. For at least 1,000 years, the valley of the Mancos River has seen natives of the Anasazi, Navajo, and Ute pass through and sometimes settle. The 1700s brought Span-

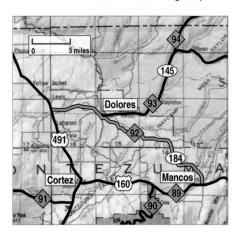

ish explorers including the noteworthy Dominguez-Escalante Expedition described on historic markers found along US 160 [089]. It is said the river-fed grasses refreshed the expedition's horses and the river was given the name of Mancos. I found the Spanish meaning of "mancos" to be "one-armed," as in doing something well with only one arm, but just how that relates to the story is still a mystery to me.

Only a quarter-mile north on Colorado 184, you will come to a sign pointing the way northeast to Mancos State Park. The shoreline of Jackson Gulch Reservoir, along with the park facilities, is just five wandering miles away. Continuing on Colorado 184, the turn northeast at 1.7 miles onto County 41 will bring you to Bauer Lake in a mile. At 8.2 miles, Summit Reservoir is a half-mile south on County 39. Then at 9.5 miles, turn on County 35.6 to reach Puett Reservoir. Finally, you can get to Lost Canyon Reservoir by turning north on County 35 at 10.2 miles.

Colorado 184 gives you a lake break as it delivers one long curve after another— through green or golden fields depending on the month, and between country homes or farms depending on the scope. There's a nice riding flow here as you lazily lean to the left then right, or right then left. You know, sometimes a ride is enlivened by passing through places where people live and work the land, and who give a wave or watch you

pass by on that sweet motorcycle of yours. Colorado 184 eventually comes to a T-intersection with Colorado 145. One mile to the right/northeast is the fine town of Dolores with food and fuel options. You can be excused if you want to bail out of 184 here, for Dolores is the southern gateway to Colorado 145 and the western leg of the San Juan Skyway [093].

Colorado 184 continues, partnering with Colorado 145 for one mile to the southwest before branching off to the northwest on its own course. At 1.5 miles there is the Anasazi Heritage Center, and three miles later, the entrance to huge McPhee Reservoir less than a mile away—also on the right/north side of the highway. Finally, the parade of lakes concludes two miles later with the very visible Narraguinnep Reservoir. You'll ride a mile of shoreline before letting off the throttle for Colorado 184's T-intersection conclusion.

There you can turn left/south on US 491 for Cortez ten miles distant, or right for Colorado 141 and Slick Rock [100] which are 26 miles away.

So, how to consider Colorado 184? Well, from the Cortez area it would make a nice, 60-minute circling ride at any time of day—easily extended by checking out one of the seven lakes mentioned above, having a picnic, or stopping at one of the many restaurants in Cortez, Dolores, or Mancos. Colorado 184 is also a shortcut for those riding the San Juan Skyway, bypassing the stoplights and traffic of Cortez, giving your iron horse a pleasing pasture on which to roam. Last, but not least, the community of Mancos has trademarked the phrase "Gateway to Mesa Verde" for good reason. If coming from the north, Colorado 184 to Mancos will deposit you seven miles east of its park entrance off US 160.

Ride 93 **Lizard Head Pass**

Colorado 145

An acclaimed 90-mile classic alpine Colorado ride, serving up some of the best riding and scenery in the state

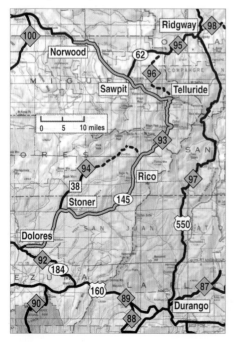

Colorado 145 is the western leg of the nationally renowned San Juan Skyway. On a map, the scenic byway has the rough shape of a rectangle. This ride explores the incredible 72-mile western side of the route, and then scoots past the Skyway's northwest corner for 18 sweet riding miles to Norwood. Of the many roads and rides explained on these pages, the scenery of the San Juan Skyway, as encountered from the saddle of a bike—from any vehicle for that matter—is among the most spectacular you will experience anywhere.

With formidable obstacles all around, early road designers had to go with the flow—literally. This meant following the designs of tumbling streams through grassy valleys and rocky canyons with a ribbon of road alongside—which never disappoints a motorcyclist. Also, with the streams up high lacking the force to carve a mighty course through mighty granite, the road had to overcome a mountain pass and other steep slopes along the way—also agreeable with motorcyclists

Dolores, just ten miles north of Cortez at the southwest corner of this Skyway rectangle, is a suitable jumping-off point. Several Cortez area rides can be easily connected to, including Colorado 184 from Dolores to Mancos [092]. The journey north on 145 here is exquisite right off the bat, with the whitewater of the Dolores River cascading beside the road. At 12 miles, County 38 [094] charts a path to the north and it is outstanding.

Thirty-six miles into this 3,200-foot climb toward Lizard Head Pass, you will come to the historic mining camp—now town—of Rico. Check out the Enterprise Bar & Grill, a historic 1892 landmark on Main Street/Colo-

rado 145. The pass summit is your next destination, and to be sure, this is in addition to the ride itself being the destination. The namesake of the pass is clearly identifiable, towering above on the west just before you arrive at the 10,222-foot crest. Look north and behold the scenic setting before you. When you are able to pull your attention away from the view, descend three miles and turn the noggin to the east to view Trout Lake with its alpine backdrop. Though you might want to pull over here, the shoulder is narrow. Go another few hundred feet, and there will be a road to the lake's shoreline.

You will continue to lose elevation as you descend the Wilson Creek drainage. At 9,200 feet, it levels off at a turnoff to small, historic Ophir with its 100 residents, three miles to the east. The turn is midway through a sweeping curve leading to a hillside-skirting ascent through thick stands of aspen. You must glance west during this mild climb and

The 400-foot pinnacle of Lizard Head at 13,113 feet. Many climbers bagging all the peaks above 14,000 feet are glad this treacherous spire isn't 900 feet taller!

Telluride, looking east in the late 1890s. Guess without snowplows even horses could get stuck in deep snow. The freighter has his 52 mules loaded with 17,000 pounds of cable for the construction of the Nellie Tramway.

admire one of the shapeliest mountains in Colorado—the 14,017-foot Wilson Peak. There is a scenic pullout on the west side of Colorado 145 for a sidestand deploy and pause at this alpine postcard place.

Seven miles north of the turn to Ophir, Colorado 145 comes to a T-intersection where a turn left/west continues the Skyway ride and a turn right leads to the National Historic District of Telluride and the ski slopes above. It is worth the turn to Telluride three miles away, just to see the dramatic

Trout Lake in its alpine postcard setting

box canyon setting of this Victorian town. Festivals and events are a common occurrence, and it could be timely for a food or fuel stop. Excellent dining establishments are present all along Telluride's Main Street.

Like many other mountain communities, Telluride's roots were planted near where miners planted explosives in search of precious ores. Silver was the lode most harvested in the vicinity. Telluride is a compound containing the element tellurium combined with some gold or silver. Curiously, the town was named Telluride even though there was no tellurium in the area.

Heading west from Telluride on the Skyway, you will get a second view of Wilson Peak's grandeur before the road dives down into the long and deep San Miguel Canyon. For 22 miles you'll relish a sequestered and winding ride along the banks of the San Miguel River before a sharp 800-foot climb pulls you out of the depths and onto plateaus surrounding Norwood three miles away. By the way, if you intend to continue riding the San Juan Skyway rectangle, don't miss the Colorado 62 [095] turnoff at Sawpit in the canyon.

From Norwood, twisting the throttle west for 18 miles will have you idling at the Naturita doorstep of three noteworthy rides—Colorado 141 through Slick Rock [100], Colorado 90 toward Utah [099], and the extraordinary Unaweep-Tabeguache Scenic Byway to Gateway and beyond [101]. I didn't touch upon the dual-sport options much in this ride, for they are everywhere in the Colorado 145 vicinity—and I mean everywhere! Dedicated dual-sporters astride nimble bikes will want to check out the high and rocky passes heading east, like Ophir, Black Bear, and Imogene. Above, I mentioned the special County 38 heading north out of Stoner for Dunton and the backsides of the incredible San Miguel Range [094]. There's also the Dolores–Norwood Road aiming north out of Dolores for an alternative route to Norwood. Finally, check out Last Dollar Road [096] for larger dual-sport bikes, which ascends the slopes north of Telluride and proceeds on to the Dallas Divide.

Two others have discovered the sweet ride along the West Dolores River.

Ride 94 **Dunton**

West Dolores Road, Dunton Road, County 38, Forest Road 535

A 32-mile mix of pavement, light dirt, and gravel, along a lonely and scenic river valley, passing by a historic town-turned-resort, then leading to a high and very scenic plateau.

About ten years ago, a climbing friend and I set off to scale the majestic peaks of El Diente Peak (14,159 feet) and Mt. Wilson (14,246 feet) in the San Miguel Mountains. We turned west off Colorado 145, just a few

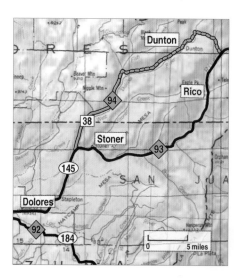

miles north of Rico, onto Dunton Road. Immediately, signs warned us that the road was closed up ahead as heavy rains had washed out the dirt road. Great. This meant driving the car way down past Stoner, then coming from the south on a lonely dirt road up a river valley. I remember how it seemed to take forever to get to the trailhead at "The Meadows." But I also remember how incredibly beautiful this tucked-away valley was, with the mineral-laden slopes of the San Miguels towering over the northeast end. So this unplanned and unappreciated detour resulted in the discovery of a great motorcycle road.

West Dolores Road/County 38 branches off Colorado 145 about 12 miles north of Dolores. For the first 13 miles, the road surface is fine pavement. If you are on a dual-sport (or even a mild street bike), Cotton-

wood Road/Forest Road 532 cuts off to the northwest for five miles of creekside riding to the Dolores–Norwood Road, which is a gateway to all kinds of off-road ventures to the west and north. Continuing on County 38 to the northeast, the West Dolores River provides a national park kind of tour through picturesque ranches in "I could see myself living here" settings.

At just under 14 miles, the surface switches to a graded, pea-gravel-sized surface. An easy-to-ride street bike would be fine, although one could turn around here and tally this up as a great motorcycle fling to this point. While the road surface changes clothes, the river keeps dancing away in its tuxedo of sparking white and mirror blue, inviting us to keep up with its moves.

Arrival at undisturbed Dunton comes 22 miles from Colorado 145. Dunton is a ghost town turned high-end hot springs resort. Precious ores nearby led to the town's formation in 1885—a post office was established in 1892. The Emma Mill was the big producer, and the population scratched together almost 300 souls before the mills became small producers as the ore ran dry. By the 1920s it was a ghost town. For decades

the structures faded and decayed until investors bought the town, refurbished and rebuilt it, transforming it into a luxury resort. Supposedly Butch Cassidy and the Sundance Kid would sneak a drink or two at the same bar where you can theoretically down one, but it isn't clear to me how "open" this establishment is. This I know: the setting is classic Colorado. I also know I felt a little conspicuous—in a good way—as the bike and I moved through the scene as guests watched this adventurer aim for the intimidating San Miguels up ahead!

To this point you will have gently ascended 1,300 feet over 22 miles. The road is now called Dunton Road and it leads you up a 1,200-foot climb in only five miles. A sweet, shelfy ledge will be the finale before arriving at a presentation of 10,000-foot views. To the north are the colorful and massive San Miguels. Looking east, the meadowy route to Rico is five miles distant and 600 feet lower, with the San Juans forming a backdrop 4,000 feet above that. By the way, on the final stretch to Rico you can see where a giant culvert was placed as part of the road reconstruction following the washout. I suppose the chance for "washed out road" angst has been minimized with this improvement, but I'm kind of glad that detour of long ago took me onto West Dolores Road!

The towns of Dolores on the south and Rico at the northwest are the service options for this 32-mile ride, with Dolores having a more plentiful selection. The historic 1892 Enterprise Bar & Grill in Rico is a draw, as noted on the Colorado 145 and Lizard Head Pass ride [093]. Since this ride is basically a parallel route north to Rico, it can be an attractive choice if you have the time and the right bike. It can also be taken as an out-and-back journey to the pavement end or to Dunton, before returning to Colorado 145.

Ride 95 **Dallas Divide**

Colorado 62

The northern 23-mile leg of the San Juan Skyway Scenic Byway, delivering a sweeping journey over a modest pass with immodest views

Colorado 62 is the highway linking the eastern and western transits of the famous San Juan Skyway Scenic Byway. It has its own character and style, with views rivaling anything, anywhere. This roadway was first a toll road built in the 1880s to link the mining camps along the San Miguel River to the Uncompahgre River Valley on the east. A relatively low pass, or divide, named after a nearby creek, was traversed to make the connection. Ten years later the Rio Grande Southern Railroad laid tracks over the 8,970-

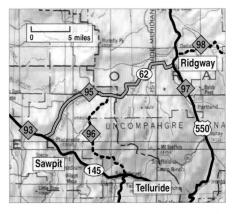

foot Dallas Divide to make the link a motorized one.

Colorado's Highway 62 is not a long-lived thing, serving only to link US 550 on the east with Colorado 145 on the west. But it lives well in these 23 miles. On the east side, you'll launch the Dallas Divide ride from the community of Ridgway. Movie buffs might know the area as the setting for John Wayne's *True Grit* and the epic film *How the West Was Won.* Originally, Ridgway was the 1890s setting for a railroad town, built to support the new connection to Telluride. The community has seen its ups and downs, including a 1950s plan to inundate the town with the construction of the Ridgway Reservoir. A 1975 decision moved the dam farther north; the town of Ridgway was spared, and thus it was called by some as "The Town that Refused to Die."

The ten-mile, 2,000-foot climb to the Dallas Divide begins soon after pointing the front wheel west on Colorado 62 out of Ridgway. The first four miles deliver a winding climb through a mosaic of small farms and pleasant fields. The next six miles serve up a broad ascent with postcard views of the jagged Sneffels Range growing in stature before you. Many of the ranches around here are of the coffee-table-book kind, though you can't always see the structures.

The descent toward Colorado 145 is less airy, with tree-covered valley slopes sneaking closer. Just one mile west of the divide summit is Last Dollar Road [096] wandering off to the south. This is a renowned dirt-road route to Telluride. Continuing west, and dropping in elevation, Leopard Creek joins the ride at it drains the higher flats and plateaus. The creek here has carved a valley deep and steep enough earn it the designation of Leopard Canyon. And as we motorcycling aficionados know, when a stream guides the way, and a canyon is involved, gratitude is sure to follow.

At the western end of Colorado 145 [093] is the sunset side of the San Juan Skyway. US 550 at Ridgway [097] is your eastern portal. Many rank the Skyway as as one of the Top Ten rides in the country. If astride a dual-sport or perhaps a dirt-friendly street bike, consider the Owl Creek Pass traverse [098] just north of Ridgway which climbs east toward Chimney Rock, or Last Dollar Road to Telluride [096]. There aren't any food or fuel options along Colorado 62, but choices are bountiful on the Ridgway side. The small community of Sawpit, two miles south of the Colorado 62 and 145 intersection, has a mercantile store with food and gas. In addition, 15 miles farther south on Colorado 145 is the historic resort town of Telluride.

Ride 96 **Last Dollar**

Last Dollar Road, Forest Road 638

A winding, ultra-scenic 20-mile country ride of mostly graded dirt, through and around meadows and mountains, with plenty of photo opportunities

When I ride Last Dollar Road, it is usually just me on a dual-sport and people on a commercial Jeep tour out of Telluride. Knowing the texture of Last Dollar's easy-to-ride road surface, I don't think a Jeep is necessary for the scenic, high-altitude climb, but folks may be looking more for the roofless "ambiance" of the ride. If they only knew what it was like to experience movement through the mountains in a truly open-air vehicle! But I can see why tourists sign up for Last Dollar Road excursions. It is one of the most visually magical journeys around. The Telluride area on the south and the Dallas Divide on the north lure sightseers from far away places every year, especially when the aspen are changing into their golden garments. You'll ride through this dressing room and then onto the stage with some amazing mountain, canyon, and ranchland vistas.

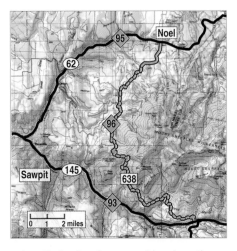

Last Dollar Road was an old and gentle wagon supply route built to connect Ouray with Telluride during the mining boom days of the late 19th century. It can be found on the south end, three miles west of Telluride, right where Colorado 145 makes the turn

south for Lizard Head Pass [093]. On the north side, it is 1.4 miles west of the Dallas Divide off of Colorado 62 [095]. When departing north out of the Telluride area, you will be greeted with a quick 600-foot ascent in the first mile. A step through the door, and Last Dollar shows you around some of Telluride's high-end residences, but—more notably—some of Colorado's high-end scenery.

The first couple of miles are paved, and then a smoothly graded, treated gravel surface takes over, which any street bike can handle. The snaking road delivers an excellent ride north toward the peaks of the Mt. Sneffels Wilderness, then south overlooking the red cliffs of the San Miguel Canyon—the resplendent Wilson Peak at 14,017 feet soaring behind and above. As experienced from your saddle, this is waaaay up there on the Why I Ride a Bike scale.

For the next six miles, to the halfway point of this ride (at ten miles), a 1,800-foot grade up to the 10,600-foot "pass" is the next act of this panoramic show. Numerous switchbacks help with the altitude gain and it is in these open meadow, wildflower-filled fields that the Jeep gang will pull over, paying customers piling out for the amazing vistas.

Against a backdrop of mountains, hillsides overrun with aspen—especially in their glorious autumn gold—are a photographer's dream. During these six climbing miles the road quality will be the most "challenging." Things are more gravelly and rutted. Dual-sports would have no problems, but I think an easy-to-ride street bike on the lighter side of the spectrum would be okay.

The northern ten miles to Colorado 62 and the Dallas Divide are defined by a moving picture of majestic ranches framed by the photogenic Sneffels Range. There is openness here, and the riding on smooth graded dirt is fun and fast. You might have to sidestep some open range cattle, and navigate through more stands of aspen, but this is Grade A scenic road riding—as is the entire length of Last Dollar. Consider this road as an alternate route to and from the Telluride area from Colorado 62 on the north end. One could also make this a sweet circling ride of around two hours by going one direction on Last Dollar Road and returning via Colorado 62 to Sawpit, then riding wonderful Colorado 145 through the San Miguel Canyon. There is an excellent full-service fuel and food station off Colorado 145 right where Last Dollar Road starts its journey north.

The technology and materials available for building avalanche sheds have evolved considerably since 1888.

Ride 97 **Million Dollar**

US 550

A spectacular, world-class 80-mile ride through deep mountain valleys, over high mountain passes, and through historical Victorian towns on the eastern leg of the famed San Juan Skyway Scenic Byway

I have separated the four sides of the 238-mile San Juan Skyway "rectangle" into four separate rides in this book, since each side deserves its own coverage. Besides, more often than not, one does not ride the whole thing, but instead enjoys a section or two at a time. (Said another way, most don't consume the whole Thanksgiving bird at one sitting, but return for another leg, then another . . . forgive me for this analogy.) Of the four appendages of the Skyway, this one from Durango to Ouray and on to Ridgway is the most famous—and deservedly so. More than a few writers employed by the motorcycle magazine press have declared this section of US 550 their favorite riding road in the country. Once you ride it, you will see why.

The Durango & Silverton Narrow Gauge Railroad has been in continuous operation for 130 years, and comes alongside on two rails while we putt along on two wheels. You

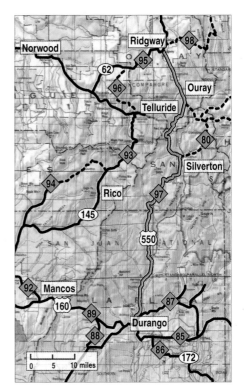

will part ways 13 miles north of Durango when the train blows a farewell whistle for a descent to the Animas River Canyon. Indeed, you will fare well as you traverse high over Coal Bank Pass and then Molas Pass, before making a great riding descent to Silverton.

From Silverton to Ouray, this Scenic Byway takes on the additional name of "Million Dollar Highway." In some circles it is the name given this entire route, but historically it has only applied to this 21-mile stretch between Silverton to Ouray. There is uncertainty as to where the name came from, but the two top legends are "It cost a million dollars per mile to build," and "A million dollars worth of gold ore was unavoidably used in the fill dirt."

And a spectacular stretch it is. I am hard-pressed to think of a more amazing, breathtaking, awe-inspiring, section of paved road anywhere.

The descent to Ouray is world-class riding (as is the ascent when riding the other direction). On the north side of Ouray, a fine Uncompahgre River ride brings you and your bike to Ridgway at the northeast corner of this San Juan Skyway rectangle, and to the conclusion of this side of the Skyway.

Ride US 550 early in the morning if you can. To be sure, it is magical any time of day, but you will be sharing the road with many others, and the chance for thunderstorms—building up and then dumping down—increases as the day goes on. Even though the early morning could be cool, there's nothing like experiencing an almost empty Skyway.

If you find that lumbering RV blocking the view or backing up traffic, pull over at a pass summit or at a wide spot. Inhale all that is around, give it some time, and then don't twist the throttle until you know there is a

Approaching Ouray from the south in 1882 . . . and today.

good gap between you and what's ahead. The few minutes of delay is a small price to pay to be able to enjoy the magnificent scenery and undulating ride to its fullest.

As with most of the rides described in this book, the Million Dollar Highway can be ridden either direction, but I lean toward going north out of Durango versus heading south toward Durango. Arguably, the first ten miles or so out of town, with the traffic, are the most ho-hum. It is nice to get this behind you right away. You will also have the sun shining mostly from behind you (morning sun versus afternoon shade) as opposed to directly into your eyes. Going north delivers more dramatic views as you ride toward the mountains, and the descent toward Silverton and Ouray is more spectacular. But to be sure, direction change can transform a ride, making it almost seem like a different road. If you can't choose, a ride up to Ouray and back (or vice versa) would be one of the best half-day rides anywhere.

Give yourself all day to ride the 238-mile San Juan Skyway Scenic Byway, which, in addition to this chapter and US 160 to the west, also includes Colorado 62 [095] at the top, and Colorado 145 [093] comprising the western slice. Clockwise or counterclockwise? Going counterclockwise gets you out of Durango before 550 gets too congested with traffic, and gives you more special breakfast and lunchtime choices in Silverton and Ouray than on the lonely west side, though you can't go wrong in Telluride. The advantage of the clockwise direction is the jaw-dropping scenery between Telluride and Lizard Head Pass filling up the space in front of your handlebars rather than the tiny canvas of your mirrors. The choice is yours. Of course, you could ride the loop clockwise one day and the other direction another day. It is amazing how different the journey can be.

Last thought—make sure your digital-camera battery is fully charged.

Chimney Rock and Courthouse Mountain stand guard over Owl Creek Pass.

Ride 98 **Owl Creek Pass**

County 8, 10, Forest Road 858, Big Cimarron Road

A 40-mile ride (for a dual-sport or lightweight street bike), through dense aspen forests, underneath intimidating rock formations, and alongside open ranch country

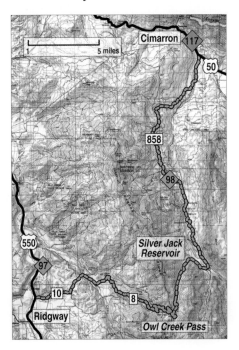

Owl Creek Pass is named after the creek draining the organ-pipe-like slopes of the Cimarron Ridge. The rock formations on both sides of the pass will have you stopping the bike and reaching for your camera—or regretting that you didn't bring one. Two of the more notable crags are Courthouse Mountain at 12,152 feet, passing judgment on all who ride by; and Chimney Rock at 11,781 feet, standing as a beacon over the pass summit.

The Owl Creek Pass begins where County 10 turns off US 550 to the east, just 1.7 miles north of Ridgway and the traffic light intersection of US 550 and Colorado 62. In four miles, County 10 connects with County 8, and this will be your road all the way to the top. By the way, County 8 also connects with US 550, but it is four miles farther north of the County 10 entrance and is less direct from the Ridgway area. Big Cimarron Road is the doorway on the north side, 22 miles east of Montrose off US 50.

Any dual-sport bike would be at home on County 8, and an easy-to-ride street bike shouldn't have any woes, if conditions are dry and the bike can handle a graded gravel road. A quick test would be to ride your bike on the smooth dirt-and-gravel surface for a short spell—either from County 10 on the west side, or Big Cimarron Road at the north. What your bike tastes here is essentially the same fare that is served the rest of the way, even up high at the pass summit.

On the sunset side of US 550, behold a 17-mile, 3,000-foot climb to Owl Creek's crest (10,114 feet). Look east, and the pinnacle of Chimney Rock will tower above you to the south. You won't always see its formidable spire because of the dense stands of white-trunked aspen trees that fill your near view. This would be an amazing place in the autumn. This road was built over an old cattle trail and it seems as though some of the bovine descendants have never left the sanctity of the aspen! Last time I rode through, it was only me and hundreds of scattered black cows. I was like a grain of salt somehow sprinkled with the pepper on an aspen salad.

The pass summit is timid, sheltered by the forest, in a small park-like setting with a bubbling stream. It does invite a sidestand-down pause. The east-side descent (now Forest Road 858) is thickly forested at first, but after several miles of elevation loss, serious panoramas unfold with wildflower carpeted meadows rolling up to the base of steeply impressive rock outcroppings. The Uncompahgre Wilderness is the undisturbed setting, and most likely you will be the only one there. This idyllic state faces only minimal adjustment as there may be a couple other people around when you approach Silver Jack Reservoir a few miles later. Silver Jack is a rustic, untouched, high mountain

Silver Jack Reservoir graces the midpoint of this wilderness ride.

lake, in a calendar photo setting. There are no facilities or services. Nothing but what a nature lover cherishes, what a photographer seeks, and what an exploring spirit rides for.

The quality of the remaining 20 miles to US 50 can't be overstated, as a gently meandering descent lowers the elevation from 9,200 to 7,200 feet. The road base continues to be unpaved but fine. The views—in your mirror or over your handlebars, depending on your direction—are drop-dead and distractingly gorgeous. Ranches begin to make an appearance as progress to the north continues, with smaller farms and country homes becoming more prevalent near US 50 [117]. All of this is an encore to a great show of a ride.

Cimarron at the terminus has two convenience stores for a snack or gas tank refill.

Ridgway on the west end presents more meal options, as well as rides like the San Juan Skyway toward Ouray [097], and Colorado 62 over the Dallas Divide [095]. Many on US 550 or US 50 have intentions of going through Montrose to get to each other. What many don't know about or consider is how Owl Creek Pass can chaperone the venturing rider to the same destination on a route that is also a destination. Give yourself plenty of time for Owl Creek Pass—40 off-road miles do not happen quickly. You will need two to three hours to make the traverse.

One last note for the movie aficionado—after a ride over Owl Creek Pass, rent John Wayne's 1969 classic western movie *True Grit,* and try to spot the scenes filmed in the area.

Ride 99 **Bedrock–Paradox**

Colorado 90

A paved 34-mile valley and canyon ride through mesmerizing solitude, leading directly to and from Utah

This is one of the better motorcycle-friendly routes to eastern Utah and US 191 running north-to-south from Moab down to Blanding, where the great Utah 95 begins its westward journey. But you don't have to ride it merely as a way to get somewhere else, you can ride this utterly lonely road in a vast, yet scenic and unspoiled place just for the journey itself.

Naturita, at the eastern side of this ride, can trace its beginnings to livestock ranching, with cattle drives to the railhead of Placerville near Telluride a once-common sight. Copper mines became a common sight in the early 1900s after ore discoveries in the Paradox Valley. Nearby deposits of uranium then took over the headlines in the 1940s and 1950s until collapsing prices in 1958 closed the Vancoram Ore Mill. This mill at nearby Uravan—which processed much of the uranium for the government's nuclear weapons research—restarted on occasion,

but its operations ceased permanently in 1983. Today, Naturita is a diversified crossroads community with several good riding highways extending out in different directions.

This Sharp Canyon ride begins south on Colorado 90, about one mile west of Naturita's town center. The first few miles skirt around the Sawtooth Ridge then ascend a 400-foot rise west to the long and narrow Paradox Valley on the other side. The road is a straight-arrow gauntlet between

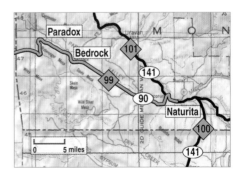

the Davis Mesa on the south and the Martin Mesa on the north. From the point of view of a turkey vulture circling high overhead, you will be the only moving speck in this sagebrush landscape. It is understandable if you feel the urge to exercise the thoroughbred saddled beneath you while shooting this 13-mile gun barrel to the general store in Bedrock. It is also understandable if you desire to lope through at a more serene pace.

Though it is hard to believe, scant Bedrock, at 19 miles, has a general store and a gas pump! For the movie buff, a scene from the 1991 movie *Thelma and Louise* was filmed here, where Louise makes a phone call to an FBI agent. Your escape will continue by pointing the bike west toward the community of Paradox and then on to the riding gift unwrapped by the Sharp Canyon.

The cluster of homes at Paradox two miles off the highway might lure you for a quick pass through, but honestly, you won't miss much by keeping the wheels planted on Colorado 90. The ten miles from here to the Utah border and beyond is outstanding. The 1,000-foot ascent up and then through the white and red rocks of the Sharp Canyon

area is motorcycle sweet, and the rush continues another four miles into Utah before the road (now Utah Highway 46) calms down and meanders 17 miles to La Sal Junction and US 191.

You'll have a small oasis at the Bedrock Store—otherwise, do not count on any services in the 55 miles from Naturita to La Sal Junction in Utah. Moreover, the last time I checked, La Sal Junction had nothing, so your best bet in Utah would be Moab, 22 miles north on US 191, or Monticello 30 miles south. Prepare thyself. This Colorado 90 ride would be an excellent route to the riding wonderland that is southern Utah. There is nothing like it in the world. By the way, two miles east of Bedrock, a sweet dual-sport journey awaits your turning north onto the Y11/River Road following the Dolores River into the canyon country of the Unaweep-Tabeguache Scenic Byway [101]. You can also connect from Naturita by riding Colorado 141 northwest out of town. Southeast of Naturita, two exceptional, but different motorcycle journeys await—the secluded Colorado 141 south to Slick Rock [100] and the renowned Colorado 145 [093] and the western leg of the San Juan Skyway.

Ride 100 **Slick Rock**

Colorado 141

A secluded 60-mile journey through canyon country, with sweeping curves and views and one special twisting climb

Two lonely rides are birthed south and west out of Naturita, this one, and the Colorado 90 journey to Utah [099]. Like fraternal twins, they start their journey together from the north in a broad canyon, make a gentle ascent, present a tempting long straight, and then make a second, but less gentle ascent above a big valley. Colorado 141 has a little more energy than its sibling, however, as it drops down again to another sweeping valley before making a ridiculously fun climb to a high and fertile plateau.

The presence of uranium and vanadium in the rocky soils near this ride is a key reason this remote road wanders through the desolate but scenic landscape. Mines near the Slick Rock area, including the big North Continent Mill, supplied ores for the 1940s wartime Manhattan Project and contributed to the U.S. Government's nuclear needs for decades, until 1982 when the mill structures were dismantled and the mining equipment removed. What does remain is this wonderful, snaking motorcycle road through a remote place, and it isn't difficult and imagine the wartime activity here 70 years ago as you pass through.

Colorado 141 toward Dove Creek from Naturita makes an eastward jaunt for four miles before turning south and then southwest toward its final destiny. The first twelve miles wind a course through shrubby pines dotting a broad kind of canyon called . . .

A Blake family moment, in 1897

The North Continent Mine, circa 1920

Broad Canyon. County U29 intersects two miles farther after emerging from the modest gulch—the last time I passed through here, a general store with food and gas was at the southeast corner. Take note and check your gas and gastrointestinal levels. This is it for the next 46 lonely and sweeping miles.

The first of two six-mile-long, ruler-straight sections of road will tempt you to air your bike out. Sneak a glance to the south if you can, and you might spot the residents of the Spring Creek Basin Wild Horse Management Area. After you cross the impressively huge Dry Creek Basin, and the five-mile-wide Big Gypsum Valley, you will wind through Gypsum Gap, two breaks (or gaps) in the high valley walls, and then enter Disappointment Valley. Here is opportunity number two to put spurs to the bike, or just go with the right flow for the moment. Whatever mode or zone you and your bike are in, the tempo is about to be modified as you enter the entertaining Slick Rock area.

There is a 1,600-foot gain in elevation over ten miles in this multi-colored Dolores River Canyon country. I remember the first time I put a bike through its paces in the tightly coiled Slick Rock riding area—unexpected curves, unexpected vistas, and an unexpectedly beautiful river setting. Despite the beehive of mining activity decades ago, a naturally scenic form is in place and it enhances the riding experience of this twisting, elevation-gaining ribbon of road.

The conclusion of the ride is a 15-mile, mostly straight shot to Colorado 141's junction with US 491. There is a wholesale change to the texture of the landscape as crops replace sage, flats replace hills, and company replaces solitude. At US 491 you can turn the handlebars to the east for services at nearby Dove Creek or Cortez 37 miles farther. A turn to the west will have you at the Utah border in seven miles, with the town Monticello 13 miles past that. At the north end, Naturita is between two amazing rides: Colorado 141 continues its amazing course north as the Unaweep-Tabeguache Scenic Byway [101], and Colorado 145 heads southeast toward Telluride and Lizard Head Pass [093]. In addition to fuel options in Naturita, there are two diners on Main Street to check out—Sandy's Cafe and Blondie's Drive-In & Cafe.

Ride 101 **Gateway**

Colorado 141

A special 90-mile scenic byway journey through through deep canyons and valleys and alongside streams and ranches, with a memorable destination community midway

This ride traverses 90 miles of a landscape filled with grandeur and heart-stopping scenery. The scale is intimidating. You'll feel a sense of humility as you pass between thousand-foot-high sandstone walls, the heights of which are enhanced when contrasted with the diminutive two-wheeled bike between your knees. And the nature of the ride will change as you swap altitudes and ride from one canyon into another. There's nothing ho-hum about this journey. Note that if you were to take away the dwarfing panoramas all around and remove the postcard settings, leaving just the strip of pavement, you would still want to ride this serpentine, tailored-for-motorcycles ride again and again.

From the north, this scenic skyway begins at the small community of Whitewater, six miles south of Grand Junction's southern suburbs on US 50. A sign points the way, you point the bike, and away you go on an always-special ride. There is no preamble or warm-up here. You will cross over the Gunnison River immediately as it flows to its rendezvous with the Colorado River, and after a lazy left-hander you'll dip into the park-like Unaweep Canyon. This canyon will be your guide for the next 30 miles, and you'll likely be inclined to give it a generous tip at the end of this tour. At 13 miles is the turn-off to the east of Divide Road [102]—a long and lonely, dual-sport ride up high on the

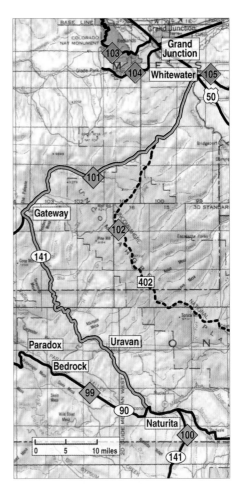

Uncompahgre Plateau—and at 20 miles you rise over modest Unaweep Divide. Unaweep means "out of two mouths" and you have a mini Continental Divide here. Behind you, a seasonal East Creek delivers water to the

Gunnison, and ahead of you West Creek aims toward the Dolores River—as you eagerly do as well!

West Creek makes a determined run for the Dolores 20 miles away, dropping 2,000 feet and bringing you engagingly along with it until you arrive at Gateway, at the confluence of West Creek and the Dolores River. As you approach, even at a distance, previews of what lies ahead will be presented over your handlebars. The contrast between this and what is in your mirrors will be striking. Say goodbye to abundant greens beneath towering granite escarpments at a coolish 7,000 feet. Say hello to shrubby scattered plant life in the shadows of red sandstone walls at a warmer 5,000 feet.

Gateway is so named because it was and is a gateway to Utah—four miles away, as the raven flies. If a dual-sport has taken you

here, great off-road rides scatter in all directions from Gateway, including the John Brown Canyon toward Utah. Gateway can trace its existence to mining, lumber, and livestock ranching, but over the years its out-of-the-way location contributed to a slow decline.

A reversal of fortune occurred when John Hendricks—founder and chairman of the Discovery Channel—decided to redevelop the town. Like an oasis appearing in a desert, a resort containing a hotel, restaurant, general store, and car museum appeared! Also, recognizing the attraction of this road to motorcyclists, plates for sidestands are bolted into the parking lot asphalt. With the Palisade landmark soaring above, the resort in Gateway is a timely place for a stop or stay. Grab a meal, fill the gas tank, check out the museum, and figure out how you can

somehow get some additional time off and extend your ride.

The 30 miles south of Gateway will be canyon riding at its finest. Utah canyon riding features similar scoots (Glen Canyon comes to mind), and its own enormously special, rock-wall journeying that is second to none, but this long stint in the deep and narrow Dolores Canyon is distinct. Those in cars and trucks, as impressive as they think this chasm is, don't know what they are missing by not experiencing it from a curve-carving, open-air, motorbike in the shadows of thousand-foot sandstone cliffs, sometimes only feet away from your throttle hand. As the mouth of the canyon begins to open up at the southern end at about 30 miles from Gateway, look for a parking area on the west side with interpretive signs. This is the Hanging Flume overlook with the visible remains of a "hanging" viaduct built in 1891 to carry water seven miles to various area mines. The flume, placed on the side of sheer rock faces high above the river, makes one consider the fortitude, if not the sanity of the suspended workers who constructed the viaduct!

Six miles past the Hanging Flume overlook you'll reach the abandoned and mostly swept-up Uravan town and mill site. Uravan (URAnium and VANadium), with 800 residents at one time, supplied milled ores for the country's nuclear weapons research. Naturita, 15 miles farther, is a small town with fuel and cafes for the bike and you, where you can connect to the Colorado 90 [099] and Slick Rock [100] rides.

Looking back at Colorado 141, as Divide Road climbs out of Unaweep Canyon

Ride 102 **Uncompahgre Plateau**

Divide Road, Forest Road 402, County 90

A lonely 90-mile dual-sport ride high up on a plateau with aspen, hidden valleys, and meadows overlooking canyon country

This secluded journey, unlike other remote rides in the Eastern Plains or the northwest corner of Colorado, has 90 miles of remoteness. Random thoughts, like, "What if the bike breaks down 53 miles into this fling? Or doesn't start?" add a little extra zip to the whole experience of Divide Road.

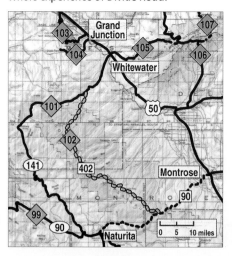

Uncompahgre is from the Ute Indian language and means, "rocks that make the water red." Long a place where the Utes would live and hunt, many of the forest roads crossing this high plateau were placed on old trails used by the Utes and subsequently ranchers and loggers over the years. Divide Road cuts a long and searching, north-south path over the heights of this high "tabletop" between the Gunnison and Dolores Rivers. The north end of this ride is 14 miles west of Whitewater off the great Unaweep-Tabeguache Scenic Byway [101]. A sign on Colorado 141 points the way. The south entrance is off County 90 linking Montrose and Naturita.

From the north canyon entrance at Colorado 141, you will engage immediately in a 1,400-foot, fun climb up to the plateau. Pause to sneak a peek to the west for a view of the Unaweep Canyon that is not commonly seen. The road surface at the north end is graded, but with loose gravel for at least 20 miles. The texture of this forest road tightens and becomes more compact as progress is made south. If loose gravel doesn't bother you, then I can see a light and capable street bike up here. Your call, but this is dual-sport Shangri-La, for sure. Be on the lookout for hidden forested canyons on the east side of the journey and hidden grassy parks on the west side.

In my opinion, the farther south the bike flies, the more exceptional the flight is. Stands of aspen are cathedral-like to ride through. What is it about a traverse through thousands of aspen that is almost spiritual? Multiple divine moments come at around 50 miles into this pilgrimage when, for about ten miles, you'll be riding high and exposed, 4,000 feet above the valleys and canyons containing the Dolores River far below and to the west. You will not be able to resist stopping and standing in the silence, taking in the magnificent panorama before you. Now, one could certainly have a picnic or snack at one of the campgrounds along the way, or anywhere along Divide Road for that matter, but I would probably claim a big rock here and make it my humble table.

At 65 miles you will ease off the throttle for County 90. A push of the handlebars toward the east leads to Montrose and to the west to Naturita. Both are about 25 smooth dirt-road miles distant. Montrose is a gateway to points east and only 25 miles north of Ridgway—which sits at the northeast corner of the San Juan Skyway [097], and at the west entrance of Owl Creek Pass [098]. Naturita tantalizes with all kinds of two-wheeled journeys commencing nearby—Colorado 141 south through Slick Rock [100],

Colorado 90 to Paradox and Utah [099], and Colorado 141 north through the Dolores Canyon, Gateway, and back to where this ride started. On the right bike, a great circling ride could be to head north/south on the Divide Road, and a return on Colorado 141 a/k/a The Unaweep-Tabeguache Scenic Byway. With all the forest roads crisscrossing the plateau, this can also deliver days of dual-sport adventuring.

As mentioned elsewhere, when a long off-road journey is in the works, it is worth repeating how it can take longer than planned, and the 90 miles here is no exception. Give yourself a healthy and relaxed three hours minimum, four with stops. Might as well call it a half-day venture! If you are making the commitment, recognize there is a 100-mile, food-and-fuel gap between Whitewater and either Montrose or Naturita. And it does take a commitment to experience the treasures of the isolated Divide Road, but as it frequently seems to be, things that are most special are often those not easily attained.

Southwest

RECOMMENDATIONS

Circling Tours

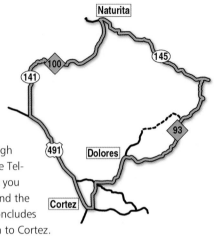

1. From Cortez, ride north on Colorado 145 through Dolores, over Lizard Head Pass [093], and to the Telluride area. Continue on 145 to Naturita where you turn south on Colorado 141 for Gypsum Gap and the Slick Rock [100] ascent. When Colorado 141 concludes at US 491, point the bike southeast for a return to Cortez.

2. From Durango, ride the San Juan Scenic Byway [097] taking US 550 north over three mountain passes, and through the towns of Silverton and Ouray, to Ridgway. West from Ridgway, ascend the Dallas Divide on Colorado 62 [095], then descend to Colorado 145 in the San Miguel River Canyon. Turn southeast toward Telluride, where Colorado 145 makes a turn south for Lizard Head Pass and the town of Dolores [093]. Colorado 184 [092] on the south end of Dolores bypasses Cortez, connecting with Mancos on US 160 [089], where you can join it for the return east to Durango. This is one of the great ones, and it delivers a much different kind of ride clockwise versus counterclockwise. Each direction has its advantages.

3. From Durango at the north side of the downtown area, find the signs on US 550 pointing the way east to Vallecito Reservoir and Florida Road [087]. Enjoy its rural winding route all the way to Bayfield. Turn the bike east onto US 160 [085] for a 25-mile cruise to Colorado 151 [088] departing south for the Navajo Reservoir and the Southern Ute Indian Reservation headquartered at Ignacio. Follow Colorado 172 north out of Ignacio for a return to Durango.

4. From Ridgway, ride west on Colorado 62 [095] over the Dallas Divide to Colorado 145 [093]. Turn northwest, ascending out of the San Miguel Canyon for Norwood and Naturita. Colorado 141 (Unaweep-Tabeguache Scenic Byway) takes over in Naturita, leading to the very special Dolores Canyon and Gateway [101]. At 141's intersection with US 50, turn the handlebars right/south for Montrose, where US 550 will bring you back to Ridgway.

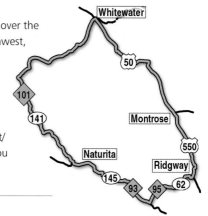

5. From Pagosa Springs ride US 84 [084] through Chromo south to Chama, New Mexico (Yes, we're being adventurous here). At Chama, ride New Mexico 17 to the north (becomes Colorado 17 at the border) and it will escort you over Cumbres and La Manga Passes [083] before dropping down to accompany the Conejos River ride all the way to Antonito. Ride north on US 285 for Alamosa, connecting with US 160 for a return over Wolf Creek Pass [081] back to Pagosa Springs.

6. From Poncha Springs, South Fork or Gunnison, ride the Silver Thread Scenic Byway [079], with US 285 and Colorado 114 [077] on the east side.

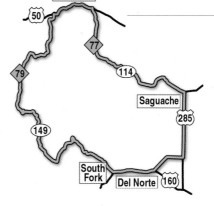

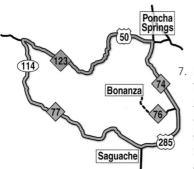

7. From Saguache at the northwest end of the San Luis Valley, connect with Colorado 114 to the west [077]. At its US 50 conclusion, ascend Monarch Pass to the east [123], where US 285 at Poncha Springs will deliver Poncha Pass [074] and a return to the Saguache area. Optionally, make a short, smooth-dirt detour to the semi-ghost town of Bonanza [076].

Linked Dirt-Road Adventures

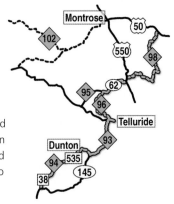

1. Twelve miles north of Dolores off of Colorado 145 [093], County 38 departs to the north for Dunton [094] and the backside of the San Miguel Range. Pavement is the surface for 14 miles before graded gravel is introduced near the historic community of Dunton. Continue on Forest Road 535 for the ascent to the San Miguels and The Meadows. Colorado 145 is rejoined a few miles later. Scoot north on 145 over Lizard Head Pass to Telluride. here 145 comes to an intersection just west of Telluride, Last Dollar Road [096] is a hundred yards or so to the east. This will bring you up and over to Colorado 62 [095] where you can scoot west for Ridgway. The Owl Creek Pass ride [098] begins its journey to the east and US 50 here. As an alternative ending from Ridgeway: ride up to Montrose instead of Owl Creek Pass and explore the Uncompahgre Plateau via Divide Road [102].

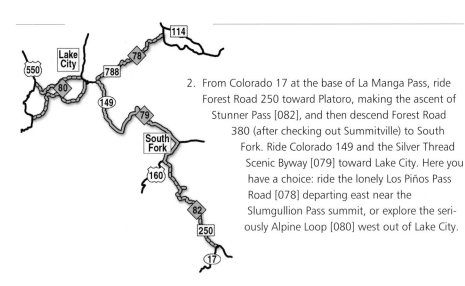

2. From Colorado 17 at the base of La Manga Pass, ride Forest Road 250 toward Platoro, making the ascent of Stunner Pass [082], and then descend Forest Road 380 (after checking out Summitville) to South Fork. Ride Colorado 149 and the Silver Thread Scenic Byway [079] toward Lake City. Here you have a choice: ride the lonely Los Piños Pass Road [078] departing east near the Slumgullion Pass summit, or explore the seriously Alpine Loop [080] west out of Lake City.

Favorite Rides

Best Cruising Journeys

- [084] US 84 from Pagosa Springs to Chama, New Mexico
- [085] US 160 from Pagosa Springs to Bayfield
- [087] Florida Road to Vallecito Reservoir
- [093] Colorado 145 from Dolores to Norwood
- [094] Paved part of County 38 toward Dunton
- [097] US 550–Durango–Ouray
- [101] Colorado 141–Whitewater–Naturita

Best Sporting Curves and Sweepers

- [077] Colorado 114 through Cochetopa Canyon and over North Pass
- [079] Colorado 149 from Blue Mesa Reservoir–to South Fork
- [081] US 160 ascent of Wolf Creek Pass
- [083] Colorado 17 over La Manga and Cumbres Passes
- [100] Colorado 141 in the Slick Rock Area

Best Dirt-Road Adventures

- [080] Alpine Loop
- [082] Forest Road 250 over Stunner Pass, to Summitville
- [094] County 38 from Dunton along the San Miguel Range
- [096] Last Dollar Road
- [098] Owl Creek Pass

Little-Known Gems

- [082] Forest Road 250–Stunner Pass–Summitville
- [087] Florida Road to Vallecito Reservoir
- [088] Wildcat Canyon
- [090] Mesa Verde
- [091] McElmo Creek through the Canyon of the Ancients
- [094] County 38 to Dunton
- [096] Last Dollar Road
- [099] Colorado 90 from Naturita to the Utah border and beyond
- [100] Colorado 141 from Naturita through Slick Rock to Dove Creek

Worthy Destinations

- [076] Semi-ghost town of Bonanza
- [079] North Clear Creek Falls off Colorado 149
- [079] Windy Point Lookout, Slumgullion Pass
- [079] Lake San Cristobal near Lake City and Colorado 149
- [079] Lake City and Creede along the Silver Thread Scenic Byway
- [080] The ghost town of Animas Forks
- [082] Ghost town of Summitville
- [083] Cumbres & Toltec Scenic Railroad
- [085] Pagosa Hot Springs
- [086] Chimney Rock off Colorado 151
- [087] Lemon and Vallecito Reservoirs
- [090] Mesa Verde
- [091] Canyons of the Ancients
- [093] Trout Lake north of Lizard Head Pass off Colorado 145
- [093] Telluride near Colorado 145
- [094] Historic town-now-resort community of Dunton
- [096] Wilson Peak from Last Dollar Road
- [097] Anything along US 550 from Durango to Ouray
- [097] Silverton and Ouray on US 550
- [097] Durango & Silverton Narrow Gauge Railroad
- [098] Autumn aspen of Owl Creek Pass and [096] Last Dollar Road
- [099] Bedrock Store in Bedrock, near Paradox, on Colorado 90
- [101] Town of Gateway in the Dolores Canyon
- [101] Hanging Flume off Colorado 141, Dolores Canyon
- [102] View of Dolores Canyon from Uncompahgre Plateau

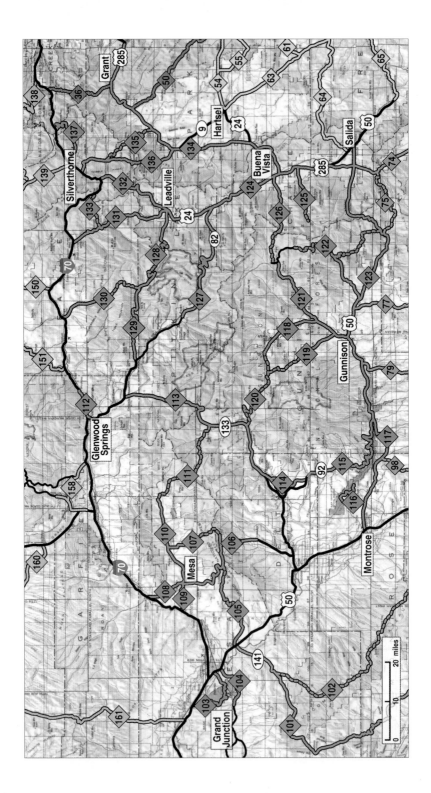

Central West

REGIONAL OVERVIEW

I've ridden most continents, twisting the throttle through places motorcyclists travel far to experience, and I would say the Central West region of Colorado holds its own against the best anywhere. In my opinion, it contains some of the finest, most diverse riding in the world. Seriously, from the alpine tundra heights of Independence Pass to the dark shadowy depths of the Black Canyon of the Gunnison, from the green meadows of South Park to the red sandstone canyons of the Dolores River—all can be experienced in a single day of riding.

This Central West region is roughly bounded by the Continental Divide on the east, the Interstate 70 corridor on the north, US 50 on the south, and the Utah border on the west. It contains a magical kingdom of motorcycle riding in the heart of the Colorado Rockies.

Rides in This Section

Ride 103 **Colorado National Monument**

Rim Rock Drive

A 23-mile tightly twisting ride through the rock canyon scenery of the Colorado National Monument

When the area was first settled, many thought the sheer-walled canyons towering above Grand Junction's western sides were inaccessible. Perhaps I am of the same unadventurous ilk, for when I look up at these

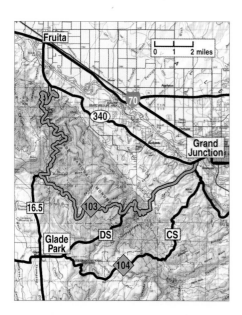

vertical rock faces rising 1,500 feet, I'm meekly thinking, "No way." Fortunately, 100 years ago John Otto, a free spirit who lived year-round in a tent in these canyons, began exploring, building trails, mapping the geography, and promoting the grand beauty of this amazing wilderness area. The Grand Junction Chamber of Commerce, hearing of his work, sent a delegation to investigate, and the rest, as they say, is history. Motorcyclists are among the many who can thank John Otto for his spirit of adventure and exploration.

To reach the eastern end of the 23-mile Rim Rock Drive, take Monument Road just off Broadway southwest of downtown Grand Junction. Numerous signs throughout the city point the way. On the west end, the entrance will be south of Fruita on Broadway, also known as Colorado 340. The fee for motorcyclists to enter the Monument is $4.

From the east, the smoothly paved road is determined to get you and your bike up

1,500 feet immediately to the plateau above the canyons. Say hello to a festival of ascending curves for the first four miles, and it is a well-choreographed party with sandstone monoliths and outcroppings in attendance to watch your progress.

The map for this ride gives you a hint just how kinked and crinkled these 23 miles are. From end to end it is only eight miles as the crow flies, but as the rider goes, it is almost three times as long! The advantage, of course, is leaning your bike into the seemingly endless variety and number of curves. The disadvantage is needing to avoid gazing at the airy spaces and deep drop-offs so you don't experience flying in a whole different way. The solution is to pull over at one or more of the 19 signed and interpretive scenic viewpoints.

There are some ride alternatives along the way. At 4.4 miles from the east entrance, you can cut over to the west via the DS Road and leave the Monument for Glade Park. You can do the same at 12.1 miles, where a turn left/south onto Road 16.5 will also lead to Glade Park and its 100-year-old store. This is the kind of place where I like to put the sidestand down. Of course, at the intersection 12.1 miles later, you don't have to turn toward Glade Park. You can continue to enjoy the buffet of curves and vistas that Rim Rock Drive serves up.

The Rim Rock ride through the Colorado National Monument is a must-do when you are in the area. You should set aside at least an hour for the 23-mile transit, and longer if stopping often, including at the Saddlehorn Visitor Center. You can extend the riding of this canyon country by linking with the nearby Little Park ride [104].

Ride 104 **Little Park**

Little Park Road, CS Road, DS Road

A paved, rural 14-mile ride through open canyon and mesa country, with sinuous stretches of twisting roller-coaster-like travel

Little Park Road is a quiet strip of rural asphalt, which runs through nameless gulches, along the rim of named canyons,

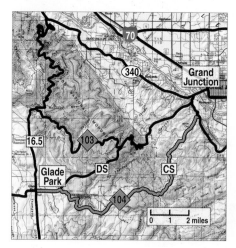

and generally ascends the flanks of the 70-mile-long, 10,000-foot-high Uncompahgre Plateau. Little Park also has the appeal of proximity to a population center, and it provides convenient access to a national monument.

Little Park Road is located southwest of Grand Junction, just off D and Rosevale Roads. It serves up a residential ride for the first mile or two before becoming a devilishly crooked road. Even the desolate, sun-baked, and rocky terrain nearby fits the theme here. For a spell, you will be riding alongside the rocky edges of Bangs Canyon and No Thoroughfare Canyon. Several parking pullouts exist with trailheads for hikes in the deep depressions.

If you're headed southwest, stealing a quick glance at your mirrors will reveal big views of Grand Junction, the Colorado River Valley, and the Book Cliffs hemming it all in. Keep the glance a quick one, for this is not a road on which to be distracted. Various curves can be tight and some of the short hills are of the "whoop" kind, which don't reveal what is on the other side until the last moment. The road surface itself has some choppy moments. It reminds me of nearby Douglas Pass [161] with its scattered undulations. I have heard the area is seismically active and that the restless earth is the source for the minor depressions and rises in the road base. Regardless, you don't want to be slightly airborne just as you need to carve your way into one of the many compact bends of the road. Stay alert!

Fourteen miles from Grand Junction, you will arrive at Glade Park. There is an intersection here, and a 100-year-old store where you can pause for a break and some snacking. You can continue straight if you find yourself in exploring mode and want to see more of the northern reaches of the Uncompahgre Plateau. A left turn/south on Road 16.5 at this intersection leads to dual-sport riding above the Unaweep Canyon. A turn right/north on Road 16.5 will have you and your bike connecting with the Rim Rock Drive of the Colorado National Monument [103] only five miles away.

Little Park is a nice quarter-day ride, good for a warm summer evening with the sun low in the sky. Linking Little Park with Rim Rock Road in the Colorado National Monument would be a fun and scenic half-day loop.

Ride 105 **Grand Mesa–Lands End**

Reeder Mesa Road, Lands End Road, Forest Road 100

A 34-mile (26 miles easy dirt, 8 miles paved) secluded, winding ride up and over the western side and rim of the Grand Mesa, with bird's-eye views of Grand Junction below

Lands End Road climbing the western flanks of the Grand Mesa, then skirting the northern rim of Deep Creek Canyon, is a road of history and one-of-a-kind scenic beauty. It was constructed in the 1930s by the Civilian Conservation Corps, which mostly employed World War I veterans looking for work. They were paid one dollar per day for their toils, and slept in army tents 11 miles below the mesa. Joining the CCC for the arduous task of hacking out a roadway to the top were inmates from the far away state prison in Cañon City. Back then and today, there are scenic rewards for being in this mostly lonely place, with its dramatic 100-mile views to the west.

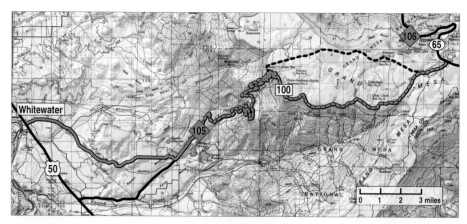

From down below, Lands End Road is reached from the small community of Whitewater on US 50. The paved Reeder Mesa Road leads five miles to the east where it intersects with the Lands End Road. Kannah Creek Road (paved), about three miles south of Whitewater, also connects with the Lands End Road. Both of these roads are flavorful appetizers before the main course is served. Make sure to check your fuel level for there is nothing to slake your bike's thirst up on the mesa.

Lands End Road is paved for three miles before turning into a hard-packed dirt surface. It is excellent here for just about any street bike. Up high the surface becomes less firm and a little rockier, and while I think a light street bike wouldn't have any woes making it to the top, I would have hesitations with a heavy bike. This is a very friendly and fun dual-sport ride. As you zigzag back and forth, gaining elevation on this serpentine road, you are continually presented with views down below, giving you a measure of your progress.

A last, edgy switchback will deposit you almost suddenly at the top. Look around as you pause at this high, flat, and lonely place on the western edge of the mesa. Continue to the east on pavement, riding airy canyon rims and rolling through fields of flowering grasses. The road surface returns to gravel for the last few miles to where Lands End concludes at the junction with Colorado 65 and the Grand Mesa Scenic Byway [106].

The eastside connection to the Grand Mesa Scenic Byway is noted above. It should be mentioned that Whitewater on US 50 is where to launch one of the best rides in Colorado—the Colorado 149/Unaweep-Tabeguache Scenic Byway to Gateway and the Dolores Canyon [101].

Ride 106 **Grand Mesa Scenic Byway**

Colorado 65

A 40-mile traverse of the world's tallest flat-top mountain, with curves winding around and between beautiful mountain lakes

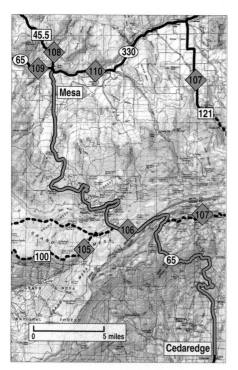

The Grand Mesa towering over the city of Grand Junction, one mile lower and to the west, is a very special destination for your bike. There aren't many places offering the diversity the Grand Mesa presents, with immense stands of aspen, far western-slope views, and 300 crystalline lakes that sparkle in the sun. As the wheels spin over the 40 miles, you will pass through noticeable contrasts of climate, vegetation, and landscape.

The communities of Mesa on the north, and Cedaredge on the south, are the bookends to this journey. You'll begin from Cedaredge, but as with every other road and ride in this book, either direction is superb. And I will confess that as the Grand Mesa looms larger in front of my visor I feel a gleeful anticipation, as if I'm getting ready to be launched on a great amusement park ride—only this is much better, and a lot longer!

The long and sweeping ascent up either side on finely cambered curves is outstanding. Look back at your progress and let your eyeballs roam far and wide at any of several pullouts along the way. As the terrain begins to flatten out, you will know you've reached the top of the mesa. Now it will be time for the lake tour.

Sixteen miles from Cedaredge, the Grand Mesa Visitor Center will be on the east side of the road. Check the interpretive exhibits, stretch the limbs, gets some snacks, and perhaps walk over to the nearby lakes.

This ride is so good, you'll be excused if you want to turn around and ride it again, or if you just want to linger at the top exploring several of the forest roads which lead to dozens of secluded lakes, big and small. A good paved road to try is the Baron Lake Drive that leads past the visitor center to a collection of small resort lakes with cabins clustered around them. The "Hotel Lake" only a half mile away has a small snack bar with outdoor seating. This road connects with dirt-road County 121 several miles later and de-

livers a beauty of a scenic and lonely ride all the way to Collbran [107]. Another alternative is Lands End Road, originally built with picks and shovels in the 1930s by convicts out of Cañon City. It takes you to the western edge of the Grand Mesa, then winds a path all the way down to Whitewater south of Grand Junction. It's a sweet one, and covered in Ride 105.

Cedaredge on the south side of the mesa is in the heart of western-slope orchard country and offers a variety of places to fill your tanks—food and fuel. There are no other services until the town of Mesa, 40 miles away on the other side of the Grand Mesa. The Wagon Wheel Restaurant and Hotel is a good place to eat and stay if stopping in Mesa is on your agenda. There are great rides are in every direction at the nearby intersection of Colorado 65 and County 330. You'll have the serious dilemma—or luxury—of choosing between Plateau Canyon [109] to the west, the De Beque Cutoff [108] to the north, and the backroad ride east to Collbran [110].

Ride 107 **Grand Mesa Lakes**

Baron Lake Drive, Lakeshore Drive, County 121, 59, 58.5

*A tranquil 23-mile mesa ride that weaves through a presentation of
sparkling lakes before delivering an entertaining descent to lower elevations*

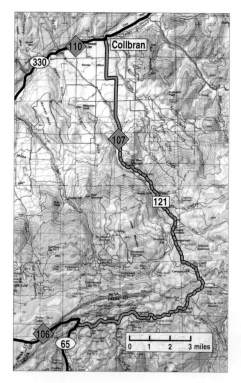

When you ride Colorado 65 and the Grand
Mesa Scenic Byway, you'll pass many pristine alpine lakes, but if you want a more intimate lake experience, this ride is for you.

At the Grand Mesa Welcome Center, just
off of Colorado 65, there is a well-marked,
poorly paved road leading past the welcome
center on the north. This is Baron Lake and
Lakeshore Drive, which becomes Forest Road
121/County 59 in about two miles. It also
loses its broken paved surface here, but in a
way, the character of this quiet ride is enhanced by the smooth dirt surface.

Pine-covered rocky outcroppings, crystalline blue lakes, and perhaps a solitary fisherman will be your companions along the
upper half of Forest Road 121. The road will
slowly bend to the south, and the flavor of
the ride will change subtly as it begins a
gradual descent to Collbran, 3,000 feet
below.

Openings through the corridor of trees reveal the stony slopes of Battlement Mesa to the east, and the steep walls of the Roan Cliffs on the horizon. The expanse before you will open up as more altitude is lost. It would be understandable if you wanted to pull over and reach for the camera, or stop just to see what distant features you could identify.

Now, you are going to have a nice surprise about eight miles south of Collbran. Pavement returns as the road base, and sweetly special riding curves are introduced to the journey. It's as if you have discovered a secret place, and have been granted insider access because you made the effort to venture this way. Enjoy sharing the twisting tarmac with no one else, until the straight, roller-coaster-like descent into Collbran.

The dirt-surfaced sections of this ride are suitable for a street bike, but as with any unpaved surface, suitability can go out the window if it is wet. Consider this ride as a supplement to the other Grand Mesa rides. What it uniquely delivers is access to more lakes, access to the quiet eastern side of the Grand Mesa, and a direct connection to Collbran where Colorado 330 [110] awaits the arrival of your bike. Of course, Colorado 65 and the Grand Mesa Scenic Byway [106], at the other side of this traverse, is one of the finest riding roads around. With the lack of services at the top, I recommend packing some food in your bags, then claiming one of the crystalline lakes as your own.

Ride 108 **De Beque Cutoff**

County 45.5

A lonely nine-mile curving, twisting, up-and-down hoot of a ride

The De Beque Cutoff begins at the intersection of Colorado 65 and 330, and ends to the north at the De Beque Exit 62 off Interstate 70. Actually this is an 11-mile road, with the the first nine miles full of twists and turns, and the northern two miles gratefully of a straighter nature. You will need to gather your wits from what you and your bike just went through coming up from the south.

Spinning the wheels north, the De Beque Cutoff winds tightly around, through, and over a series of rocky bluffs and dry, sandy, creek beds. There are modest rock formations and spires competing for your attention, but don't gaze away too long—there

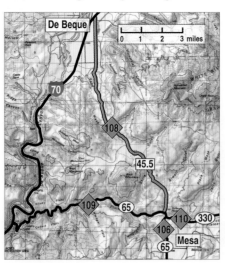

are places where the road opens up briefly, then gets bored and wants to tighten and coil up again.

The sinuous pavement skirts the eastern edge of the Kimbell Mesa at around mile eight, then as the Roan Cliffs on the other side of Interstate 70 come into view, there is a catch-your-breath coast to the road's conclusion. Reverse the direction, and you will be lured by the docile approach into an inescapable snake pit of a ride.

With De Beque on Interstate 70 not really being a destination, I often think of this as an out-and-back kind of ride. From the intersection of Colorado 65 and 330 at the south entrance, that's what I'd do. Then I would consider which of the other three tasty choices I would point the bike toward—the S-curves of Plateau Canyon [109], the backroad ride to Collbran and beyond [110], or the south ascent of the Grand Mesa [106]. If one is droning east or west along Interstate 70, one might get off at exit 62, ride south, and make a run at the roller-coaster ride of the De Beque Cutoff—perhaps even taking advantage of Plateau Canyon (Exit 49) as part of the east-west traverse. There are limited food and fuel options at De Beque, and in Mesa just south of the Colorado 65–330 intersection.

Ride 109 **Plateau Canyon**

Colorado 65

A ten-mile ride through a steep-walled canyon filled with S-curve after S-curve

Colorado 65 along the Plateau River through Plateau Canyon is 20 or so enticing curves snaking back and forth, back and forth, delivered in a sweet package of river and rock-wall accompaniment.

There is a rhythm to it, and when you are on a bike it is almost like you are dancing, with the road as your willing partner. Find the right tempo, the perfect rpms and gear, and you can keep it unchanged as you tango the entire length.

As you approach Interstate 70 on the western side, the Plateau River cuts deeply and dramatically into the rocks before it flows into the Colorado River. The gorge is deeper, the rock walls more intimidating, and you feel ant-like in size as you follow the paved path through the granite cliffs.

The flow and motion of Plateau Canyon is so special that if a lumbering truck or RV were in front of me, I would pull over and al-low enough space up ahead to be able to ride at my own pace. It's safer, less frustrating, and far more enjoyable.

If you're looking for ride options in the Grand Junction region, this area around the Grand Mesa needs to be on your short list. While the Grand Mesa Scenic Byway [106] is a jewel, the roads to and from the mesa are worthy of their own attention. The De Beque Cutoff [108] at the eastern terminus of Plateau Canyon is a hilarious ride. I can see combining that one with this one, maybe even going out and coming back. The ride to Collbran and beyond on County 330 [110] delivers a paved, country backroad experience, and adds nice visual diversity after the rocks of Plateau and De Beque. The town of a Mesa has a selection of food and fuel options, as does Collbran. The Wagon Wheel in Mesa is good base camp (restaurant and hotel) for rides in the area.

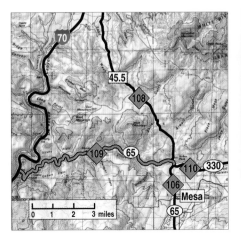

When entering the canyon from the east, or Mesa side, you get the first hint that this isn't going to be a road that cups your tires.

Ride 110 **Collbran**

Colorado 330, County 330E

A rural 26-mile backroad ride up a broad river valley dotted with farms, orchards, ranches, a state park, and distracting views of the Grand Mesa's north slopes

Colorado 330 leads east of the great ride intersection of Colorado 65 and the De Beque Cutoff. As noted elsewhere, when you arrive at this junction just north of the small town of Mesa, you can turn your front wheel in any direction and launch yourself on a great motorcycle ride.

This meandering road follows the wandering ways of Plateau Creek as it drains the forested slopes of the Grand Mesa to the south, and Battlement Mesa's rocky ramparts to the north. The ascent is gentle as you climb east up the valley. You'll take in a little bit of everything along the way—tree-lined road-

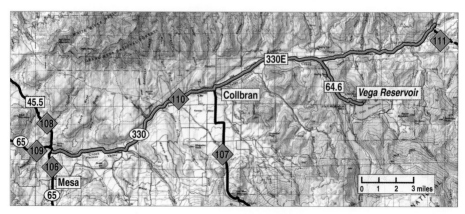

ways opening up to fertile, irrigated farms, cattle grazing on lush grasses, small communities in between. Personally, I enjoy having a bike take me up close to where people live and work, and especially so when the journey is serene and picturesque.

At 12 miles, you will lower the rpms for the small, tree-lined town of Collbran. This area was homesteaded in the late 1800s, and cowboys and ranching are their legacies. A circuit of the downtown area can lure you to pause a moment, stretch the legs, or perhaps make a snack or fuel stop.

Continuing on, the road will ascend a rocky shelf, and as you rise above the eastern side of Collbran with the valley dropping away a few hundred feet, you will have grand views of the Grand Mesa's carpeted northern face. Just below the slopes you will see idyllic farms with open fields displaying a rainbow of storybook colors. If you are here within an hour of sunrise or sunset, and you happen to have your camera with you, you may consider going into the postcard business.

The road becomes County 330E east of Collbran, and for the next 14 miles it will be a more secluded and lonely place. Most of the way, it will be just you and the two wheels beneath you. The flow of the ride can be modified at 6.4 miles east of Collbran by turning right/south on Peninsula Road/

County 64.6. A well-marked sign here notes that this is the way to Vega State Park and the Vega Reservoir three miles away. Check it out. It is a good-sized body of water, at 8,000 feet, in a sub-alpine meadow on the western edge of the Grand Mesa National Forest. Campgrounds, cabins for rent, picnic areas, and various recreational activities can make Vega the destination as much as this ride is.

Eight miles past the Vega State Park turn-off, the pavement concludes its run, and leading away from you are long, dual-sport rides to incredibly remote and solitary places. The Forest Road 265 ride is described in Ride 111, but I wouldn't recommend journeying farther on a heavy street bike.

In Collbran, Forest Road 121 [107] is an alternative to Colorado 65 as a route to the the top of the Grand Mesa. A good chunk of it is dirt, but if you have a lightweight street bike you should be okay. It is worth noting how FR 121 winds along and around numerous isolated lakes at the top.

If you're going to ride 330, and continuing past the pavement is not in your plans, you could either ride the 52 miles out and back, or throw some food in your bags and ride to the State Recreation Area. Grab a picnic table or big flat rock, and with your bike cooling off nearby, consume the vittles with the scenery your place setting, and the ride back your dessert.

Ride 111 **Grand Mesa National Forest**

Forest Road 265

A secluded 33-mile dual-sport ride through a landscape of deep forests, hidden valleys, and wildflower meadows

This ride is a journey through a rolling landscape defined by the remote eastern and northern knobby sides of the Grand Mesa. If isolation has its attractions for you, Forest Road 265 is worthy of being on your need-to-ride short list. You may not come across anyone else the entire 33 miles. This ride has a quality to it, a defining texture threaded by wilderness and distinct scenery. Plus, the two paved roads at either end of this journey are among the most special you'll find.

Forest Road 265 on the east connects with Colorado 133 at the southern base of

McClure Pass [113]. A sign points the way to the northwest, seven miles south of the McClure Pass summit. At the western terminus, it directly connects to County 330E [110] 14 miles west of Collbran.

With your wheels spinning west, the first few miles are about as busy as it will get. You will pass by a scant few ranches before entering a zone of you and . . . you. Here, you will ascend to the lower eastern shelves of the Grand Mesa. Look in your mirrors, and then turn the bike slightly to take in the spurs of the Elk Range clogging the views to

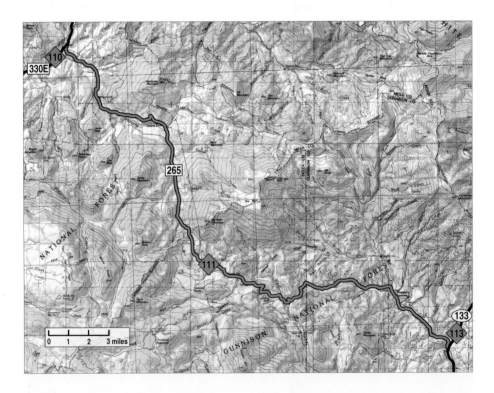

the east. With aspen trees everywhere you look, near and far, this would be a flaming golden place in September.

After 13 miles you will come upon the deserted West Muddy Ranger Station and a mile past that is Forest Road 705 to the south, which you can explore for six miles to the hidden Overland Reservoir. Along the way you will be tempted by stray dirt roads leading toward deep and unknown sites . . . and sights. You will be deeply amidst the Gunnison and Grand Mesa National Forests. If two-wheeled camping casts a spell, then you will be entranced with all the options presented along Forest Road 265.

On the western side of this ride, trees loosen their grip on the terrain and grassy meadows get the edge. It is more open, the streams no longer sheltered by thirsty plants. Ranches and cattle begin to greet you. Forest Road 265 concludes at County 330E. A turn to the northeast will lead you to the town of Silt, 26 miles away on Interstate 70. A turn southwest will take you toward Collbran, with pavement appearing in a few miles.

A dual-sport bike would devour Forest Road 265, and want more. A lightweight street bike would survive, but I'm not sure about the wanting more part. Food and fuel services are non-existent. Collbran on the west, and Paonia on the east, are the load-up options to get you through the 74 miles of wilderness in between!

An engineering masterpiece, with cars, a truck, a raft, a train, and a motorcycle idling just out of view

Ride 112 **Glenwood Canyon**

Interstate 70

A 15-mile ride through a famous high-walled canyon on an award-winning engineering marvel of the Interstate Highway System, with viaducts, bridges, tunnels, scenic pullouts, rest areas, and hiking trails

Much of Interstate 70, as it winds through Colorado's Rocky Mountains, is quite entertaining, but this 15-mile stretch along the

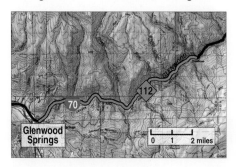

Colorado River through narrow Glenwood Canyon is especially noteworthy. Glenwood Canyon has long been the traffic route for points west. In 1887, railroad tracks were laid down in the narrow canyon. A primitive dirt road was hacked out in the early 1900s, and 30 years later a paved auto route was constructed—US 6. Increasing traffic over the decades in this twisting and constricted place resulted in sky-high accident rates. It was a dangerous highway. After 20 years of study and ten years of controversy, a mas-

The road through Glenwood Canyon in 1915

sive engineering project was launched, challenged with shoe-horning a four-lane freeway into a long river canyon barely wide enough for two lanes. Finally, in October of 1992, this last leg of the original US Interstate system was finished, utilizing a series of cantilevered bridges, tunnels, and massive retaining walls. The result is a spectacle to ride—a combination of nature's wonders and man's achievements.

Whether you are entering the canyon from the east or west, the introduction isn't dramatic, but once you are past the first few appetizing curves, the main course comes into view. The 3,000-foot walls are the tallest anywhere along the Colorado River, except for that modest ditch called the Grand Canyon.

The impressive design of the highway is easily observed as you lean into its shapely curves while considering how the thing was built. During the summer, you will probably see people on rafts on the Colorado enjoying a different kind of river ride. Chances are excellent a train will be riding the rails on the opposite bank. By the way, if you're thinking about pitching a tent at one of the camp-

grounds in the canyon, be prepared for the thunder of enormous diesel engines and the whine of singing rails occurring at every hour. That's all I'm gonna say.

Ten miles from Glenwood Springs, Exit 125 leads to a rest and parking area with a foot trail to Hanging Lake. If you have your hiking legs, a mile away and 1,000 feet higher is a stunning, sight-to-behold place. Waterfalls and a limestone lake teeming with trout resemble a page from a storybook. It is worth the 90-minute round trip hike.

The fun town of Glenwood Springs, with its famous hot springs, anchors the western side of the canyon. There's plenty to do here, and plenty of services for both motorcycle and pilot.

A ride south out of Glenwood on Colorado 82 will take you to Frying Pan Road [129] and toward Independence Pass [127]. If you turn south in Carbondale onto Colorado 133, McClure Pass [113] awaits. Twelve miles west of Glenwood on I-70 is New Castle, and the roads of Grass Valley and Rifle Gap [158]. Tie a selection of these together for some great day rides.

Heading north on Colorado 133, approaching a drained Paonia Reservoir

Ride 113 **McClure Pass**

Colorado 133

A supremely scenic 58-mile ride over a mountain pass, with special approaches on each side delivering attractions found on every motorcyclist's checklist

McClure Pass is the key feature of this very special ride. Its 58 miles contain three distinct and equally wonderful riding sections. First there is the 25-mile bliss of pavement north of the town of Paonia to the southern

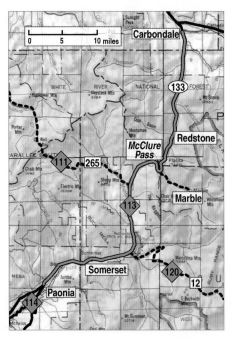

foot of the McClure Pass ascent. For the first ten miles or so of curving valley riding, you will pass by some serious coal mining activity in the vicinity of the town of Somerset. Personally, I find it fascinating to see these major league operations up close. Then there will be 15 miles of A+ riding as you follow the outlines of Paonia Reservoir.

Now you'll enter into the McClure Pass portion of this Colorado 133 ride. The southern ascent is a beautifully bending roadway weaving its way through lush groves of aspen trees. In the autumn, it's like riding through a painting. The pass summit is brief, and then you will be on a heady decline to the Crystal River Valley—and a dramatic panorama it is! Western spurs of the Elk Range will have you downshifting to pull over for a photo. The grade is steep here and places to stop are not plentiful, but about halfway down on the east side of the road there is a very broad shoulder where you can pause. I think it is better to stop here than at the rather ho-hum summit, unless getting a picture of the McClure Pass sign with some aspen trees behind it is on your to-do list.

At the bottom of the north side of McClure, there is a turnoff to the small town of Marble. In a way, it is a semi-ghost town, for the place is much smaller than it was 100 years ago when it could boast of having the largest marble mine in the world—supplying special stone for the Lincoln Memorial and the Tomb of the Unknown Soldier. The road to Marble is paved for the first mile or so, and then it is an easy dirt surface to town. Along the way, you can note evidence of a time when the place was more bustling and populous.

Seven miles north of Marble on Colorado 133 is the National Historic District of Redstone. The curving road follows the cascading waters of the Crystal River. Redstone was developed in the early 1900s by industrialist John Cleveland Osgood for those who worked his coal mines and coke ovens. It is said he wanted to take care of those in his employ and, indeed, the 84 cottages and 40-room inn he built included luxuries like indoor plumbing and electricity. Nearby, he constructed a 42-room mansion for his second wife, completing it in 1902. Today it is often referred to as the Redstone Castle.

On the west side of the road at Redstone, you will see the beehive coke ovens used to transform raw coal into high-grade coke needed for the production of steel. I suggest hanging a right (to the east) at the Redstone sign, and riding through the quaint and very charming town. You will see the famous inn, and as you ride the main road you will also be paralleling Colorado 133 to where the roads merge after a mile or so. There are several excellent places at which to stop for a meal.

This ride is near others described in the book. Just south of the Paonia Reservoir is the Kebler Pass Road [120] leading east toward Crested Butte. At the southern base of McClure is long and lonely Forest Road 265 [111] leading one on a tour of the northern flanks of the Grand Mesa. Both of these routes are off-pavement, but many can make the Kebler Pass journey on a street bike. Not far from this ride's northern Carbondale terminus is the town of Basalt on Colorado 82 toward Aspen. Here you can connect with the Frying Pan River ride [129]. It should be noted there are restaurants in Paonia and Carbondale, and on the north side of McClure Pass in Marble and Redstone. As for fuel, I would make sure you have enough in the tank for the 58 miles when you set out.

Ride 114 **Crawford–Back River**

Crawford Road, Back River Road

Two rural backroad alternatives (11 miles and 7 miles) to a busy nearby highway, delivering a hilly and winding tour of farms, orchards, and irrigated fields

These two roads are examples of the kind of journey you can find when you are in explorer mode. Tucked around communities big and small, you will find wandering, solitary roads that generally aren't too long, but definitely look intriguing. The two motorcycle roads described here are representative of what you can find when you take a road less travelled. There's something about riding a road you've never been down, seeing places through your visor that you never knew were there, and if the journey offers a more pleasing alternative route to somewhere you need to go, well that's just a bonus!

Chances are, if you are in the Crawford area and have just ridden the exquisite Colorado 92 along the north rim of the Black Canyon described in the Gunnison ride [115], your destination is Paonia and Colorado 133 [113]. A mile west of Crawford on Highway 92, there's a sign pointing to Paonia via Crawford Road. If you are already in Paonia, Mathews Lane leads out of town to the southwest. At two miles, turn onto this nice rural passage at the intersection.

For eleven miles, the Crawford Road climbs sandy bluffs, descends to thirsty dry creek beds, and goes around or through the rest of the scenery. Green water-fed fields contrast starkly with arid sage-covered soils. Small ranches and rural homes dot the landscape, and higher up, dry mesas are in every direction, including Oak Mesa above Hotchkiss and Paonia.

Back River Road also joins Mathews Lane and Crawford Road at the junction noted above. The southern terminus is one mile east of Hotchkiss on Colorado 92. It is a seven-mile, curving, farm-filled ride that avoids a busy Colorado 133 between Hotchkiss and Paonia. The adjacent North Fork of the Gunnison River is the apt source for the name of this road. Its flows enable the thriving fruit industry you will see, if not smell, as your open-air vehicle cuts through vineyards of grapes, and orchards of apples, cherries, nectarines, and peaches.

These two backroads are alternatives to more ho-hum and congested routes. Food and fuel services exist in Crawford, and are plentiful at nearby Hotchkiss and Paonia on Colorado 133.

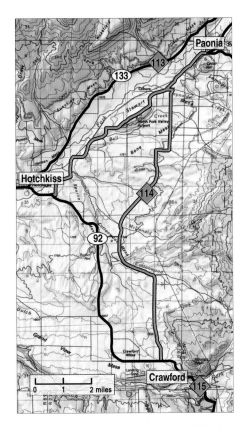

Ride 115 **Black Canyon North Rim**

Colorado 92

A premier 41-mile motorcycling road along the north rim of the Black Canyon of the Gunnison, delivering an amazing buffet of riding delights to even the most discerning of ride connoisseurs

More than a few riders I know have declared Colorado 92 to be their favorite Colorado road. There aren't enough superlatives in the English language to describe its twisting transit along the north rim of the Black Canyon of the Gunnison.

From US Highway 50, you will find the well-marked turnoff to Colorado 92 near Sapinero on the western side of the Blue Mesa Reservoir, 26 miles west of Gunnison. Motorcycle bliss begins immediately as the pavement closely sketches the edges of the drop-offs and contours of the Black Canyon.

The bends, creases, curves, and sweeps go on and on. And on. Since this is basically a road from one quiet place to another quiet place, there isn't much "noise" from other vehicles. The features of this road, combined with its emptiness over many miles, is definitely a gift to motorcycle riders. As for its

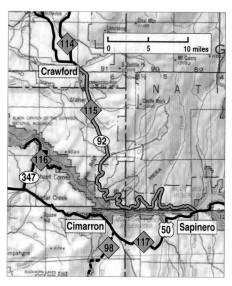

scenic attractions, glances stolen to the south reveal the deep gorges of the Gunnison River and they add extra dimensions (literally) to the ride. There are several

wide spots along the way, and in 17 or 18 miles, there is a scenic overlook with parking and facilities.

I need to mention that this road does demand attention. Most of the curves and bends are clean, well-cambered, and of a good and predictable radius. There are, however, two or three curves that can surprise you with their tightness, or with unexpected grit on the surface. Keeping this awareness in the back of your mind would be a good thing.

Colorado 92 departs to the north after the overlook, and continues to be one hoot of a scoot. There are two state parks with small lakes are along the way, and forest roads for dual-sport exploration depart to the east and west, including one that returns to the edge of the Black Canyon.

Crawford is the first community you will come to after joining this ride. There is a convenience store with gas pumps south of town, and two restaurants—the Branding Iron and The Boardwalk—with bikes occasionally in front. That's it for services between here and the spread-out communities on US 50 to the south, so be prepared.

This ride on Colorado 92 needs to be on your short list of must-do rides in Colorado. Fortunately, you do not have to drone on uneventful roads to get to this eventful place. Check out the US 50 ride between Gunnison and Montrose [117] and Colorado 133 over McClure Pass [113].

On this day, these riders at the scenic overlook were among the few I saw the entire length of this ride.

Ride 116 **Black Canyon–Portal**

Portal Road, County 347

A 12-mile ride to the Black Canyon of the Gunnison National Park, then down an extremely steep and twisting road to the shy, secluded, river canyon floor

You may have heard about the Black Canyon of the Gunnison National Park. You may have traveled past its entrance, or ridden along its north rim via Colorado 92 [115].

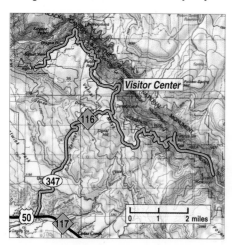

On this ride, you'll take your bike into the depths of this dark canyon. This national park has its own unique and special features. No other canyon in North America has its combination of narrow entrance, harrowing depths, and sheer rock walls. The canyon has long intimidated those coming to the rim to cautiously peer over its steep cliffs. Indeed, early expeditions revealed no evidence of a human presence in the gorge.

The main entrance to this national park is 7.7 miles east of Montrose in US 50. There is a dual-sport north rim ride off of Colorado 92, but it is this south entrance that you want for the park facilities, interpretive areas, South Rim Drive, and Portal Road. The main course is Portal Road, but for almost six miles, County 347 offers a nice introduction to the ride on your way toward the main gate. After entering the park and paying the park entrance fee ($7 for a motorcycle), go past the nearby Portal Road turnoff (it is well marked), and take your bike along the South Rim Drive. Plan to pause at the visitor center and/or several of the 12 Black Canyon scenic overlooks.

When you think you are ready, head back toward the park entrance and turn left/southeast onto Portal Road, and get ready for a 2,000-foot drop on a paved road containing hair-raising 16 percent grades! At first, the road tentatively circles near several canyon walls, like a predator looking for a weakness, then it makes its move, making a beeline for the opening to the bottom.

That beeline doesn't last long, for the only safe way to plunge deep in a limited amount of space is to tie the road into knots. So if you like pretzel shapes, you're going like the taste of this one. Actually, the road designers have not made this into a frightening thing. Just keep your bike in the lower gears, don't get too distracted as the canyon swallows you up, and in five miles you will be at the floor of the canyon along the banks of the Gunnison River.

You will be at a T-intersection when you complete the descent. To the left is a short cul-de-sac with a camping area. To the right, the road continues for another two miles, passing a picnic area with restrooms, and joins the Gunnison River for an utterly scenic and placid ride to the dam. This is a special place, with the crystal clear river pouring over scattered rocks, and verdant foliage decorating its banks. With just two cul-de-sacs down here, you'll have an equally fun ride back up to the top.

Ride 117 **Blue Mesa**

US 50

A sweeping 64-mile ride through valleys, over mountain divides, and alongside Colorado's largest body of water

This section of US 50 largely follows the pioneering trail of General William Jackson Palmer's railroad as it forged westward from Gunnison. The general enjoyed engineering challenges, and he certainly was faced with a stiff one when driving the Denver and Rio Grande through the deep narrow gorge of the Black Canyon. This obstacle is the reason for the slight deviation between the train route and your motorcycle route. There is no highway going through the shadowy recesses of this nearby national park, but you can be dwarfed by its depths by riding to the bottom via Portal Road [116]. Heading east from Montrose on US 50, the turn north to the Black Canyon of the Gunnison National Park is 7.7 miles from downtown.

Continuing east, you will gain 1,200 feet

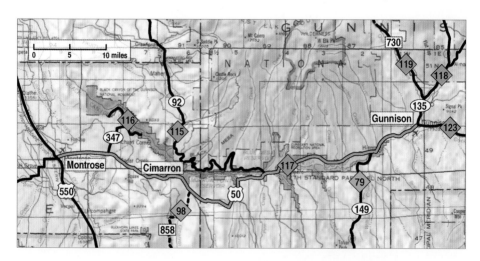

to the top of Cerro Summit, the first of several high mountain humps, and like a big roller-coaster for giants, the road winds down 1,000 feet before the next climb.

Consider making a stop in Cimarron at the eastern bottom of Cerro. This is where Palmer's narrow-gauge emerged from the Black Canyon. With the steep grades of Cerro to the west, and the recognition that helper engines would be required, Cimarron was developed into a full-fledged railroad town with a station, a roundhouse, and even the popular Black Canyon Hotel and Eating House. Not much remains, but if you are interested in train history, a half-mile north from Cimarron take Morrow Point Dam Road toward the canyon and check out the Cimarron Canyon Rail Exhibit and Museum. Locomotive #278, its coal tender, a boxcar, and a caboose sit atop the last remaining canyon trestle. This short detour is worth it.

The ups and downs and lefts and rights continue. You'll have two more summit tops to overpower before glimpses of big Blue Mesa Reservoir and the Curecanti National Recreation Area sneak up on you. There is a longish descent to this massive water stor-

age project, completed in 1965, and then there will be a refreshing and extended shoreline ride for almost 20 miles.

The fishing here is serious. Blue Mesa is recognized as the world's largest lake trout and Kokanee salmon fishery. It is also a body of water with some of the most vivid, yet changing shades of the color blue I've ever seen. Every time I scoot by it seems to be painted another vibrant hue. Fortunately, the ride alongside Big Blue here is serene, great for cruising, and safely permits lingering glances at the scenery on both sides of the road.

Montrose and Gunnison at both ends of this journey provide all kinds of riding services, from food and fuel, to lodging and leisure. Gunnison is one of the better base camps in Colorado for staying at one place and riding in a different direction each day. At the western end of Blue Mesa is the stellar Colorado 92 [115]. Not to be outdone, sublime Colorado 149 [079], on the eastern side of Blue Mesa, is also not to be missed. Dual-sporters may want to bail off of US 50 near Cimarron and head south to scenic Owl Creek Pass [098].

Ride 118 **Almont**

Colorado 135

A curving 28-mile ride through a resort crossroads town to a charming Victorian ski community, with two rivers showing the way, and stirring peaks providing the backdrop

The ride from Gunnison to Crested Butte is sweet. From rivers to ranches, and towns to talons, Colorado 135 escorts you through and past a variety of sights to see from your

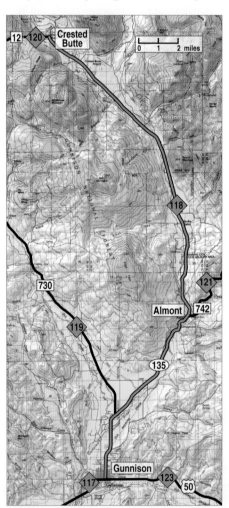

saddle. It is frequently noted that the difference between traveling by car and by bike is that one observes scenery through a car window, while one is a part of it on a bike. It is an apt description for this journey.

Colorado 135 departs for the north out of Gunnison at the main downtown intersection. It is well marked. The fertile countryside will start to envelope you as you cross over the Gunnison River. At 2.5 miles there is the stunning Ohio Creek Road [119] leading off to the northwest.

The chilly and churning Gunnison River will be your riding partner for seven miles, until you come to the quiet crossroads and cross-rivers town of Almont. Here, the East River from the north says hello to the Taylor River from the east, and from that little intimacy, the Gunnison River is born. You'll stay on Colorado 135 and head north, but some future riding agenda will need to include your pointing your front wheel to the east to ride the Taylor River Canyon, described in Ride 121.

Three miles north of Almont you'll enter the Roaring Judy State Wildlife area, and one mile later there is a road to the left leading to the fish hatchery. The East River south of the hatchery is a designated Wild Trout Stream, and the trout here are like Steppenwolf—born to be wild. Their relatives at the hatchery are destined to swim in other Colorado rivers. Did you know that ev-

ery autumn, between 50,000 and 150,000 Kokanee salmon make a run from Blue Mesa Reservoir to the hatchery? Well, I think the bald eagles know this. Keep your eye out for these majestic raptors when riding alongside the East and other nearby streams. Also, consider making a turn at the hatchery road and walking among the pond-like tanks teeming with trout fry.

You will know you are approaching the old-mining-town-turned-ski-resort community of Crested Butte, when you see its towering namesake gain girth and height on the horizon. The southern peaks of the Elk Mountains are a dramatic, if not intimidating, backdrop to this valley where the Utes would set up their summer camp. This is a wild and beautiful place in every direction.

Sometimes there are roads where winds whisper in your ears, suggesting an active throttle, and sometimes those same soft voices suggest a ride in cruise mode, letting what you see come to you. This is a ride of the latter persuasion.

Gunnison offers a great launch to this traverse with all kinds of lodging and restaurant options. The Firebrand Deli, a few steps north of the Colorado 135 and US 50 intersection, is a motorcyclist favorite. Crested Butte's main street is stacked with great places to eat. If you are up for turning more miles on your odometer, the Kebler Pass ride [120] takes off from the west side of Crested Butte. While unpaved, the dirt is street-bike easy, and the aspen forests are among the largest in the world.

Ride 119 **Ohio Pass**

Ohio Creek Road, County 730, Forest Road 730

A deeply scenic ride (12 miles paved, 11 dirt) through impressive ranching country and amazing aspen forests, and over a 10,000-foot pass

The Ohio Creek Road, three miles north of Gunnison off of Colorado 135, is on my short list of one of the most beautiful rides in Colorado. The road may not twist and turn to the degree of some others, nor does

it go up and down like a folded ribbon, but it sure does deliver top-quality panoramas. Whether it is the resplendent ranches you ride through, the craggy spires of the West Elk Wilderness you steal glances at, or the looming Anthracite Range before you, this is a totally mesmerizing motorcycle journey.

After you turn north onto County 730/Ohio Creek Road, you will have a mile or so of residential views before the distance between the dwellings spreads. The country road will then start to wind its way through lush fields and manicured farms, taking advantage of what flows between the banks of Ohio Creek. There is a sense of fertility here, one that's apparent regardless of the season. Some of the pastures are immense, and some of what you will ride by is 2,775 acres of conservancy land set aside as habitat for the sage grouse. Actually, the grouse here was only recently recognized as a separate species, and is called the Gunnison Grouse. Petitions have been made to have this ground nesting bird listed as endangered, but the Fish and Wildlife Service has not yet acted on this.

Around mile 14, if you look east up a hillside, the ghost town of Baldwin is visible. It flared to life in 1897 because of a rich gold strike nearby, but for several decades what mostly sustained it was cattle ranching and nearby veins of "black gold," or coal. If you look closely you will see blackened evidence of what lies under the soil and rocks. The

road surface here is a dirt-gravel mix, and is street-bike rideable.

Heading north, there is a different texture to the ride. Fields give way to the grandest of aspen tree groves. The scale is enormous, just as it is on the other side of the Anthracites as experienced from Kebler Pass Road, to which this route connects [120]. Hills and curves are amplified as the road hunts for a route to the Ohio Pass summit, eight miles away and 1,600 feet higher. You will pass through hallways of aspen, and slice around a big S-curve before making a final climb up a shelfy ledge to the top. An Anthracite spur is just to the west and seemingly only a snowball toss away.

The road surface near the top of Ohio Pass is rocky in places. A dual-sport bike would be at home here, and an easy-to-ride street bike is probably okay. If you don't want to venture onto the dirt, at least point your bike up the very special Ohio Creek Road for another dose of this graceful valley, and then turn around where the tarmac ends.

Just 1.4 miles north of the Ohio Pass summit is Kebler Pass Road. For a longer journey, turn left/west toward Paonia and Colorado 133 [113]. For a shorter day ride, turn right/east for the resort community of Crested Butte and Colorado 135 [118], which provides a wonderful escort along the East and Gunnison Rivers back to where you started. One last suggestion—for dazzling views, place your bike on the Ohio Creek Road when the aspen have put on their autumn clothes of fiery gold and blazing orange.

The remains of Baldwin, nestled beneath a hill of aspen trees, have gradually deteriorated between 1952 and the present day.

Ride 120 **Kebler Pass**

Kebler Pass Road, County 12

A smooth 30-mile dirt-road ride renowned for its alpine scenery and immense aspen forests

Kebler Pass Road delivers a deeply scenic ride between Crested Butte on the east, and Colorado 133 north of Paonia on the west. It is a mild pass, in that the grades are not steep and the curves not tight, but it isn't mild when it comes to the over-the-top views and vistas you will have in every direction. Bring the camera.

From Crested Butte on the east end, take Whiterock Avenue to Kebler Pass Road just two blocks south of downtown Crested Butte's main drag. Signs point the way, as they do on the Colorado 133 side, where the pass road starts just south of the Paonia Reservoir. When heading west out of Crested Butte, the road begins with a meandering 1,000-foot climb to the pass summit seven forested miles away.

I find the 23 miles west of the pass sum-

mit, all the way to Colorado 133, to be where the scores on the grandeur scale climb significantly. Several miles west of the pass, the bony spine of the Ruby Range scrapes the sky to the north, and the Raggeds Wilderness will be your ride companion the rest of the way. Two solitary peaks are visible to the south—East Beckwith Mountain and West Beckwith Mountain. Both are 12,000-foot monarchs with the eastern sibling 300 feet higher at 12,432 feet. On the northern slopes of these two sentinels, shaggy carpets of aspen trees extend as far as you can see. Numerous reports describe the panorama before you as containing the world's largest groves of aspen.

As you can see, the dirt surface is smooth and wide. The ride is fun, and you know about the scenery. Toward the western end,

you and the bike will lose 1,000 feet of elevation as the road descends to the Anthracite Creek Valley, and after a few sweet miles following the creek, you will come to the conclusion of Kebler Pass Road at Colorado 133.

During the autumn, with the aspen ablaze in shades of yellow and orange, this could be quite the ride. The downside would be that your neighbor, and your neighbor's neighbor, will probably be dusting up the road at the same time. It is key to motor through on this journey when others aren't, like early in the morning. Then again, this ride over-delivers any month it is passable. It should be noted, 30 miles on a dirt road takes a lot longer than 30 miles on a paved one. Stir in a few stops for photos, perhaps a snack, and the time adds up. Between Paonia on Colorado 133 to the west [113], and Crested Butte to the east [118], there are no food or fuel stops for 47 miles. There's nothing but you, your trusty steed, and deep wilderness . . . and this, I think, will be okay with you.

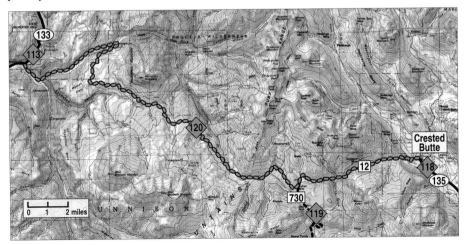

Ride 121 **Taylor River Canyon**

Cottonwood Pass Road, Forest Road 742

A paved, sweetly curving 20-mile canyon road following the course of the Taylor River to the high mountain parks surrounding the deep blue Taylor Reservoir

The Taylor River drains the 9,400-foot-high Taylor Park area, and the surrounding western slopes of the Sawatch Range. Here's a coincidence—the Taylor River and Park are named after Jim Taylor, who was one of the first to discover gold in the area. But the Taylor Park Reservoir takes its name from Glenwood Springs Congressman Edward Taylor, who secured funds in a congressional bill for its construction in 1935.

The reservoir is parked right at the eastern

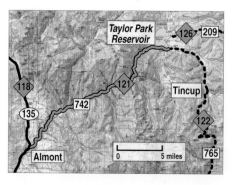

entrance of the 20-mile canyon. For centuries, the canyon has always conducted descending traffic to the west, whether it is of the foot kind hundreds of years ago, or the wagon kind a hundred years ago, or more recently, the internal-combustion kind. Heading west from the reservoir into the canyon, the nicely paved roadway plays tag with the river, toying back and forth via several bridges. This is scenic river riding at its best.

Halfway into this two-wheeled tour of the canyon, the river drifts away a little farther, with rows of trees standing at attention filling in the gap. It will be a gauntlet ride here for several miles, and the road surface will have noticeably switched to one with a bigger chip. It is still sealed, but just not as smooth, like going from a fine, 200-grit sandpaper, to a medium-coarse 100 grit.

As you approach Almont on Colorado

135, the river sneaks closer, fields and farms establish a presence, and activity supporting the recreational offerings of the Taylor area becomes more visible. There are dude ranches, rafting outfitters, and fishing guide services open for business. And there are numerous self-service options, as well. With the feds building, owning, and maintaining the Taylor Park reclamation project, extra money has been devoted toward campgrounds, picnic places, and hiking trails. There's much to do in the Taylor Canyon and Taylor Park recreational area. Getting there and experiencing it on a motorcycle is one of the better choices, in my most humble of opinions!

This Taylor River Canyon ride is between Colorado 135 [118] on the west and two, high-alpine pass rides on the east—the Pitkin area passes [122] and Cottonwood Pass [126]. With Cottonwood being "passable" on a capable street bike, string this pass together with the Taylor Canyon to Colorado 135, and you'll have an alternative route from Buena Vista to Gunnison (versus US 50's Monarch Pass [123]). A good place to stop on this ride is at the Taylor Park Trading Post just past the reservoir. In addition to food (a general store and cafe) and fuel, there is a gift shop, cabins for rent, and RV hookups. This place could be ideal as a base camp for riding (especially dual-sport) in every direction over multiple days.

Ride 122 **Pitkin Passes**

County 888, Forest Road 765, 763, 887

Three rides totaling 38 miles over easy dual-sport passes in the Pitkin area, with history, old mines, hidden valleys and meadows, and plenty of scenery

The historic mining town of Pitkin is ground zero for this and other rides nearby. Back in the 1880s, it was a center of mining activity and was productive over an extended time. The surrounding forested slopes harbored prodigious amounts of iron, silver, gold, lead, and copper. At one point, 36 mines were in operation, and on average, they produced more riches than any other camp in Colorado at the time. Today the mines are quiet, but their silent remnants still tell a story.

There are several ways you can experience this area from your bike.

Option 1

From the town of Parlin on US 50, ride the very sweet and paved Parlin–Pitkin Road north 15 miles, all the way to Pitkin. I could do this 100 times, back and forth, and never tire of this wandering rural route that follows a lazy Quartz Creek through ranches and forested valleys. At eight miles, you will pass the townsite of Ohio, also a bustling place—more than a hundred years ago. Unless you have a dedicated dual-sport bike, Pitkin should be as far as you go. But before you turn around, ride the town briefly, pausing before old places, including the crumbling foundation of a large mill on the west side. You can also stop at the general store for a snack and beverage.

Option 2

With a dual-sport bike, head northeast on US 50. At the western base of Monarch Pass, 1.2 miles from Sargents, turn left/north onto County 888. There will be signs noting that this is the direction for the town of White Pine (a ghost town), Black Sage, and other passes. It will be paved for two miles before turning to a dirt surface. At six miles from US 50, take a sharp left onto Forest 887. Continuing up, County 888 will take you to the ghost town of White Pine, and the more challenging and rocky Hancock Pass.

Black Sage Pass, at 9,745 feet, offers a twisting, but easy ascent up its eastern slopes, with scenic views of the bucolic Tomichi Creek Valley below. You will know you are approaching the summit when you pass underneath cathedrals of aspen trees.

Descending the west side of Black Sage Pass, you'll lose 800 feet of elevation before your wheels reach the Waunita Hot Springs area. There's a popular dude ranch here offering guests all kinds of amenities and activities, including a year-round pool and spa with a water temperature of 95 degrees. But sorry, the ride is the destination here, so turn right/west just before the ranch, and bag pass number two. Waunita Pass, at 10,302 feet, is six miles up Forest Road 763. The first four

miles follow the lead of Hot Springs Creek, taking you past old abandoned cabins, and recently built, currently inhabited beaver lodges. The last two miles contain two fairly large switchbacks, and then you will be at the pass crest.

Continuing west, aim the bike toward Pitkin, four miles away and 1,200 feet lower. This side of the pass presents a somewhat tedious, rocky ride down. This section makes me hesitate to suggest that a lightweight street bike would be okay for this ride. Could it be done? Probably. Would it be fun and would the bike emerge unscathed? Possibly. Upon arrival at Pitkin, you could turn south and ride option number one back to US 5. If you're ready for more, option number three will certainly deliver it!

Option 3

You're in Pitkin, have a bike that can handle dirt and modestly rocky surfaces, and want to ride north 20 miles to the semi-ghost town of Tincup via Cumberland Pass. In my opinion, this is a great Colorado dual-sport ride. It is more alpine than option number two above, and what one sees—close and far—distinguishes this adventure from many others.

County 76 leads northeast out of Pitkin, becoming Forest Road 765 in two miles. You

Remains of abandoned mines can be found throughout the Pitkin area.

will ride up a steady grade in a valley drained by the North Quartz Creek. Seven miles from Pitkin, your bike will strain a little more as the grade steepens. At eight miles, you will have a close-up view of the remains of the large Bon Ton Mine. You might want to pause and consider what life was like here 150 years ago, harvesting ores from the surrounding slopes.

At eleven miles, you will be at a lofty 12,010 feet, and the broad Cumberland Pass summit will offer up to you—the conqueror of its heights—360-degree views of mind numbing scenery. I suspect you will want to hang around for a while taking it all in. When you are ready to proceed to Tincup,

you will be greeted with a series of gravelly switchbacks, dropping you to a ride through a fine, beaver-populated wetland valley. Tincup is nine miles from the top of the pass.

The historic town of Tincup has an occasional cafe open for business during the summer. If you continue on toward Taylor Park Reservoir, you can ride the Taylor Canyon described in Ride 121, or take the Cottonwood Pass Road to Buena Vista [126]. With no fuel options in the Pitkin area or along these remote roads, fill the tank before starting your adventure, but several miles northwest of Tincup, there is the Taylor Park Trading Post with a gas pump, general store, and cafe.

At the Cumberland Pass summit, the surface resembles that of the planet Mars.

Ride 123 **Monarch Pass**

US 50

A 64-mile sweeping, curving ride over the Continental Divide, with a destination pass at the top, delivering seriously scenic vistas and a crest house

The centerpiece of this ride is Monarch Pass, straddling the Continental Divide at a thinly aired 11,312 feet. I remember when I first saw the postcard panoramas from the Monarch summit and, even now, decades later, the panoramas still inspire with their pristine and untouched beauty. Indeed, I can't think of anything you can see, in any direction, that has changed. The vivid greens of the Gunnison National Forest still lead to the southwest horizon in lumpy fashion. To the northeast, jagged peaks of the Sawatch Range stand at attention, seemingly only an arm's length away.

Monarch's past can be traced to an 1878 gold strike by Nicholas Creede on the east side of the pass. Eleven years later, he literally struck gold again near the town that bears his name, south of here. Within

months, 3,000 miners swarmed to Monarch's eastern approaches, establishing towns like Maysville and Garfield of which you will see only traces as you throttle past. You will be riding a road built in 1939 that replaced a wagon road known as Old Monarch Pass, which actually replaced an even older wagon road known as Old Old Monarch Pass Road! Near the top, a sign points the way to Old Monarch Pass Road, which is a graded dirt-road alternative, primarily for traverses of the western side of the pass. By the way, here's a piece of useless trivia: Charles Vail, the state highway engineer, originally named the new pass after himself! He had Vail Pass signs placed at the summit, but local residents didn't care much for the non-collaborative decision, and painted out the name on the signs, and the historic

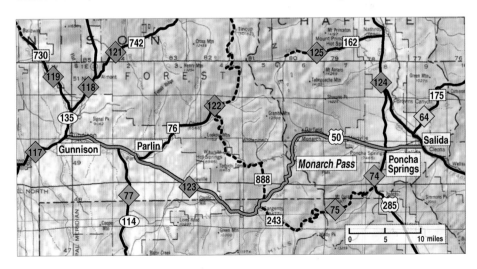

name was reinstated. In the end, Vail had his name more permanently attached to a pass on Interstate 70.

While Monarch's summit is widely known as one of the more scenic passes around, it also has a European Alps-style cafe and gift shop at the top. There isn't another pass in Colorado with this kind of facility at its summit, and let me tell you, there are times when this can be a welcome sight at 11,312 feet!

The best part of this ride is the winding, climbing US 50 on the west side of Monarch Pass. The ascent coming up from the west has few peers. The surface is sublime, the curves beautifully cambered with mostly even radii, and you'll have two lanes at your disposal—meaning there won't likely be a lumbering truck or RV forming a rolling roadblock in front of you and all other traffic. This unimpeded, 2,800-foot change in elevation, on ten miles of scenic sweetness, is unparalleled bliss for those on two wheels.

The distant approaches to Monarch on ei-ther side are tranquil, with US 50 following the meandering Tomichi Creek on the west and the South Arkansas River on the east. Fields of hay and pastures of cattle are nurtured by the flows of these streams. Whether you are heading toward Monarch with anticipation, or grateful for the respite as Monarch fades in your mirrors, these pastoral sections of US 50 are good for the riding soul.

Between the full-service and plenty-to-do towns of Salida and Gunnison, numerous journeys for your bike are called out on these pages as they depart from US 50. Five miles west of Salida, at the crossroads town of Poncha Springs, you have the Collegiate Peaks Scenic Byway [124] pointing toward the north, and Poncha Pass [074] rising 180 degrees the other direction. The Gunnison side of Monarch presents the dual-sport Marshall Pass journey [075], and be sure to check out the Parlin–Pitkin Road described in Ride 122. Finally, Colorado 114 going south eight miles east of Gunnison is a road designed for motorcycles if there ever was one [077].

Ride 124 **Collegiate Peaks**

US 285, US 24

A sweeping 57-mile ride on scenic byways through a major river valley at the base of eight peaks towering more than 14,000 feet

US 285 and 24, running together between Poncha Springs to the south and Leadville to the north, host two of Colorado's 25 scenic byways. Riding north on the Collegiate Peaks Scenic Byway, you come across the largest concentration of peaks higher than 14,000 feet to be found anywhere between Alaska and South America. At the small riverside town of Granite, the byway becomes the Top of the Rockies, defined by Colorado's two tallest peaks. You will have rarified company with you on this ride—and this doesn't include the bashful 14,000-plus foot monarchs of La Plata, Oxford, Missouri, and Belford, hiding behind their more visible and up-front granite neighbors. Enhancing the scale of these giants is the relatively low Arkansas River Valley—"just" 7,500 feet above sea level at the south end—through which US 285 and 24 run. With Leadville at 10,152 feet, there is a 2,500-foot elevation

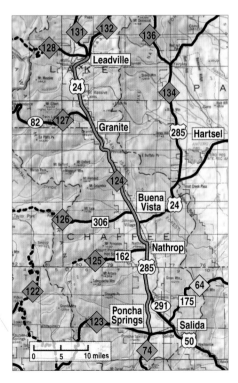

The road, river, and rails point the way to the townsite of Granite, and the almost-touch-the-clouds summit of Mt. Elbert.

change over the 57 miles between the two ends of this journey. Stir in the national historic districts of Salida and Leadville, and you have a unique place toward which you can point your motorcycle.

If you are wandering Colorado on two wheels, or perhaps heading for a special destination, the chances are excellent you will find yourself motoring along on this stretch of roadway. It forms one of the main north-south routes in the Colorado Rockies, and with the formidable array of peaks on its western sides, one often has to ride this highway to get westward to conquer those guarded heights. On the south end at Poncha Springs, US 285 starts its march north from US 50. The Monarch Pass ride [123] is just to the west from here. A few miles farther south, the Poncha Pass [074] and Marshall Pass [075] rides are waiting for you. The historic river town of Salida, with its galleries, cafes, parks, and shopping is just five miles to the east on US 50.

The mountains of Shavano and Tabeguache are the first of the 14,000-footers as you ride north. If you are here in May or June, look up at the high crease on Shavano's eastern slopes and you will see a snow-melt pattern in the form of angel, known famously as the "Angel of Shavano." I find myself always checking what shape the angelic snow is in whenever I ride by.

Farther north is the Colorado 291 turnoff to Salida. If Salida on US 50 is your destination as you head south on US 285, this cutoff is an enjoyable countryside ride, with all the scenic appeal of US 285, plus it shaves 10 to 15 minutes off the route going through the Poncha Springs crossroads. County 162/Chalk Creek Road, departs to the west at Nathrop, eight miles south of Buena Vista. This is a fun, yet reflective ride to the ghost town of St. Elmo [125]. Two miles south of Buena Vista, US 285 turns east and aims for the mountains and meadows of South Park [134].

From here, US 24 will take over escort duties for you and your iron horse. Main Street heading west from downtown Buena Vista becomes County 306, and makes one of the finest paved pass ascents around—to the top of Cottonwood Pass [126]. North of Buena Vista, there is a soil and terrain transition. Green fields of hay give way to the minty green of sage. There will be a rougher texture to all that is around you. Rocky, boulder covered hillsides approach the definition of cliffs, and there is some sweeping canyon riding here to the semi-ghost town of Granite, 17 miles north of Buena Vista, where the two scenic byways meet and exchange the baton of your bike. North of here, the Top of the Rockies is on the stage. Also north of here about three miles is Colorado 82 and the grand Independence Pass ride [127]. Open park riding is the name of the game from here north to famous Leadville, which was at the forefront of the silver boom in the 1870s. Leadville offers elegant Victorian structures, less elegant (but perhaps more moving) abandoned mines, and plenty to see and do. Of course, the riding will be the destination as US 24 continues with an assault on Tennessee Pass [131], and Colorado 91 does the same at Fremont Pass [132].

This journey is primarily one of sightseeing. The road is gently winding, with mild grades and straight sections. With popular towns along its length and the access it gives to the heart of the Colorado Rockies, it can have its share of traffic. This all means that the way to experience these two conjoined byways is to be in cruising mode. Go with the flow. Smell the wildflowers. Kick back in the towns. And with the overdose of outstanding riding in every direction, the area can be a great base camp for rides that span one day or several.

Ride 125 **St. Elmo**

Chalk Creek Road, County 162

A 16-mile ride (half paved, half packed dirt) up a high mountain canyon to a historic town

This ride visits what is considered to be one of Colorado's best-preserved ghost towns. Note the word is "preserved" and not "restored," for the buildings remain in whatever condition the high-altitude elements have permitted. Founded in 1878 in a heavily forested area, the community was first called "Forest City," but the soon-to-arrive post office objected to this common name. So Griffith Evans, one of the founders, suggested St. Elmo, after a romantic novel he was reading. Well, so much for a classic and descriptive high-altitude mountain moniker!

The fortunes of nearby mines and the construction of the nearby Alpine Tunnel in the 1880s exploded the town's population to more than 2,000. With a uniform demo-

graphic profile of mostly single young men, it is said this town, originally founded with high moral intent, soon became a raucous place of saloons, dance halls and houses of questionable repute. I guess Saturday nights were quite a spectacle. Anyway, the flame only burned brightly for a few decades. The number of productive mines began to fade, the Alpine Tunnel closed, and fire took out the business section of town. In 1922, the railroad tracks were pulled up and the remaining residents supposedly rode the last train out. Today you'll ride your iron horse in on the old road and train bed.

This is a ride of two destinations: the engaging road itself, and the ghost town at the end. Get started by turning west eight miles south of Buena Vista onto Chalk Creek Road,

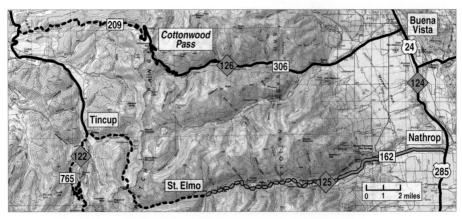

also known as County 162. This turnoff is just a few hundred yards past the small community of Nathrop on US 285 [124].

At five miles, you will pass the famous Mt. Princeton Hot Springs Resort with its steamy waters ready to soothe body and soul any day of the year. At eight miles, the pavement will have run its course, and the remaining eight miles will be smoothly packed dirt.

There are deeply shaded campgrounds, picnic places at the sides of the road, and resorts beckoning for you to stay a spell. The rushing whitewater of Chalk Creek provides visual and audio accompaniment, and more placid fishing waters lure you as well. You will find the 2,000-foot ascent over 16 miles a gentle one, but the rocky and steep surrounding peaks are not so gentle, and they add a stunning backdrop to this "I sure feel small" ride.

The town will appear quite suddenly around a bend, and if your throttle hand is enjoying the fine and fun dirt-road scoot, a steady quick brake may be needed as you enter the slow zone. Take time to park your bike and walk a main street that has seen a lot. A hundred years ago, the street would have been teeming with people and fortune seekers. Thick black smoke from the Denver, South Park & Pacific train at the nearby station would have hung in the air, while a whistle shrieking its intent echoed off the canyon walls. Quite a place—then and now.

Any street bike can make the 16-mile ride. If you happen to be astride a serious and lightweight dual-sport bike, Forest Road 267 west of St. Elmo will take you 2,000 rocky feet higher to Tincup Pass high in the Sawatch Range, over the Continental Divide, and down to the semi-ghost town of Tincup [122], just south of the Taylor Park Reservoir area.

Had you arrived in St. Elmo 130 years ago, you could have been greeted by the town band.

On this busy Saturday, only local shopkeepers will celebrate your visit to St. Elmo.

These buildings still stand, 80 years after the town closed its doors.

Ride 126 **Cottonwood Pass**

Cottonwood Pass Road, County 306, 209

A divinely bending 35-mile high-alpine ride over a quiet pass (21 paved miles on the eastern side, 14 miles packed dirt to the west), with 360-degree views along the way and at the top

The route over Cottonwood Pass began as a footpath used by the Utes, and was widened to accommodate horse- and mule-drawn coaches in the late 1870s, when silver was discovered in the Taylor Park area. Though nearly twice as long as the roads hacked out over nearby Tincup and Cumberland Passes, the Cottonwood Pass Road offered a more gradual ascent and descent. This meant a freighter could use fewer horses and mules to haul heavy loads over the divide, thus saving money. Cottonwood suffered some traffic loss when narrow-gauge trains laid track to the mines of Taylor Park and Aspen, but the fat lady really started singing the Cottonwood refrain when the mines began to close. The mining

industry faded into the history books with tales of toils and triumph, and the demise of companies in the business of transporting the precious metals soon followed.

Two-wheeled enthusiasts can set aside some gratitude for the hearty explorers searching for high-altitude ores—their discoveries have had the delayed benefit of delivering outstanding roads for bikes. The Colorado tourism industry, noting the wide and far vistas offered by Cottonwood Pass, worked with Gunnison and Chaffee counties to refurbish the rutted wagon road into one suitable for automobile traffic, and in 1959 the auto route was opened. Chaffee County took an extra step in 1987, paving their 21-mile side of the pass, completing the project in 1990.

The ride to the summit of Cottonwood Pass from the east begins from Buena Vista's Main Street intersection with US 24. Signs point the way west toward Cottonwood. The road name becomes the Cottonwood Pass Road or County 306. After two miles of suburban Buena Vista riding, the traffic empties out, and ahead of your handlebars you will have one of the most blissful 19 miles of serpentine road anywhere. Seriously. With the wandering and rushing waters of Cottonwood Creek showing the way, the tarmac follows the stream's lead for 18 miles, before leaving to forge its own route to the summit 1,100 feet higher. The remaining three miles contain a mix of lazy and more energetic switchbacks. You'll pass the last few hardy trees able to survive in this rarified air, and after one more bend in the road, your bike will accelerate up a short straight to one of the highest passes in North America, at 12,126 feet.

You did bring your camera, didn't you? Whether it is looking back toward the east at the exhilarating climb you just made, or west to the Taylor Park area down below, this is one photogenic place. To be sure, while the images of this ride provide a glimpse of what you can expect, there's nothing like being in the postcard yourself, transported there by the best of open-air vehicles.

I don't mean to minimize the western side of Cottonwood Pass. For more than a few, it will be a blast letting your dual-sport or lightweight street bike have its way with this fun, hard-packed dirt road. The curves will be tighter at the top, as it is with the east side, then it will be a more meandering affair through dense stands of pine, with breaks in the trees to gaze upon the Taylor Park Reservoir below you and the jagged rooftop of the Sawatch Range above you. It is a 14-mile journey to the park, where the razor blue colors of the reservoir will greet you. Point your front tire south for a mile, and just to the east is the Taylor Park Trading Post, where you can stop, grab a snack, and reflect on what you have just ridden—and anticipate what is to come!

At the eastern end of the Cottonwood Pass ride are two nearby journeys: the US 24 Arkansas River Valley ride paying homage to ten peaks over 14,000 feet [124], and the US 285 journey over Trout Creek Pass into the high meadow expanse of South Park [134].

For a side journey on the east side of the pass, there is a dual-sport ride 8.7 miles from Buena Vista. Turn south onto Forest Road 344 to Cottonwood Lake three miles up the road. Very, very pretty. The Taylor Park side, to the west, presents two ride options, a dual-sport journey south through the semi-ghost town of Tincup, over Cumberland Pass to Pitkin [122]; and the Taylor River Canyon ride [118] to Almont.

Ride 127 **Independence Pass**

Colorado 82

A famous 43-mile alpine journey over one of the highest paved passes in North America, with the well-known resort town of Aspen on the west side

The road over Independence Pass has recently been recognized by Congress as a national scenic byway. Few paved roads in North America, if not the world, go as high as this baby. When your bike gulps the thin air at the 12,095-foot summit, realize that you will have arrived at an uncommon place. But it is the ride there that is really the destination. You can make this above-timberline journey on a narrow and exposed road in a vehicle with doors, with maybe the heater on or the windshield wipers going back and forth, but for me, nothing compares with being out in the wind on the airiest of transportation devices.

Both sides of the pass are dramatic. From the east, Colorado 82 leaves US 24 just north of Granite. After circling Twin Lakes Reservoir, you'll start the 4,300-foot climb alongside the whitewater of a cascading Lake Creek. The elevation gains are fairly mild as the road bends and curves gently through

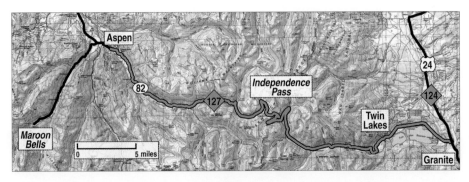

bench layers of trees and rock. As you enter a broad, flat, wetlands area, look ahead and up at the shelf road you will soon be ascending.

The real climbing begins when you make a sharp left around a hairpin curve, and over the handlebars you'll see a narrow strip of asphalt squeezed between two cliffs that climb toward the sky. There is no guardrail, and basically no shoulder except for small pullouts here and there, so don't be too distracted by distant sights! The airy openness of this journey, with its deep drop-offs just feet away helps to amplify the white-knuckle quality of this ride.

The western, or Aspen side of the pass has its own unique character, including passage on ledges of rock only one and a half lanes wide. There have been times when I've been confronted by a super-wide SUV coming the other way and was glad to be on a skinny bike!

Aspen as a town may not be everyone's cup of tea, but it is an amazingly historic place, with many fortunes won and lost, earned and spent. There's always something going on in Aspen, and a pause to check out the festival of the moment, or to just to grab a meal, always seems to work out. When wandering around town, or taking Colorado 82 through it, you might note the historic Jerome Hotel.

One side trip in the Aspen area that you should not pass by is a scoot up Maroon Creek to see the famous Maroon Bells. The turnoff to Maroon Creek is well marked just one mile west of Aspen on Colorado 82. Not only is this curving, climbing, nine-mile ride excellent, with thick aspen groves cloaking the nearby steep slopes, but when the 14,000-foot Maroon Bells make their appearance before you, you will understand why this is considered one of the most beautiful sights in the world.

For connecting rides on the east, you have US 24 [124] and its tour of the Fourteeners (peaks over 14,000 feet in elevation). West of Aspen is the Frying Pan ride [129] and the McClure Pass [113] traverse. You are going to find food and fuel options very limited on the east side of the Independence Pass, though in Twin Lakes there is a small restaurant and a small general store. The Aspen side, understandably, is loaded with restaurants for whatever mood you're in, but if you top off your tank in Aspen you also will find top prices per gallon as well! Enjoy a memorable ride over Independence Pass.

Ride 128 **Hagerman Pass**

Turquoise Lake Road, Hagerman Pass Road, County 4, 41, 105, Ivanhoe Lake Road

A historic 31-mile alpine pass ride with eight miles of scenic, paved lake riding and 23 miles of high-altitude dual-sport adventure

The ride around the south shore of Turquoise Lake, then up and over the lofty heights of Hagerman Pass is a Colorado classic. Now, it should be mentioned that the stony road over Hagerman pushes the boundary of what makes the cut for inclusion in this book. There is some rough rock riding on either side of the summit, and a water crossing, but a heavy dual-sport bike ridden carefully will make it, and the reward will be worth the effort.

Like many passes in Colorado, Hagerman's development can be traced to a railroad company's sometimes overly ambitious attempts to reach paying customers on the other side of a soaring mountain range. The 11,925-foot

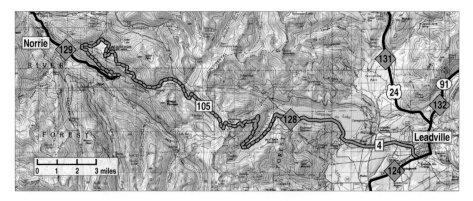

pass is named after James Hagerman, who extended his Colorado Midland Railroad from Colorado Springs to Aspen in 1887. Rather than place rails over the top, he drilled a 2,100-foot tunnel 400 feet lower, but it was a troublesome thing, and six years later in 1893, the line was sold. A new, more direct tunnel, the Busk-Ivanhoe, at a whopping 9,400 feet in length, was bored at an elevation 600 feet lower . Alas, hard times followed, and trains ceased rolling on the ribbons of steel, and the tracks were pulled up during World War I. In 1922, the train bed was converted to an auto road, and the lower bore became the Carlton toll tunnel, which carried traffic for 20 years. There were concerns about the safety of the tunnel, and a serious collapse in 1943 ended the tunnel chapters of Hagerman Pass.

From the east, access to the route to Turquoise Lake and Hagerman Pass is gained from US 24 on the south side of Leadville,

turning north on McWethy Drive, then left onto Turquoise Lake Road. From the west, Hagerman is reached by the Frying Pan Road east out of Basalt [129]. From the Leadville side, you might not have a dual-sport underneath you, but you can still enjoy a most assuredly beautiful ride for eight miles alongside the lake that should more accurately be called "Deep Blue Lake." A sign and turnoff to the south will point the way to Hagerman Pass. The next four miles will be unpaved, but graded, and should be no problem for a heavy street bike. This was the autoroute used for two decades to access the Carlton Tunnel located four miles past the Turquoise Lake Road turnoff.

It is common to see a few cars parked here, with sightseers checking out the history and reading the interpretive signs at this 10,900-foot-high place. It is uncommon to see many people going beyond this point, however. From this point, the altitude and

Looking east, just shy of the Hagerman Pass summit

difficulty of the road and journey increase. The pass summit is 1,000 feet higher and 4.4 miles away. Two switchbacks later, there will be an airy and smooth shoulder, then a snowfield that could be problematic if it is early in the season. Just on the other side of this snowy guardian is the summit.

The western side of Hagerman offers its own heavy hitting line-up of vistas, history, and road "texture." To the south are the soaring 13,000-foot sister peaks of Mt. Elbert, which is Colorado's tallest, at 14,433 feet. The road base is gentle dirt in places, but mostly rocky, with a maneuver or two over a bouldery surface. A fun water crossing presents itself about 1,000 feet down the west side, then a long gravelly valley descent leads to a curvy forest ride.

At lower elevations, cow camps and meadow scenery will have you squeezing the brakes. Shortly after joining the pavement of

Frying Pan Road, you can see the semi-ghost town of Norrie toward the south. This old lumber camp is distinguished by the red roofs atop the refurbished structures.

Leadville on the east and Basalt on the west are your sources for food and fuel. In between is 62 miles of "be prepared," but it's also amazing riding. The approaches on both sides are paved, including the 31 miles of the delicious Frying Pan Road. If you are astride a dual-sport, you can make this a great day of riding by connecting the Hagerman Pass journey with the unbeliev- able Crooked Creek Pass ride [130], north off of Frying Pan Road, just east of Ruedi Reser- voir. Street-bike exploration of the Turquoise Lake area can be connected with the rides sprouting in every direction out of Lead- ville—Tennessee Pass [131], Fremont Pass [132], and the US 24 tour of the Fourteeners [124].

Ride 129 **Frying Pan River**

Frying Pan Road, Forest Road 105

A snaking 31-mile paved river road providing access to a recreation area and two special dual-sport rides

Before Second Creek Raceway near Denver International Airport closed in 2005, I signed up for a two-day track school. With me for those sessions were half a dozen sport-bike riders from Aspen. During a break, I asked them what their favorite ride in the Aspen area was. The hesitation wasn't long and the vote was unanimous—Frying Pan Road.

Midland Avenue is the main east-west road through downtown Basalt. If you ride it east, following the signs pointing the way to Ruedi Reservoir, you will end up on Frying Pan Road. The reservoir is an appetizing 13 miles away, offering its own eight-mile sec-

tion of tasty riding, before you consume another ten miles for dessert.

You might assume that Frying Pan River, or "The Pan" as locals sometimes call it, is named for the ultimate destination for some of the residents of this Gold Medal fishing stream. But according to legend, the stream is named after a frying pan that was left in the crook of a tree to mark the spot where a fallen comrade had died in a fight with Indians. I haven't seen this pan-in-a-tree, but I sure do see fly fishermen working the stream hoping to tempt the river's residents with their array of flies. Likewise, those of us on motorcycles will be working to ride the lines,

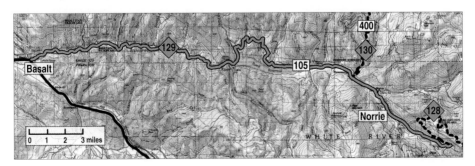

hit the apexes, and be one with the bike and road.

The castle-like southern slopes of Red Table Mountain are barricades to the north, and there are places where spires of deeply colored rock will draw your gaze upward. There are also occasional breaks in between the kinks of the road, where pleasing views of pastures and farms provide a respite from the pace of the ride. To be sure, the Frying Pan can deliver delights at any speed. The nearby and constant presence of the rushing stream, coupled with the hues of reds and green all around you, make this a scenic journey, as well.

Near the 13-mile mark, the road ascends up and away from the river as you approach the dam and reservoir. When you round a left-hand curve and see the azure blue waters, consider a pause at one of the several wide spots on the right. I hope you have a camera with you. Continuing on, you will wind around, and up above Ruedi Reservoir, before descending closer to the water on the eastern side of the lake. There are another ten miles of more secluded riding before the journey becomes a dirt, off-road one.

If you are on a street bike, you have choices for out-and-back destinations, whether it is the reservoir or the termination of the surfaced road base 31 miles from Basalt. If a dirt-worthy dual-sport bike is moving you through the wind, two of the best off-road journeys in Colorado are on the eastern side of this ride. Crooked Creek Pass Road departs to the north 25 miles from Basalt [130]. In a word—stunning. If you just stay on Frying Pan Road, it leads to high and historic Hagerman Pass [128]. In two words—also stunning. Regardless of your plans, your main food and fuel options will be in Basalt, before you take off.

Ride 130 **Crooked Creek Pass**

Forest Road 400, Brush Creek Road

A very special 32-mile ride winding through abundant wilderness, complete with lakes, a state park, and fun riding sections

Years ago, someone mentioned to me how I needed to ride Crooked Creek Pass. Sure, I thought to myself, I'll get around to it some day, but it took a while. When I finally rode it, my immediate reaction was, "Why did I wait so long?!"

I try not to use superlatives like cheap Mardi Gras beads, casually and abundantly tossed about, but there isn't anything cosmetic or superficial about this Crooked Creek Pass ride. It is one of the best in Colorado, and it delivers a real gem of an experience.

On the north end, the Brush Creek Road out of Eagle leads to Crooked Creek Pass. Coming up from the south, is well-marked Forest Road 400, three miles east of Ruedi Reservoir off Frying Pan Road [129]. The ride up from the south is an ascending one initially, with 1,200 feet of altitude gained in seven miles. The road base is mostly smooth dirt with a light mix of rock, but it can be rutted from hard rains. To escort you and your bike higher, it winds lazily back and forth, climbing through hillsides of wildflowers and hallways of aspen.

At seven miles, you will break out into a magical place of epic dimensions. Before you, to the east, will be enormous fields and meadows clothed in grasses and colored in wildflowers. Nature's carpet rolls away from you to valleys below, where the texture changes to shaggy pine and remains that way all the way up to timberline, below the alpine peaks of the Holy Cross Wilderness.

This is a pristine and unchanging place—the faint dirt road your bike is on is the only visible intervention from man. I have to admit that my memory of this place is probably enhanced by the perfect conditions of my first ride there—the low level of the sun, the terrain dappled from cottony clouds, the rainbow of wildflowers, the hues of green, and

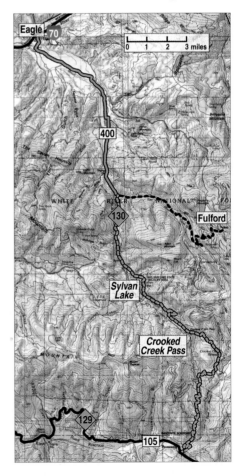

the undisturbed wilderness. But regardless of when you ride to this area, your senses will get a workout.

Three miles to the north and 600 feet higher, you will come to the modest Crooked Creek Pass summit at 9,995 feet. It isn't a glorious one, but after the painting you've been through, you're still on a motorcycling artistry high. At just under seven miles to the north, as you descend toward Eagle, you'll enter the Sylvan Lake State Park area. Oh, my. What a setting. You will not be able to resist squeezing the brake. There's a parking area at the lake, or you can pause above it on the road and get a view many below don't know about.

If more dual-sport adventure is on your brain, the fine Gypsum Creek ride via Forest Road 412 heads to the northwest just south of Sylvan Lake. If you continue north, the pavement returns in four miles. This is also where you intersect with Brush Creek Road. A turn to the right/east, will take you to the Fulford ghost town and Fulford Cave, five miles up a dirt-and-rock road. Staying with Brush Creek to the north, you will be in Eagle in ten miles, and it is a fun winding road following the meandering whims of Brush Creek.

If you are on a street bike, from Eagle you can just ride the ten miles south up Brush Creek to where the pavement ends, then turn around, or if you are up for it, continue on the easy dirt road to Sylvan Lake. It is above and south of Sylvan where conditions are more favorable for dual-sport. Connections to the southern end of this ride include Frying Pan Road mentioned above, and the Hagerman Pass dual-sport ride [128] to the east.

Ride 131 **Tennessee Pass**

US 24

A superb 30-mile motorcyclist's road with a variety of features from ascending mountains to descending gorges, with circling meadows to curving rivers, and some history along the way

US 24 between Leadville and Minturn offers numerous excuses for owning and riding a motorcycle. There isn't a boring strip of asphalt the entire route. The diversity of sights and scenery is a bonus. The history—from mining camps and towns, to a famous military camp—is bonus squared.

Start by pointing your bike north out of Leadville on US 24. About a mile from the downtown area, the highway forks: the left tine continues as US 24, while the right tine is Colorado 91 aiming for Fremont Pass [132]. The ride on US 24 over the 10,424-foot Tennessee Pass—on a hump between the monster 14,000-foot peaks of the Sawatch Range and puny 13,000-foot peaks of the Mosquito Range—traverses the Continental Divide only eight miles from Leadville, and is only 272 feet higher (Leadville is already sky-high at 10,152 feet). So it is accurate to note the climb to Tennessee from the south is on the modest side of the scale. The scenery on this stretch is pastoral, with fields of cattle leading to slopes of trees, which give way to the granite tops of Colorado's two tallest mountains, Mt. Elbert at 14,433 feet, and Mt. Massive, 12 feet lower at 14,421 feet.

The pass summit is not the most dramatic, but still, it is worth pulling over for. There is a memorial here in honor of the men of the World War II 10th Mountain Division from nearby historic Camp Hale (the next stop).

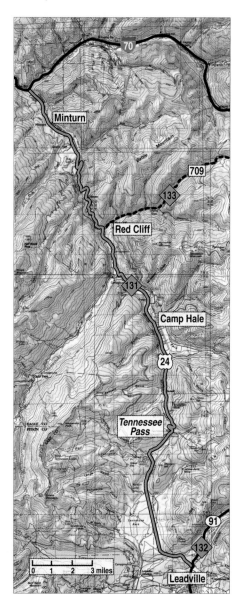

A dirt road leading east from the summit ascends a grade to Ski Cooper less than a mile away. Much of the ski area is above timberline and was used as a training ground by soldiers skiing and fighting in the Alps of Europe. The pass area also possesses an extensive railroad history, going back to mining's heyday, and even continuing today as one of the few passes where trains continue to sing the song of the rails.

The north side of Tennessee Pass is a little more lively and spirited than the south. There's nothing hairy, but a nice curly coif of a road figures out how to manage the gap between the summit of Tennessee Pass and Camp Hale, 1,200 feet lower. The highway here also takes on another name—the 10th Mountain Division Memorial Highway. There are banks of interpretive signs at several scenic pullouts, and you will know you have arrived when you see the broad and flat meadows to the east. Briefly, the light infan-

try division that trained here fought in some of the most challenging terrain and fiercest weather conditions the planet has to offer as they evicted two Axis powers out of the well-defended Italian Alps. There's much more to read at the Camp Hale site, a big place of big history 70 years ago.

There is more heavy-duty motorcycle action the next seven miles as you ride through Eagle River country. When you cross the historic and commemorated Red Cliff Truss Bridge high above the Eagle Gorge, take the signed turn to the right for a quick tour of the old mining town a half-mile away. More information on what some say is a counter-culture town today can be found in Ride 133, for the town lies at the base of the dual-sport Shrine Pass ride.

The remaining eight miles to Minturn do not give you any relief from the steady diet of fun and challenging riding. Immediately north of Red Cliff is the cliffy jaunt on the steep western slopes of Battle Mountain. You will be between a literal rock and a river-gorge place. Another 1,200 feet of elevation change will be express delivered before you can catch your breath, when you'll join the Eagle down below for the winding river finale to Minturn.

There aren't many rides anywhere with so much stuffed into only 30 miles. The towns of Minturn and Leadville, the bookends for this ride, both offer many food and fuel options, but they are more numerous in Leadville. The downtown main street, US 24, is popular for those on two wheels. Continuing south on US 24 is the launch of Fourteener Alley [124], and if you ride 15 miles south out of Leadville, to the right will be Colorado 82 and the great Independence Pass [127]. A popular option for those in the Minturn area is to head west on Interstate 70 for 14 miles and take the exit to Wolcott and superb Colorado 131 [150]. Dual-sporters have the Shrine Pass option mentioned above, as well as Hagerman Pass [128] west of Leadville, and also several side adventures along this Tennessee Pass ride. A fine one is County 703 three miles south of Red Cliff, wandering along Homestake Creek to Homestake Reservoir ten miles farther.

The present-day image of the Camp Hale site was most likely taken from the opposite side of the valley from where the 1940 photo was shot. The faint dirt road on the far side of the original photo is probably the location of US 24 today.

Ride 132 **Fremont Pass**

Colorado 91

A 23-mile sweeping, scenic, high-altitude journey over a pass rich with mining history

Fremont Pass was named for explorer John C. Fremont who discovered this pass in the 1840s. Colorado 91 is the road ascending and descending the 11,318-foot heights, linking Copper Mountain on Interstate 70 to the north with Leadville on US 24 to the south. Leadville possesses a rich history steeped in tales of gold and silver mining. Nearby Fremont Pass can write its own chapters on mining, but the ores beneath its surfaces are not of the kind you would put on a ring finger!

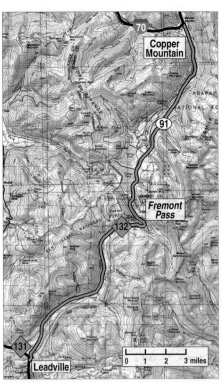

This pass differs from others in that instead of a tightly coiled snake ready to strike, the serpent of Fremont Pass is more stretched out and retreating, avoiding confrontation with its fangs. The climb heading south from Interstate 70 is gradual, with sweeping curves and above timberline peaks guarding the eastern flanks.

As you approach the pass summit you will see enormous tailing ponds to the west, hinting of mining activity, which will become evident when you reach the pass summit and you see the enormous Climax Mine area.

In 1879 Charles Senter, while looking for deposits of gold and silver, came across an ore that was different, and he didn't have a clue what it was. Nevertheless, he staked a claim but continued to look for the gold with which he was more familiar. He did the necessary assessment work each year so the could retain his claim as he worked a nearby gold placer, living in a cabin near the summit of the pass with his Ute wife. In 1895, the ore was identified as molybdenum, but at the time there was no significant market for it and Senter never realized the monetary value of what he discovered. Eventually, molybdenum was noted for its ability to harden steel, and in 1915 the first deposits were shipped out. The place quickly became a beehive of activity, with World War I and its need for armaments. The Climax Mine became the largest molybdenum mine in the world, and met three-quarters of the world's

demand before other alloys and hardening alternatives weakened market prices. The mine shut down in the 1980s. It is still owned by a large company who keeps the operation ready for the day when more attractive market prices for molybdenum make a comeback.

On the west side of the pass summit there is a place to view interpretive signs and exhibits. Consider pulling your bike over and putting the sidestand down to reflect on Charles Senter, his discovery, and the "busyness" of this place more than 100 years ago.

The descent to Leadville 13 miles south of Fremont's summit continues the gradual theme of the north-side incline. With Leadville already at a high-altitude location, the 1,000-foot descent is spread over a distance.

I like the diversity of this pass. It can be ridden at a wonderful cruising speed, and peaks near and far deliver 360-degree vistas as the bike flies between these giants.

Fremont Pass offers several enticements to those who ride it. By itself, it is a serene high-altitude journey with a notable history. Fremont also provides direct access to the Interstate 70 or US 24 areas. From Leadville you have great rides in every direction, including Fourteener Alley on 24 to the south [124], the great Tennessee Pass on 24 to the north [131], and the dual-sport Hagerman Pass to the west [128]. There are some basic food and fuel options in Copper Mountain to the north, and an abundance of choices in Leadville, with the downtown area presenting the best selection of places to dine.

Looking from the top of Fremont to the southeast in the 1880s, and looking from the same location and direction today.

Ride 133 **Shrine Pass**

Shrine Pass Road, Forest Road 708, 709, 712, 16

An easy 12-mile dirt ride known for its wildflowers and special views, with an old mining town anchoring the western approach

Shrine Pass Road was the main route between the Blue and Eagle River Valleys before US 6 was constructed over Vail Pass and became the principle autoroute. US 6 was later replaced by Interstate 70, which Shrine Pass now links to US 24 and Red Cliff on the west. The rush of traffic on the interstate to the north will be in contrast to you, your bike, and maybe a few cars on Shrine Pass Road. This old wagon road has a heady statewide reputation for its amazing fields of wildflowers.

The name "Shrine" comes from the vistas

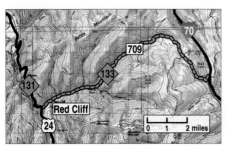

the pass provides of a high, shy peak—the Mount of the Holy Cross, at 14,005 feet. Indeed, when I climbed Holy Cross, the only view I had of its famous east face was looking down the snow couloir, or column, of the cross from the top. Chances are you've only seen photos of the Holy Cross, unless you've been on Shrine Pass, skied a back bowl of Vail and looked up in the right direction at the right place, or climbed a peak far to the east, to view the famous cross from a distance.

Kick off a ride on Shrine Pass Road at Exit 190 off I-70, east of Vail Pass, or from the historic mining town of Red Cliff on the west—there is a sign downtown which points the way to Shrine Pass. From the I-70 side heading west, you'll have a modest ascent of 500 feet over two miles before arriving at its flat, grassy, and flowery summit. The road consists of dirt for its entire length, though it has been improved and can be ridden by a light and capable street bike. There are some mild rocky places here and there but nothing that should cause undue concern.

While it is a gentle 500-foot ascent to Shrine Pass from the east, the elevation gap with Red Cliff to the west is 2,300 feet. Basically, this journey is one of a long climb or a long descent depending on your direction. Personally, I'd opt for a traverse toward the west so you can have the postcard views in front of your visor most of the way. The west side of the pass follows Turkey Creek as it drains the high terrain, with water tumbling over boulders and through fallen timber, playing a nice whitewater instrumental background to your approach to Red Cliff.

Red Cliff, named for the red quartzite cliffs surrounding the town, was founded in the 1870s during the heydays of the Silver Rush. Miners coming north out of Leadville over Tennessee Pass first settled here looking for better fortunes. It once was a bustling place, serving as the first county seat of Eagle until 1921. Today it is a small mix of the old and new, eclectic and common, and worth stopping for a visit.

Shrine Pass Road packs a lot into 12 miles. On the west side, several miles down from the top, there is a small parking area for the

The Holy Cross can be seen from the Shrine Pass road.

Shrine Trail on the south side of the road. Viewing areas for The Mount of the Holy Cross are a short hike away. Enjoy the fields of flowers, the old miners' cabins, and the quiet ride between US 24 and Interstate 70. Red Cliff offers a few options for fueling the digestive tract. For fueling the bike, the closest sources are Minturn eight miles north of Red Cliff on US 24, and Copper Mountain six miles east of the Shrine Pass exit. And by the way, Red Cliff is just half a mile from US 24 and the riding nirvana of Battle Mountain and Tennessee Pass [131].

Looking north at the "suburbs" of Redcliffe in the 1880s, and today

The Jefferson railway depot still services travelers—those riding the roads now, rather than the rails, as they did in 1937.

Ride 134 **South Park**

US 285

A cruising 74-mile ride through immense high country, mountain-ringed meadows, over three gentle passes, along a river, and through historic frontier towns

A trip through South Park is at the heart of this ride. It is a high, inter-montane grassland or meadow, at an altitude of almost 10,000 feet, comprised of almost 1,000 square miles. Mountain ranges protect the park on three sides, with distant Pikes Peak the anchor to the south. The combination of 100-mile views, snowcapped peaks, and fertile meadows, give this journey special scenic status. In 1896, while gazing upon South Park from the summit of Kenosha Pass, the poet Walt Whitman wrote,

> I jot these lines literally at Kenosha summit, where we return, afternoon, and take a long rest, 10,000 feet above sea-level. At this immense height the South Park stretches fifty miles before me. Mountainous chains and peaks in every variety of perspective, every hue of vista, fringe the view . . . so the whole Western world is, in a sense, but an expansion of these mountains.

Many have passed through South Park over the years. It was a favorite hunting ground of the Utes, and they defended it vigorously from other tribes who wanted a share of the action. It still remains a wild and largely unspoiled place with big game roam-

Motorcycling Colorado

ing the meadows and forest. Pioneering ranchers and miners came onto the stage in the second half of the 19th century, and trains soon followed. For years, the only motorized access to this basin was the Denver, South Park & Pacific Railway. Once during a winter blizzard in the park, a train engineer decided he could go no farther, and shut down the train to wait out the raging whitewash of snow. In the morning when the storm let up and visibility returned, he realized that his train had left the tracks miles behind and had been churning across open frozen fields!

From Bailey at the foot of Crow Hill, US 285 follows the curving path of the North Fork of the South Platte. You will be enclosed in the Platte Canyon here, and riding on the old narrow-gauge train bed. Old resorts and towns like Glen Isle and Shawnee were frequented by vacationers 100 years ago coming up from Denver on the trains. Soon the gentle, 10,001-foot summit of Kenosha Pass is attained, and if you look up and to the west while making the climb, you will see scars on the grassy hillsides indicating the train route up the Kenosha grade.

Kenosha Pass isn't the most alpine of passes. It doesn't have gnarly approaches or steep, exposed drop-offs, or vertical rock walls passing close by. But it does have vistas of the expanse below to the south, bordered on the west by a spur of the Mosquito Range that is unlike any other in Colorado. And when seen from the saddle of a bike, well, it is truly special.

The feel of the ride changes once you descend to the park. The terrain levels out. Bends straighten out. Eyes focus far. Look for big herds of elk and small herds of pronghorns. You will pass through the small town of Jefferson a few minutes after descending Kenosha. The Jefferson Market has gas pumps, a short-order kitchen, and for your sweet tooth, famous fudge. About ten miles farther, Red Hill Pass, marked by an S-curve at the top, begins to fill your visor. A glance to the west on the south side will grant you bird's-eye views of two Fourteeners—Mt. Bross (14,172 feet) and Mt. Lincoln (14,286 feet).

The county seat town of Fairplay is a nice halfway stop for this ride. Long ago, the town was founded on the principle of "We Play Fair." With graft and corruption the way

it was in the nearby mining camps, the town of "Play Fair" wanted miners to know they would be treated justly and equitably in the town. The order of the two words was switched later on.

The shapely peak just north of Fairplay is Mt. Silverheels at 13,822 feet, named after a dance hall girl who looked after local miners when a smallpox epidemic swept through the camps. Eventually she contracted the disfiguring disease, but managed to struggle through before retreating to her nearby cabin. The miners raised $5,000 to thank her, but when they arrived at her cabin to present it, she was nowhere to be found. The money was returned to the miners, but out of gratitude, the nearby peak was named for her. To this day, folks claim to have seen her ghost tending the miners' graves at the old Buckskin Joe Cemetery.

For a hearty breakfast or lunchtime meal, the Brown Burro south of Fairplay on Colorado 9 just a few hundred yards from US 285 is a good place to put your sidestand down.

The meadows of South Park continue as you ride south out of Fairplay. You will as-cend the modest Trout Creek Pass 22 miles from Fairplay, and then enjoy an extended and winding descent to Buena Vista and the Arkansas River Valley 13 miles farther and 1,500 feet lower.

This is a go-with-the-flow ride. A cruising ride. A look-around ride. Going at any other kind of tempo will be unfulfilling, if not frustrating. Just take it all in.

Here are some of the other rides described that can be linked with this ride:

- The Wellington Lake, Stony Pass, Matukat, dual-sport ride out of Bailey [049]
- The Guanella Pass Scenic Byway from Grant to Georgetown [036]
- The 43-mile, trip-through-time Tarryall Road out of Jefferson [050]
- The historic Boreas Pass dual-sport ride from Como to Breckenridge [135]
- Rustic and lonely Colorado 9 from Fairplay south toward Guffey [063]
- An alpine Colorado 9 north of Fairplay over Hoosier Pass to Breckenridge [136]
- The Collegiate Peaks and Top of the Rockies Scenic Byways at Buena Vista [124]

Ride 135 **Boreas Pass**

County 50, Forest Road 33, 10

An easy 20-mile dual-sport ride on a historic train bed, over a high mountain pass between the old frontier town of Como and the modern ski resort town of Breckenridge

In the early 1860s, Boreas Pass was a foot and burro path for miners seeking golden ore in the Blue River Valley. It was known then as Breckenridge Pass. In 1866 it was widened to accommodate wagons and stagecoaches. In 1882 the Denver, South Park & Pacific Railroad began laying narrow-gauge track up the wagon road, and the company renamed the pass to Boreas, after the ancient Greek god of the North Wind.

Originally, the line was just a spur to Breckenridge and the railroad found it convenient to build a roundhouse in Como at the junction with the spur. Considered a noteworthy engineering feat, the Boreas line ascended four percent grades to the wintry and snow-laden summit at 11,481 feet. A small company town was built at the top for

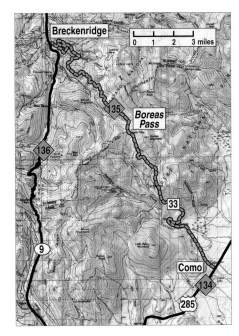

Como is still recognizable after 60 or 70 years.

workers maintaining the line, and several refurbished structures remain today. The railroad lines throughout the area were abandoned in 1938. In the 1950s the U.S. Army Corp of Engineers pulled up the tracks and put down a road base.

The town of Como on the east side of Boreas Pass Road was given its name by Italian miners, perhaps for the similarity this high-alpine place has with Como in the Italian Alps. Today it is small, western, frontier town with a dirt road for Main Street and a few dozen small hardscrabble dwellings, many of which housed the miners and train workers of years ago.

The well-marked main road west out of Como becomes Boreas Pass Road. It turns to a combination of small gravel and dirt just past the town, and remains that way for the next 16 miles until just above Breckenridge. Just over three miles from Como there is a sharp turn to the right/north, and the 1,400-foot climb begins to the lofty heights of Boreas Pass, six miles away.

The mostly compacted dirt surface is fast and the scenery is among the finest. To the east is the high meadow expanse of South Park, and if you stop for a look, you'll be challenged to find anything that has changed from what the Utes would have seen from the same place centuries ago. To the south, a deeply forested valley will be below you, with towering Mt. Silverheels, at 13,822 feet, your guardian along the way.

The Boreas Summit is worth a stop. Pause at the interpretive signs, check out the old narrow-gauge train car parked at the top, and perhaps walk over to the fixed-up section house where rail-line maintenance workers would live year round—even through the fierce cold and snowy winters.

The western descent toward Breckenridge ten miles away has a different texture and flavor than the eastern side. The road surface can be rockier, and the journey passes through tunnels of trees more frequently. A restored water tower, originally built for passing trains a century ago, is visible about halfway, and you might be engine braking and slowing for a picture when you see the snowcapped Ten Mile Range stretched out before you on the horizon, with the immense bulk of Quandary Peak at 14,235 feet. anchoring the south end. Three miles before Breckenridge, pavement returns and you will have a fun, curving descent the rest of the way. At the road's conclusion, there is a re-conditioned narrow-gauge train and a small museum to visit.

You have a time-hasn't-changed town on the east; a modern day glitzy ski resort on the west; and in between, a high, above timberline adventure for you and your bike. The surface would not be friendly to a heavy street bike, but a light one should be okay, especially on the east side. Dual-sport bikes would be at home on Boreas Pass Road.

You can grab a snack in Como at the general store when it is open, and even a meal at the Station House—now a bed, breakfast and restaurant. For fuel, Breckenridge is your closest option to the west, or the towns of Jefferson and Fairplay on US 285. You can connect with rides on either end of this journey—Highway 9 and Hoosier Pass [136] and US 285 from Bailey to Buena Vista [134].

Two wheels and two rails, same location, different years

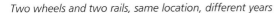

Ride 136 **Hoosier Pass**

Colorado 9

A 30-mile alpine traverse over a high pass possessing two distinct riding personalities, leading to a river ride and ski resort towns

The heart of this ride is the ascent and descent of Hoosier Pass and the Continental Divide at 11,542 feet. Named after men from Indiana who worked on the pass as a WPA project in the 1930s, Hoosier Pass sits between the headwaters of the Blue River to the north, and the headwaters of the South Platte in South Park. I am always amazed that rain falling or snow melting at two places a few hundred feet apart will ultimately arrive at different destinations a few thousand miles apart.

This 30-mile Colorado Highway 9 journey takes you from the Park County seat of Fairplay to the Summit County playground of Frisco. It is a classic ride for your bike with just about everything stirred in—from special towns, to sweeping curves, hairpins, and a river ride.

When you depart Fairplay for the north on Highway 9, you will come to Alma at 5.5 miles. At one time it was the country's highest incorporated town, but nearby Leadville on the other side of the Mosquito Range didn't appreciate Alma incorporating a cemetery on a hillside to wrest the altitude

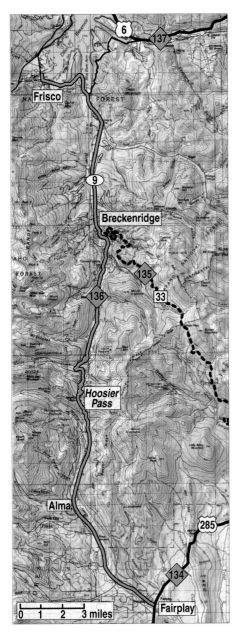

"Puhlease!" was the Leadville response, and they incorporated a similar, up-high subdivision. Alma ultimately raised the figurative white flag of surrender, and this means you only get to spin your two wheels through highest city number three at 10,578 feet—but wait a minute, what do you mean number three? Well, several years ago the cheaters at Winter Park incorporated the ski slopes above town into their city limits. You just can't win!

The road rises up to Hoosier Pass shortly after Alma. Hoosier Pass, in a way, is a tale of two different passes. The south side presents a gentle and sweeping ascent up 1,000 feet to the summit. The north side is a different animal—a coiled serpent of a road with eight percent grades hissing back and forth.

The dramatic peaks you see to the west while cruising along on Colorado 9 have the numbers to back them up. Mt. Bross, at 14,172 feet, is the sentinel above Alma. Mt. Lincoln, at 14,286 feet, towers over the Hoosier Pass summit, and 14,271-foot Quandary Peak is the massive granite mount dominating the north side.

The ride through Breckenridge to Frisco is more sedate, with the Blue River coming alongside for the passage. Breckenridge is a major resort town and you can choose to ride through it, or take a bypass that only saves a few minutes. I tend to go through the scenic heart of town if traffic isn't too bad. Frisco, a ground zero Summit County town, is another ten miles away. There's much to do here, as well. Between Breckenridge and Frisco you will ride around the southwest shore of immensely beautiful Lake Dillon.

This 30-mile ride can easily be turned into a long day, with all kinds of mountain and crown away. So Leadville did the same, expanding the town limits to include a burial site on nearby and higher eastern slopes. Oh yeah? "Well, we're gonna incorporate a high new subdivision," was Alma's retort.

Colorado 9 from Boreas Pass Road, as it approaches the ski slopes of Breckenridge

city stops to lure you. You will find food and fuel readily in most towns, but there is no fuel in Alma. The Brown Burro restaurant in Fairplay is a popular motorcycle stop for breakfast or lunch.

This section of Colorado 9 can also be linked to other nearby roads and rides. Briefly, to the north of Frisco, Colorado 9 goes on to Rabbit Ears Pass and Steamboat Springs [139], and if you turn east at Lake Dillon onto Swan Mountain Road, you will find the Keystone Ski Resort—which lies at the foot of the great Loveland Pass [137]— only four miles away. South of Fairplay, Colorado 9 delivers one of my favorite lonely rides from Hartsel—Ride 63.

Ride 137 **Loveland Pass**

US 6

A stirring 15-mile ride over a classic high mountain pass, with scenic views and easy access from Interstate 70 and Summit County resorts

Loveland Pass, as well as the ski resort at its northern base, was named after William A. H. Loveland, who was president of the Colorado Central Railroad. This railroad was active with the expansion of lines up Clear Creek Canyon, which is essentially the cut through the mountains Interstate 70 follows west of Floyd Hill.

Prior to the opening of the nearby Eisenhower Tunnel on Interstate 70 in 1973, the US 6 Loveland Pass was one of the main east-west routes over the Continental Divide. One of the highest paved roads in North America, it is said to be the highest pass in the world that is regularly maintained in the winter. In can be an unpredictable place any month of the year. This 11,990-foot pass, with its exposed turns and drop-offs, makes it one of the more exhilarating rides around, whether in the driver's seat of a snow plow or holding on to the bars of your motorcycle.

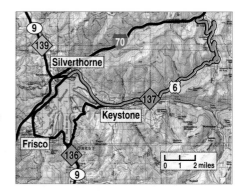

The north end of this ride is at the Loveland Pass/US 6 exit on I-70. It is just before the Eisenhower Tunnel, which can be seen to the west. The Loveland Ski Area is at this exit as well. From the south, you can ride and climb the other side of the pass by heading east on US 6 from the Keystone Ski Resort. Both routes offer a combination of short straights, glorious sweepers, and tight bends.

While on your ascent or descent, you will be tempted to look left and right at the postcard-like vistas. Steal those glances, but with the recognition there is a 100 percent chance a curve will be quickly approaching your front wheel, I would resist any extended trance-like stares!

Since you will be riding well above timberline in this scant-air place, be prepared. You should expect anything, from thunderstorms and electrical activity, to cold sleet, and possibly snow in the summer. But still, this is a pass for which your bike was made. This ultimate convertible ride will deliver an experience to the top that no four-wheeled vehicle could hope to come close to.

Consider making a turn toward Loveland if you are riding east or west on I-70 and have the time (or the desire) to avoid the rush and commotion of interstate traffic near the Eisenhower Tunnel. Also, you could point your bike in this direction if you want to beat the heat in the Denver area. You will be less than an hour away from significant temperature abatement. During a heat wave several years ago, temperatures were forecasted to climb north of 100 degrees along the base of the Front Range, so I decided it was time to ride to the refreshing Loveland Pass and bask in its balmy 50-degree temperatures.

At the summit there is a parking area with views begging to be photographed to the north and south. There are also short hiking trails for higher ascents. You won't find services at the top, nor on this road, but the Keystone Ski Resort, six miles away, is food- and fuel-friendly.

This ride links to the Colorado 9 and Hoosier Pass venture [136]. By taking short Swan Mountain Road southwest out of Keystone to Colorado 9, you can be at the base of Hoosier Pass in less than 15 minutes. If you stay on US 6, not taking Swan Mountain Road, you will intersect with Colorado 9 heading north, connecting with US 40 to Steamboat Springs [139], which is the gateway to a number of special rides.

Central West

RECOMMENDATIONS

Paved Mountain Pass Tours

1. From the Summit County area of Interstate 70, ride west to Copper Mountain. Take Colorado 91 south over Fremont Pass [132] to Leadville. Return north to I-70 via US 24 over Tennessee Pass [131] to Minturn. Take the bike east over Vail Pass back toward Summit County. Three passes in an easy-riding triangle over a few hours.

2. Ride Interstate 70 west from the Front Range foothills for Loveland Pass [137]. Scoot through Keystone turning left on Swan Mountain Road for Colorado 9 and the Breckenridge [136] area. Cruising south, ascend Hoosier Pass and enter South Park. Turn left at US 285 [134], returning east for Red Hill and Kenosha Passes. Four passes, half a day.

Unpaved Mountain Pass Tours

1. From Georgetown on Interstate 70 ascend Guanella Pass [036] to the south. Continue on to Grant on US 285 [134], turning right for Kenosha Pass (bonus) to South Park. At the community of Como, point the bike west for Boreas Pass [135] and Breckenridge. Two easy, scenic, high passes in an easy half day.

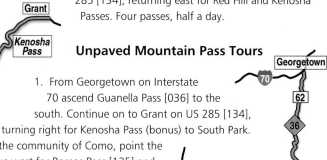

2. From the Interstate 70 and the Vail Pass area, exit for Shrine Pass [133]. Descend to Red Cliff on US 24 [131], taking it south over Tennessee Pass (bonus) to Leadville. Aim the bike west for Turquoise Lake and Hagerman Pass [128]. At the western base of Hagerman, turn right onto Forest Road 400 for Crooked Creek Pass [130] and Eagle on I-70.

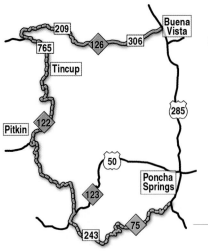

3. From Buena Vista, ascend Cottonwood Pass [126] to the west (It is paved on the east side). Descend to Taylor Park, then ride Forest Road 765 south past the semi-ghost town of Tincup for Cumberland Pass and the other dirt-road passes in the Pitkin area—Waunita and Black Sage [122]. If up for more, find the entrance to Marshall Pass [075] on nearby US 50 for an alternative to paved Monarch Pass [123]. A full day of five easy off-pavement passes.

4. On the north side of Gunnison, ride Ohio Creek Road over Ohio Pass [119] to nearby Kebler Pass [120], turn east on Kebler Pass Road for Crested Butte and a return to Gunnison on Colorado 135 [118]. Alternatively, don't turn east for Crested Butte, but ride the bike west on Kebler Pass Road for Paonia and Colorado 133 [113].

Sweet Rides That Aren't Over a Pass

1. Ride US 50 west of Gunnison along the Blue Mesa Reservoir [117]. Turn right/ north on the western edge of Blue Mesa at Sapinero, joining Colorado 92 for the northern-edge traverse of Black Canyon [115]. Continue to Hotchkiss, then west to the Colorado 65 turnoff to the Grand Mesa [106]. Ride atop the world's largest mesa descending to the town Mesa. At the intersection of Colorado 65 and 330, proceed across onto the De Beque Cutoff [108], riding it to Interstate 70. Go west on I-70 for 13 miles to Exit 49, pointing the bike east on Colorado 65 through the Plateau Canyon [109]. At Mesa, turn south for the Grand Mesa and return. Four twisting roads are connected for a great day of riding.

2. From Whitewater south of Grand Junction, ascend the dirt-surfaced Lands End Road [105] to the top of the Grand Mesa. At Colorado 65 [106], journey south to the Grand Mesa Visitor Center and County 121 [107]. Ride east through the lakes descending to Collbran. Turn west on Colorado 330 [110] for Mesa, connecting with Colorado 65, continuing west through the Plateau River Canyon [109] to Interstate 70 and a return to Grand Junction. An easy half-day, scenic, and secluded ride.

Favorite Roads

Most Scenic (Mountain Passes)

[113] McClure Pass
[120] Kebler Pass
[123] Monarch Pass
[126] Cottonwood Pass
[127] Independence Pass
[128] Hagerman Pass
[130] Crooked Creek Pass
[137] Loveland Pass

Most Scenic (Not Mountain Passes)

[103] Colorado National Monument
[106] Grand Mesa
[112] Glenwood Canyon
[115] Colorado 92 above the Black Canyon
[116] Portal Road, Black Canyon of the
      Gunnison National Park
[119] Ohio Creek

Best Sporting Roads

[106] Grand Mesa
[108] De Beque Cutoff
[109] Plateau River Canyon
[113] Paonia to McClure Pass
[115] Black Canyon of the Gunnison
[123] Western ascent of Monarch Pass
[131] Tennessee Pass

Little-Known Gems

[104] Little Park Road
[105] Lands End Road
[107] County 121 to the Grand Mesa Lakes
[108] De Beque Cutoff
[109] Plateau River Canyon
[110] Colorado 330 to Collbran
[116] Portal Road, Black Canyon
      of the Gunnison National Park
[119] Ohio Creek Road
[122] Parlin–Pitkin Road
[130] Crooked Creek Pass

Best Dirt-Road Adventures

[105] Lands End Road
[107] County 121 to the Grand Mesa Lakes
[119] Ohio Creek Pass
[122] Pitkin to Tincup via Cumberland Pass
[130] Crooked Creek Pass
[135] Boreas Pass

Worthy Destinations

[106] Grand Mesa Visitor Center
[107] The lakes of Grand Mesa from County 121
[110] Vega State Park east of Collbran
[112] Hanging Lake hike
      from Glenwood Canyon
[113] Town of Redstone north of McClure Pass
[115] Black Canyon of the Gunnison Overlook
[116] The Black Canyon via Portal Road
[117] Cimarron Narrow Gauge Train Exhibit
[119] Ghost town of Baldwin
      on Ohio Creek Road
[120] Kebler Pass in the autumn
[122] Town of Tincup below Cumberland Pass
[123] Monarch Tram at the top of Monarch Pass
[125] The ghost town of St. Elmo
[127] Top of Independence Pass
[128] Turquoise Lake west of Leadville
      before Hagerman Pass
[129] Reudi Reservoir at
      the east end of Frying Pan Road
[130] Sylvan Lake State Park
      north of Crooked Creek Pass
[131] Camp Hale north of Tennessee Pass
[132] Molybdenum exhibit top of Fremont Pass
[133] Town of Red Cliff at the base
      of Shrine Pass and at US 24
[134] Through South Park to Fairplay
[135] Boreas Pass Section House
[136] Summit County resorts and restaurants
      from Breckenridge to Frisco

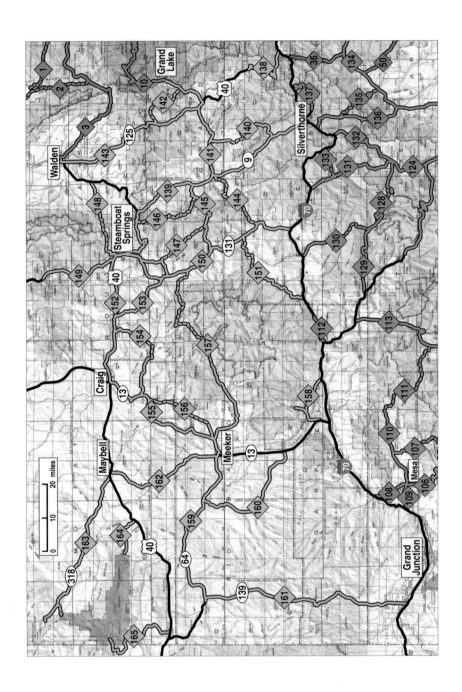

Northwest

REGIONAL OVERVIEW

US 40, as it runs mostly straight through the flat, ho-hum sea of sage west of Craig, is hardly an accurate representation of the northwest section of Colorado. While the region may lack the scale of alpine scenery found elsewhere, or the kinds of roads required to access those lofty places, it does have sweet riding zones everywhere delivering their own brand of perfection.

Often when cruising elsewhere in the state, a truly enjoyable stretch of road may last little more than five or ten miles before your joy is sadly interrupted by traffic, a town, or a stop sign. In northwest Colorado, your grin may go unchecked for 40 or 50 miles.

For example, if you were to take Straw-berry Road north out of Meeker, you could likely count on one hand the number of cars you'd pass on the 40 miles to Maybell. True, if a knee-dragging sport ride is what stirs your hot chocolate, then this stretch might be a lukewarm concoction, but if you hit that open zone of endless undulations with the right frame of mind, you'd have the makings of a perfectly brewed ride.

From the Continental Divide on the east to the Utah border on the west, from Interstate 70 on the south, up to Wyoming, this whole area is brimming with intoxicating routes for all kinds of riders. So, saddle up whatever steed is in your stable and prepare to drink deeply of its charms.

Rides in This Section

Ride 138 **Berthoud Pass**

US 40

A 24-mile ride over a grand sweeping mountain pass, with much-appreciated passing lanes, easy access from Interstate 70 on the south, and a mountain resort town on the north

Back in 1861—the first year of the Civil War—Chief Surveyor of the Colorado Cen-

tral Railroad, Edwin Berthoud, discovered the pass which now bears his name while searching for possible railroad routes. Accompanied by famed mountain man Jim Bridger, Berthoud decided the pass was too steep for a train and that it would be more suited as a road for horse-drawn wagons. Well, today our modern horses like it just fine!

For the southern approach of Berthoud Pass take the Empire exit from Interstate 70—from the north take US 40 as it departs south from the Winter Park Ski Resort. As you pass through Empire, you will be riding through a historic community, one that flourished in the late 1800s during the silver

Traveling over Berthoud Pass in 1915

boom. The Peck House on the northwest side of town is one of the oldest hotels operating in the state. Numerous objects and furnishings inside came with the Peck family by oxcart in 1862.

The approach to the pass, whether from the north or south, is park-like, with high imposing peaks anchoring the horizons. You will feel quite small on the motorized thing between your knees but, nevertheless, anticipation will build knowing a climb is about to begin!

While the dirt rang true for many years, motorized carriages began making the adventurous trip to the top in the 1920s. For decades, traversing US 40 was a harrowing experience. It was a narrow, two-lane affair with tight switchbacks and frequent crashing slides of earth or snow—depending on the season. Only recently was it reconstructed as a broader and safer roadway, but the curves remained, some sweeping and some less so. Do be careful on some of the tighter curves. They can sneak up on you just as your bike is gaining speed on a longer straight. And, they sometimes can be sandy.

At the top of the 11,307-foot pass, there is a dirt parking area with a newly built warming hut to welcome backcountry travellers on both snow and two wheels. There used to be a lodge with a gift shop back in the 1980s, but the Colorado Department of Transportation is returning this pass, along with several others, to a more natural state.

I always enjoy the special views from the top Berthoud Pass. The expanse to the north is especially far-reaching and soul-enriching as you gaze at the bony spine of the Continental Divide with US 40 winding away down below. This pass is both a destination in itself and a gateway to other riding destinations. The resort town of Winter Park, at the northern end of the pass, offers everything from lodging, to fuel and food.

Peck House in 1905

Peck House now

Ride 139 **Rabbit Ears Pass**

Colorado 9, US 40

A sweeping 90-mile rider's road—an always entertaining, bending, and climbing roadway, showcasing reservoirs, resorts, and a major mountain pass

Colorado 9 and US 40, between the resorts of Summit County on the south and Steamboat Springs to the north, cut through the heart of some of the best motorcycle roads in Colorado. If a journey all the way to Steamboat is on your menu, then you've made a great and fulfilling choice in this route. If you decide to order a smaller portion of Colorado 9, combining it with another road, that's another good call. Some of the options available are noted below.

Riding north out of Silverthorne on Colorado 9, you will be soon joined by the Blue River heading the same direction. Take a quick scan for bald eagles, as I've seen them cruising above the Blue while I rolled alongside. Other scans easily take in the Williams Fork Mountains to the right/east, and the jagged skyscrapers of the Gore Range to the west. I've always felt the imposing Gore Range, with its lineup of 13,000-plus foot peaks—including Mt. Powell at 13,448 feet—to be one of the more impressive scenic ranges in Colorado. At 18 miles, the "blue" waters of Green Mountain Reservoir take over accompaniment duties from the dammed Blue River. This is one of the better big water shore rides in the state. At 36 miles, the town of Kremmling comes into view. This community, founded upon silver mining, is sustained today by ranching, hunting, and the trains of the Union Pacific.

At the end of Colorado 9, US 40 takes over

Staring down the namesake for the pass

road duties north out of Kremmling. After passing Wolford Mountain Reservoir ten miles farther, you will enter into some of the finest curve riding in Colorado, which continues for the next 40 miles all the way to Steamboat. Welcome to sweeper heaven. Halfway to Steamboat you will ascend the relatively low Muddy Pass at 8,772 feet, then climb another 700 feet to the broad Rabbit Ears Pass summit. A look to the north between Muddy and Rabbit Ears will reveal the source of the pass's name. After crossing back over the Continental Divide at Rabbit Ears Pass, you will have a seven percent grade to descend to Steamboat Springs.

The resort town of Steamboat Springs is surely a destination for motorcyclists. One will see bikes parked in almost every hotel or motel parking lot. The downtown US 40 main street is an amphitheater of bikes passing by on its stage, from morning to night.

I'm not even going to try to suggest a restaurant, for they are all good, regardless of the kind of food you are in the mood for. There is fine riding in every direction from Steamboat Springs, as well as off Colorado 9 and US 40. Here is a listing of all the motorcycle fun roads you can turn toward from Silverthorne to Steamboat, starting from Silverthorne heading north:

- Ute Pass Road east to Williams Fork [140]
- Trough Road west to Colorado 131 [144]
- US 40 east of Kremmling through Byers Canyon to Granby [141]
- Colorado 134 west over Gore Pass to Colorado 131 [145]
- Buffalo Pass Road north of Steamboat then east to North Park [148].
- Elk River Road north of Steamboat to Steamboat Lake [149]
- US 40 west of Steamboat to Craig [152]
- Colorado 131 south to Wolcott [150]

Ride 140 **Ute Pass–Williams Fork**

Ute Pass Road, Forest Road 15, County 3

A 27-mile ride consisting of a wonderfully curving, paved mountain pass ascent with hardly any traffic, leading to a descent toward an impressive mill, and concluding with a fun and scenic, smooth dirt ride toward a recreation area

This is a split personality ride. On the south end you have a paved, mountain pass basically all to yourself. On the north end you have a sweet, hard-packed dirt road following a river through open rolling ranchland, and a paved conclusion at a large and scenic mountain reservoir. In between you have a massive mill operation processing ores delivered by a tunnel through the Continental Divide.

The turn to the east onto the Ute Pass Road from Colorado 9 is about 12 miles north of Silverthorne on Interstate 70. For years, I would pass the sign and turnoff with a shrug of the shoulders, continuing my merry way north or south on Colorado 9. It wasn't until I was poring over a map looking at off-road ventures in the Winter Park area that I noted this 27-mile route and kicked myself for so blissfully ignoring it.

The first order of business will be the climb up to Ute Pass, its summit five miles away and 1,300 feet higher. The sweetly paved surface presents a mixture of curves and sweepers that would meet with the approval of a discerning sport rider. You would be excused for minimizing glances at your mirrors on the ascent, but as your bike turns more to the north, not gazing at the dramatic Gore Range is less excusable.

The penthouse views of these rugged peaks on the other side of the Blue River Valley are worth pulling over at wide shoulders along the way or at the pass summit, but the views are better before the summit. The east decline to the Williams Fork Valley is

matched with a decline in the quality of the pavement. It's not bad, just not as good as on the west side.

The extensive operations of the Henderson Mill will appear as you approach the valley. I can't help but be mesmerized by large-scale projects and all they entail—in this case, the largest molybdenum mine in North America. The mill processes the steel-hardening ores mined from its sister operation 15 miles away on the other side of the Continental Divide, not far from the base of Berthoud Pass. The ore is transported via tunnel and train to the Henderson Mill.

Once you reach the valley floor you can enjoy a fun, weaving, and hilly ride on smooth firm dirt. Most any street bike should be okay on this if maneuvered with a steady hand. The Williams Fork River helps lead the way for a spell, but then the road departs for a smorgasbord of ranches, meadows, and patches of forest. As the odometer clicks off more miles on this fast dirt surface, the views open up, and sweeping vistas will fill the horizon as you approach the Williams Fork Reservoir Recreation Area. From camping and picnicking, to fishing and boating—this mountain lake has it.

The northernmost four miles of this ride are paved. Given the dual nature of this ride, one could just ride a section and then head back. For example, you could ascend Ute Pass from Colorado 9 [140] and then return. Same for the Williams Fork Reservoir side. If you are on a dual-sport bike, ride theportion south from US 40 [141], and just before the Henderson Mill, find Forest Road 139 heading east toward Fraser and Winter Park. This Ute Pass ride is a great connector between Colorado 9 and US 40 if you want to avoid going all the way to Kremmling. There are no food or fuel services between Silverthorne on the south and Hot Sulphur Springs on the north, so give this some consideration, and possibly bring some food with you for a picnic at the reservoir.

Ride 141 **Headwaters**

US 34, 40

A 40-mile leg of the Colorado River Headwaters Scenic Byway following the river's journey through impressive lakes, fertile fields, and the first canyon carved by its waters

The Colorado River starts its canyon carving journey toward the Pacific Ocean below the Continental Divide just north of Milner Pass on the west side of Rocky Mountain National Park, 15 miles north of the eastern end of this ride at Grand Lake. You'll join the river south of the national park entrance as it enters a series of water conservancy reservoirs and projects. Even Grand Lake, Colorado's largest natural lake, has its water level managed by the conservancy district. The big blue pond of water here is Lake Granby, Colorado's second largest reservoir, filled in 1949 with water from the Colorado River after its large earthen dam was com-

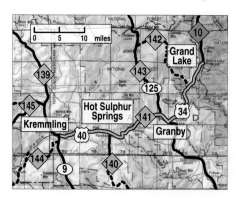

pleted. Together, the five lakes in the vicinity are sometimes referred to as "The Great Lakes of Colorado." The river is soon released to its more free-flowing natural state, and this will be what you follow for 31 more miles to Kremmling.

The ride south out of the resort community of Grand Lake on US 34 is one of lakeshore riding, marinas, small businesses, and forested housing development. There will be traffic here, so it is best to ride in cruise mode, with the big water on the east side of the road calming your throttle hand. After ten miles, you will rise over a small bluff and then descend five miles toward the town of Granby and US 40, where you will turn right/west to continue on the Colorado River Headwaters Scenic Byway.

Though you are riding down the river valley, the river isn't always right there next to you and your bike. Its flows will sometimes be distant and hidden by dense stands of cottonwood trees. This is the case for the eight miles to the town of Hot Sulphur Springs, as US 40 traverses a gentle valley through low rising hills. This town is one of the older communities in Colorado, first sinking roots in 1840 when William Byers was the first white man to discover the hot-water springs—already well known to the Ute Indians. With a little courtroom deception, coupled with some assistance by the U. S. Cavalry, he was able to "acquire" the land from the Utes, and thus began the colorful history of this small town and the hot-springs resort that remain today.

A five-mile gorge and canyon named after Mr. Byers swallows traffic just west of Hot Sulphur Springs. For many of us on a motorcycle, this will be the riding highlight of these 40 miles. There is a chance the Union Pacific will race you through this cut in the earth, but you already know what the outcome will be, right? Byers Canyon is the mighty Colorado's first rock-cutting work of art; it's the first canyon of many on its 1,450-mile journey to the Gulf of California and the Sea of Cortez. The second is just west of Kremmling—the truly tremendous and intimidating Gore Canyon [144]. The ranching town of Kremmling is 16 miles farther, after you emerge from Byer's western portal. The road and river will be more neighborly on this stretch of US 40, and they'll accompany each other most of the remaining distance to Kremmling.

You won't be far from amenities and services on this ride. I particularly enjoy the old mining-turned-lake-resort town of Grand Lake. It still has that historic village feel, with a main street enticing you with all kinds of restaurants and shops. On July 4th, its fireworks show is one of the finest in Colorado, with the lake reflecting the sparkling show above. You're also at the doorstop of the western side of Rocky Mountain National Park with the classic Trail Ridge Road ride [010] only two miles to the north.

If you are on a dual-sport bike, you might want to check out the nearby Stillwater Pass Road [142]. The town of Granby on US 40 is Grand County's most populous, and is less resort-like than Grand Lake. It may be more of what you'll be looking for as a place for a pause or stop.

Colorado 125 and the Willow Creek Pass ride is just two miles west of the US 34 and US 40 intersection [143]. Two miles west of Byers Canyon, a smooth and graded dirt road leads to Williams Fork Reservoir and on to the paved Ute Pass [140]. And when your bike is idling in Kremmling and you're wondering which direction to turn the handlebars, consider Trough Road over Gore Canyon [144], which continues the Headwaters Scenic Byway, or the ride between Silverthorne on the south and Steamboat Springs to the north [139].

A river, a road, and rails share the narrow and cliffy spaces of Byers Canyon.

Ride 142 **Stillwater Pass**

Stillwater Pass Road, County 4, Forest Road 123

A 23-mile dual-sport journey over a lonely mountain pass, through a country filled with moose, placer gold, and hidden valleys

This is an off-road venture, visually exploring the southern peaks of the Never Summer Range. Both ends of the ride are watery tours down low, and this would include the massive Lake Granby on the eastern edge. But more humbly, this would be Stillwater Creek on the east and Willow Creek on the west. Lush wetlands with trickling water

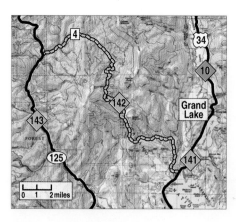

feeding thirsty aspen groves will accompany you as you gain altitude. Corridors of pine frequently block far-ranging views, but gaps in the trees permit close-up observation of some shapely, if not colorful peaks. The thin veins of gold in the area were mostly mined out in the 1880s, but placer gold—flakes that have made it to the surface of hillsides and into the flows of creeks—can be found in every burbling stream draining this side of the Never Summer Range.

From Colorado 125 on the west end, the well-signed Stillwater Pass Road is 17 miles north of the intersection of Colorado 125 and US 40. There is an interpretive display at the beginning to introduce you to what will be ahead in this chunk of the Arapaho-Roosevelt National Forest. The first four miles deliver a gently ascending valley ride on a smooth dirt surface, with Willow Creek your willing but wandering companion. The greenery around the stream stands in contrast to the beetle-killed forest around.

I haven't touched upon this elsewhere in the book, but the mountain pine beetle's catastrophic, if natural infestation is predicted to claim all of Colorado's large diameter lodgepole pine forests in the next several years. Currently, the devastation is especially noticeable in the state's northern forests, and also extends to southern Wyoming. A Canadian riding friend tells me there are explosions of the same epidemic in the Canadian Rockies as well. If we were to ride these forests decades from now, I suspect we might see quite a flourishing scene, vibrant with replacement vegetation, including aspen trees.

At seven miles, you will have urged your steed to gain 800 feet in elevation. It is time to leave the Willow Creek Valley and put

spurs to the bike to climb another 1,000 feet over the next 3.7 miles for the pass summit at 10,620 feet. Stay alert up to this seven-mile point, for you will be riding through prime moose country. This tallest of North American mammals has a thing for the wetland salad bowls of this area's drainages. The North Park region just on the other side of nearby Willow Creek Pass [143] was a key re-introduction point for 24 moose brought here in 1978. Colorado living has expanded their numbers to more than 600 today.

It is the traverse from here to the pass summit where I question the ride's suitability for a street bike. With the 1,000-foot altitude gain comes an increase in the number and size of the rocks populating the road. Oh sure, a capable street bike could probably pick its way around and through the bumpy surface, but it does get tedious without a suspension-ready dual-sport. There is a devi-

ous network of unmarked and stray forest roads near the top that could tempt a wayward turn. If you're not interested in turning this into another kind of adventure, just stay the course on the road looking the most "main."

The east side of Stillwater resembles the west side up high, then transforms itself into a terrain of broader valleys, farther views, and milder curves, with a fast dirt surface encouraging a little extra twist of the throttle. It's a fun section here as the Trail Creek and Stillwater Creek drainages host the entertainment, both riding and visual. Whether ascending or descending, be sure to pause and look east at the grand views of Lake Granby's blue waters with the sentinels of the Indian Peaks guarding the eastern shore-line. At the very eastern end of this 23-mile pass ride, a smooth dirt, then paved surface, is the roadway as it winds through a housing development near Lake Granby. A sign on US 34 points the way toward Stillwater Pass.

Colorado 125 [143] is at the west end of this ride. You have Rocky Mountain National Park and Trail Ridge Road [010] just a few miles north of Lake Granby. Just to the south is the Colorado Headwaters Scenic Byway described in Ride 141. Think of the Stillwater Pass ride as a dual-sport alternative to the paved US 40 and Colorado 125 route. With no food or fuel services on the west end except for Walden to the north or Hot Sulphur Springs to the southwest, the nearby towns of Granby and Grand Lake are where you can pause or stop to stock up.

Ride 143 **Willow Creek Pass**

Colorado 125

A exquisite 52-mile rider's road—a destination road if there ever was one— with a lonely mountain pass and divine curves on each side

Those I know who ride for the thrill of it, who definitely view the ride as the destination, put this section of Colorado 125 over Willow Creek Pass on their short list of Colorado favorites. It has a delectable combination of lazy and lusty curves, dips and rises, for miles and miles. In addition, with almost vacant North Park on the north side, it's basically a forlorn highway going to or from a remote and quiet place. You will essentially have the 52 miles to yourself and those with whom you ride. Last time I rode Colorado 125, it was me and, for a brief moment, a beater truck with some logs in tow.

From the south going north, the entrance to Colorado 125 is three miles west of downtown Granby, or two miles past the US 40 and US 34 intersection. When you join the road you will have in front of you a 21-mile, 1,800-foot ascent to the Willow Creek Pass straddling the Continental Divide. As passes go, this isn't a lofty one—the mountains separating North and Middle Park not as high as those in neighboring ranges—but it is a lofty pass in the minds of those who know what it delivers as a motorcycling road.

The first few miles contain a few homes and ranches, and then the few become isolated homestead cabins in the trees or meadows, as Colorado 125 cuts a path, first through the Arapaho National Forest and then the Medicine Bow-Routt National Forest on the other side of the Continental Divide. Glorious sweepers will be on your flight plan, as Colorado 125 follows wetlands fed

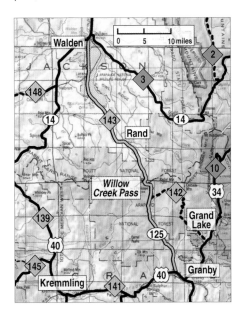

by the flows of a wandering Willow Creek. The forested pass summit is rather undramatic compared to the riding zone you are now in. So unless you want a Continental Divide photo, you will be flying on by without interrupting the flow. The north side of the pass serves up wonderfully tighter bends, but there's nothing unexpected or hair-raising here. The zone continues for another six miles until the road flattens and straightens out for the high meadows of North Park.

If you don't want to go all the way to Walden, 25 bone-straight miles farther, I would ride five miles to Rand and turn around there, especially if the Rand Store is open. There you can grab a snack and have a break before returning for another run. Every time I pass through Rand, the store has had a sign out front noting it was open Thursday through Sunday, 10 a.m. to 5 p.m. There is no fuel in Rand, with Walden the closest option once you are in North Park. For the taste buds, the Moose Creek Cafe on Main Street is popular with motorcyclists.

Pointing your bike west from Walden, you have Colorado 14 heading toward the Rabbit Ears Range where you can connect with the US 40 ride toward Kremmling or Steamboat Springs [139]. If you are on a on a dual-sport, Buffalo Pass [148] is your ticket to Steamboat. Taking Colorado 14 in the other direction from Walden, toward the east, will bring to you the peerless Cache La Poudre Canyon and Cameron Pass [003]. If a dual-sport is underneath you, the Rand–Gould dirt-road cutoff means you don't have to ride all the way to Walden to head toward the Cache la Poudre Canyon. This cutoff delivers penthouse views of North Park. Be sure to check your gas gauge first, however!

South of Willow Creek Pass, there is a well-marked turnoff to the east for Stillwater Pass. This dual-sport traverse to the Grand Lake area is described in Ride 142. At the southern end of Colorado 125 on US 40, you have the Colorado Headwaters Scenic Byway shadowing the Colorado River [141].

There is one thing I must caution you about this Willow Creek Pass ride: the North Park area and its surrounding forests are teeming with moose. I've never seen one step out of the woods here, nor have I seen the aftermath of a collision, but ride with awareness. That's all. Be at the top of your game and enjoy this immensely special road.

Ride 144 **The Trough**

The Trough Road, County 11, 1

A 24-mile smooth, treated dirt-road ride through scenic Colorado River country, with a deeply cut gorge on the east end

The Trough Road contains the western 24 miles of the Colorado River Headwaters Scenic Byway. With the exception of short Byers Canyon near Hot Sulphur Springs, this is the best section of the byway—visually and as experienced from a bike. From high on Gore Canyon's towering walls, where the Colorado River down below looks like a skinny little creek, down to where the river is only a few feet from you, this is a superb ride. And if trains bring out the ten-year-old in you, like they do for me, then this is even a "superber" ride! Since "The Trough" is a state scenic byway, it gets a little extra road-condition attention, and while not paved, the chloride treatment and smooth, graded surface compressed by other traffic makes it passable for any kind of street bike.

From the small cluster of structures called State Bridge on the west side at Colorado 131, point the front wheel east. The remains of the historic State Bridge Lodge, destroyed in a 2007 fire, can be seen on the south side of the road. In 1901, then Vice President Teddy Roosevelt stayed at the lodge on a hunting trip. Look around and you will see trusses from the original wagon road bridge commissioned by the state in 1890 (thus, State Bridge!). Rails for trains were first placed in 1905 to bring cattle and sheep to market, and at one time the area hosted a huge cattle stockyard. Today, black coal is the primary paying passenger for the 20 to 25 trains passing through daily, but Amtrak trains carrying the human cargo also sing by on the rails.

Your first mile or so will be a 200-foot ascent, and then you'll see the curving river, curving rails, and a curtain of valleys before you. At 3.6 miles you will cross the unsullied waters of the Colorado River and then depart the river and rails as they ply north through Red Gorge, while you fly south over a 400-foot ridge, then down into another valley. Before another ascent is made, there is a fork in the road with County 11 jogging off to the northwest, and the Trough Road becoming County 1 trotting off toward the northeast. The County 11 cutoff drifts down to the tracks and river, and to the small, old train stop town of Radium. This is a rafting area and state wildlife area. Rainbow trout are plentiful in this clear water stretch of the Colorado. Elk and other big game are abundant up and behind the town. There is a "se-

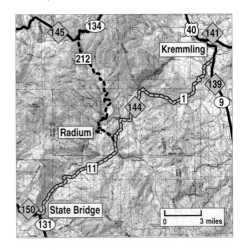

cret" hot springs nearby, but it isn't marked and one has to ask a local to take pity on your commitment to get there and show you the way.

From here, the scenery and ride get ramped up a bit as you continue east on the Trough Road. The snaking circuit visibly twists below as you gaze down into the next valley. Lift your eyes and note the eastern sides and steep 1,000-foot cliffs of the mighty Gore Canyon rising above you. It's a fun ride down 400 feet then up 600 feet to a ledge perched on the south walls of the canyon. The road surface turns to pavement for a mile and there is an Inspiration Point Lookout on the south side of the road. You must put your sidestand down here. Look west at where you have been, and down at where you haven't been.

The canyon hosts Class V rapids and was deemed unnavigable in the 1800s. It was first successfully rafted in the 1970s and now one can even sign up for a commercial river trip through its crashing whitewater. Most outfitters acknowledge the Colorado River in Gore Canyon as the wildest white-water rafting in the state and possible the country. So yes, maybe you have been to the bottom of the canyon on a different kind of "ride"—in a bucking raft, or as a passenger on Amtrak's California Zephyr train, or as an employee of the Union Pacific Railroad!

From here to the east you will have eight more miles of this 24-mile excursion. The Trough Road aims south, away from the canyon, and toward the high, grassy ranchland slopes of the Gore Range above Kremmling. The road surface continues to be off-road excellent, as are the views, as you squint at Kremmling far in the distance. Kremmling is a good place to sit a spell, with a fine Mexican cantina (Restaurant Los Amigos) at the Colorado 9 and US 40 intersection. On the north side of the intersection is Our Family Kitchen, also excellent. The connecting Colorado 9 ride is covered in Ride 139 and the Colorado Headwaters Scenic Byway continues on US 40 to the east toward Grand Lake and Rocky Mountain National Park [141]. On the west side of the Trough Road ride is sweet Colorado 131 [150], and if you're up for joining the river for some more touring, the Colorado River Road [151] guides to the west just 7.7 miles north of State Bridge on Colorado 131.

Ride 145 **Gore Pass**

Colorado 134

A lonely, supreme 27-mile mountain pass ride with sinuous textbook approaches on each side

Gore Pass isn't that high at 9,527 feet. It doesn't rate high in terms of scenic vistas. But it is certainly high on the motorcyclist's list of favorite riding passes in Colorado. There is a motion to the road that invites those on two wheels to join the promenade. If swaying to the music of perfect curves is your idea of a fine ride, then this is for you. Since Colorado 134 has no towns along the

way, only a smattering of dwellings on the east side, and connects two somewhat quiet highways, chances are that you will encounter very little traffic on this road.

The eastern start of Colorado 134 is six miles north of Kremmling on US 40. The first two miles are benign, then the road winds along Pass Creek briefly before starting the 2,000-foot ascent to the pass summit, nine

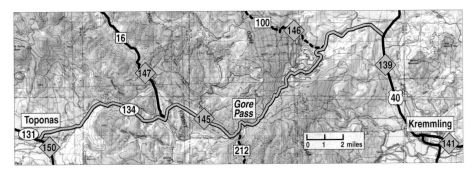

luscious miles away. There are old home-steads, cabins, and some ranches here at which to steal some glances but the sweet bends before you will be the main attraction. At seven miles you will come to a small meadow with an old log home on the south side of the road. The forest starts here and so does some of the best four miles of motorcycle riding anywhere.

From here to the top of the pass, your bike will enter a zone of superb back-and-forth S-curves. The cambers are perfect, the radii consistent, and the grippy surface tends to be clean. The first time I rode this section, my riding friend turned his bike around at the top of the broad summit, looked over at the rest of us and yelled, "I'm going back down to do that again!" In contrast, the pass summit is uneventful. But on the south side, a short walk from the small parking area leads to a marker that notes how the pass was named after Sir St. George Gore from Ireland. He arrived in the area in 1854 to hunt, hiring famous mountain man Jim Bridger as a guide. In three years time, his hunting party killed an estimated 2,000 buffalo, 1,600 elk, and 100 bear.

Another attraction of Gore Pass is the different flavor of the west side. If the east side is sharp cheddar, the west is mild mozza-rella. The remaining 16 miles to the western terminus at Colorado 131 are more sweeping and open—motorcycle divine. This is open range country with modestly hilly terrain. Limited traffic is still the norm, except for the stray logging truck hauling beetle-killed wood out of the surrounding forest. The lumbering trucks won't be an issue, but if where they pull out from the dirt forest roads happen to be near a curve or two, I've seen some carryover debris on the road right where you don't want to see it.

If you're in the dual-sport frame of mind or mode, check out Forest Road 212 leading to the south two miles west of Gore Pass. It is a ten-mile journey to Radium in the middle of the superb Trough Road venture of Gore Canyon and the Colorado River [144].

Kremmling, six miles from the east side of Gore offers a full range of services. Check out Restaurant Los Amigos or Our Family Kitchen if your stomach is growling. Both are at the Colorado 9 and US 40 intersection. The Toponas Country General Store is at Colorado 134's conclusion on the west end. Fuel and snack food is available there. The bookends of US 40 on the east [139] and Colorado 131 [150] on the west link to this ride. If astride a dual-sport, check out the Buffalo Park [146] and Lynx Pass [147] explorations leading to the north toward Steamboat Springs, directly off of Colorado 134.

Ride 146 **Buffalo Park**

Forest Road 100, County 19

A secluded 30-mile off-road ride from one mountain pass to another, through deep meadows and forests, with range cattle your only witnesses

The Buffalo Park ride is a trip through small and huge meadows, open and dense forests. There are wildflowers and the aftermath of wildfires. There are views of Middle Park down below and the Rabbit Ears Range up above. I think what strikes me most when I ride this route is how quiet and remote it is. The last time I made the 30-mile transit I came across one forest service vehicle and a car touring the park area, and that was it. There are side forest roads to check out, but they don't seem to provide access to other explorations. It will be you, your bike, and open range cattle trying to figure out what you are.

The north entrance to Buffalo Park is on the west side of Rabbit Ears Pass, 3.5 miles west of the intersection of US 40 with Colorado 14. The south end is on the Colorado 134, or the Gore Pass Highway, 4.1 miles west of US 40. Turning your handlebars south from US 40 on Rabbit Ears Pass to Buffalo Park or Forest Road 100, a sign will greet you immediately to assuage any hesitations you might have

about making a wrong turn. If you are at this 9,300-foot altitude in midsummer, fields of wildflowers will welcome you as you wind

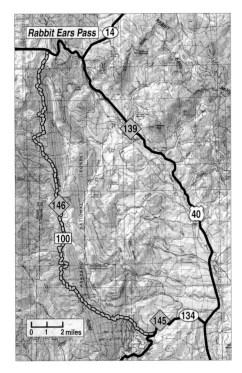

through high meadows and the numerous drainages of Muddy Creek.

Swampy wetlands will have you scanning for moose, and riding through blackened stands of asparagus-like spears of trees will have you wondering when and how you might encounter one. Open range cattle will be scattered alongside the road, and there might be some are on the road. They'll stand, sizing you up with little movement as you approach. You'll wonder if they are simply shocked to see a moving object with an audible growl, or are they considering making a stand for their domain. Or both.

At 13 miles, you'll reach the namesake for this road and ride. The scenic park is immense and will stand in contrast to the vast wooded lands around. It's like a major bald spot among a crew cut of trees, covered with dense carpets of wildflowers. This is a fine place for a pause, a stop, a short stroll, or maybe a snack sitting atop a rock. You will probably have the park all to yourself.

After the park, you'll ascend 500 feet to a 10,000-foot elevation. The best views are to the lumpy wilderness below and to the east, near and far away. The west side consists mostly of trees hugging the roadside. A ten-mile-long 2,000-foot decline to Colorado

134 will be the next serving and a fast road on a good road base makes this a fun chunk of the ride. To clarify, it is all fun, with the northernmost 20 miles tighter and hillier, but the southern ten miles is a nice and open change. It isn't long before ridgelines of the Gore Range come into view, with scattered housing appearing in the meadows above Colorado 134 [145]. In a way, after the 30 miles of seclusion, this will be a welcome shift.

By itself, the quiet journey through the national forest to Buffalo Park can be a riding destination. But this ride could also be a quiet alternative to the traffic of US 40 between Kremmling and Rabbit Ears Pass. [139]. To be sure, 30 miles of dirt, with much of it zigzagging gleefully back and forth, will take a long time, as do most off-road ventures. A dual-sport bike would be at home on this ride. A light and capable street bike ridden steadily and smoothly could make it without a hair-raising incident. Be sure to be food- and fuel-ready as there are no services between Kremmling on the southeast and Steamboat on the northwest. A nice dual-sport loop would be to take this ride on the east side of Gore Pass, and return via Lynx Pass [147] on the west side.

Ride 147 **Lynx Pass**

County 16, Forest Road 250

A 22-mile smooth dirt-road ride over a mountain pass, winding through aspen forests and a series of ranches and small lakes, with a state park at the northern end

While flying over the Colorado Rockies one autumn, I was studying the landscape, identifying features and "riding" the roads. I followed US 40 to Kremmling and then Colorado 134 over Gore Pass. On the west side of the pass summit I spotted this very visible, but secluded road heading north toward the countryside surrounding southwest Steamboat Springs. It was a solitary path through a vast forest of glowing aspen gold and more diminutive fields, with no other roads nearby, and it led to a large body of water. I was eager to identify just what this road was, and to fly over it from three feet, instead of 30,000.

From the south, this Lynx Pass to Stagecoach Reservoir ride is identified by a graded dirt road pointing north off of Colorado 134 [145]. This junction is 8.5 miles east of the Colorado134–131 intersection, or seven miles west of the Gore Pass summit. The first act of this ride is a gentle 300-foot ascent over 2.5 miles on a kindhearted road base to the modest Lynx Pass summit at 8,969 feet.

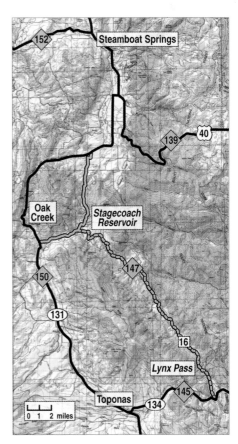

The lodgepole pine devastation wrought by the mountain pine beetle is evident in this section of the Medicine Bow-Routt National Forest. The prevalence of needled pines here on the south end of the ride gives way to leafy aspen on the north end. From Lynx Pass, the bike has a meandering descent of 1,700 feet toward the Stagecoach State Park area, 17 scenic miles away. Morrison Creek will be your guide as you wind through groves of trees, around numerous and picturesque lakes, and past bucolic ranches. It isn't difficult to imagine putting down roots here. The national forest is in every direction, and this includes the never-to-be-molested Sarvis Creek Wilderness Area, hugging the east side of this ride.

With the azure blue waters of Stagecoach Reservoir in the distance, and a greater density of housing, you'll realize that you are approaching the northern terminus of this 22-mile tour. Stagecoach is one of Colorado's pre-eminent state parks, with facilities and recreation options not always found at other parks in the system. It was named for a stagecoach line running from Steamboat Springs to Toponas that closed down in 1907. When you reach County 14 on the western side of the lake, you'll have two options. A turn to the left brings you to Colorado 131 a few miles south of Oak Creek [153]. A push of the handlebars to the right delivers a nice, hilly curving ride to Steamboat, 17 miles away. Both destinations are your best nearby options for food and fuel services, and both are in the middle of superb rides going in every direction. With Gore Pass [145] on the south end, this Lynx Pass ride will likely be one leg of a multi-legged riding animal.

Perhaps the ride described in this chapter is best considered as a little-known alternative going to or from the Steamboat area. Despite the surface of dirt and small rocks, most any motorcycle can make it without travail. Just take your time. No matter what you are riding, these are 22 miles to soak in rather than blast through.

Ride 148 **Buffalo Pass**

County 38, 24, Forest Road 60

A 30-mile dual-sport, dual-personality ride over the Continental Divide, with aspen forests on one side, deep pine forests on the other, and fishing lakes at the top

This is a tale of two rides. On the west side of Buffalo Pass is the all-season destination resort community of Steamboat Springs. It is a bustling place during ski season, and

equally so when the snow is gone. The homes, the businesses, and the activities all reflect the economy and commerce of the area. Even the west side of the pass has a

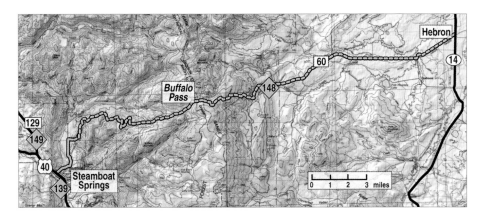

distinct flavor. But reach the 10,300-foot summit on your bike and descend toward the east and it will be as if Scotty has beamed you to another place far away. Bustling becomes bucolic, ski lodges are exchanged for ranch structures, and views of ski runs are replaced with vistas of vast, fertile meadows.

Buffalo Pass Road, or County 24 and Forest Road 60, was originally the main horse-drawn wagon road between Walden and Steamboat. Today, horses of a different kind still traverse it, and it delivers sojourners to a quiet place of fishing lakes and forest service campgrounds. On the west end, the route to the pass can be found in downtown Steamboat by taking Second, Third, or Fourth Street northeast to where they end at Maple Street. Turn right/east onto Maple. Follow it for half a mile to the first crossroad, and turn left/north onto Amethyst Drive. This pretty and twisting paved road merges with County 36 in a mile, and then after one more mile, the signed Buffalo Pass Road will be to

the right/east. You will be at 6,800 feet, and have a 3,500-foot climb over which to spur your bike for the next 11 miles.

Pavement gives way to a smooth, treated-dirt surface in only a few hundred yards and the ascent begins immediately. For several miles you will be riding through vaults of aspen trees and the views behind you toward the Elk River Valley are worth pulling over for. At midsummer, this is ground zero of wildflower central. Most any street bike could make the ascent to these heights and sights, but over the next seven miles your tires and suspension will be introduced to Mr. Rocky Surface. If you are on a street bike, you will know your limits, as well as those of your bike. A dual-sport should have no problems. Switchbacks and stony alpine meadows will be the fare until you reach the broad pass summit.

Up high, aspen trees have waved the white flag (or trunk) of surrender to the elements, leaving hardy Douglas fir and lodgepole pine to make a stand. When you head east from the summit, pause at the blue waters of Summit Lake on the north side of the road. If you have a backpacker's fishing pole in the saddlebag, you can try your luck here, or at one of six other fishing lakes within a half-mile, just behind and to the north through the woods. The descent to the east couldn't be more different. The dirt and rock surface is smoother, the elevation change is more gradual, vegetation is of piney woods, and the views through gaps in the trees are on a bigger and grander scale.

As you descend, resist the temptation to take forest roads going north or south, even if they look more "main," and stay the east-west course. Signage could be better on this side of Buffalo Pass. I once made such a turn and ended up miles away on a dead-end trail, sharing its conclusion with a bunch of displeased and bellowing open range cattle.

Seven miles east of the summit, and 2,000 feet lower, you will arrive at a fantastically beautiful and wild meadow setting. The old Grizzly Creek Ranger Station is here. Place your sidestand down at this place if you can. The unfolding vistas probably haven't changed much since a time many decades ago when rangers would spend summers here. Actually, except for a distant and stray ranch, I wonder if anything has changed over many centuries. County 24 will continue its stroll east, turning to pavement a few miles farther, and then concluding its run at Colorado 14. A turn north leads to the ranching community of Walden, 13 miles away, where food and fuel await. The Moose Creek Cafe at 508 Main Street could be a welcome destination if your digestive tract is making demands. A turn the opposite direction, to the south, will transport you 21 miles to Muddy Pass and Rabbit Ears Pass on US 40 [139].

Ride 149 **Elk River**

Elk River Road, County 129

A 25-mile curving and sweeping river valley ride past impressive ranches, historic towns, and ghost towns, to a lake and a state park

The Elk River Valley is one of the most pristine alpine ranching valleys in the west. The irrigated hay meadows, rustic ranches, shapely mountains, and winding road through it all makes this a very scenic and pastoral ride. Gold and silver in the Hahn's

Peak area lured settlers and treasure seekers in the 1860s with towns sprouting soon after. The Laramie, Hahn's Peak & Pacific Railroad placed tracks more than a century ago, helping to bring ores, cattle, and sheep to market. Glances left and right as you turn your wheels through this valley will have you spotting traces of the old rail bed and witnessing the testimonies of old hand-hewn structures still standing. Put all the above together, along with two state parks, and you have a very special ride.

The Elk River Road, or County 129, can be located at the first stoplight west of the Steamboat Springs downtown area. Easily observed signs pointing the way to Steamboat Lake help with the navigation. A turn to the north here starts this 25-mile ride. There's a mile or two of commercial activity and suburbia before you enter the harmonious ranch and river country, and if you're riding this road in cruise mode, it will be a three-part harmony. There is a flow to this ride best joined by taking it easy with the throttle.

At almost 17 miles, you will come to the small, rustic town of Clark. There's a general store full of character here that's worth browsing through. Clark was supposedly named after a stagecoach rider, and has deep roots as a community. Well-known and stylish Hahn's Peak will come into view as you approach the lake and park. At 10,839 feet, it is the sentinel of the Steamboat area.

The views from the top of the mountain are magnificent, and the views of it from the road are equally so.

Eight miles later, the placid waters of Steamboat Lake will be on your left/southwest. There is Forest Road 409 to the righ,t and just a few hundred yards away is the old ghost town of Hahn's Peak. I recommend exploring the old town on two feet rather than two wheels. In the late 1800s, with the Wild West mining economy booming, this was quite the busy place. Even unsavory characters like Butch Cassidy were hosted . . . in the jail. The full-service state park is just a mile farther up the Elk River Road, and is a fine destination for a picnic lunch or even a camping stay.

The paved surface of the road continues to the small community of Columbine four miles past the lake, and then it is off-road dual-sport exploration all the way to Wyoming. County 209 three miles south of Steamboat Lake delivers an easy two-mile dirt-road ride east to another state park with a centerpiece lake—Pearl Lake State Park. Poring over a forest road map of the area will reveal a network of off-road riding for adventuring dual-sporters. The Steamboat Springs area can be a base camp for great motorcycle rides in every direction [139].

OPEN RANGE

Ride 150 **Toponas**

Colorado 131

A 70-mile course tailored for those on two wheels, serving curvy hors d'oeuvres valley, after valley, after valley

Colorado 131 is a road that motorcyclists (including myself) often rave about. While there isn't a dramatic mountain pass to conquer along the way, it is still one of the hilliest roads around, and this means arcs, bends, and constantly changing elevation. A twisting roller coaster comes to mind, and comes courtesy of the Eagle, Colorado, and Yampa Rivers, and getting from one valley,

to the other, to the other. The duration of this appeal is a noteworthy 70 miles. In addition, there is minimal traffic.

The southern end of Colorado 131 is in the small town of Wolcott on Interstate 70 at Exit 157. In the beginning, you will weave a climb up 1,000 feet, then unravel yourself on a descent to the Colorado River, 1,200 feet lower and 14 miles away. Look for the big diesel engines of the Union Pacific along the river as they emerge from the Gore Canyon to the east.

The preceding 14 miles are just an appetizer. You now will be served an ascending, 20-mile buffet of serpentine roadway up to the high plateaus feeding the Yampa River. You will gain 1,400 feet in elevation but lose what little traffic there was. The solitary general store in the town of Toponas offers a place to catch your breath, top off the tank, grab a snack, and consider your way from here. And there are several options. You could re-ride the 34 miles back to Wolcott. If you take a peek east, you'll see isolated and outstanding Colorado 134 heading off to tackle Gore Pass [145]. Or you could maintain course and continue north.

At Toponas you will be about halfway between Wolcott and Steamboat, and the best part of this ride will be the section from here south to Interstate 70. The next 15 miles north are mostly open meadow riding with a few mild bends here and there until you reach pleasant Oak Creek. This town is see-

ing a modest revival as an alternative to pricey Steamboat Springs, 20 miles to the north. If you ride for the road, with its variety of shapes and textures, then I want to call to your attention the alluring Twentymile Road pointing northwest on the north side of Oak Creek [153].

Between here and Steamboat Springs, Colorado 131 returns to its amusing ways, with the highway following Oak Creek up a narrow and twisting valley. By the way, there is another paved alternative route between Steamboat and Oak Creek. Two miles south of Oak Creek, Routt County Road 14 shoots off to the east, wraps around the western shores of Stagecoach Reservoir, ascends a wide bluff, then winds down toward Steamboat, reconnecting with Colorado 131 ten sweet miles away.

For fuel, you can quench the bike's thirst at Toponas, Yampa, or Oak Creek, where there are general or convenience stores. For quenching your thirst or appetite, I recommend the Yacht Club in Wolcott with its out-

door seating, or the quaint Mexican cantina on the south side of Oak Creek. Of course, you'll want for nothing at the resort of Steamboat Springs.

Here are some ideas for connecting rides, listed in order going north on 131 from Wolcott:

- At 14 miles, when you reach the Colorado River and the cluster of structures at State Bridge, the graded Trough Road travels east toward the Gore Canyon and Kremmling [144]
- At 22 miles, the graded and paved Colorado River Road curves toward the west and runs beside the mighty river all the way to Dotsero on Interstate 70 [151]
- At 34 miles near Toponas, you'll experience one of the best riding passes in the state if you take Colorado 134 to Gore Pass [145]
- At 52 miles, on the north side of Oak Creek, take note of outstanding Twentymile Road, briefly described above [153]

Ride 151 **Colorado River**

Colorado River Road, County 301

A special and distinct 34-mile (half paved, half hard-packed dirt) scenic river and high plateau ride, with access to recreation sites and wilderness areas

Colorado River Road is one of my favorite river rides in the state. So how do these 34 miles fare in my ranking system? Well, descriptively, they have duration, seclusion, curvation, attraction, and juxtaposition. The

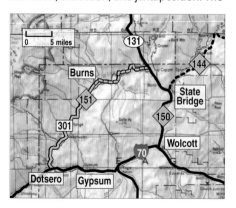

translation? At 34 miles, Colorado River Road is a longer river ride than most, with minimal traffic. The road bobs and weaves with the river, the views will have you pulling over, and for much of this two-wheeled journey, the mighty Colorado is very close.

From the south, the River Road starts at the small town of Dotsero at Exit 133 on Interstate 70. The delights begin immediately as you ascend the side of a shelfy bluff, bank to the left, and see your watery and curving companion below waiting for you. At two miles, Coffee Pot Road, and at seven miles, Sweetwater Road, will take those of you on dedicated dual-sport bikes westward into the southern reaches of the Flat Tops Wilderness Area. There are sweet mountain lake destinations on these dirt-and-rock roads.

Crossings bridges and swapping sides with the river adds extra pizzazz to the ride, as does the possible appearance of the Union Pacific rumbling through the steep valley slopes nearby. Remarkably, there is a place where the road squeezes between a cliffy wall and the train tracks only a few feet away and at the same level as the road! It would be a major hoot to face off with the train, coming or going. At 17 miles, or about halfway, the pavement concludes its run and a hard-packed dirt surface takes the baton. Any street bike can handle this road base. The river and rail continues to be extremely close for the next six miles, until you come to the small cluster of homes at Burns.

From Burns, there is an ascent to a plateau and you'll depart the Colorado for a striking high meadow ride with superb vistas of the Flat Tops to the west. If heading east, be sure to take a gander at your mirrors, then pull over. Turn the key to the off position. Step away from the bike. Breathe in the solitude, detect the faint aroma of the sage meadows, listen for the light breeze, and gaze at the shapes and hues of the surrounding mountains. And then? Well, get back in the saddle, thumb the starter, and get those wheels a turnin'. There is 250-foot descent back to your river companion, and a twisting seven miles to the conclusion at Colorado 131 [150].

On the I-70 end of this ride, the pickin's are slim in Dotsero, with Gypsum seven miles east on the interstate the better place for food and fuel. Or you could ride the amazing Glenwood Canyon and Interstate 70 [112] seventeen miles west to Glenwood Springs. On the northeast end, Colorado 131 [150] is outstanding north and south of River Road's terminus. If you're in the mood to continue some river riding, scoot eight miles south on 131 to State Bridge and take Trough Road [144] east to Kremmling.

Ride 152 **Yampa River**

US 40

A cruising 40-mile ride along a river, with sweeping views of ranch country and proximity to state parks and wildlife areas

This is a route where you just let the meandering US 40 guide you on a go-with-the-flow cruising ride. Let the rolling landscape come to you. The Yampa River will accompany you all the way from the Moffat County Seat (Craig) to the Routt County Seat (Steamboat Springs). Hayden is a pleasing tree-lined community at about the halfway point. Ranches, fertile fields, old homesteads, parks, and more, all make this a sweet 40 miles of riding. Finally, there are four outstanding journeys you can turn your bike toward along these 40 miles.

Craig was founded in 1889 by a William H. Tucker and named for one of its financial backers, the Reverend William Bayard Craig.

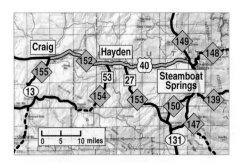

Located at the confluence of the Yampa River and Fortification Creek, Craig was the heart of serious ranching country and remains so today. It also sits amidst serious big game country, home to one of North America's largest elk herds. For those of us on two wheels, Craig is close to other destination rides, beginning with Colorado 13 [155] pointing south toward Meeker. Six miles east of Craig on US 40, you will be introduced to the Yampa River State Park system, with paved Lower Elkhead Road cutting off four miles to the north to one of Colorado's newest state parks, Elkhead Reservoir.

Nine miles of serene US 40 riding later will have you scooting by the Yampa River State Park on the south side of the road. This is the "headquarters" site for the 13 access points along US 40 from Hayden to Dinosaur. Speaking of Hayden, this inviting community is only two miles farther east. The heavily treed Main Street Park across from a full-service convenience store is a fine place to take a break. Hustle across US 40, grab some food, hustle back, and watch the world pass

Turn-of-the-century Craig could have been the scene of a John Ford western, complete with horse racing.

by, including like-minded others on two wheels. Before pointing the front wheel farther east of Hayden, consider the remote and bucolic Pagoda ride that departs to the south via downtown's Poplar Street to County 53 [154].

Throttling east out of Hayden, the smooth pavement and sweeping bends will have you in a riding zone, but before you get too locked into this enchantment, you must read about Twentymile Road, five miles east of Hayden [153]. Whether coming from or going to Steamboat, this alternative through Oak Creek should be in your bag of tricks. The best riding of the 40 miles is between Hayden and Steamboat. There is an amplitude gain of the hill-and-curve variety, and views of Mt. Werner's ski runs above Steamboat will begin to fill the eastern horizon.

At the first stoplight on the west side of Steamboat, there is the Elk River Road journey up to Steamboat Lake [149]. It is worth checking out. Dual-sporters could tackle Buffalo Pass [148] on the northeast side of Steamboat. Colorado 131 southwest out of Steamboat is a bliss-filled 72 miles all the way to Wolcott on Interstate 70 [150]. You can see why Steamboat Springs has received base camp status in my statewide recommendations.

Ride 153 **Twentymile**

Twentymile Road, County 27

A rider's road, delivering 23 miles of empty, twisting, ascending, descending roadway fun

Several years ago I was chatting with a couple at the motorcycle hangout of Deckers. Understandably, the conversation drifted toward great Colorado riding roads. The couple gushed over a sweet road they had recently ridden in northwest Colorado, and while they couldn't remember the name,

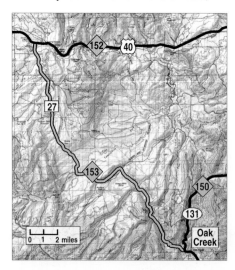

they described how it deliciously departed northwest out of the pleasing small town of Oak Creek. A quick check on a detailed road atlas of the state revealed it to be Twentymile Road. Now having turned two wheels on Twentymile many times, I heartily agree with this couple's enthusiasm!

For me this road offers 23 of some the best riding miles in the state. I don't mean it is the most scenic, or the most dramatic, or that it is populated with all kinds of things to see and do en route. What I mean is if you ride for the ride, becoming one with the bike and road, and that road invites you to a mesmerizing and twisting dance, then this is one of the best two-steps around. There isn't a ho-hum moment over the entire secluded course, as you arc over hills, carve through valleys, then repeat. And repeat again. And if you're in a riding zone, in sync with this swaying and seductive ribbon, then the choreography will be something to behold.

On the south end, Twentymile Road/ County 27 departs to the west from the north side of Oak Creek, over a set of train tracks. The north end of Twentymile Road is five miles east of Hayden on US 40. Going either direction will have you patting your bike's gas tank, leaning forward, and giving it a grateful smooch.

When heading out of Oak Creek onto Twentymile, there isn't any kind of easing into the relationship. You will be committed as soon as you slip your transmission into second gear and lean your willing bike into the first turn. A series of knobby hills and tightening, but not alarming curves are the southern introduction, before a scenic and broad valley takes the partnership to the next level.

A matrimony of ascents and descents will be the next challenge until you come to the massive Twenty Mile Coal Mine in its own valley. While I was parked here on the side of the road taking photos of the operation, with a riding friend nearby, a state trooper pulled over and asked if all was okay. We asked about the mine and he mentioned that it was one of the largest coal mines in the country, stretching underground 20 miles all the way to Hayden. Peabody's Twenty Mile Mine is indeed one of the biggest, shipping almost nine million tons of high-quality coal to utility customers worldwide.

From the mine to this ride's conclusion, 14 swooping miles to the north, you might share the road with a heavy-duty coal truck or two, but passing lanes are thoughtfully built into the ascending traverses. The destination for many of these trucks is the immense coal-fired Hayden Station operated by Xcel Energy. The transmission lines will be a part of the landscape here, but they do not disturb the rolling roadway. The riding marvels of Twentymile continue all the way to its conclusion at US 40 [152]. Don't hesitate to turn around and fly these 23 miles again. You won't be the first to do so.

Oak Creek and Colorado 131 [150] are at the southern terminus of this ride. Oak Creek has a service station and a fine Mexican cantina on the south side of town for a picnic table kind of meal—burritos are their specialty. A good two-hour circuit from Steamboat Springs would be riding to Oak Creek, to Hayden, and back to Steamboat. All three legs of this ride are in the book.

Ride 154 **Pagoda**

Colorado 317, County 29, 53

A lonely, 32-mile river ride with a mix of pavement and dirt, passing through idyllic ranch and wilderness country

You have here a 32-mile ride of exploration. Both ends of this journey are paved but there is a ten-mile section in the middle serving up a stew of dirt and gravel. Yes, this is a ride of exploration, because we're talking roads many simply have not ridden before, and these roads skirt the border of an immense and scenic wilderness. This is another one of those special northwest Colorado rides.

Colorado 317 departs to the east from Colorado 13, at the small cluster of buildings called Hamilton. For 12 miles you'll have a paved road cruise along the north banks of Williams Fork, and the mode, indeed, should be one of "cruise." This is a ride to absorb all that is around you; it isn't one where you try to hit the apexes in every curve. Try to make this tranquil journey last. You won't want it to end. Perhaps it is the peaceful river, or the undisturbed hills and mountains. All I know is I wish it went on for 120 miles instead of 12.

Up above you on the north side of 317 will be the shrubby, cliffy slopes of the Williams Fork Mountains. River-fed fields of grass and hay, with sheltering cottonwood and aspen, will be below you to the south. Horses and cattle graze in the placid meadows. Traffic will be limited to those who live in one of the small homes, or at one of the large, picturesque ranches . . . and of course, the occasional adventurous motorcyclist.

If you look at a map, you will see that

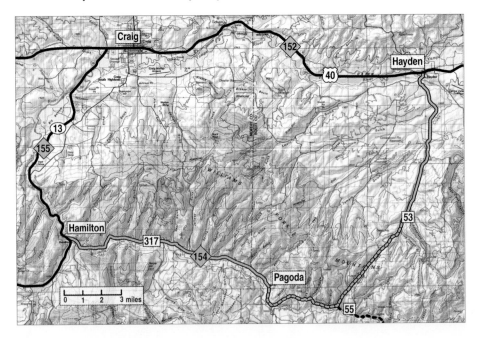

there is nothing but massive wilderness to the south. You can scan the horizon far away and see only the carpeting of pristine forests on low-rising hills, and on the other side is the huge Flat Tops Wilderness Area. Seriously, the last time I was on this road, I pulled over several times, turned the bike off, stepped away, and then just stood in the silence. It isn't classic alpine, above timberline scenery, but I find this ride to be exceedingly memorable, perhaps because it isn't.

I've seen smoother pavement, but the rural aspect of the chip-and-seal goes with the flow here. Because the road follows a river, it has plenty of bends and curves to keep things interesting, if not lively. The pavement runs its course at Pagoda, and gravel becomes the surface you'll surf across for the next five miles. Literally. I've explored much of Routt County's off-road offerings and I've noticed something common to many of these roads: heavy and deep layers of gravel. It is unlike any other county in Colorado. By the way, essentially the only way you will know you have arrived in Pagoda is when the gravel has arrived. There is nothing resembling a town or community, past or present, here—unless I stretch my imagination and say that a forlorn structure over there might have been a part of Pagoda.

If you are astride a heavy street bike, survey the gravel scene and see if you want to proceed. Turning around is certainly a viable and acceptable option. Continuing east, you will have five miles of this crud before turning north onto County 53, which will escort you to Hayden 15 miles away. But who knows, by the time you read this, weather and wheels might have beaten the large chip down to submission. When turning the handlebars onto County 53, you still have five miles of off-road riding, but the surface is more likeable here, mostly dirt and hard pack, except for occasional 100-yard stretches where Routt County Road and Bridge couldn't resist continuing their gravel love affair. You will know you have ten more miles to Hayden when asphalt surfaces return, and it will be a fun, sweeping ride through pasturelands the rest of the way. Be sure to check out the old Hayden Speedway on the outskirts of town. Perhaps, like me, you used to go to these kinds of racing events years ago!

I think you can surmise that this isn't a place offering a variety of food and fuel choices! Hayden, at the northern end, is the best place to refill, replenish, and relieve. Craig, to the west of Hayden, would be an option if you're in that area, or turning this into a nice circle of a ride. Colorado 13, on the west end, is described in Ride 155. US 40, to the east of Craig, is described in Ride 152. If you want an outstanding dual-sport adventure to get away from it all, take County 55 south into the heart of the Flat Tops. The turn for this road is three miles east of the turn onto County 53 that you took to Hayden in this ride.

Ride 155 **Williams Fork Canyon**

Colorado 13

A quiet and rustic 48-mile tour delivering a sweeping and scenic pass, river, and canyon ride through ranching country

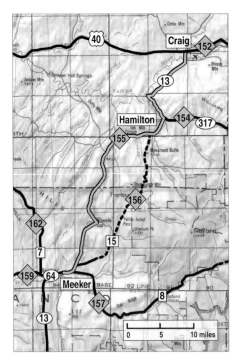

Colorado 13 between Meeker and Craig is an uncluttered curving highway with homesteads, abandoned mines, lakes, and rivers. The countryside is lonely and the shrubby hillsides and rocky canyons seem wild and unexplored. It isn't unusual to come across a cattle or sheep drive, with fertile and productive ranches helping sustain the two active communities on either end of this ride.

Meeker, at the southern end of this ride, was named for Indian Agent Nathan Meeker, who, along with 11 others, was slain in a Ute uprising in 1879. Since the massacre site is west of town along Colorado 64, the details are described in the White River ride [159]. Ranching is a significant chunk of the economy here, but big game hunting is also important. Theodore Roosevelt once stayed at the historic Meeker Hotel across from the courthouse while on a mountain lion hunt-

ing trip. Today you'll be hunting for a sublime riding road and Colorado 13 delivers it. About ten miles north of Meeker, there is a sweeping, 1,000-foot ascent to a modest pass, Ninemile Gap at 9,475 feet. The Jensen State Wildlife Area will surround you on all sides.

It will take twice as long to lose the 1,000 feet on the north side of Ninemile as it did to gain it from the south. For 20 miles you will have a sweet riding descent to Hamilton, with the road bending back and forth, following the whims of Good Springs Creek. In ten miles, the valley widens, as do the views. You will pass the small Wilson Reservoir, a favorite of waterfowl, before you arrive at the small town of Hamilton on the banks of Williams Fork.

Here is where the ride changes clothes— the garment becomes tighter, revealing some nice curves. For almost seven miles north of Hamilton, the Williams Fork Canyon is a snaking river ride, and it is sublime. Last time I was on this stretch of

tarmac I rode it twice—and considered turning around to do it again! After the seven miles, where Williams Fork flows into the Yampa River, the valley expands again, and in three miles you will enter the outskirts of Craig, where there are a variety of lodging, food, and fuel options.

For almost 50 miles, between Meeker and Craig, there's nothing along the way to help you quench or replenish. Plan accordingly. Chances are you will be riding Colorado 13 as a component of a larger journey. West of Meeker you have the White River ride of Colorado 64 mentioned above, and the "secret" Strawberry Road [162]. East of Meeker is the road to Buford and the Flat Tops Scenic Byway to Trapper's Lake and over Ripple Creek Pass [157]. Northeast of Meeker is the graded dirt-road ride over Yellowjacket Pass to the Thornburgh Battlefield [156]. From Hamilton and the Williams Fork Canyon described above is the journey to Pagoda and Hayden [154], then you have the Yampa River ride on US 40 east of Craig to Steamboat [152].

Downtown Meeker in 1920 and today

Ride 156 **Thornburgh–Milk Creek**

Thornburgh Road, County 15, 45

A smooth 27-mile dirt-road venture over a mountain pass to a scenic mountain valley with a historic Indian battlefield site

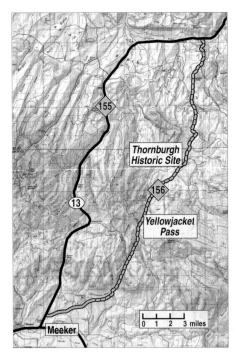

In the late 19th century, tensions were rising between the Utes and the Indian Agency headed by Nathan Meeker in the White River Valley. Sensing both sides were on the brink of armed conflict, Meeker sought reinforcements and a show of force from the U.S. Cavalry. The Utes, aware of, and threatened by the cavalry's approach 20 miles away, attacked the agency on September 29, 1879. You can observe the site of the Meeker Massacre from Colorado 64 in Ride 159.

When Major Thomas T. Thornburgh led 120 troops across Milk Creek, northeast of present-day Meeker, he knew crossing this northern boundary of the Ute Reservation would bring war. It did so immediately in the form of a rambling ambush between the water-fed meadows of Milk Creek and the Yellowjacket Pass summit. In the first hour, Major Thornburgh died with a bullet to the chest. After a hasty retreat back to Milk Creek, the soldiers established defensive positions with a classic circle of wagons and animals. For seven days, Thornburgh's troops held out until reinforcements from the 9th Cavalry (the famed African-American "Buffalo Soldiers") and 5th Cavalry arrived. Casualties on both sides were heavy. This Milk Creek battle was the last military conflict between the Utes and white encroachment, and it resulted in the relocation of the Utes to Utah from their ancestral Colorado lands.

So, with this brief background, you'll ride to this isolated battlefield park. The scenery is not of the high-alpine variety, but is of sweeping vistas, with evenly curved mountain slopes sliding down to sweet fertile fields, to form a seamless, harmonious union. The smooth and improved dirt-road surface is a perfect fit with the secluded environment and terrain, with its echoes of its historic conflict.

The ride to the battlefield site begins two miles east and north of Meeker off Colorado 13, where you will want to turn the handlebars right/east onto the paved Thornburgh Road/ County 15. The paved surface becomes fast dirt after three miles, and you'll enjoy a delightful curving descent down to Coal Creek before ascending 600 feet to the modest Yellowjacket Pass summit at 7,428 feet. A gentle five-mile decline will bring you to this stunningly pastoral place. What a contrast to the heated events that took place here more than 130 years ago. Chances are you will be the only visitor in the park. Perhaps a quiet pause, with the wind brushing by, will evoke the silent echoes of battlefield cries.

This ride parallels the differing journey on Colorado 13 [155] from Meeker to Hamilton, and could be linked with numerous other off-road rides in the area, or with other adventures spreading out in every direction from Meeker. Meeker is also your closest source for food and fuel, but if you are continuing north after joining Colorado 13, Craig is a fun 16 miles of riding away.

The northern descent from Yellowjacket Pass to the battlefield site

Ride 157 **Flat Tops Trail Scenic Byway**

County 8, 132, 17, Forest Road 8, 16

An 83-mile mix of pavement and graded off-road riding along a scenic byway, through remote wilderness accompanied by a river, a mountain pass and matchless views

The Flat Tops Wilderness is one of the country's wilderness jewels. The deep, pristine beauty of this place is said to be the inspiration for establishing a wilderness preservation ethos in the west. When you experience the solitude of Ripple Creek Pass, with 360 degrees of stop-the-heart vistas, you will know your bike has brought you to a special place. This 83-mile journey is a memorable one.

The Flat Tops Trail Scenic Byway runs from Meeker to Yampa. Point the bike east out of Meeker for a mile before coming to a sign pointing the way to the Flat Tops Trail Scenic Byway. This is paved North Fork Road, or County 8. The "north fork" refers to the North Fork of the White River, but for the first 21 miles, you will be actually riding alongside the marriage of the North and

South Forks of the White River. As you probably already know, when a road follows a river's course, the road is made for a motorcycle. The serene valley through which you will pass is one of the blissful components of this ride. At the small community of Buford, you can spot the distinct lineages of these rivers. The paved surface will continue for another ten miles before you enter the designated wilderness area.

At this point, you will have almost 50 miles of graded gravel or dirt if you want to continue east all the way to Yampa. I have Harley riding friends from out of state who have ridden the whole thing without complaint. There is nothing tricky about this route, but 50 miles of off-road riding can be tedious and time consuming—especially if

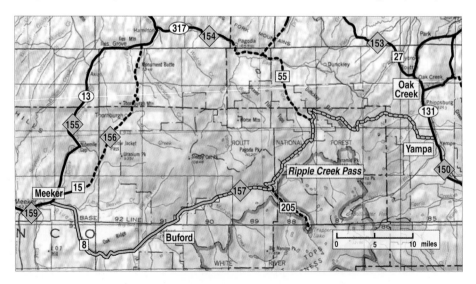

you are on a street bike you don't feel comfortable with, and particularly if the surface is potentially squirmy gravel. Even if you turn around here and head back to Meeker, you will have ridden 60 miles of magical tarmac. If continuing on, the ascent begins toward Ripple Creek Pass, 14 miles farther and almost 3,000 feet higher.

The flavor of the ride will change as altitude is gained. The taste of valley riding, while divine, has been on the plate for awhile, and the front forks of your bike will be moving on to a fresh dish of horizon-to-horizon wilderness views.

One mile shy of the unremarkable pass summit is the remarkable Ripple Creek Overlook on the south side of the road. Pull in here, put your sidestand down, and do some . . . overlooking! There are restroom facilities, picnic tables, and a short interpretative trail with signs pointing out what is before you. One of the signs describes the huge number of thriving elk in the area, with the herd being one of the largest in the country. I suppose this might have been the case 100 years ago as well, when Teddy Roosevelt hunted here for "wapiti" (Shawnee for "white rump").

The east-side descent will be a mesmerizing mix of huge aspen forests and meadows, looking as if they'd been lifted out of an oil painting, and views attempting to reveal

how wide and far this wilderness is. Other areas of Colorado are known for their golden aspen colors in the autumn, but this area west of Yampa on this remote scenic byway—though not widely known among the leaf peepers—is probably just as spectacular. Route finding is not difficult here—just follow the scenic byway signs or markers pointing toward Yampa.

This journey is a link between the riding meccas of Meeker and Yampa (Colorado 131 [150]). Meeker is ground zero for a cluster of great rides if there ever was one:

- Piceance Creek Road [160]
- The Strawberry Road [162]
- Colorado 64 to Rangely [159]
- Colorado 13 to Hamilton and Craig [155]
- The ride to the Thornburg–Milk Creek Battlefield Site [156]

Be prepared before venturing into this no man's land of services. The first time I placed a bike on these roads I mistakenly assumed Buford would have something—fuel or food, especially the former. The gas gauge was an object of my attention for awhile until I calmed down with the calculation that I wouldn't be pushing the bike to Yampa. For a meal, I would heartily recommend throwing some food in the saddlebags for a picnic at the Ripple Creek Overlook, or take Forest Road 205 seven miles south from the west base of Ripple Creek Pass to scenic Trapper's Lake.

Ride 158 **Rifle Parks**

Buford Road, Grass Valley Road, Colorado 325, County 245, 226

A curving 26-mile paved backroad tour of three state parks, two reservoirs, and small country farms

Next time you are flying down Interstate 70 west of Glenwood Springs, instead of blasting the throttle for the 15 miles between New Castle and Rifle, consider exiting at either town and extending your ride a bit, taking in two nearby scenic reservoirs and a roaring three-headed waterfall. Better yet, make this rural ride your main destination, with its twisting course weaving through farms, ranches, and state parks.

From New Castle, take Grass Valley Road

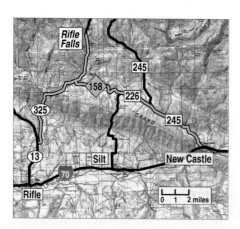

directly at Exit 105 on Interstate 70. You can shoot directly north from the intersection on the Castle Valley Road, which becomes the Buford Road, and then Grass Valley Road all seamlessly. On the west end, Colorado 325 heading toward the signed Rifle Gap Reservoir will be the road you want. From Exit 90 on Interstate 70, take Colorado 13 two miles north to Colorado 325. Together, Buford Road, Grass Valley Road, and Colorado 325 comprise this fine country ride. From the New Castle side, the Buford Road takes you west through a small valley containing the flows of Elk Creek. If you are in the mood to explore, several roads, initially paved, depart to the north where they become dual-sport adventures in the White River National Forest. Six miles from Exit 105, New Castle–Buford Road wanders all the way up to the Flat Tops Scenic Byway covered in Ride 157. This is where Grass Valley Road seamlessly takes over touring duties for the ride.

At 9.3 miles, Harvey Gap Road arcs off to the south. Turn your handlebars here for a pretty 190-acre lake only a mile away. Harvey Gap State Park encompasses the area, with a visitor center, a picnic area, and a boat ramp. If you're not towing a boat behind your bike, maybe you will have your backpacker's fishing rod with you. Harvey Gap is known for its fishin'! You can bail out of this ride here, and continue on the Harvey Gap Road to the south, connecting with Silt and Interstate 70 only seven miles away. But if you're up for some more, backtrack to Grass Valley Road, then turn left/west for five fun, twisting miles to the road's conclusion at Colorado 325.

You'll want to go north on 325 at this intersection for two reasons. The first is checking out the namesake for the Rifle Falls State Park three miles away, and the other is the sweet curling nature of this ribbon of road. The $6 park fee allows you to see the falls and take advantage of other park facilities and attractions.

You can continue north past Rifle Falls State Park and check out the fish hatchery only a mile away. Beyond that, it is dual-sport country into the national forest. So let's point the bike south, returning on 325 past the Grass Valley intersection and to its termination at Colorado 13. Four miles south of Rifle Falls will be the sky blue waters of the 350-acre Rifle Gap Reservoir. This third state park will be a respite before you engage the road on a twisting, 500-foot descent over seven miles, through a meadow- and tree-lined golf course, along a tumbling Rifle Creek. When you arrive at Colorado 13, you can turn left/south toward Rifle two miles away and continue your Interstate 70 blitzkrieg or head north for some spectacular motorcycle rides in the Meeker area. The towns at both ends of this state park and backroad tour, New Castle and Rifle, offer food and fuel services, but the choices are more numerous in Rifle.

Ride 159 **White River**

Colorado 64

A serene and scenic 57-mile rural river ride over rises and through valleys, with working ranches competing for your attention

One thing I have observed over many miles of riding is that when a road follows a river, chances are that it will be a good road to ride on two wheels. One such road is lonely Colorado 64 as it sweeps over and around rocky bluffs, arching through fertile valleys fed by the crystal waters of the White River. Also, which would you prefer? A shorter road with more twists and turns, but choked with traffic, or a longer journey with sweeping bends, but zero traffic before or behind you? If you're raising your hand for the latter, then Colorado 64 and its 57 miles is waiting for you and your bike.

Rangely, on the western terminus of this ride, is not as old as many other Colorado frontier towns, only having been incorporated in 1947, with paved roads reaching its boundaries a decade later. Today, it is a vibrant community, supported economically by ranching and significant reserves of coal and natural gas nearby. Departing east on 64 toward Meeker, in five miles you'll be introduced to fairly new Kenney Reservoir (filled in 1984) and its full-service recreation area of boating, fishing, camping, and picnicking.

What makes this ride fine is the right mix of lazy serpentine roadway and safe oppor-

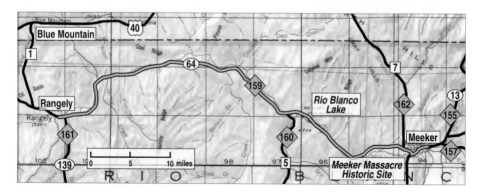

tunities to glance left and right as you pass old homesteads, working ranches, the wandering river, and the shadows of distant mountains. This is a sightseeing journey, but it can be taken at cruise speed, or even at a more accelerated pace. As the distance to Meeker narrows, keep an eye out for sheep on the road, either loose or as part of a drive, and note the size of some of the sheep ranches.

Six miles west of Meeker there is a roadside historic marker. Pull over to the south side of Colorado 64 and read about the Meeker Massacre of September 29, 1879. The monument and sign will point to a marker in a nearby grassy field where Indian Agent Nathan Meeker fell, along with 11 others connected to the agency, slain in a Ute response to a threat of U.S. Cavalry action. A separate interpretive sign a mile away provides additional details. The military confrontation at Milk Creek northeast of Meeker followed soon after, and you can learn more about this battlefield site in Ride 156.

Both Rangely and Meeker have lodging, fuel, and excellent diners on their main streets. If you are so inclined, 37 miles east of Rangely (20 miles west of Meeker), the Rio Blanco Lake offers camping and picnicking, along with water sports and wildlife viewing in the surrounding state wildlife area. The Meeker area is ground zero for glorious rides in literally every direction.

Rangely is a launch pad for other motorcycle forays as well. Colorado 139 over Douglas Pass [161] embarks to the south, and the Dinosaur National Monument area [164] is 20 miles north. For a shortcut to US 40, instead of Colorado 64, try out County 1 leading to the north, three miles west of Rangely. This 11-mile paved backroad is a secluded thing, leading to Blue Mountain on US 40.

Now, I must point you toward two paved country roads with entrances right on Colorado 64 between Rangely and Meeker: Piceance Creek Road [160] going south and Strawberry Creek Road [162] pointing north. They deliver two of my favorite Northwest Colorado rides.

Ride 160 **Piceance Creek**

Piceance Creek Road, County 5

A paved 42-mile lonely and scenic valley ride, with the road curving through and around mesas, bluffs, gulches, meadows, and working cattle ranches

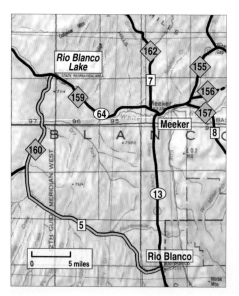

Piceance Creek Road is 40-plus miles of un-interrupted riding—totally uninterrupted riding. It doesn't have dramatic high-alpine scenery or the tightest of curves, but there is a rhythm here, and when you hit it at the right speed, you'll be in a zone all the way to its distant conclusion.

Riding west and north from Colorado 13 on the east, you'll immediately begin to feast on a steady and sustained diet of sweepers. Piceance Creek also comes to the dining hall at the beginning, and it really sets the course for the entire journey, until it empties into the White River at Colorado 64. This is one big, long, valley ride.

Continuing west, small farms and big ranches take a sip at the contents of

Piceance Creek. There are valley shades of green and tan blending with different shades of green and tan on the hillsides. Speaking of hillsides, the first half of this ride is gulch central, with gulch names like Sorghum, Jessup, and Big Jimmy spaced out about every mile. The frequency decreases to about every two miles on the northern half. You will see scattered roads, paved and unpaved, drifting off to the left and right. Many of these lead to oil company facilities tapping into the huge natural gas fields underneath you and your motorcycle. However, if you were to turn west onto the paved Ryan Gulch Road/County 24, at 14.4 miles south of Colorado 64, it would go to the Piceance Creek East Douglas Wild Horse Management Area about 12 miles away. I have yet to explore my way down this road, but definitely plan to do so the next time I'm there!

Nine miles from Colorado 64 [159], this ride enters the Piceance Creek State Wildlife Area. The area is populated with big game, and you will be in the midst of it all the way to where road and creek terminate at a bigger road and a bigger river. The Rio Blanco Lake is at this junction, and is known for its teeming populations of shorebirds. Fishing is also said to be decent. Picnic areas and campsites could certainly be worthy of placing your sidestand down. This is not a congested or busy area. Last time I was there, I think I only saw one solitary vehicle at the lake—other than the one I was astride.

If there is a nuance to this inviting 42-mile-long ride, it is the potential for sharing it with gas company vehicles—pick-up trucks and tankers. Fortunately there are plenty of places to pass. But in a unique twist, instead of this having more traffic on a weekend, when most of us can escape to ride, it is the opposite here. Workers drive the road on weekdays, but operations are mostly shut down on the weekends!

Be sure to have plenty in the tanks, food and fuel, for there is nothing out here between Rifle to the south and Meeker to the northeast.

Ride 161 **Douglas Pass**

Colorado 139

A 70-mile tour of Western Slope topography, with canyons, forests, sage, views, a mountain pass, and a national historic district on the north side

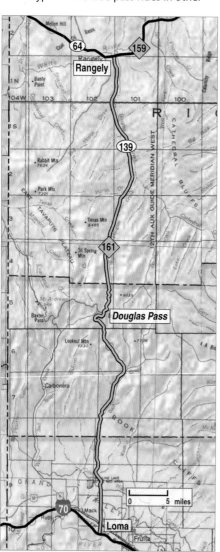

The proximity of this pass ride to Utah and its arid landscape make it unlike any of the stereotypical Colorado pass rides in other parts of the state. There is also the sheer diversity of Colorado 139 and how it seems to pass through, go alongside, or climb over just about everything anyone would want to see and experience from a motorcycle in Colorado.

Access Colorado 139 and Douglas Pass on the south via Exit 15 on Interstate 70, and from the town of Rangely on the north. Now, Douglas Pass, topping out at only 8,268 feet, isn't as high as Colorado passes tend to be, but when you start your journey from the south, 35 miles away, you will be almost 4,000 feet lower in Loma, the farming community at Exit 15. Fertile, irrigated fields will be to the left and right out your frameless windows as you throttle north. Then like an on-off switch, you'll enter unirrigated and sandy lands. The road will begin to dip and turn as it approaches the valley of East Salt Creek. There is a little more greenery in the valley as you continue to moderately gain elevation.

You will enter Trail Canyon 13 miles south of the pass summit. Here is where the grade steepens and the hillside stiffens. You will also note a choppiness to the road. I once was chatting with a motel clerk, impressing her with my suave ways, and learned she was from Rangely and well acquainted with Colorado 139, driving it often to Grand Junction. She said the road gave her the creeps, with the surface seeming to shift around as she death-gripped the steering wheel. Indeed, this is a seismically active area, and I think shifting soils account for the asphalt's unevenness in places. On the other hand, the need for a little extra concentration is offset by the lonely nature of this ride. There just isn't a whole lot of traffic sharing the road with you and your bike.

Soon after riding into the canyon, within five miles, you'll really begin the climb to Douglas. Valley-floor riding becomes mountain-hugging shelf-road riding. Gentle curves will now have tight creases to them, and your front wheel will be definitely higher than the one behind you. The dramatic ascent delivers dramatic views to the south, and just shy of the summit, there is a pullout on the side of the road. This is a good place to pause, grab the camera, and look back at where you have been. A riding friend told me about standing here with his father after the two of them had just ridden the southern ascent on their bikes, and how magical the moment was with the vista below and the road snaking a path through it all.

The pass summit is halfway between Loma and Rangely. The north side resembles its south-side cousin—steep and tight up high before mellowing out to a fine creekside ride. This time it will be rambling West Douglas Creek showing the way to Rangely, 3,000 feet lower. Beginning about 20 miles north of Douglas Pass, and encompassing the remaining 15 miles to Rangely, is the Canyon Pintado National Historic District, which contains rock petroglyphs and painted pictographs on sheer sandstone walls, left behind by Fremont and Ute civilizations long before Europeans crossed the Atlantic and pushed west. More details will be waiting for you at the eight, well-marked sites along Colorado 139 south of Rangely.

Looking south and north from the Douglas Pass summit

Be sure your food and fuel needs are taken care of before venturing onto Colorado 139. It will be just you, a few other hardy travelers, and vultures circling overhead. From Rangely, there's the great Dinosaur National Monument [165] and Colorado 64 [159] ventures. A fine riding circle from Grand Junction would be Colorado 139 up to Rangely, Colorado 64 east to the Piceance Creek Road [160], south to Colorado 13 to Rifle, then a return. If you happen to be heading south on 139 around sunset, check out the Colorado Monument on the southern horizon and its low-sun shadows. Very impressive and scenic.

Ride 162 **Strawberry Creek**

Strawberry Road, County 7, 57

A mesmerizing 40-mile paved backroad ride through a deeply beautiful landscape, with sweeping hills and curves to entertain, ranches old and new to distract, and most of it shared with no one else

Strawberry Road is a magical ride that follows the whims of Strawberry Creek, descends through Coyote Gulch, carves a path through the Danforth Hills, and concludes with a jaunt through a wildlife area at the north end. This recently paved road is secluded, which according to my subjective

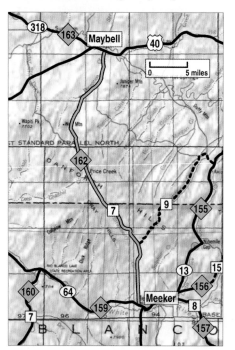

ranking system earns major points for delivering a winding and scenic journey uncluttered with traffic. There simply aren't hordes of trucks and cars trying to get from Meeker to Maybell. So you'll share Strawberry Road with those who live in the scattered, picturesque farms and ranches along the way, plump hawks and eagles who will size you up from the power poles, grazing cattle who'll lift their heads at the sound of approaching internal combustion, and big game who are probably observing you from afar.

Strawberry Road comes to life three miles west of Meeker off Colorado 64 [159]. It is one mile west of the Colorado 13 and 64 intersection. With Rio Blanco County's largest town nearby, the first few miles of Strawberry are the most populous of the entire route, but we still aren't talking bustling 'burbs. The ride will be fairly flat and straight the first five miles, before the road begins to respond to the entertainment provided by Strawberry Creek and Coyote Basin.

At seven miles, a graded and smooth County 9 departs to the northeast up Devil's Gulch. It connects directly with Colorado 13 [155] and with other dual-sport adventures

15 miles away. Strawberry Road, from here to its conclusion 32 miles away, changes its posture. Its backbone has kinks to it, the elbows and knees are more bent, things are less stretched out and more hunched over. The texture of the landscape will be changing as well. Shrubby trees, sage cover, and empty fields are more common, with evidence that some tried to make a go of the place, but ended up walking away.

Soon, there will be a descent into the Coyote Basin with the Danforth Hills rising in the distance. The middle 20-mile chunk of this ride is one of the finest anywhere. The lonely Danforth Hills are strikingly beautiful, and fertility returns in the basin with fields and idyllic ranches competing for your attention. Note the jagged rock formations and outcroppings ringing this place. The views are distant, and in a way, intoxicating, as if some kind of happy juice is flowing through your veins. The road doesn't disappoint either as it delivers a serpentine ride around and through nature's obstacles. I could turn around and ride this area again and again.

Oh yeah, I paused here once for a photo of an enormous bird of prey on a nearby pole, and a solitary car came by, slowed and paused, and asked if everything was okay. It was, and I thanked them.

The remaining seven miles to the north will be along Deception Creek and through the Bitter Brush State Wildlife Area. The terrain is mild, and the road equally so. When you arrive at US 40 you will be only two miles east of Maybell, where there is a general store for food and fuel, along with a nearby cafe. Maybell is where you can launch a magical Colorado 318 ride to the Gates of Lodore and Browns Park [163], and continuing west on US 40 you have the Dinosaur Monument access via Twelvemile Gulch [164] and Harper's Corner [165]. The Meeker area to the south has four great rides as described on these pages:

- Piceance Creek Road [160]
- The Flat Tops Scenic Byway [157]
- Colorado 13 to Hamilton and Craig [155]
- The ride to the Thornburg–Milk Creek Battlefield Site [156]

Ride 163 **Gates of Lodore**

Colorado 318

A secluded and sweeping 60-mile ride to the ultra-scenic Gates of Lodore, Browns Park National Wildlife Refuge, and the north side of Dinosaur National Monument

From a map it looks like Colorado 318 is a long ride from nowhere to nowhere. Technically, this may be true, but an empty road before you can have real appeal, especially when there is also a special scenic destination or two. Such is 318. The solitude on this road can be mind-numbing, but the lack of vehicle traffic can be refreshing. Being an excellent riding road to boot adds to the appeal.

Colorado 318 takes off from US 40 less than a mile west of Maybell and heads to

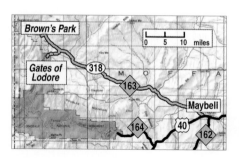

the Utah border, which is 60 miles distant. Cross the Yampa River at five miles near the small community of Sunbeam, and ten miles later, you will drop into a scenic and colorful rock valley containing the Little Snake River. North of here is the Sand Wash Basin Wild Horse Management Area. I was talking to an ATV owner the other day who rides the Sand Wash area frequently, and he often sees the wild mustangs running free. Even on 318, be on the lookout for these spirited animals.

Arid mesas, shrubby bluffs, and miniature canyons harboring small creeks will look on as you move through the landscape. As I think about it, the birds of prey flying above you—and you flying below them—could be the only moving objects from horizon to horizon. At 40 miles from Maybell, County 34, a graded dirt-and-gravel mix, departs south and west eight miles for the Gates of Lodore. While signs point the way here, an alternative way to get to the mouth of this memorable and incredible canyon is to continue down 318 another six miles and look for County 34N cutting off to the south. It connects with County 34 in two miles and will save you four off-road miles. If you can make it to the Gates of Lodore, please do so. The placid Green River will join you on the right as you approach what the John Wesley Powell Expedition discovered in 1869, naming it after the English poem "Cataract of Lodore." You will be stunned when you see its towering walls and the narrow entrance swallowing the no-longer-placid Green River. There is a campground, picnic area, and boat ramp at road's end. I spoke with a river guide preparing to lead three rafts and five people on a three-day trip, and he noted the view from this place is the best in all of the Dinosaur National Monument area—and I don't question his assessment.

You will need to retrace your riding steps back to Colorado 318. From here, if proceeding westward for the next scenic destination, you will only need to spin your wheels five more miles to the Browns Park National Wildlife Refuge. This park is only two miles

south, down graded County 164. You can stay on 164 for an eight-mile loop with camping, picnic places, overlooks, and Wildlife Drive, before the road reconnects with 318. The life-giving Green River is the centerpiece here, attracting moose, elk, deer, bear, mountain lion, and all kinds of waterfowl. A long-time Browns Park ranger at the Maybell General Store told me how Butch Cassidy would use the remote Browns Park Valley as a hideout. Sharpshooter Annie Oakley often stayed in the area as well, but didn't have to lie as low as Butch.

When you return to Colorado 318 you will be only a few miles from the Utah border. The pavement continues to the state line. US 191 at the Utah and Wyoming border will be 27 miles away. The journey back to Maybell is sublime. The scenic destinations have inspired, the winding sweeping road has entertained, and a celebration of this remote tour awaits at the Maybell General Store, where you can grab some food and fuel. There's a diner next door, and a city park. The weather should be fine. I'm trying to remember if I've ever seen a cloud in the sky above Maybell!

Ride 164 **Twelvemile Gulch**

Twelvemile Gulch Road

A paved 12-mile road over hills and along the untamed Yampa River to a lonely and scenic entrance of the Dinosaur National Monument, with nearby park and camping facilities

This is not a well-known road, even among the locals. Despite losing book "points" for being essentially a 12-mile cul-de-sac, it still more than comes through with its combination of lonely hilltop, river, and canyon riding, along with parks and scenery.

Twelvemile Gulch Road is 16 miles west of Maybell. It wanders to the north from US 40, up its namesake gulch. You already know you are in for a secluded ride, since you have just jumped off a secluded main highway. For four miles the road winds through small ranch country and then ascends a small saddle between two hills. On the other side you will be introduced to wild Yampa River coun-

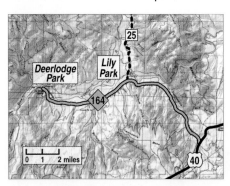

try. As the only free-flowing, major river in the state, the Yampa is the last undammed river in the immense Colorado river system.

At the bottom of the north-side descent, just before the road banks to the left to join the river up ahead, glance to the right and check out an almost camouflaged canyon. This is the stream-carved Cross Mountain Canyon, and it is striking how it simply and abruptly starts its high-walled cut right there! There is a small parking area at the mouth of the canyon where you can put your sidestand down and walk to the water's edge . . . and maybe skip a few rocks farther than I did.

At six miles, your bike will enter the Lily Park area. This is where untamed nature makes a presentation not seen routinely in Colorado today, in the form of a wide and wild riverbed ready to accommodate an unruly Yampa River. I'm reminded of a historic marker seen next to the Rio Grande River in Conejos County [071] describing how, 200 years ago, the Rio Grande was 250 feet across and ten feet deep at most places before dams, irrigation, and other controlling methods had reduced it to the small and subdued stream it is today. Back then, early explorers were faced with a stiff challenge trying to cross most of the major rivers in Colorado, especially during the snowmelt in the spring or early summer! I've only ridden Twelvemile Gulch in the autumn, but I'd love to return in the spring to see the difference.

You'll have six more miles of meandering chip-and-seal beneath your wheels before it ends at a parking area. You will know you approaching the end when you pass the Deerlodge Park on your right, and canyon walls of the Dinosaur National Monument begin to alter the landscape before you. Deerlodge contains a boat launch, seven camping sites, and a picnic area with vault restroom facilities. There is a ranger on duty during the summer. At the end-of-the-road turnaround there is a faint hiking trail leading to a rocky overlook of the Yampa, with a view of its canyon to the west.

Essentially, this improved Twelvemile Gulch Road is a federally funded eastern access point for the monument. It delivers a journey that should be ridden in cruise-and-look-around mode. Whenever I'm in the area traveling along on US 40, I often make the turn to check the place out again—to see if the river has changed its mood.

If you are on a worthy dual-sport, there is County 25 leading to the north at Lily Park, six miles from US 40. It follows a Yampa tributary, the Little Snake River, for five miles before dividing to the east and west for a lonely backcountry adventure, and eventually Colorado 318 [163].

Make sure you have gas in the tank, for there isn't a drop of it out here for the 55 miles between the towns of Dinosaur and Maybell on US 40. And unless you want to catch and skin a lizard, I would throw some food in the bags and have a picnic at Deerlodge, or grab a meal at the small diner in Dinosaur or Maybell.

Ride 165 **Harper's Corner**

Harper's Corner Road

A quiet 31-mile paved, scenic ride into Dinosaur National Monument with stunning lookouts and a sweet serpentine roadway

Harper's Corner Road is the main paved route into Dinosaur National Monument. For more than 31 miles, the winding road takes you to some of the most stunning overlooks in Colorado, if not the U.S. Indeed, as I stood alone at some of these lookouts gazing at the massive canyons below,

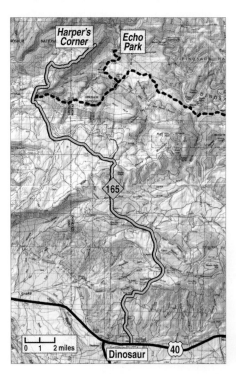

with their deep, earthly scars stretching to the horizon, I was reminded of the Grand Canyon. There is nothing like it in Colorado.

The monument gets its name from extensive fossil beds discovered in 1909 by Earl Douglas, a paleontologist working for the Carnegie Museum in Pittsburgh. Thousands of fossils were excavated, crated, and shipped back to Pennsylvania for examination and display. The allosaurus, a T-rex like predecessor, was among the fossil finds. Six years later in 1915, President Woodrow Wilson proclaimed the fossil beds in Utah the Dinosaur National Monument, and in 1938 the boundaries were extended east to include the 200,000 acres encompassing the magnificent canyons of the Green and Yampa Rivers. It is this canyon country on the Colorado side of the border that this ride takes you through.

Harper's Corner Road is found two miles east of the small town of Dinosaur on US 40. There is a visitor center here, but there is no fee to enter and ride the monument. Even if this weren't an amazingly visual place, I'd place the bike on Harper's Corner just to experience its "cornering" ways. The first 15 miles will be a gradual 2,000-foot ascent to an elevation of 8,000 feet. Sweeping arcs, ups, and downs, are the steady diet with views to the south (behind you) and to the west. At nineteen miles, you will want to make the turn to the right/north to the Canyon Overlook. Bring the camera.

At 25 miles, there is an overlook with the dual-sport Echo Park Road descending to the east. Bring the camera again. This dirt road is a stunning 13-mile ride to the confluence of the Green and Yampa Rivers deep in the canyons. You can see this winding road from up high here. If you are astride a bike appropriate for this kind of surface, I would make this Dinosaur National Monument tour longer by going for it. Interpretive signs at this pullout describe what you are seeing, and what you will see if you descend the 2,000 feet to Echo Park. If you do embark on this venture, the dirt Yampa Bench Road at 7.6 miles optionally winds through the southern heart of the monument going east, eventually becoming Bear Valley Road (also dirt), ending 30 miles away on US 40 at Elk Springs.

There will be six more curving miles to the road's conclusion at Harper's Corner and the overlook there. Signs have previously noted your entering Utah several miles ago, but you return to Colorado again on this last stretch of chip-and-seal. There are restroom facilities here and a picnic area. The views astound (again). By the way, there are additional lookouts on this ride I didn't mention, so certainly check them out as well. This is a quiet, if not lonely ride. Last time I put the bike on this snaking road it was just me and one other car. We kept leap-frogging each other as we would alternately pull over for the spectacular vistas.

As you can surmise, there are no food or fuel options in the monument, so the town of Dinosaur on US 40 west of the entrance is your best source—and the pickin's are slim there. A picnic deep in the monument would be my chow time recommendation. For other nearby rides, the Rangely area, 18 miles south of Dinosaur, launches the Douglas Pass (named after the paleontologist) journey south on Colorado 139 [161] to Grand Junction. From Rangely you can also point your bike east for the White River ride on Colorado 64 to Meeker [159]. If canyon country is still bouncing around between your ears, two other Dinosaur Monument rides are noted on these pages: Twelvemile Gulch Road [164], and Colorado 318 [163] northwest out of Maybell to the north side of the monument and Canyon Lodore.

Northwest

RECOMMENDATIONS

Twisting and Sweeping Rides

1. From Kremmling, ride six miles north to Colorado 134. Enjoy Gore Pass [145] all the way to Colorado 131. Turn right/north for Oak Creek. North of town join Twentymile Road [153] to its termination at US 40. Backtrack to Oak Creek for a second serving of Twentymile. Ride Colorado 131 [150] south to Wolcott.

2. Traverse Berthoud Pass [138] into Middle Park via US 40. On the west side of Granby turn the handle bars north for Willow Creek Pass [143], riding Colorado 125 to Walden. Join Colorado 14 to the southwest for sweepers to Muddy Pass and US 40. Ride south on US 40 to Kremmling. From here, continue on US 40 through Byers Canyon [141] back to Granby then Berthoud Pass, or take Colorado 9 [139] to Silverthorne.

3. From Silverthorne on Interstate 70, ride Colorado 9 and US 40 over Rabbit Ears Pass [139] to Steamboat Springs. Return to Interstate 70 via Colorado 131 [150] to Wolcott.

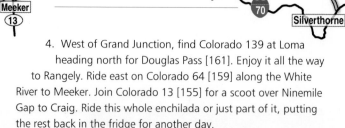

4. West of Grand Junction, find Colorado 139 at Loma heading north for Douglas Pass [161]. Enjoy it all the way to Rangely. Ride east on Colorado 64 [159] along the White River to Meeker. Join Colorado 13 [155] for a scoot over Ninemile Gap to Craig. Ride this whole enchilada or just part of it, putting the rest back in the fridge for another day.

Backcounty Tours

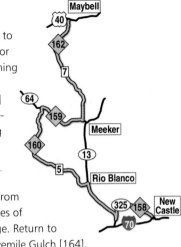

1. From New Castle on I-70, ride Grass Valley Road [158] to Colorado 325, turning south past Rifle Gap Reservoir for Colorado 13. Join Colorado 13 north for 18 miles, leaning the bike left/west onto Piceance Creek Road [160] at Rio Blanco. Cruise to its terminus at Colorado 64 [159] where you'll turn right/east for Meeker. Three miles before Meeker, look for Strawberry Road [162] departing to the north, to Maybell and US 40 at the north end.

2. Explore three sides of Dinosaur National Monument. From Maybell on US 40, ride Colorado 318 [163] to the Gates of Lodore and Browns Park National Wildlife Refuge. Return to US 40 heading west 16 miles to Twelvemile Gulch [164].

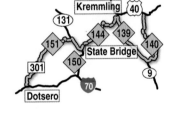

Follow it to where the Yampa River enters the monument. Return to US 40 and ride west to the main monument entrance at Dinosaur, cruising the special 28-mile Harper's Corner course [165] high above the canyons of the monument.

Dirt Road Ventures

1. At Dotsero on I-70 ride north on Colorado River Road [151]. At its Colorado 131 [150] conclusion, descend south almost eight miles to State Bridge. Connect with Trough Road [144] heading east. Follow its route to Colorado 9 [139], where you'll lean the bike right/south, looking for Ute Pass on the east side of Colorado 9 at about 22 miles. Ride Ute Pass [140] over to Williams Fork Reservoir on US 40 at the west side of Byers Canyon.

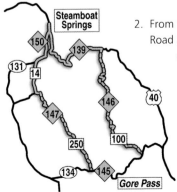

2. From the west side of Gore Pass [145] ride north on Forest Road 250 over Lynx Pass [147], continuing to Stagecoach Reservoir. On the west side of the state park, find County 14 charting a course north for Steamboat Springs. It connects with Colorado 131 [150] where you turn right/east for its nearby connection to US 40. Ascend Rabbit Ears Pass [139] and on the west side of the pass Forest Road 100 begins its journey south through Buffalo Park [146], ending up at the east side of Gore Pass.

3. From Meeker, ride one mile to the northeast on Colorado 13 [155], turning east onto County 15 or Thornburgh Road [156]. Ride to the battlefield site, then continue on to where the county road reconnects with Colorado 13. Bear right and cruise four miles up to Hamilton where you'll lean east onto Colorado 317 for Pagoda [154]. Three miles past Pagoda, ascend County 53 for Hayden and US 40.

Favorite Rides

Best Curves

[138] Two-lane Berthoud Pass ascent
[140] Ascent of Ute Pass from the west
[141] Byers Canyon on US 40
      west of Hot Sulphur Springs
[143] Willow Creek Pass
[145] Gore Pass
[150] Colorado 131 from Wolcott to Toponas
[153] Twentymile Road
[161] Douglas Pass
[165] Harper's Corner Road,
      Dinosaur National Monument

Best Cruising Rides

[139] Colorado 9 and US 40 from Silverthorne
      to Steamboat Springs
[149] Elk River Road
[152] US 40 from Craig to Steamboat Springs
[155] Colorado 13 from Meeker to Craig
[159] Colorado 64 from Rangely to Meeker
[160] Piceance Creek Road
[161] Douglas Pass Road
[162] Strawberry Road

Best Dirt-Road Adventures

[144] Trough Road
[147] Lynx Pass
[151] Colorado River Road
[156] Thornburgh Road to the Battlefield Park
[157] Ripple Creek Pass via
      the Flat Tops Scenic Byway
[163] County 34 to the Gates of Lodore
[163] Browns Park National

Most Scenic Spots

[138] The Berthoud Pass summit
[144] Gore Canyon from the Trough Road
[149] Hahn's Peak from Elk River Road
[151] Colorado River from Colorado River Road
[156] Thornburgh-Milk Creek Battlefield Park
[157] Ripple Creek Pass—Flat Tops
[161] Douglas Pass summit
[162] Danforth Hills—Strawberry Road
[163] Gates of Lodore
[163] Browns Park National Wildlife Refuge
[164] Dinosaur National Monument Canyons
[164] The Yampa River
      from Twelvemile Gulch Road

Little-Known Gems

[140] Ute Pass
[144] Trough Road
[149] Elk River Road
[151] Colorado River Road
[154] Colorado 317 to Pagoda
[157] County 8 from Meeker to Buford
[160] Piceance Creek Road
[161] Douglas Pass
[162] Strawberry Road
[164] Twelvemile Gulch
[165] Harper's Corner Road

Eastern Plains

REGIONAL OVERVIEW

There is much to see and savor in the eastern third of Colorado, below the mountains. To truly appreciate the enchantment of the rolling, open plains, and the small country towns that call them home, resist the temptation to blast on through, and you will be amply rewarded.

Several years ago, at around 6 p.m. I crossed the Colorado–Kansas state line on US 36 heading toward Denver. The fireball of the sun put on a colorful show before me as it descended in the western sky. A look in the mirrors revealed a vivid palette of colors created by the low-angle light as it merged into a deepening sky made all the more blue by soft, white puffs of clouds. Below it, cattle grazed on a brilliantly verdant background, serenaded by countless songbirds. Completing the painting were manicured picturebook ranches in the distance. As I neared Denver, the sun finally slipped behind the peaks of the Front Range, drawing a curtain on the artwork through which I'd been riding.

Maybe it's just the country boy in me, but I find it special to visit places where things are rooted and real—to have a meal at a country diner at a fair price and tour a small town swelling with pride. When I ride the plains I see the greatness of America—the

vastness of the country and its productive potential.

But at one time, this land told a different tale, back when it was known as The Great American Desert. Pioneers once streamed from the East, some passing through, some staying put, and their trails and tales are everywhere upon the landscape, written with evidence of prosperity alongside abandoned homesteads and towns that have seen better days. Other chapters tell of bitter conflicts with those who previously roamed and resided on these plains.

There aren't many journeys covered in this region—in a way, the essence of riding on the plains isn't that much different from road to road, but rather is determined by the sights and experiences you will encounter along the way. The defining differences of this unique section of the state contribute to the dazzling diversity that is Colorado.

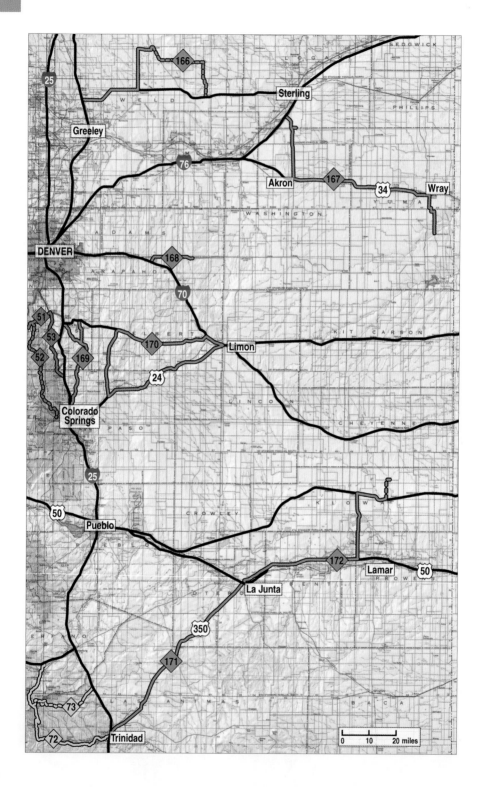

Motorcycling Colorado

Ride 166 **Pawnee Buttes**

Colorado 14, County 77, 120, 390, 112, 127

An 80-mile ride (half paved, half graded dirt) along the Pawnee Pioneer Trails Scenic Byway, through small towns, impressive grasslands, and distinctive buttes

The ride to the Pawnee National Grassland and Pawnee Buttes is different from the typical and common mountain-fest journey, but a scoot to these high plains is rewarding in more ways than one.

The National Grassland here contains an immense 192,000 windswept acres, just over 300 square miles. And I mean "windswept" literally. At the turn of the last century, there was an attempt at scratchy agriculture, with checkered results. The Dust Bowl years of the 1930s had those who tried to eke out a living raising the white flag of surrender. Today, towering white windmills rise above the fields east of Grover, taking advantage of the constant wind. When you ride this area, you will also see immense short grass prairie on all sides, with song

birds your constant companions. They are everywhere.

There's a good chance, with a keen eye looking left or right, you will see herds of pronghorn antelope. Recently, just before I turned into the Pawnee Buttes entrance, I saw the largest pronghorn herd I had ever seen, and what was amazing was when they

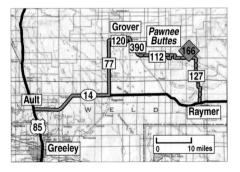

took off, they moved out as a unit at Mach 1. There was no spreading out, or antelope stragglers trying to keep pace, they hauled like a big homogeneous blob. Something to behold.

Of this 80-mile ride, about half is paved—the quiet and lonesome journey from Ault on Colorado 14, to Grover via County 77 and 120. Grover is ground zero of the Pawnee National Grassland. Even if you have no interest in riding the dirt to the buttes about 16 miles farther, I would still point your front wheel to Grover as a destination, and for the experience of being swallowed up by the grasslands. There is a cafe in town, and a small grocery store which might be open. (It wasn't the last time I rode through. Maybe it was too early in the day, for it looked like an ongoing operation.) I would fuel up before leaving the Ault area to be safe. Grover is a small community with a park and minimal services—it is this kind of off-the-beaten-track place I always find to be a worthwhile visit.

A faint sign at the east side of Grover points the way southeast to the Pawnee Buttes. County 390 is the route. Look at the road surface and see if grading efforts and recent weather has made it acceptable to what you have between the knees. Dual-sport riders will have no problem. At 5.5

miles, you will turn left/east onto County 112. There is another sign here pointing the way. Actually, the route is well marked, the roads are looked after, and I think this is because it is a state scenic byway. At just under ten miles, the U.S. Department of Agriculture sign points the way north to the Pawnee Buttes access area.

The two solitary buttes rise three hundred feet above the prairie, and remain standing as anomalies in an area where erosion has lowered everything else around them. Quite the contrast. It should be noted that erosion hasn't sunk everything, for the Pawnee Buttes access and overlook area sits atop ledges of yet-to-be-fully-eroded, cliffy rock. The views are far and panoramic, and one could easily spend extended time here, perhaps hiking the trails to the buttes. From March through June though, the trails are roped off 200 yards from the cliffs to protect nesting falcons, eagles, and hawks.

After gawking at the Pawnee Buttes, you could ride more fine dirt east to County 127, then south to Raymer on paved Colorado 14, or return the way you came. I would give serious consideration to packing a lunch for the visit at the Buttes. It is a place to stay for awhile, taking it all in, including the unimpeded, 360-degree views stretching to the horizon.

Ride 167 **Summit Springs–Beecher Island**

Colorado 63, County 2, 60, US 34, 385, Beecher Oil Road

A 104-mile mostly paved, high plains tour to two historic Indian battle sites

The Great Plains Indians Wars includes three major battlefield sites on Colorado's eastern plains. The battle that caused years of mistrust and revenge was the 1864 Sand Creek Massacre described in Ride 172. During the late 1860s there was a schism among the Cheyenne, with a conflict-weary faction retreating south to Oklahoma, leaving behind a more youthful gang of warriors intent on keeping up the raids on homesteads, trains, and pioneers pointing their wagons west. Both of the battlefields sites you ride to here were U.S. Cavalry attempts to suppress the terror on the plains.

The Summit Springs Battlefield site is not far south of Sterling, and is only nine miles from Exit 115 on Interstate 76. Summit Springs is where Tall Bull and his marauding band of Cheyenne "Dog Soldiers" finally met their July 1869 end after an extended period of murderous raids in Kansas. Pawnee scouts (no friend of the Cheyenne) and William "Buffalo Bill" Cody located the Cheyenne in a shallow valley with a small canyon or cleft on the southeast hillside.

The U.S. Cavalry, led by Colonel Eugene A. Carr, wanted badly to not only exact payback for the Kansas attacks, but also to rescue two kidnapped white women who were with the Cheyenne. Carr skillfully deployed the soldiers into positions on three sides of the Indian camp, then launched the surprise attack. Tall Bull had time to plant a tomahawk into the forehead of one of his prisoners, then joined the battle with his warriors by moving defensively to a small canyon on a nearby hillside (seen above in photo). At one point when Tall Bull poked his head up above cover, he was killed by a U.S. Cavalry

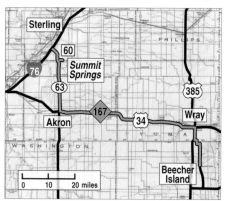

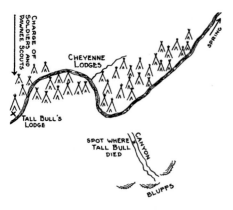

The Summit Springs Battlefield map, from the November 1929 edition of Colorado *magazine.*

bullet. As the Cheyenne bullet and arrow supply ran out, the Pawnee asked Colonel Carr for permission to finish the task. Their request granted, they changed into ceremonial fighting clothes and jumped into canyon, emerging minutes later. The Cheyenne warriors had been completely decimated with no loss of Pawnee lives.

At Exit 115, head south five miles then turn left/east onto County 60. Looking ahead over your handlebars you will see a dirt road stretching out before you. A capable street bike, ridden smoothly, can navigate the four-mile two-track road. Note that Summit Springs is on private property. Sometimes it is chained off and you will have to walk the half mile to the historic marker area. Sometimes it isn't, and you can ride out to it if you don't mind the narrow track.

After the short ride to Summit Springs, and walking the grounds of this unchanged place, you, of course, have the option of turning around. If you're ready for more, you can ride through some high plains towns and check out the Battle of Beecher Island. Head south from Summit Springs on Colorado 63 for 20 paved miles to US 34. The sizeable plains town of Akron will be your gateway east to 54 miles of high country riding all the way to Wray. This isn't a highway tour of times-better-seen, but is actually one of vibrant towns and active communities. I always enjoy throttling down and cruising through small towns. At Wray, you'll turn to the south on US 385 for 4.7 miles, then left onto County 30 for 1.2 miles, then take a right onto County JJ, which zigzags to County 27 three miles later, then finally a

This is the location where the first relief scouts spotted the besieged cavalry.

right to County KK taking you to Beecher Island six miles farther. Sorry about all these turns, but this paved route (cumulatively known as the Beecher Oil Road) is in contrast to the dirt ones surrounding, and well marked by signs pointing the way.

In August 1868, Frank Hall, the acting Governor of Colorado, asked Union Army General Philip Henry Sheridan for assistance following the deaths of 79 settlers from repeated attacks upon farms, way stations, and wagon routes. Sheridan asked Major George Alexander Forsyth to form a com-

pany of civilian scouts willing to fight the Cheyenne warriors using Indian-like techniques, instead of the showy saber rattling methods of the Civil War. About 50 men signed on and all were armed with Spencer repeating rifles. The scouts were ordered to respond to a raid on a Kansas Pacific train station, and they traced the trail of the retreating Indians to Colorado, just across the border.

On September 17, 1868, despite being significantly outnumbered, the scouts con-

Beecher Island in 1917, during an annual reunion of the scouts

A 1940 artist's rendition of the Beecher Island Battle

The Beecher Island battle was fought in the treed river valley seen in the distance.

tinued to shadow the Cheyenne until they were detected by a rifle shot that leveled an Indian who was on reconnaissance. Chaos ensued, the scouts hunkered down on a sandbar in what is now called the Arikaree River, and the battle was on. The great war leader of the Cheyenne, Roman Nose—with a strength of 200 to 300 warriors compared to the 50 U.S. Army soldiers on the sandbar—planned a surprise dawn attack, but premature movement by a few jumpy Indians gave the scouts time to prepare for the offensive. The superior firepower of the Spencer repeating rifles (20 rounds per minute versus the 2 to 3 of a muzzle-loading rifle) enabled them to repel the attack, with one of the rounds mortally wounding Roman Nose. So began the ten days of conflict and stalemate, with Forsyth's scouts subsisting on stirred-up river water and decaying horse flesh. Two scouts were able to escape and bring notice of the situation to commanders at Fort Wallace. Relief started trickling in on September 25th, and by the 27th, the siege was over. Six of Forsyth's scouts died in the extended conflict, including Lieu-

tenant Fredrick H. Beecher (nephew of Henry Ward Beecher) for whom the battle was named. The Cheyenne would call the engagement, "The Fight When Roman Nose Was Killed." More than 100 Cheyenne warriors are estimated to have died during the ten-day encounter. General George Custer called it the "Greatest Battle on the Plains."

This ride out to the eastern edge of Colorado only seven miles from the Kansas border is a journey under a spacious sky, with views to the edge of the earth, leading to a destination of historic worth. You can continue on to the Sand Creek Massacre site and Old Bent's Fort [172], making this a two-day trip. The town of Burlington is 40 miles south on I-70 and is a fine halfway point with multiple lodging, food, and fuel options. The town of Wray to the north of Beecher Island is a pleasing town with full services. You could throw some food in the saddlebags and take advantage of the picnic facilities at Beecher Island, and if you want to sleep under the stars as Forsyth's scouts and the Cheyenne warriors did, there are camping spots at Beecher Island as well.

Ride 168 **High Plains Raceway**

US 36

A ride to Colorado's newest racetrack facility

Well, we have something different here—a track facility for your bike. I debated whether to dedicate a chapter to this place, but I believe it offers a unique destination for your more-than-you-think capable bike, and it delivers dividends that will enhance your two-wheeled experience.

High Plains Raceway opened for the 2009 season after several years of diligent collaborative work among amateur road racing clubs and their members. The Denver area was in serious need of a place to exercise high-octane machines after several older facilities all coincidently closed in 2005. In a remarkably collaborative kind of way, the clubs came together to locate, design, finance, and build the track, while working with officials on the zoning and permitting process.

HPR is 17 miles east of Interstate 70 and Byers on US 36. With Byers only 26 miles east of the E-470 and Interstate 70 exchange, the track is within an hour of many in the Denver area. So let's answer a few tactical questions, and then a strategic one:

Q. Can anyone circle the track?

A. If you have completed an organized track day or track school, you are qualified. Any written documentation you have regarding this would be helpful. If you haven't, you will be required to go through a short orientation with the track manager on duty.

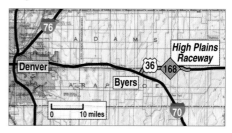

Q. How do I get my bike to the track?

A. You can ride it, trailer it, or throw it into the back of a truck.

Q. How do I prep the bike?

A. You want a safe bike . . . tires, brakes, no leaks, nothing loose. If your bike is liquid cooled, you will want to drain the slippery glycol-based coolant and replace it with water or a track-friendly replacement like "water wetter." You will need to remove or tape the mirrors. Light-adhesive painter's tape is good for this. You will need to have one- or two-piece leathers (two-piece must zip all the way around), gloves covering the wrists, and boots covering the ankles.

Q. Can I show up with any kind of bike?

A. Technically yes, if it is a safe bike. I've seen many kinds circling various tracks, but have yet to see a low-slung cruiser or heavy touring bike. Not that it isn't possible, but there are better choices.

Q. When can I show up and how much does it cost?

A. Typically, on what is called "Lapping Day." There is a calendar, and information at www.highplainsraceway.com. The calendar will list the dates when there is open motorcycle lapping, and what the full- and half-day costs are.

The strategic question is, "Why should I consider this?" Unquestionably, riding time spent in a controlled, closed-course environment improves your skills, and thus makes you a safer rider. Now of course, skill enhancement can come from many sources, but a track environment takes your ability and capability to another level. To be sure, you don't wander the track, thinking a few laps will, by osmosis, have a positive effect. It will work best if you have a foundation, and for this I recommend a track school at HPR, or individual instruction.

A web search will reveal the season's training opportunities. The Star Motorcycle School is one such school to look into. They tend to make an appearance every summer. By the way, those of you in southern Colorado have a closer track facility near Pueblo, the Pueblo Motorsports Park. For more information, go to www.pueblomotorsportspark.net/motorcycles.html.

There's something about using more of that bike beneath you. Most of the time, the bike is more willing and more capable than you are. You'll learn to trust it more at the track, and this will translate directly to your experience on the road.

The Colorado 83 bridge over Castlewood Canyon

Ride 169 **Castlewood**

Colorado 83, Lake Gulch Road

A 30-mile alternative to Interstate 25, winding through creek-fed valleys and horse ranch country

Colorado 83 scores points as an alternative to the traffic gun-barrel gauntlet of Interstate 25 between Denver and Colorado Springs. It also has the attraction of proximity to metro areas. Ranch country, horses grazing in green or golden fields, and seasonal creeks are common sights from Colorado 83 as it meanders over small rocky bluffs and through or around broad, seasonal drainages. There are places where the views are classic Colorado.

Franktown is at the intersection of Colorado 83 and 86, which is about seven miles south of better-known Parker. Actually, the Colorado 83 of this chapter is Parker Road extended. You don't have far to scoot before coming across a small canyon carved by Cherry Creek. Castlewood State Park, five miles south of Franktown, harbors this seemingly out-of-place canyon amidst grassy fields and low piney hillsides. The daily use fee of $6 gives you access to several scenic overlooks, hiking trails, and an opportunity

to check out the remains of the Castlewood Dam, which burst in 1933 under the pressure of a swollen Cherry Creek, sending a 15-foot-high wall of water toward Denver. A

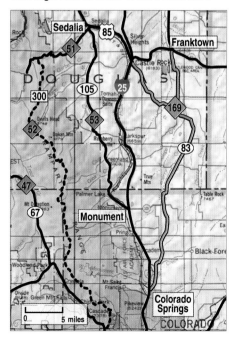

catalog of Denver historic images almost always includes the devastation of the 1933 Cherry Creek flood. With the dirt streets back then, it was one muddy, messy place for a long time.

Continuing on, in less than four miles you will be the Lake Gulch Road, which runs west to Castle Rock. For almost nine miles, Lake Gulch presents a serpentine journey through manicured ranches and farms, old rural homes, and not-so-old homes, with a fine mix of hills and bends to make it one of the nicer riding roads in the area. Lake Gulch Road in Castle Rock kicks off its journey east toward Colorado 83 at the intersection of Plum Creek Parkway and South Gilbert Street.

The remaining 22 miles to the north side of Colorado Springs is one of semi-rural and relaxed riding. There are mild ascents over broad hilltops, and calm descents to shallow valleys. As distance to the Springs narrows, the slopes of Pikes Peak rise. It is difficult to ignore this solitary 14,110-foot giant looming before you and towering over the west

side of the city. Five miles before Colorado 83 joins the northern reaches of the Springs, open fields and meadows will be in your mirrors but the Ponderosa pine of the Black Forest will be ahead of you. There is a short hilltop climb though the needled trees, then a curving 600-foot descent to the intersection of North Powers Boulevard and Interquest Parkway.

As an alternative to the zoo on Interstate 25, and as a get-out-of the-city rural ride, Colorado 83 and Lake Gulch Road is a short-list option for you. Think of Colorado 83 as the "avoid I-25 alternative" on the east, while Colorado 105 [053] is the parallel choice on the west. You could make a circling ride out of the two by cutting over to Castle Rock via Colorado 86 west of Franktown, or via Lake Gulch Road. Then 86 continues (also known as Wolfensberger Road) west over to Colorado 105. In Monument, Colorado 105 also shoots east over to Colorado 83.

Heading north on Elbert Road

Ride 170 **Limon Loop**

Colorado 86, US 24, Elbert Road

A 127-mile eight-town, high plains tour through broad valleys, over broad hills, and under a broad sky

Ride this high plains excursion as a change of pace from all the mountain rides that Colorado is famous for.

You'll begin with the western leg of this triangle—Elbert Road stretching 26 miles between US 24 on the south and Colorado 86 on the north. Its southern end is five miles east of Falcon and the northern terminus is at the town of Kiowa. The route delivers a nice medley of farms and ranches, fields and forests, and a roadway with gentle curves and hills. You'll pass through the town of Elbert, named after the 1870s Colorado Territorial Governor Samuel Hitt Elbert, 16 miles north of US 24. It is a town that's seen more populous times, but I can see a rebound over the years as Front Range sprawl works its way toward the east.

The rural nature of this cruising ride continues nine miles north of Elbert until it arrives at Colorado 86 and the county seat town of Kiowa, named after the Indian tribe.

This is a good-sized and vibrant plains town with nice cafes on the Colorado 86 main street, fuel options for the tank, and places for picnics. If you're short on time, a ride to here via 86 or Elbert Road is definitely worthwhile, and I could do it many times without ever tiring of it. If you venture east from here, then you are making a commitment! There is nothing but you, your bike, the strip of asphalt, and the rolling prairie—for 50 miles until you reach Limon. Shortly east of Kiowa you're poised on a high ridge

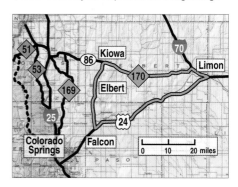

Elbert county courthouse in Kiowa in 1910, and today

with a 500-foot valley descent before you. There are more of these ups and downs until you reach Interstate 70 at 43 miles, and then seven miles to Exit 359 and Limon where you'll find services and US 24 awaiting your two wheels.

If you can time it, Limon is a convenient halfway stop with plenty of choices for replenishment of the food and fuel kind. There are options at Exit 359. A turn of the handlebars toward main street Limon brings you additional choices. The journey west on US 24 is a contrast to the dearth of towns on Colorado 86, with Matheson, Simla, Ramah, Calhan, and Peyton being the small communities you pass by or through. Perhaps the railroad had something to do with this. You will see the old train bed alongside, a grassy and brown hump as if a giant mole has burrowed a long tunnel.

This Eastern Plains ride is not far from the Front Range. It could be a destination for a one- to two-hour journey by riding one or two of its legs, or a longer half-day scoot by circling the entire pie-shaped traverse. Just jump in where you want.

Ride 171 **Comanche–Santa Fe Trail**

US 350

An 80-mile ride along a historic trail with distinctive grassland features, sweeping views, and old places

For sixty years, the Santa Fe Trail was *the* route for travel between Missouri and the Southwest. It wasn't until the rails of trains reached Santa Fe, New Mexico, in 1880 that its days as a principle transportation link were over. It was initially developed as a trading route with Mexico, but was also used by the U.S. to send troops to New Mexico during the 1846–1848 Mexican-American War. The Trail passed through Comanche country, and while the Comanche sometimes required "tolls" to pass through their territory, trade with the natives was often profitable, with Bent's Fort on the Arkansas River [172] at the center of these dealings.

Pointing your bike southwest out of La Junta on US 350, it is not difficult to imagine what it must have been like to be bouncing along in a wagon, or loping along on your horse, seeing the mountains fill the horizon for the first time since the start of your journey. Many have traveled this route the past

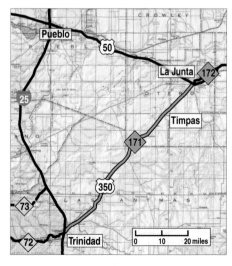

two centuries, but today it isn't such a busy place. Chances are, for much of this 80-mile ride between La Junta and Trinidad, you won't see a vehicle in front of you or in your mirrors. You'll enter the expansive 440,000-acre Comanche National Grasslands soon after twisting the throttle toward the southwest, and you'll see an ancient landscape unchanged except for the presence of a road, some crooked posts, and perhaps a windmill turning in the wind for a purpose no longer needed.

A sign to the Sierra Vista Lookout appears 13 miles into the ride, and a turn north onto Colorado 71 will take you to its parking area a half-mile away with a panorama of high peaks and wide prairies. Three miles farther southwest on US 350 you'll come to the Timpas Picnic Area. There is a half-mile trail leading to the creek, which was the first source of water for 1800s travelers since last refilling at the Arkansas River.

At mile 27 is the historic Iron Springs stage stop, but it is one mile away after a turn left/south onto a graded County 9. Trail ruts from 150 years ago are visible from the parking area. When you ride a lonely county road like this, one mile from a companion lonely road, you can expect it will probably be only you and your bike at Iron Springs,

except for the whispers of those who passed through long ago.

The remaining miles to Trinidad tell a tale of towns possessing a more prosperous past, containing the remains of hopes dashed by the realities of arid and quiet isolation. One can't help but be reflective when riding by faint signs of advertising hanging over drafty structures, with neighboring decaying and abandoned buildings feeling the weight of a steady wind. Perhaps this isn't everyone's kind of ride. Maybe I just think more about the past as I age. You'll cross the Purgatoire River a few miles from Trinidad, and to the east is a network of great dual-sport roads in the Purgatoire River Canyon area. The river also brings about a visible change in vibrancy the rest of the way to Trinidad.

Be sure to top off the tank before venturing the 80 miles between La Junta and Trinidad. Food is nowhere in between either. Trinidad is a beautiful historic town with 6.5 miles of brick streets, primarily in the restored downtown area. If you like Mexican, ride to Exit 11 on Interstate 25 just south of Trinidad for Tequila's Family Mexican Restaurant. If you're ready for more, the Highway of Legends Scenic Byway [072] awaits you west of Trinidad, as do the rides in the nearby Aguilar and Cordova Pass area [073].

Ride 172 **Bent's Fort–Sand Creek**

Colorado 94, 96, US 50, 287, County 54

A 90-mile high plains tour between two historic sites on fine country backroads, through fine eastern plains towns, with fine horizon views

You'll have two noteworthy historic sites to ride to and visit. As eastern plains riding goes, this journey is diverse, with farms close by, a state wildlife area, and a leafy green river all part of the mix. From the major US 50 town of La Junta, you'll want to follow a series of well-placed signs calling out the way to Bent's Old Fort. Essentially, you exit south off of US 50 to Adams Avenue or Colorado 109. Go north back over 50 about a mile and turn east onto Colorado 194. A seven-mile mix of suburban and country riding will have you at this national historic site located on the south side of 194.

Bent's Old Fort is on the 1833 site of the only major permanent white settlement between Missouri and Mexico. For 16 years it was a major stop on the Santa Fe Trail for the U.S. Army, for adventurous explorers, and for those engaging the Cheyenne and Arapaho Indians in the trading of buffalo

robes. Now, compared to most historical dates contained in this book, the 1833 to 1849 operation of this fort is almost prehistoric! We're talking serious Colorado territory frontier with few non-native residents before the invasion of fortune-seeking miners. As your bike cools and you walk to the faithfully reproduced fort, it isn't difficult to imagine what a kaleidoscope of people, animals, and activity this riverfront place was back then.

Continuing east on Colorado 194, you'll

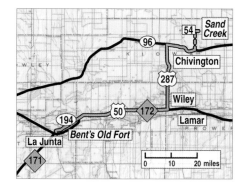

be riding a horse of the times, and aiming toward a destination of solemn significance. The Arkansas River is refreshing to have nearby, along with the occasional shade tree. East of Old Bent's Fort about two miles, pause next to a farm on the west side of Colorado 194, and you will see an exotic collection of African animals, from zebras and antelopes, to ostriches and emus.

The journey to the Sand Creek Massacre National Historic Site continues via US 50 east to US 287 north, where the quiet town of Wiley offers pause and replenishment for you and your steed. From here on north, it will be a lonely and seemingly abandoned country, with scattered and decaying structures telling a tale of past hopeful times. In a way, there is a slow return here to the visual state of things 150 years ago.

Kansas settlers at that time were accusing the Cheyenne Indians of raiding and stealing their livestock. Skirmishes, small battles, denials, and the like continued for several years until a peace conference at Fort Weld, noted by a historic marker in a parking lot just two miles north of downtown Denver, resulted in a treaty whereby the Cheyenne, led by Black Kettle, would relocate to an area under the protection of Fort Lyon on the Arkansas River. With U.S. assurances of peace, Black Kettle dispatched many of his warriors to hunt while making camp at Sand Creek, 40 miles north of the fort.

Fueled by a hatred for Indians and heavy pre-victory drinking at Fort Lyon, Colonel John Chivington, with the support of territorial governor John Evans, led 800 territorial guard troops to the Sand Creek encampment, ordering a dawn attack on a cold gray 1864 November morning. Despite the American flag and white flag of peace flapping above Black Kettle's teepee, the rout was on, with more than 130 Cheyenne casualties, mostly women and children. Black Kettle escaped but his wife was seriously wounded. Repercussions would be felt for years, including revenge battles, such as those at Beecher Island and Summit Springs [167].

The ride to Sand Creek does involve almost six miles of dirt-road riding on County 54 to the entrance. It is graded, but there are places where the wind will have deposited sand on the surface (I guess there are reasons it is called Sand Creek), and this can cause uncertain, if not tense moments if you happen to hit the soft spots at speed. County 54 will go north just east of Chivington off of Colorado 96. There are rangers on site to help guide and answer questions, and there is no fee, but donations are accepted. Consider linking this ride with the Beecher Island and Summit Springs ride mentioned above. It would be a memorable two-day journey through a momentous time. The Interstate 70 town of Burlington would be a good halfway stop for the night.

Eastern Plains

RECOMMENDATIONS

A Northern Tour

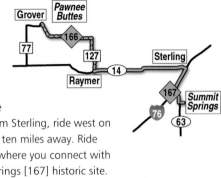

Combine a visit to Summit Springs with a tour of the Pawnee Buttes not far away to the north. After a visit to the Pawnee Buttes [166], ride south to Colorado 14, turning left for Sterling where you can pick up some lunchtime chow. From Sterling, ride west on US 6 or Interstate 76 for Colorado 63, only ten miles away. Ride south on Colorado 63 almost five miles to where you connect with County 60, turning east for the Summit Springs [167] historic site.

A Southern Tour

Connect the ride of the Comanche National Grasslands [171] along the Santa Fe Trail with a stop at Bent's Old Fort in La Junta. If you're ambitious, continue on to the Sand Creek Massacre National Historic Site [172]. Both journeys include La Junta at their ends so this would be a seamlessly connected ride.

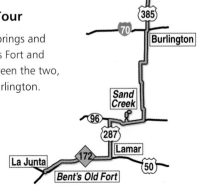

A Two-Day Indian Battlefields Tour

Commence with either the Summit Springs and Beecher Island ride [167] or the Bent's Fort and Sand Creek Massacre ride [172]. Between the two, ride US 385, spending the night in Burlington.

Favorite Rides

Distinct and Special Views

[166] Pawnee Buttes
[167] Hillside canyon of Summit Springs
[167] Peate Hill north toward Beecher Island
[168] US 36 east of Last Chance
[169] Colorado 83 toward Pikes Peak
       from the Black Forest area
[170] Colorado 86 east of Kiowa
[170] US 24 to the southwest out of Limon
[171] US 350 between Tyrone and Delhi
[172] US 385 north toward Cheyenne Wells

Sweet Riding Sections

[166] County 112 toward the Pawnee Buttes
[167] County LL north and south
       of Beecher Island
[169] Colorado 83 south of Franktown
[169] Lake Gulch Road
[170] Colorado 86 east of Kiowa
[170] Elbert–Kiowa Road south of Elbert
[171] US 350 from Trinidad to Tyrone
[172] Colorado 194 east of La Junta

Worthy Destinations

[166] Pawnee Buttes
[167] Summit Springs Indian Battlefield Site
[167] Overland Trail Museum, Sterling
[167] Beecher Island Battleground
[167] The town of Wray
[167] Bonny Reservoir south of Beecher Island
[171] Purgatoire Canyon east of US 350
[172] Bent's Fort
[172] Eastern Colorado Historical Society
       Museum, Cheyenne Wells
[172] Sand Creek Massacre National Historic Site
[172] Amache Japanese WWII
       Internment Camp, Granada

Colorado Statewide

RECOMMENDATIONS

The entire state is your playground.

Six Easy Mountain Passes from the Central Front Range
207 miles from Morrison

Ascend Bear Creek Canyon [037] for Evergreen, continue west toward Bergen Park but turn southwest onto the Squaw Pass Road [034]. Bag Squaw and Juniper Passes on the way to Echo Lake. Descend Colorado 103 to Idaho Springs. Go west on I-70 exiting just before the Eisenhower Tunnel for US 6 and Loveland Pass [137]. Ascend Loveland, pass the Keystone Ski Resort, and at the stoplight on the west end of Keystone, turn left/south onto Swan Mountain Road. This winding road concludes at Colorado 9 where a turn south toward Breckenridge delivers Hoosier Pass [136], with Fairplay and South Park on the other side. If you're in Fairplay around lunchtime, the Brown Burro is a good place to put

your sidestand down. US 285 [134] on the east end of town is where you turn north for the passes of Red Hill and Kenosha.

A North and Northwest Tour
220 miles from Empire

From US 40 at the Empire exit, ride over Berthoud Pass [138] for Middle Park and Granby. Continue on US 40 through Byers Canyon, past Kremmling, over Muddy and Rabbit Ears Pass [139] to Steamboat Springs. If you're time-pressured, ride Colorado 131 [150] south toward Oak Creek. If you want to experience Twentymile Road [153], ride US 40 west out of Steamboat toward Hayden [152]. Just east of Hayden, turn south on Twentymile [153] for Oak Creek. At Oak Creek continue south for Toponas. For a more westward conclusion, Colorado 131 from here to Wolcott on I-70 is sweet. But so is Colorado

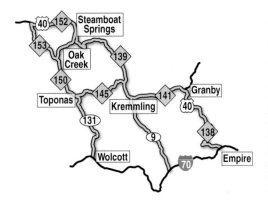

134 east over Gore Pass [145]! This latter choice will have you at Kremmling, for Colorado 9 to I-70 and the Summit County area.

A Southern and Western Slope Circle
280 miles from Hotchkiss

From Hotchkiss, where Colorado 133 [113] and 92 [115] connect, cruise west on 92 for 16 miles to Colorado 65 as it departs north for Orchard City and the Grand Mesa [106]. At the north end of Mesa, Colorado 65 carves west through the Plateau Canyon [109], terminating at I-70 where you'll follow signs for US 50 south out of Grand Junction. At the town of Whitewater join Colorado 141 to Gateway [101] and ride through the canyons of the Dolores River. After descending into the San Miguel River Canyon east of Norwood, Colorado 62 ascends the Dallas Divide [095] to Ridgway, where you can ride US 550 and 50 north to Montrose or Delta.

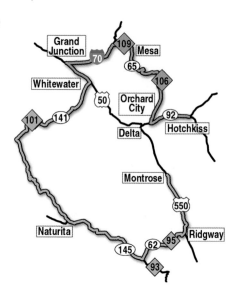

A Southern Front Range and Backroad Journey
250 miles from Morrison

From the Denver area, ride US 285 southwest to Deckers Road [047] and on to Woodland Park. From Colorado Springs, join the ride here. Cruise west on US 24 from Divide, taking Lower Twin Rocks Road 1.6 miles past Divide to Teller County 1, where you'll ride south six miles to Teller County 11 departing toward the southwest. At an upcoming three-way intersection, lean left for High Park Road [062] to Colorado 9 [063], where a left/south turn will have you at US 50 in a little over eight miles. Turn east for Cañon City, and seven miles later lean the bike left for the whoops of Skyline Drive [066]. From downtown Cañon City, find Colorado 115 wandering through the southern burbs toward Florence, where you'll join Colorado 67 south for Wetmore, then McKenzie Junction on Colorado 96 [069]. Turn south here on Colorado 165 for Bishop's Castle [070] 13 miles away. Return to McKenzie Junction and push the handlebars left/west on 96 for Westcliffe. Colorado 69 will escort you from Westcliffe to Texas Creek in the Arkansas River Canyon

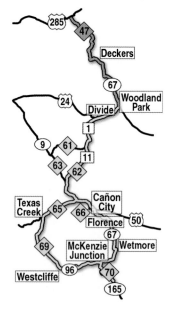

[065], where an eastward cruise on US 50 completes a circle back to the Cañon City and Florence area. If short on time, Colorado 115 north out of nearby Penrose offers a straight shot to Colorado Springs.

Central Mountains Horseshoe
310 miles from Poncha Springs

Start at Poncha Springs, which can be approached from the south via US 285 and Poncha Pass [074], or from the north on US 285 through Buena Vista [124], or on US 50 from the east as it emerges from the Arkansas River Canyon [065]. Ride west on US 50 over Monarch Pass [123] to Gunnison and past Blue Mesa Reservoir [117] to join Colorado 92 [115] to the north at Sapinero. Ride the north rim of the Black Canyon of the Gunnison. One mile west of Crawford, turn right onto Crawford Road [114] for a backroads scoot to Paonia where Colorado 133 [113] north skirts Paonia Reservoir, ascends McClure Pass, and connects with Colorado 82 at Carbondale. Take 82 east through Aspen, over Independence Pass [127] to US 24. North on US 24

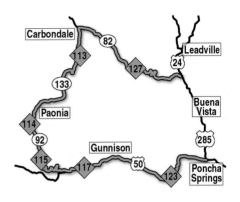

leads to Leadville, then Tennessee Pass [131] or Fremont Pass [132] and Colorado 91 to I-70. South on US 24 will have you at Buena Vista [124], then Poncha Springs.

A Northern Front Range and Mountain Loop
265 miles from Lyons

Grab a light breakfast at the Stone Cup in Lyons. Scoot north past Carter Lake [007] for US 34, where you turn east for Buckhorn Road less than a mile away. This connects to Stove Prairie Road [005] by turning left/west at the T-intersection in Masonville. Ride Stove Prairie to Colorado 14 and Cache la Poudre Canyon [003]. Aim left/west for Cameron Pass, then to North Park and Walden for some lunchtime chow at the Moose Creek Cafe. Take Colorado 125 south out of Walden for Rand and Willow Creek Pass [143]. If headed back north, US 34 here will bring you through Rocky Mountain National Park via Trail Ridge Road [010] to Estes Park. But if the fee and potential park traffic has you hesitating, take the southerly return on US 40 over Berthoud Pass [138] to I-70 for a return to Denver. To close the loop to Lyons, take the Central City Park-

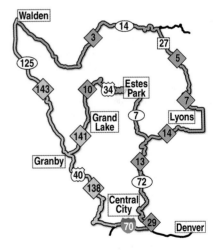

way [029] exit from I-70. This connects to the Peak to Peak [013], which takes you to Colorado 7 [014] and a return to Lyons.

Weekender Trip to the Northwest
510 miles from Buena Vista

From the Buena Vista area, ride US 24 [124] north for Leadville, and over Tennessee Pass [131] to Minturn and I-70. Ride 16 miles west on I-70 for Colorado 131 [150] at the Wolcott exit. Take 131 past Oak Creek all the way to Steamboat Springs for the evening. If this is a one-night venture, return via US 40 over Rabbit Ears Pass [139] to Kremmling, taking Colorado 9 back to I-70; or follow US 40 riding east to Granby [141] and then Berthoud Pass [138] to I-70. If a two-nighter is on the ride agenda, either spend a day in the Steamboat area (check out Elk River Road to Steamboat Lake [149] and Twentymile Road [153] between Hayden and Oak Creek), or pack up and ride west on US 40 to Craig [152] and then Colorado 13 to Meeker [155]. Check in mid-day and explore Strawberry Road [162], or the road to the Thornburgh Battlefield [156]. For the return home, ride south on Colorado 13 to Rifle, joining I-7 to the east. If you have time and are headed south, consider

exiting at Glenwood Springs for Colorado 82 through Aspen, over Independence Pass [127] to US 24, where you started. Or, ride I-70 east through Glenwood Canyon [112], then Vail Pass on to points east.

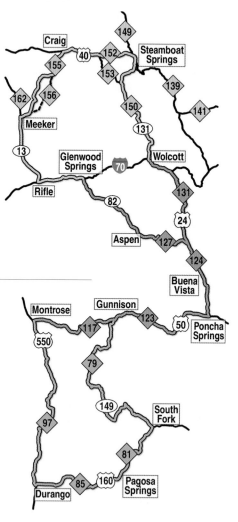

Weekender Trip to the Southwest
560 miles from Buena Vista

From the Buena Vista area, ride south on US 24 [124] to Poncha Springs, engaging US 50 west over Monarch Pass [123] to Gunnison. Connect with Colorado 149 and the Silver Thread Scenic Byway [079] on the east side of Blue Mesa Reservoir, riding south to South Fork where US 160 to the west traverses Wolf Creek Pass [081] to Pagosa Springs. Stay in Pagosa Springs, or continue on US 160 [085] for Durango. For a one-nighter, leave for US 550 and the Million Dollar Highway [097] early in the morning, riding north to Montrose where you'll turn east on US 50 over Cerro Summit [117] toward Gunnison, Monarch Pass, and then return home. If a two-nighter is the plan, wander the Durango area perhaps for a day . . . maybe Mesa Verde

[090] or Florida Road to Vallecito Reservoir [087]. Or, savor the San Juan Skyway, stopping at Silverton, Ouray, etc. See the narrow-gauge train at Cimarron on US 50 and stay in Gunnison for night number two.

The Grand Tour

If you are inspired to cover a lot of ground and have a week or two to sample the wonders of Colorado, this statewide tour links many of its premier riding roads into one incredible trip that you can join at any point, and travel in any direction. Enjoy!

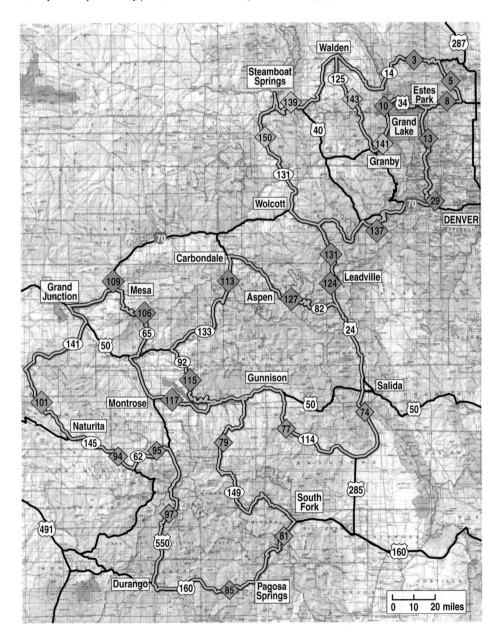

Favorite Rides

Except for the list of Best Distinctive Scenic Rides, the lists are exclusive, meaning that roads are not repeated on two different rankings. Thus, while Trail Ridge Road in Rocky Mountain National Park is a great cruising road, it is already on the "Best Riding Roads More Than 20 Miles in Length" list and hence, isn't repeated.

Best Distinctive Scenic Rides

[003] Cache La Poudre Canyon to Cameron Pass
[008] Big Thompson Canyon
[010] Trail Ridge Road
[011] Bear Lake Road, Moraine Park
[028] Apex Valley Road to Mammoth Gulch Road
[035] Colorado 5 over Mt. Evans
[036] Guanella Pass
[057] Pikes Peak Highway
[064] The Ute Trail and Tallahassee Road
[079] Colorado 149 between Lake City and Creede
[080] Alpine Loop
[082] Platoro to Stunner Pass to Summitville
[093] Colorado 145 over Lizard Head Pass to Ophir
[096] Last Dollar Road
[097] US 550 between Durango and Ouray
[098] Owl Creek Pass
[101] Colorado 141 to Gateway
[103] Rim Rock Road
[106] Colorado 65 to Grand Mesa
[113] McClure Pass
[119] Ohio Creek Road over Ohio Pass
[120] Kebler Pass
[127] Independence Pass
[130] Crooked Creek Pass
[144] Trough Road
[151] Colorado River Road
[157] Ripple Creek Pass
[162] Strawberry Road–Danforth Hills
[163] Colorado 318–Gates of Lodore
[165] Harper's Corner Road

Best Roads More Than 20 Miles in Length

[003] Colorado 14 from Ted's Place to Walden
[005] Stove Prairie Road
[010] Trail Ridge Road
[013] The Peak to Peak Scenic Byway
[034] Colorado 103 from Bergen Park to Idaho Spgs
[047] Pine Valley, Deckers Road
[070] Colorado 165 from McKenzie Junction to Colorado City
[072] Colorado 12 from La Veta to Stonewall
[077] Colorado 114 from Saguache to US 50
[079] Colorado 149 from Blue Mesa Reservoir to South Fork
[083] Colorado 17 from Antonito to Chama, NM
[093] Colorado 145 from Dolores to Norwood
[097] U.S. 550 from Durango to Ouray
[101] Colorado 141 from Whitewater to Naturita
[106] Colorado 65 over the Grand Mesa
[113] Colorado 133 from Paonia to Redstone
[115] Colorado 92 from Sapinero to Crawford
[127] Colorado 82 from Twin Lakes to Aspen
[131] US 24 from Leadville to Minturn
[143] Colorado 125 from Rand to Granby
[145] Colorado 134 over Gore Pass
[150] Colorado 131 from Wolcott to Toponas
[153] Twentymile Road

Best Roads Less Than 20 Miles in Length

[009] Devil's Gulch through Glen Haven
[014] St. Vrain Canyon
[015] Lefthand Canyon to James Canyon
[025] Coal Creek Canyon
[027] Golden Gate Canyon
[062] High Park Road
[108] De Beque Cutoff
[109] Colorado 65 through Plateau Canyon
[123] US 50 west ascent of Monarch Pass
[126] Eastern ascent on Cottonwood Pass Road
[137] US 6 over Loveland Pass
[138] US 40 ascent of Berthoud Pass

Best Cruising Roads

[008] US 34 Big Thompson Canyon
[011] Bear Lake Road
[012] US 36, Lyons to Estes Park
[021] Boulder Canyon
[032] Clear Creek Canyon
[056] Colorado 67, Divide to Cripple Creek
[063] Colorado 9, Hartsel to Parkdale
[065] US 50 through the Arkansas River Canyon
[069] Colorado 96, Wetmore to Westcliffe
[112] Interstate 70 through Glenwood Canyon
[117] US 50 from Gunnison to Montrose
[139] Colorado 9 and US 40,
       Silverthorne to Steamboat Springs
[155] Colorado 13, Meeker to Craig
[159] Colorado 64, Rangely to Meeker
[161] Colorado 139 over Douglas Pass
[170] The Limon Loop

Best Short and Tightly Twisting Rides

[018] Sunshine Canyon
[019] Fourmile Canyon
[023] Magnolia Road
[024] Flagstaff Road
[033] Lookout Mountain Road
[037] Bear Creek Canyon
[039] Stanley Park, North Turkey Creek
[041] City View, Crystal Drive, Hilldale Pines
[042] Deer Creek Canyon
[043] High Grade Road
[044] Conifer Mountain Road
[056] Colorado 67 between Victor
       and Cripple Creek
[116] Portal Road, Black Canyon of the
       Gunnison National Park

Best Rural Backroads

[001] Red Feather Lakes Road
[004] Rist Canyon
[020] Sugarloaf Road
[046] South Platte River Road
[050] Tarryall Road
[051] Jarre Canyon Road
[061] Park County 102
[087] Florida Road
[091] McElmo Creek Road
[094] West Dolores Road to Dunton
[104] Little Park Road
[110] Colorado 330, Mesa to Collbran

[119] Ohio Creek Road
[121] Taylor River Canyon Road
[122] Parlin–Pitkin Road
[129] Frying Pan Road
[149] Elk River Road Steamboat Springs
       to Steamboat Lake
[151] Colorado River Road
[154] Colorado 317 From Hamilton to Pagoda
[157] Buford Road
[160] Piceance Creek Road
[162] Strawberry Road

Best Dirt-Road Journeys

[002] Laramie River Road
[028] Apex Valley Road to Mammoth Gulch
[036] Guanella Pass
[049] Stoney Pass and Matukat Road
[060] Shelf Road
[064] The Ute Trail and Tallahassee Road
[073] Cordova Pass
[080] Alpine Loop
[082] Platoro to Stunner Pass to Summitville
[096] Last Dollar Road
[098] Owl Creek Pass
[105] Lands End Road
[107] Forest Road 121, Grand Mesa to Collbran
[120] Kebler Pass
[122] Cumberland Pass
[128] Hagerman Pass
[130] Crooked Creek Pass
[135] Boreas Pass
[144] Trough Road
[157] Ripple Creek Pass

Best Base Camps (Unpaved)
For Touring Colorado

Salida
Ouray
Steamboat Springs
Meeker

Best Base Camps (Paved)
For Touring Colorado

Durango and Pagosa Springs
Gunnison and Montrose
Steamboat Springs
Meeker
Estes Park

DUAL-SPORT OPPORTUNITIES

Colorado has no shortage of noteworthy dirt and gravel roads, and many rides in this book guide you beyond pavement, on routes that can be traversed with a heavier dual-sport bike or even a versatile street bike. The routes listed below either describe, lead to, or are in the middle great off-pavement adventures. See the text for more details.

Northern Front Range

[001] Red Feather Lakes
[002] Laramie River
[003] Cache La Poudre
[005] Stove Prairie
[010] Trail Ridge
[013] Peak to Peak
[015] James Canyon
[016] Lefthand Canyon
[018] Sunshine–Gold Hill
[020] Sugarloaf Mountain
[022] Eldora–Caribou
[023] Magnolia
[024] Flagstaff Mountain

Central Front Range

[028] Apex–Mammoth Gulch
[029] Central City Parkway
[031] Fall River
[047] Deckers
[049] Matukat
[050] Tarryall
[051] Jarre Canyon
[052] Rampart Range
[053] Perry Park

Southern Front Range

[055] Elevenmile
[056] Cripple Creek
[058] Gold Camp
[059] Phantom Canyon
[060] Shelf–Red Canyon
[064] The Ute Trail
[068] Oak Creek Grade
[069] Westcliffe
[073] Aguilar–Cordova Pass

Southwest

[075] Marshall Pass
[076] Bonanza
[078] Los Piños Pass
[079] Silver Thread
       Scenic Byway
[080] Alpine Loop
[081] Wolf Creek Pass
[082] Stunner Pass
[085] Pagosa–Bayfield
[089] Durango–Mancos
[091] Canyons of the Ancients
[093] Lizard Head Pass
[094] Dunton
[095] Dallas Divide
[096] Last Dollar
[099] Bedrock–Paradox
[101] Gateway

Central West

[111] Grand Mesa
       National Forest
[115] Black Canyon North Rim
[119] Ohio Pass
[121] Taylor River Canyon
[122] Pitkin Passes
[125] St. Elmo
[126] Cottonwood Pass
[128] Hagerman Pass
[129] Frying Pan River
[130] Crooked Creek Pass
[135] Boreas Pass

Northwest

[140] Ute Pass–Williams Fork
[141] Headwaters
[142] Stillwater Pass
[143] Willow Creek Pass
[145] Gore Pass
[146] Buffalo Park
[147] Lynx Pass
[148] Buffalo Pass
[149] Elk River
[152] Yampa River
[154] Pagoda
[158] Rifle Parks
[162] Strawberry Creek
[164] Twelvemile Gulch
[165] Harper's Corner

Eastern Plains

[166] Pawnee Buttes
[171] Comanche–Santa
       Fe Trail

INDEX

ABOUT THE AUTHOR

As a longtime resident of Colorado, Steve Farson has roamed all over the state in search of mountains to climb, trails to hike, and roads to ride. He bought his first bike, an old Honda, from a neighbor at age 12 with money from his paper route. By the time he was married, he and his wife would hop on a bike to explore whatever back roads they could find. Though travels in his corporate life have enabled him to ride motorcycles in many places around the country and abroad, he has yet to find any other place that offers the wide diversity of riding opportunities available in Colorado.